A WORLD OF EMPIRES

A WORLD OF EMPIRES

The Russian Voyage of the Frigate *Pallada*

Edyta M. Bojanowska

THE BELKNAP PRESS OF
HARVARD UNIVERSITY PRESS

Cambridge, Massachusetts
London, England
2018

Printed in the United States of America

First printing

Library of Congress Cataloging-in-Publication Data
Names: Bojanowska, Edyta M., author.
Title: A world of empires : the Russian voyage of the frigate
Pallada / Edyta M. Bojanowska.
Description: Cambridge, Massachusetts : The Belknap Press of Harvard University
Press, 2018. | Includes bibliographical references and index.
Identifiers: LCCN 2017045047 | ISBN 9780674976405 (alk. paper)
Subjects: LCSH: Goncharov, Ivan Aleksandrovich, 1812–1891. Fregat "Pallada." |
Goncharov, Ivan Aleksandrovich, 1812–1891—Criticism and interpretation. |
Pallada (Ship) | Voyages and travels. | Russia—Foreign relations—1801–1917.
Classification: LCC G490 .B7255 2018 | DDC 910.4/5—dc23
LC record available at https://lccn.loc.gov/2017045047

Contents

Note on Primary Sources, Transliteration, Ethnonyms, and Place Names

To avoid confusion, I refer to the ship as the *Pallada* and to Ivan Goncharov's book as *The Frigate Pallada.* Unless otherwise noted, references to Goncharov's texts come from the following edition, cited in Notes as *PSS*: I. A. Goncharov, *Polnoe sobranie sochinenii v dvadtsati tomakh*, 20 vols. (St. Petersburg: Nauka, 1997–). The text of *The Frigate Pallada* appears in vol. 2 (*PSS* 2). All translations from the Russian are mine.

In the endnotes, I use the Library of Congress transliteration system for Russian. In the main text, except for quoted Russian, I use a simplified version of this system that omits palatalization markers, transcribes Russian surnames ending in -skii or -ii / yi as -sky or -y, uses initial "Ye" for "E" in first names, and spells surnames and place names of non-Russian origin in the language of origin (Kronstadt instead of Kronshtadt). However, I use Russian phonetic spelling of foreign names of famous persons (Ivan Kruzenshtern instead of Johann von Krusenstern).

For Chinese, I use the pinyin romanization system, with the exception of names better known in English in the older system (such as Canton). Except for quotations, I replace Goncharov's Peking with Beijing.

In the main text, I adopt currently accepted neutral names for African ethnic groups in place of the derogatory colonial labels commonly used in Goncharov's time. I therefore use Khoikhoi for Hottentot, Xhosa for Kaffir, San for Bushman, and Mfengu for Fingo. Likewise, I replace Goncharov's ethnonyms of Siberian indigenous groups with currently accepted names:

Evenki for Tungus, Sakha for Yakut, and Luoravetlan for Chukchi. By contrast with African neutral ethnonyms, the autonyms of Siberians are less commonly known; I therefore gloss them with older equivalents both at first use and periodically throughout the text. In all cases, I preserve Goncharov's original terms in quoted material.

Whenever accurate dating is important, I convert Goncharov's dates in the Julian calendar, which Russia observed until 1918, to the Gregorian calendar, which ran twelve days ahead in the nineteenth century. When rough dating suffices—as when orienting events by months—I follow Goncharov's Julian designations as stated in *The Frigate Pallada.*

A WORLD OF EMPIRES

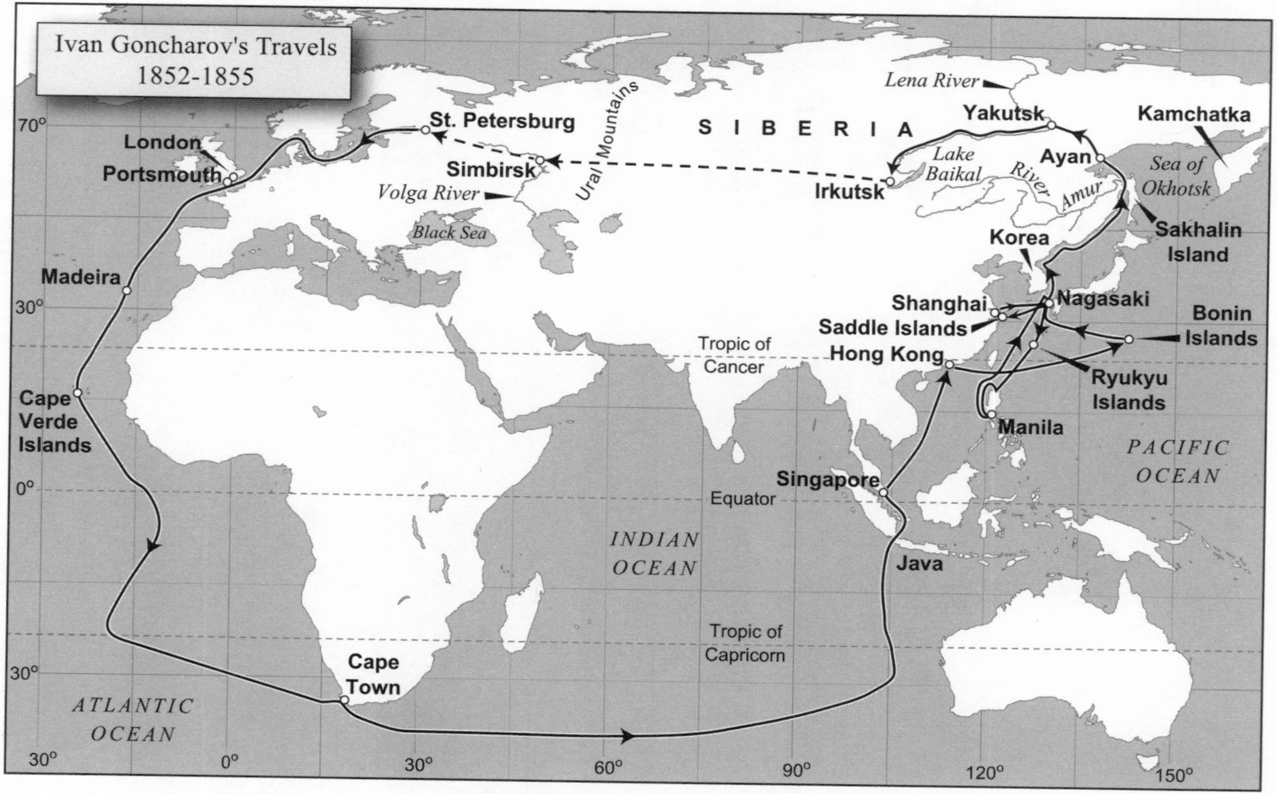

Map 1. Goncharov's Travels in 1852–1855. The travelogue breaks off when Goncharov arrives in Irkutsk, Siberia. He later journeyed to St. Petersburg, stopping over in his hometown of Simbirsk.

Introduction

He thumbed the pages. "You made notes in Russian?" I asked. He nodded. "I thought they were written in cipher," I said. He laughed, then became serious. . . .

—Joseph Conrad, *Heart of Darkness* (1902).
The book in question is a seamanship manual,
annotated by a Russian whom the narrator
calls "Kurtz's last disciple."

On October 9, 1852, the Russian sailing frigate *Pallada* weighed anchor at the naval base at Kronstadt, in the Gulf of Finland, and departed for a high-profile, government-sponsored voyage around the world. It carried 465 men, 52 guns, and about 1,300 pounds of gunpowder. The official goal was to inspect Russia's North American possessions, at the time not yet sold to the United States. The condition of the twenty-year-old frigate was not perfect. A stormy passage through the Baltic necessitated lengthy repairs in Portsmouth, England, causing the *Pallada* to miss the wind currents needed to sweep it around South America's Cape Horn. The projected circumnavigation became a semi-circumnavigation. The *Pallada* sailed instead along Africa's western seaboard, around the Cape of Good Hope, and crossed the Indian Ocean, with brief stops on Dutch Java and in the British ports of Singapore and Hong Kong. Then it headed for Japan, where it would pursue its unofficial goal, the most important, top-secret mission.

This mission was to open up Japan, a country that for two centuries had kept a strict isolation from Europeans, to western trade. The Russians knew they had competition in the steam-powered US squadron headed by

Commodore Matthew Calbraith Perry. The Americans reached Japan first, sailing into the harbor at Tokyo (then called Edo) on July 14, 1853. The Russians arrived at Nagasaki five weeks later, on August 22. Over the next several months, the Japanese negotiated separately with the two missions, eventually signing treaties with both. In the course of the negotiations, the *Pallada* also visited Shanghai and the Bonin and Ryukyu (Okinawa) Islands south of Japan. After visiting Spanish Manila, it later sailed up the Korean coast toward Russian Siberia's Pacific shores.

In *A World of Empires*, I explore the story of this remarkable voyage as it was told by Ivan Aleksandrovich Goncharov, a Russian writer who held the post of secretary to Vice Admiral Yevfimy Putiatin, the expedition's commander. Goncharov's account became a bestselling travelogue and is read in Russia to this day. Born in 1812 to a family of merchants, the writer grew up in the provincial town of Simbirsk on the Volga River. After attending Moscow University, he moved to St. Petersburg where he worked as a government official and began his literary career. He is known today mainly as the author of a quirky Russian classic, the novel *Oblomov,* about a quintessential Russian couch potato, a man so sedentary in his ways that he renounces the woman he loves not least because marriage would entail the hassle of moving to a bigger apartment. Oblomov cannot summon the energy to cross a bridge over a river, let alone cross oceans. The inertia of this famous character has come to be associated with its author, whom many unjustly picture as a slothful homebody.

Yet the sheer scope of the *Pallada* voyage, which allowed Goncharov to see so much of the world, makes him unique among major Russian writers, who tended to confine their international itineraries to Europe. Goncharov was offered the position of Putiatin's secretary when a friend refused and recommended him instead. At the time, Goncharov had been working as a translator in the Russian Ministry of Finances' Department of Trade. He was feeling sapped by bureaucratic drudgery, and hoped that exotic sights of "savages" living in "primordial simplicity" would rejuvenate his spirits, as he later explained in his travelogue. The authorities specifically sought a literary man for the position, very much hoping that he would immortalize this important voyage by producing a popular book.[1]

Goncharov was initially apprehensive about stepping into the role of the expedition's Homer, as he put it. Yet he did end up publishing a hugely popular travel account of his seafaring adventure. The first book edition of *The Frigate Pallada* came out in 1858. This seven-hundred-page tome takes

Figure I.1. Ivan Goncharov, 1856.

its title from the expedition's flagship, which was named after the Greek goddess of war and wisdom Pallas Athena ("Pallada" in Russian). It is written in the casual form of letters to the friends back home whose advice to stay put went unheeded. Alternately humorous and lyrical, ironic and earnest, prejudiced and insightful, Goncharov's account has been hailed by some Russian specialists as the best travel book in world literature. While perhaps exaggerated, this claim attests to the Russian reading public's enthusiasm. That the world may not yet be in an ideal position to judge is to a large extent due to the book's incomplete translations into English.[2]

Goncharov's travelogue serves as a fascinating lens on mid-nineteenth-century global imperial history. The *Pallada* navigated Africa and Asia, from European trading enclaves on the coastal rims of Asia, to older settler colonies, to new imperial frontiers in Japan and Korea. Goncharov then trekked back to St. Petersburg through Russia's own Siberian colonies. The range of events discussed by Goncharov is truly impressive: the British-Xhosa Wars in the Cape Colony, London's devolution of power to the Cape in 1852, the Taiping Rebellion in China (which Goncharov personally experienced in Shanghai), the operation of Chinese treaty ports in the aftermath of the Opium Wars, the push to "open up" Japan, the Russians' prospecting of Korea, and preparations by Russia to annex the Amur-Ussuri region from China. Among the broader topics that captivated Goncharov were the relative strengths of mercantilism versus free trade, the progress of economic globalization, the methods and merits of informal imperialism, the management of settler colonies (in southern Africa and Siberia), the responses to the anti-colonial resistance of restive indigenes, the best methods of "civilizing" them, and the pertinence of "race" and other conceptions of human difference for modern imperial regimes.

To top it all off, the Crimean War broke out while the voyage was in progress, complicating Putiatin's diplomatic mission to Japan. In this war, Western Europeans backed the Ottoman empire in order to repulse Russia's expansion into the Black Sea region. In response to a Russian attack on their Danubian principalities, the Ottomans declared war on Russia in October 1853. In March 1854, around the time the *Pallada* was docked in Manila, the British and French followed suit, joined by the Kingdom of Sardinia. Though fought mainly in Crimea, the war also had its Pacific theater, where the Russians were more successful.[3] The *Pallada* became a potential target for British and French attacks.

The Crimean War was a watershed event for Russians. They saw it as Europe's betrayal, especially galling after the Russians had liberated Europe from Napoleon. (They were disinclined to share this glory with their allies.) As the scholar of Russian culture Susanna Soojung Lim frames it, the Russians were chagrined that the Europeans decided to side with the "infidel" Turks rather than accept Russia's legitimate imperial aspirations. So they redirected those aspirations to Asia, where they hoped to realize their imperial potential "without Europe's hostile meddling." David Schimmelpenninck van der Oye calls Russia's expansion into Asia "a tonic for the empire's wounded pride." The Crimean War made modernization a pressing concern. This eventually led to Alexander II's internal reforms—most importantly, the emancipation of serfs—but also to a renewed focus on modernizing the instruments of imperial rule, such as the navy and colonization policy. At the time it was published, *The Frigate Pallada* meshed perfectly with the ambitions and concerns of reform-era Russia.[4]

Goncharov's gripping narrative is a rich document of the Russian imperial worldview that broadly resonated with the tsarist-era Russian public.[5] It records a Russian image of Western European imperialism that circulated widely in Russia for the remainder of the century. It also offers insight into how Russians understood their place in the global imperial arena. By considering it in the larger political and cultural context of mid-nineteenth-century Russia and comparing it with other accounts of this expedition we see what is typical and what is unique in these images and understandings. Goncharov's travelogue sometimes diverges from his private writings. He reshaped his experiences where they might undercut his overall message, risk running afoul of censors, or antagonize the Russian public. This, in turn, offers a tantalizing view into the ideological tensions, public debates, and political anxieties that informed discussions of imperial questions in Russia. The travelogue's reception charts the arc of changing ideologies, political priorities, historical understandings, and emotional valences that have accompanied discussions of imperial questions in Russian culture from the nineteenth century to today.

The Russians are here the observers of the imperial world while also acting within it. It is unusual to see them in this role because they remain marginal in common accounts of European imperialism and because they had a complex relation to Europe. While feeling culturally marginal to it, the Russians nonetheless increasingly regarded themselves as central to its imperial enterprise. Domestic anxieties about their European status receded from view when nineteenth-century Russians turned outward and faced other nations. This was especially true when they found themselves on imperial frontiers in Asia. However, Russians were also aware of being treated by Western Europeans as inferior "Orientals," and felt intellectually colonized by them. Postcolonial philosopher Madina Tlostanova has argued that Russians emphasized their European identity in order to compensate for a deep-seated anxiety about being "second-rate" Europeans saddled with a "second-rate" empire.[6]

If Goncharov felt this anxiety, he compensated for it well. His Russians firmly belong in the same civilizational community with Europeans. That the travelogue projected this affiliation strongly was a big part of its appeal.[7] Politically, the Russian empire shared the global aspirations of this imperial vanguard (which also included the Americans), keenly following its modernizing innovations. This was clear to the Polish-born writer Joseph Conrad, who in *Heart of Darkness* made an enigmatic Russian the "disciple" of the rogue extractor of African ivory, Kurtz—the western literary canon's paradigmatic colonialist. At the same time, Russia was developing confidence in its own impressive rule which extended over three continents and hundreds of ethnic groups. While the Russian empire was about to get a cold shower in the Crimean War, at the time of the *Pallada*'s departure its army was the largest in the world. It had knocked at the gates of Constantinople in 1829 and taken over former Persian territory. By the 1840s, the Russians were pushing into the Caucasus and warming up to the idea of annexing the Amur-Ussuri region from China. Slow to be integrated into accounts of European imperialism, mid-nineteenth century Russia emerges in my book as an increasingly assertive empire that understood itself and operated—diplomatically, economically, and discursively—within the global imperial world order based on imperial expansion and competition.[8]

Certainly, observing is not all the Russians did during the *Pallada* mission. Their officials negotiated with European and non-European counterparts. Russian sailors aimed cannons at those perceived as hostile or obstreperous. Although Goncharov attenuated the mission's imperialist activism, portraying Russians as bystanders to Euro-American exertions, this pretense became untenable the moment the frigate dropped anchor in Nagasaki Bay. The same goals united Perry and Putiatin, and Putiatin's slightly later treaty was more comprehensive and arguably more advantageous. *A World of Empires* therefore also contributes to efforts aimed at countering Perry-centrism, which makes the so-called "opening" of Japan an episode in the history of the West. Imperial-era Japanese in fact considered their country to have been opened up by Russians. As testimony to their impact, "Putiatin" for a while became a synonym in Japanese for "foreigner."[9] The Russians were not, however, trying to win a race to Japan, as is sometimes assumed. The Russian government's instructions to Putiatin were to let Perry do the heavy lifting and to hover close enough to profit from Perry's success, whether peaceful or violent. Any haste that ensued had more to do with the unfolding Crimean conflict that imperiled the Russian Navy in the Pacific.

The nature of what the Russians were doing in Japan in the 1850s has also been distorted for Russian audiences. (Goncharov wrote about Japan because by the time he published his travelogue this mission was no longer secret.) In introductions to the Soviet editions of *The Frigate Pallada,* readers were informed that the tsarist government's business, beyond settling a border dispute about the Kurile Islands, was to sign a trade treaty with a neighboring country. This was whitewashing plain and simple. The so-called "unequal treaties" that Perry's Americans and Putiatin's Russians eventually signed with the Japanese government, just like earlier British treaties with China, violated the sovereignty of Japan and extracted at gunpoint trading rights that favored the imperial intruder. This was an attempt at economic exploitation

Figure I.2. Vice Admiral Yevfimy Putiatin, commander of the *Pallada* expedition.

without the messy and costly business of a territorial takeover. The *Pallada* Russians also proposed trade to Korea and explored the navigability of the Amur River, the heart of a huge region Russia annexed from China in 1860 in rather devious ways. Though Goncharov did not mention it, Putiatin eventually managed to secure access to Chinese ports for Russians, who were apparently more eager to join the rapacious Euro-American vanguard than to take the moral high ground. The *Pallada* expedition thus marks Russia's important push into East Asia.

Global voyages encouraged global visions.[10] Mutual learning and emulation among empires contributed to homogenizing effects. Best-practice comparisons were par for the course. Goncharov's travelogue vividly captures the impetus of nineteenth-century globalizing processes. His grand tour of the imperial world with its exotic peoples and places acquainted Russian audiences, both governmental and recreational, with the maritime colonizing empires—British, French, Portuguese, Spanish, Dutch, and American—that had transformed much of the globe. Everywhere Goncharov went, he keenly observed the imperial practices of other empires and reflected on Russia's own: Are the Dutch or the British better at colonizing? How does Russia fit into the global network of empires? What can we learn?

From the beginning of their expansion, European empires kept watchful eyes on one another. As historian Anthony Pagden argues, they "measured their behavior against each other, and, far more frequently than has been supposed, borrowed from each other in their continuing attempts to understand the evolving shape of the empires which they had created." At stake was not just understanding, but what Ann Laura Stoler calls "a competitive politics of comparison" that fostered the production of imperial knowledge and its exchange. This included, in Stoler's account, a search for new forms of rule and a "poaching" of practices, which were carried across imperial systems. Western empires borrowed technologies of empire from one another and from Russia. The Russians borrowed them from western empires. At times, both the Russian and western empires borrowed from the Ottoman and Persian empires. What the historian of Russian empire Willard Sunderland calls "the intellectual headquarters of Russian colonization"—the St. Petersburg library of the Resettlement Administration—included a variety of western works on European colonization of various places around the globe. Empires, including the Russian one, made extravagant claims to exceptionalism, but the reality of how they operated involved a heavy reliance on comparison and mutual borrowing.[11]

Travelogues were an important point of imperial knowledge transfer. This knowledge was considered of strategic and sometimes sensitive importance to the imperial state. Some printed travel accounts deemed not suitable for the general public were classified by the Ministry of Foreign Affairs as confidential.[12] This was not the case for *The Frigate Pallada.* Russian readers had a chance to learn from Goncharov's wildly popular book about such innovations as London's devolution of rule to the Cape Colony, gunboat diplomacy, the economics of free trade, and the Spanish empire's racial caste system. They were also encouraged to think of their own empire as cognate to others. Goncharov explicitly identified parallels in the colonial wars of conquest in the Eastern Cape region of southern Africa and Russia's wars in the Caucasus Mountains. His depiction of Russia, a traditional overland empire, as a seafaring empire made it look like western ones.[13]

The importance of travel writing as a conduit of such knowledge and such comparative sensibility cannot be overstated. One scholar puts it this way: "Travel writers offered up their expertise as historians, geographers, demographers, anthropologists, and authorities on the natural and built environments, and displayed their talents as prose writers, all to a highly receptive and sizeable reading public. . . . In the nineteenth century, publishers earned much of their income, and, more importantly, the reading public gained much of its knowledge about the world, from travel books."[14] Having been dismissed until recently by cultural critics as a middlebrow literary genre, it may well be the most socially salient of them all. Travel writing is revelatory on three levels, in that it reports on unfamiliar places and peoples; conveys the values, interests, and assumptions of travelers; and reflects those of their home cultures. Culture and ideology shape geographic visions, as historian Mark Bassin's work shows well. He observes that "a society's picture of foreign peoples and places is above all an expression of its own mentality. It informs us accordingly not so much about the object of representation as about the beliefs, hopes, prejudices, and frustrations of the group that authors it." *The Frigate Pallada* reflects the society that in some sense coproduced it, and that reacted vividly to it as finished product.[15]

Though less well known in the West, Russian travel writing was voluminous, ubiquitous, and socially significant.[16] Excerpts from travel books and sundry travel notes inundated periodicals, that key cultural vehicle of nineteenth-century Russia. Travel accounts were the quintessential popular reading of the 1800s, valued for combining entertainment with useful knowledge. Mostly read for pleasure, *The Frigate Pallada* was also read in governmental circles and taught in schools and military academies. Much of it appeared in the journal of the Naval Ministry, which sponsored the *Pallada* expedition. Against all odds—given the ostensible anti-colonialism of the new regime—it remained Party-recommended reading even in the Soviet period.

Beyond popularizing specific imperial technologies, travelogues played a key role in popularizing imperialism as such. As Mary Louise Pratt has influentially argued, travel books made imperial expansion "meaningful and desirable" to the citizens of imperial countries. They created "a sense of curiosity, excitement, adventure, and even moral fervor about European expansionism." They gave European reading publics "a sense of ownership, entitlement and familiarity with respect to the distant parts of the world that were being explored, invaded, invested in, and colonized."[17]

Such was the role that *The Frigate Pallada* played in Russian culture for the remainder of the tsarist period and beyond. It reflected popular imperial attitudes, opinions, and aspirations. It also tried to mold them. No mere collection of impressions, this was a book that made arguments, at times polemical ones. Contrary to Soviet critics, who—incredibly—declared the book anti-colonial in its orientation, *The Frigate Pallada* championed Europe's and Russia's imperial expansion and colonial activity, presenting them as hallmarks of modernity, progress, and global capitalism. It promoted imperial globalization, free trade, and Europe's and Russia's mission of civilizing subject peoples. Of lasting legacy, for example, was Goncharov's boosterist image of Siberia: the writer masked Siberia's colonial status, Russified its public image, and exaggerated the government's benevolence. Ironically, some of Goncharov's ideas may have actually imperiled the empire in rather unexpected ways. So influential was his book's reckless condescension toward Asians, for example, that some historians have blamed it for contributing to Russia's defeat in the Russo-Japanese War of 1904–1905.[18]

The naval voyages themselves, like the travelogues that described them, imported to Russia western models of modernizing colonial administration. They helped generate colonial knowledge useful for governing peripheral lands and peoples in increasingly uniform ways. As historian Ilya Vinkovetsky argues, visits to various European-run colonies around the globe deeply impressed Russian circumnavigators who were eager to apply the observed techniques in Russia's imperial domains. Their accounts, Vinkovetsky writes, "tipped the scale toward more West European–oriented models for Russian elites to perceive and act upon empire's various peoples." Many Russian naval officers trained directly with Britain's Royal Navy and travel literature was part of their education. Just as bureaucrats back home did, circumnavigators at sea had libraries filled to the brim with travelogues and western sources about various colonial sites around the globe. The *Pallada* had a library of eight thousand volumes, and Goncharov also kept his own collection, to which he added new acquisitions at various ports of call.[19]

It was the nature of the genre that Goncharov would channel these sources to some extent. Borrowing that in today's parlance would be called outright plagiarism is more charitably referred to by scholars as the "citationary structure" of travel accounts. It involved routine repetition and copying from other travel accounts, often without attribution. So entrenched was this practice, especially in eighteenth- and nineteenth-century travel accounts, that Simon Gikandi questions their discovery value, calling them "an elaborate reworking of the colonial library, a rediscovery of the already discovered." That colonial library filtered and often displaced travelers' personal experiences with ideas and assumptions culled from their reading. To know this

Figure I.3. The officers of the *Pallada*. Goncharov is seated front row, fifth from left, between the ship captain, Ivan Unkovsky, on his right, and the expedition commander, Yevfimy Putiatin, on his left. Daguerreotype from 1852, reproduced from "Solntse Rossii," 1911, No. 47.

might lessen our expectation of authenticity, though Goncharov's work, luckily, is not an egregious case.[20]

The western experience in colonial modernization flowed through written documents of naval voyages, but also through the subsequent professional trajectories of their crews. The *Pallada* expedition yielded a worldly cadre of government officials, made up of men who had already been accomplished in their prior careers. Yevfimy Putiatin, having concluded the treaty with Japan, later negotiated one with China, and went on to became a Russian attaché in London and a Minister of Education. (In a morbid irony for a seaman, he died in the bathtub of a French hotel.) Prior to the expedition, he had participated in military expeditions to the Caucasus and negotiated, with the aid of military pressure, a trade treaty with Persia.[21] The *Pallada*'s resident naturalist and Sinologist (and an official of the Ministry of Foreign Affairs), Iosif Goshkevich, became the first Russian consul to Japan. With the help of a Japanese refugee smuggled out of Japan on the *Pallada*, Goshkevich authored the first Russian-Japanese dictionary—for which he received the Russian equivalent of the Nobel Prize, the Demidov Prize. The natural history collection he brought from the voyage is housed in St. Petersburg's Hermitage Museum.

Prior to the expedition, he had spent nine years with the Russian Orthodox mission in Beijing.[22] The Dutch interpreter in Japan, Konstantin Possiet (Pos'et), a member of the Russian Geographical Society and of the Russian Academy of Sciences, became Minister of Communication. Goncharov himself, who was a published novelist and an official in the Department of Trade during the voyage, later became a high-level censor.[23] Putiatin and Possiet both joined the State Council, the tsar's highest advisory body.

While his colleagues may have recorded their experiences of the voyage in their governmental capacities, Goncharov did so through his travelogue. Its overriding, if implicit, message was that Russia must catch up to its colonial rivals, especially the ever-energetic British. It must become a global contender in trade, resource extraction, and access to cheap labor markets, in both current and future areas of imperial control. Goncharov was impressed with the British empire most of all, especially its new cost-sustainable model of an informal empire, which relied on naval and economic power and did away with the need for territorial annexations. The central geopolitical confrontation of the nineteenth century—Russia's Great Game with Britain over Asia—hovers on the travelogue's horizon. Less overtly, the travelogue suggests that Russia must compete with other empires also in humanitarian arrangements and infrastructure improvements for its imperial peripheries. In the nineteenth century, territories and profits were not the sole platforms of imperial rivalries. Ideologies of civilizing mission comprised such a platform, too. In one richly allusive passage Goncharov even tentatively sketches distant prospects for indigenous self-rule in Siberia, Russia's largest colony—a scenario he also vaguely contemplated for Africans. Ideas of imperial trusteeship, it seems, which treated colonialism as temporary stewardship of "backward" places, also infatuated Russian elites desirous of giving empire a moral uplift.[24]

This imperial humanitarianism, however, had its sordid flipside. Paternalistic policies appeared less benign to native people. Civilizing bromides alternate in Goncharov's book with wholly self-interested considerations of raw power and profit. Violent means toward "civilized" ends did not overly trouble him. *The Frigate Pallada*'s descriptions of colonial sites and peoples employ classic rhetorical tropes of European colonialism. Russians were capable of mentally Orientalizing "uncivilized" lands and peoples just as any other Europeans were.[25] Despite moments of sympathy and understanding, Goncharov's perceptions of Japan in particular offer an ample record of unvarnished Eurocentric arrogance. In this case, the book's sentiments contrast with the actual conduct of the Russian expedition in Japan. As compared to Perry's men, Russians went about their gunboat diplomacy in ways more respectful toward their hosts. Individual non-European people everywhere could appear to Goncharov good and kind and wise, but lumped into ethnicities and "races," they tended to be harshly stereotyped and slotted into demeaning Eurocentric hierarchies. The stereotypes Goncharov peddled therefore did not always align with his recorded experiences, but he typically avoided using his experiences to revise his stereotypes. He viewed a confident civilizing mission, in Russia's own Siberian "Orient" and Asia more generally, as the Russian's birthright and duty. Everywhere he went, he ignored or diminished the negative impacts of European imperialism on its non-European subjects. Their mistreatment occasionally invited critique, but only if the perpetrators were not Russian. European imperial elites protested most keenly the colonial ills of empires other than their own.

While this indeed is the large-scale vista of the travelogue's imperial terrain, in many places this message falters, or becomes ambivalent, contradictory, or rife with anxiety. To be sure, the book does express imperialistic and racist attitudes. But these attitudes have convoluted genealogies and complex rhetorical strategies, and often intermix with more benign sentiments.

The travelogue's imperial terrain is therefore a shifting one, more like swampland than firm ground. I endeavor to understand this complex ecosystem by peering into that swampy underside. Categories are in flux; clashing perspectives coexist without being reconciled; consistency is hard to come by. Goncharov trumpeted the primacy of enlightened, white, modernized Europe, but sometimes missed a beat. Regarding Japan, for example, he promoted a plan of Europeanizing it, yet at times judged its people to be on a par with Europe's most civilized nations. In their knack for fine workmanship, the English were said to be just like the Chinese, for whom Goncharov prophesied a leading role in world affairs despite witnessing a particularly low point in their history. The category of race structured Goncharov's perceptions of human difference, yet indigenous African women momentarily appeared to him quite similar to their sunburnt counterparts back in Russian villages. Some of Goncharov's evocative assertions of imperial authority seem rooted in deep-seated anxieties.

A World of Empires does not reduce Goncharov's text to a tale of ineluctable top-down colonial oppression in zealous service to political authority, with no shades of gray allowed. I examine instead the diversity of Goncharov's ideas about empires and imperialism, their intellectual genealogies and ideological complexity, what cultural assumptions or anxieties they fed on, and how richly they interacted with history. I also venture beyond Goncharov's travelogue to material that completes the picture merely sketched by him, or fills out the contours of the voyage itself, or enriches this particular slice of Russian imperial history. Though they imitated Britain's gunboat diplomacy, whose efficacy in China impressed all imperial regimes, the Russians' diplomatic success came, paradoxically, when they lost their boat and their guns. Their vaunted opening of Japan petered out without the expected follow-through of exploitative trade.

I also contrast the travelogue with what we know of the actual histories of the places Goncharov visited, including those likely to have been known to the writer himself. As the scholar of travel writing Carl Thompson warns, even when complete fidelity is the goal (not always a given), "the inevitable filtering of the original travel experience gives a writer considerable scope to be, if not exactly deceitful, certainly economical with the truth." Sins of omission, lapses of memory, embellishments, and fictive coloring are all tricks and perils of a travel writer's trade. Economy with the truth, moreover, becomes even more pronounced on topics where authors have an ideological ax to grind. Despite their claims to eyewitness authenticity, travel books, Thompson writes, "should never be naively read as just a transparent window on the world."[26] Their obvious ethnocentrism clouds that window even more. In short, travelers' ideas about the world should not be taken as the truth about it. Travelogues, Goncharov's included, are sets of representations that may or may not be related to actual reality.

That said, Goncharov was a fairly acute and often accurate observer. The basic events, itineraries, and interactions of the voyage are verifiable by other accounts of the expedition and by the official report delivered to Emperor Alexander II, which Goncharov penned on Putiatin's behalf and which Putiatin authorized. Some of Goncharov's comments about the Taiping Rebellion in China or the gathering forces of globalization anticipate cutting-edge historical research of today. Yet his Eurocentric bias also distorted much history, especially on the subject of empires' relations with indigenous people. I credit Goncharov's time-tested insights where such credit is due, but do not take him at face value. I aim instead for a productive conversation between the writer's crafted vision of the world he saw, the history known then, and the history known now.[27]

Unlike some historians who have been drawn to this travelogue, however, I do not treat its literariness as a liability, or a distracting fog to be quickly dispelled in the rush to get at the historical facts. The potency of this document and the source of its lasting power lie in its combination of fact and fiction. *The Frigate Pallada* deserves our attention not only because of the historical limelight of the events it describes, but also because of the powerful and sophisticated literary dimension that made it such an influential cultural phenomenon. "The literary image of another country and its inhabitants," Barbara Heldt notes, "is often the image that most people hold."[28] Moreover, literary devices, rhetorical patterns, and narrative techniques are the very things that help us glimpse the person and the worldview that produced the book. Like other forms of human activity, literature is a form of sense making. The travelogue's literary dimension thus helps reveal a lively, unique human mind trying to make sense of the worlds encountered on a voyage. As imperial historians have recently begun to discover, this kind of individual, human focus offers important gains, for which one may want to sacrifice some of the synoptic breadth afforded by armies of soldiers, missionaries, and administrators.[29] An intimate, creative encounter with history, and with a world so evidently and exhilaratingly in flux, is what I hope to capture in this book.

The need for this kind of intimacy and focus has also been articulated within the realms of postcolonial and travel writing studies. Both have critiqued a bird's-eye, homogenizing view of colonial writing, to some extent unavoidable in surveys of vast scope that traverse many epochs, authors, and texts. Both also decry the overwhelming focus on Western European cultures, and especially literature written in English. More fine-grained analysis is called for to ferret out complexity, nuance, and variance and connect texts to operations of power in more subtle ways. My work on Goncharov is sympathetic to these critiques.

Yet what makes this particular Russian travelogue worthy of focused attention? More than its being a great read, the answer lies in its incredible popularity. Because this travelogue clearly resonated with Russian readers, it has something to tell us about that public's tastes and interests. Enduring popularity also means enduring social impact. I was surprised to discover just how popular this book was, especially in the imperial period. Yet few non-Russian specialists of Russian literature know that Goncharov was so well traveled, or that he wrote this book. Even fewer have read it. He is mostly known for his three novels—*An Ordinary Story*, *Oblomov*, and *A Precipice*—the second being most famous. However, the nineteenth-century Russian reading public seemed most drawn to the travelogue. *The Frigate Pallada* enjoyed vastly greater readership than Goncharov's celebrated *Oblomov*.

At a time when few books saw two or three editions in Russia, *The Frigate Pallada* reached ten by 1900 (compared to six of *Oblomov*) and even this fell far short of actual demand for it.[30]

There were other Russian nineteenth-century travel accounts of exotic, faraway places, but none as popular, influential, or literarily accomplished. *The Frigate Pallada* was widely reviewed by prominent cultural commentators. Beyond men of letters, its socially diverse audience included women, government officials, and students of naval and military academies. This book was taught in schools.[31] Anton Chekhov read it as a young man, and then reread it when preparing for his own trek across Siberia to Sakhalin Island, north of Japan. The Orientalist painter Vasily Vereshchagin was obsessed with it. Vladimir Nabokov mentions it in one of his novels as a staple of middlebrow pre-revolutionary reading. Goncharov's account of the Cape of Good Hope reverberated in the Russian press during the Anglo-Boer War of 1899–1902. Soviet Communist Party leaders recommended the travelogue to young writers. It is mentioned in Secretary General Leonid Brezhnev's memoir. The renowned Russian literary scholar Viktor Shklovsky spoke of it in 1955 as a book that for over a century "has never left readers' desks." Goncharov himself reportedly called it his own favorite and recommended it to his fans above his novels. He warmly labeled *The Frigate Pallada* "a rose without thorns," unique among his own books in that it gave him "exclusively pleasure," causing "no bitterness at all." The book is available to Russian readers today in e-book and audiobook formats.[32]

For the remainder of the century, *The Frigate Pallada* became a model for Russian travel writing, including the kind sponsored by the government.[33] It also became a staple of young adult literature in Russia, similar to such imperially-themed Western European classics as Charles Kingsley's *Westward Ho!*, Jules Verne's *Around the World in Eighty Days*, and Rudyard Kipling's *Kim*. Like these other texts on which generations of Europeans were brought up, Goncharov's book played a vital role in shaping and transmitting imperialist attitudes and cultural stereotypes of non-European peoples and places. It confirmed for Russians their belief that empire was their natural and logical aspiration.

Readers of *A World of Empires* will find here a snapshot of the mid-nineteenth-century imperial world. This transitional moment saw experiments in gunboat diplomacy and informal colonialism based on free trade. It was a time of structural changes in the world economy. Europeans and Americans gained a commanding lead in Asia. For Russia, too, the 1850s mark a transition when the empire pivoted to Asia and embraced modernization, processes that accelerated after the Crimean War, when Goncharov's travelogue began capturing the attention of the Russian public. The story of this high-profile government expedition illuminated the stakes of Russia's Asian politics and presented an argument for modernization.

It is particularly striking how precociously, in the 1850s, this insightful Russian traveler identified the approach of globalization. This was Goncharov's biggest discovery of his voyage. He was amazed to find the unprecedented network of interconnections and increasing homogeneity that we today associate with globalization. He thought in parallels and comparisons. Seclusion-era Japan appeared to him not dissimilar from pre-westernization Russia; the wars of conquest in Africa seemed quite like Russia's own in the Caucasus. In each port, he watched international imperial elites engage in flurries of networking. Imperialism was for Goncharov a distinctly global phenomenon.

And his Russia was part of it. Historians have illuminated the internal workings of the Russian empire: its expansion, institutions, administrative policies, and management of multiethnicity. The Russians in this book, by contrast, face outward, looking beyond their own empire. They orient themselves on the global stage among their imperial peers. When *The Frigate Pallada* eventually turns its gaze on Russia's own colony (Siberia), its author's mental framework has been shaped by encounters with global imperial frontiers and other empires' ideologies of rule.

Historians have turned to Goncharov's book before, but mostly as a repository of historical facts, purging it of what are arguably its most compelling assets: an image of a certain mindset, a rhetorically ornate ideology, a way of thinking *about* history.[34] *A World of Empires* makes the case for the study of Russian empire as a joint enterprise of historians and literary scholars. Far from serving as inert backdrops for each other, history and literature here dynamically interact. I check Goncharov's representations against empirical sources, especially those he surely knew. This allows for concrete arguments about the text's ideological shaping and helps avoid perpetuating myths that should instead be critiqued. How events are refracted in this text matters because seductive literary packaging gave these manipulations long afterlives. Literary analysis, by contrast, probes the rhetoric, context, and innuendo of Goncharov's text, revealing how an arsenal of artistic tropes may be harnessed for ideological effect.

The spotlight here is on a major Russian writer's forgotten masterpiece. It is a profoundly complex document of Russian literature's engagement with the problems of race and of empire, both relatively understudied.[35] Given its astounding dissemination and lively reception, the travelogue offers insight into the connection between literature and society. As a literary work it is far from pedestrian. It is a fascinating text, full of humor, irony, descriptive charms, and occasional lyricism—truly among the best examples of nineteenth-century Russian prose.[36] It escaped attention due to traditional literary hierarchies that have privileged fiction. In-between genres such as travel books have been little heeded; the taint of popular culture has contributed to this neglect. Thus the novel *Oblomov* became canonized as Goncharov's most important work. It also helped that *Oblomov* meshed more easily with the Soviet regime's anti-feudal critique and made no mention of Russia's complicity in European imperialism. While in the early decades of the Soviet Union imperialism was eagerly criticized as a distinct iniquity of the tsarist regime, the political orthodoxy soon turned to denying it altogether. The perceived ideological harms of *The Frigate Pallada* were thus carefully managed in the Soviet period.

The Frigate Pallada also casts new light on *Oblomov,* by placing this classic novel's "Russian" questions within the global worldview of its creator. The travelogue provides a powerful deterrent to nostalgic readings of *Oblomov,* which excessively leverage the author's purely human sympathy for his flawed protagonist into an idealization of the values he represents.[37] The foil to the novel's slothful Oblomov is his best friend, a Russified German named Stolz, a resourceful entrepreneur reminiscent of *The Frigate Pallada*'s British merchants. His business ventures keep him perpetually on the road. Readers have tended to find Stolz artificial and unconvincing, a somewhat wooden contrast to Oblomov's warm and fallible humanity. Yet he may well be key to the novel's social meaning. The *Pallada* voyage showed Goncharov how the British empire benefitted from the activities of such intrepid, middle-class businessmen. Implying a connection between knowledge and power, his travelogue makes Russian competitiveness in the imperial race contingent on greater public interest in travel, particularly seafaring. Goncharov gently rebuked the Russian homebodies with the example of English ladies, who nonchalantly traversed the globe and for whom a trip from India to London was about as daunting as one from Tambov to Moscow was for a Russian.[38]

For all the novel's nostalgia for Russia's feudal past, epitomized by the character of Oblomov, the context of the travelogue makes it clear that Stolz is the type of hero the modernizing Russian empire really needs. Indeed, within the text of *Oblomov* itself, Anne Lounsbery finds stasis to be the threat to Russia's economic future. In her interpretation of the novel, in order to join history, "Russia must get connected—intellectually, economically, and also spatially—with the rest of the world."[39] The novel and the travelogue thus appear to be consistent. According to *The Frigate Pallada,* to keep up with other empires, Russia must become a nation on the move, a nation of Stolzes—itinerant doers, well apprised of the wider world. Oblomovism, however quaint and touching, represents a historical dead end for Russia. A belief nourished in Goncharov by the *Pallada* voyage was that Russia's modernity and imperialism depended on mobility and connectivity. This belief also infused his novel.

A World of Empires follows the *Pallada*'s journey yet avoids merely chronicling it. This is not a gallery of Goncharov's "images" of various places. Instead, chapters are focused on particular problems and topics. Together, they survey Goncharov's imperial vision.

Goncharov's first two longer visits, to London and to southern Africa's Cape Colony, show his penchant for imperial comparisons. He was fascinated with the British empire and the global reach that made it an acknowledged—and resented—imperial leader by mid-century. London emerges in his travelogue as the center of the colonial world and its economy. The Cape Colony becomes the icon of the Britons' formidable colonizing competence, which contrasts starkly with the lackluster performance of the Dutch, the colony's former masters. Looking at southern Africa, Goncharov pondered the challenges of running a distant settler colony perpetually imperiled by the indigenous population's resistance, a problem Russia then faced in the Caucasus. As he studied various imperial regimes, Goncharov sought instructive lessons for Russia.

Trade, tariffs, flows of global capital, and skyrocketing profits captured Goncharov's attention as he visited European-run ports and trading enclaves on the coastal rims of Asia. In them he truly came to appreciate the increasing interlocking of the world. Manila, Singapore, Hong Kong, and Shanghai emerge in his travelogue as vibrant trading hubs whose networks encircle the globe, and as testaments to the emergent world economy, the globalizing forces of Euro-American imperialism, and Asia's incredible economic potential. Also vividly captured are the collaboration and exchange of expertise among international imperial elites in these coastal footholds. Moderating his starry-eyed adulation for the British, in Shanghai Goncharov turned critical of their demeaning treatment of indigenous populations. He castigates the European and American opium trade in China as immoral and exploitative.

When they reached Japan, the Russian observers of imperialism became actors: they muscled in with their gunboats to compel Japan to open its ports. Compared to Perry's Americans, the Russians showed greater respect for Japanese customs and protocol. Goncharov, however, was impatient with such moderation. *The Frigate Pallada* mingles humanitarian sentiments with brutal realpolitik. It indulges in grandiose plans for remaking Japan into a fully Europeanized country. Though its author barely set foot on land, the travelogue confidently assesses Japan's own cultural resources as unsustainably meager. Japan brought out the full-throated Eurocentric in Goncharov. He articulated Russia's bold civilizing mission in Asia. The Russians turned aggressive when prospecting Korean shores for future Russian expansion. Claiming the classic rights of European explorers, they named various landmarks with Russian names. This is how Korea acquired Goncharov Island (today Mayang-do Island, site of a North Korean missile base).

Gears suddenly switch when the travelogue lands its author in Siberia, Russia's biggest resource and settler colony. This is the Russian piece in Goncharov's mosaic of the global imperial world order. While all rhetoric of colonialism is screened from descriptions of Siberia, the region is shown to operate in recognizably colonial ways. It took delicate ideological footwork for Goncharov to convey his belief in Russia's manifest destiny of continental expansion. His account Russifies the image of Siberia, presenting it as an inalienable part of the Russian land. It lauds the successes of Russian colonization (calling it settlement) and of Orthodox missionary activity, crediting them for humanizing the indigenous people. It entices future settlers with boosterist images of a thriving colonial enterprise, spectacularly diminishing its hardships. As he wrestled with the meaning of his own empire, Goncharov claimed Siberia to be Russia's civilizing miracle to rival western models.

Between Africa and Siberia, the voyage exposed Goncharov to bewildering human diversity. His conceptual grid included race, ethnicity, nationality, hybridity, and miscegenation. Russian critics have tended to celebrate Goncharov's purported sympathy and humanism in portraying other ethnicities. He did display these qualities. Yet, as a general characterization, that assessment is flawed and ultimately untenable. Goncharov mixed glaring racial prejudice with more benign sentiments, certitude with ambivalence, insistence on difference with assertions of similarity, instinctive superiority with anxieties of identity. My term for this pervasive inconsistency in the travelogue is to call it an imperial kaleidoscope. The writer could not fathom why some Russians in Siberia "went native" and adopted the culture of the indigenous peoples. The enigma of Russianness became a tantalizing question for him in these exotic settings.

What polemics has the travelogue inspired from Goncharov's times to today? What have been the sources of its appeal? The book had a huge following in tsarist Russia. But how was this paean to global imperialism made palatable to the Soviet regime? Under the guise of condensing the text, some Soviet editions cleansed it of its most egregiously racist or fervently procolonial passages, making key portions of the travelogue vanish into thin air. Since 1989, the replica of a three-mast frigate named after Putiatin's *Pallada* has been sailing the seven seas. Post-communist Russia is finding new sources of appeal and discomfort in *The Frigate Pallada*.

For readers today, Goncharov's book creates a stage on which nineteenth-century European and American empires can be seen to engage in a diplomatic tango—a dance in which Russia was by no means a wallflower. Like the tango, the interaction among them was full of tense energy, dramatic lunges, and close contact, at once uncomfortable and exciting. Rivalry and cooperation went hand in hand. For all their differences, the French, the British, and the Russians could engage one another because they all knew the steps and generally respected the common rules of the dance floor. With perspicacity and prescience, Goncharov's travelogue detects the interconnections and synergies that we today call globalization. So let us follow Goncharov's Russians to the imperial dance floor, and watch them tango.

CHAPTER ONE

From London to Cape Town, or How to Run a Successful Empire

I may say without any vainglorious boast, or without great offence to anyone, that we stand at the head of moral, social, and political civilization. Our task is to lead the way and direct the march of other nations.

—Lord Palmerston, Britain's foreign secretary, 1848

Deeply impressed by Britain's uncannily reliable postal service that spanned the globe and treated each letter as caringly as "a newborn baby," Ivan Goncharov explained to his readers back home: "In England and its colonies a letter is a cherished object. It passes through thousands of hands, on railroads and other roads, across oceans, from one hemisphere to the other, and unfailingly finds the addressee, so long as he is alive. If he is dead or has moved, the letter just as ineluctably returns to the sender."[1] Since Goncharov's letters sent to friends from London and Hong Kong did nonetheless disappear, he went on to surmise that Dutch or Prussian intermediaries must be to blame. His framing of such exemplary postal service as peculiar to the British obliquely disparaged the Russian equivalent's lower levels of customer satisfaction. Goncharov's readers could also have read between the lines that the letters just as likely disappeared while in the care of the notoriously unreliable Russian mail service. This little anecdote sounds the first note of what will become a persistent pattern of *The Frigate Pallada:* a comparison, whether implied or overt, between Britain and other empires, including Russia, with respect to imperial objectives, policies, strategies, and achievements. Like other European empires, Russia saw plenty to fret about regarding Britain, which by the mid-nineteenth century had left its competitors in the dust and challenged Russia in the Great Game over Asia.

The greatest success story of nineteenth-century European imperialism, the largest by far in territory and population, the British empire was the envy of all rivals with global aspirations. Goncharov captures the dominance of the British in global terms, which is how the British themselves had viewed their empire since the late eighteenth century. According to historian Jürgen Osterhammel, Britain was the first nation to shift imperial operations into global gear. It built a cohesive transoceanic empire that spanned the globe, advancing its interests through a flexible repertoire of formal rule and informal control. Thanks to an immense demographic boom—the population of the British Isles nearly quadrupled between 1750 and 1850—it mobilized huge waves of eager migrants ready to spread the English language, customs, and lifestyle to imperial frontiers. It had the world's most advanced and efficient industrialized economy and a robust financial sector actively searching for investment opportunities abroad. As the chief beneficiary of government funding, the Royal Navy made Britain the supreme maritime power. By the end of the nineteenth century, Osterhammel writes, "there was no major waterway or strait in the world where the Royal Navy did not have a say." Rather than shut out competitors, the British policed sea routes for the benefit of Europe's imperial nations. Along with the abolishment of trade and tariff protections, these unilateral actions were, in Osterhammel's estimation, "unprecedented, indeed revolutionary." They helped establish Britain among its Western peers as the benign hegemon of the worldwide imperial system.[2]

European and American imperial elites—including Britain's own elite, as this chapter's epigraph's shows—found it difficult not to be impressed with the British empire by mid-century, and Goncharov was no exception. As Susanna Soojung Lim notes, Goncharov was acutely conscious of being "a Russian traveling in an Englishman's world"—a world "created, owned, and maintained, essentially, by England."[3] This caused resentment, to be sure, but also fascination with the secrets of British success. Goncharov's awe speaks loudest in his descriptions of southern Africa, which unfold in the travelogue as the story of a spectacular British makeover of a lethargic Dutch colony. As in other Russian travelogues of this era, Britain is the mirror in which Russia studies its own image—the precedent with which it contends.[4]

Depicting Russia's chief geopolitical rival required a careful ideological balancing act. While Goncharov's attitude toward England has been mostly seen as critical, there's more ambivalence and complexity to it than meets the eye. Snide put-downs of the philistine English bourgeoisie alternate with inspirational messages about the wise arrangements of England's public life and the successes of British overseas colonization. To read Goncharov's comments as transparent reflections of the author's views carries risks—the same hazards that are inherent in reading travel literature in general. Like its cousin, autobiography, travel writing always conveys crafted reflections of travelers' personas and of the worlds through which they journeyed.[5]

Moreover, the historical context in which Goncharov wrote mattered. Russia's loss in 1856 to the British-led coalition in the Crimean War was the setting for *The Frigate Pallada*'s first publication as a book, in 1858. Britain's brutal suppression of the Indian Mutiny of 1857, which in the eyes of many Russians exposed the falsity of Britain's much vaunted humanitarianism, perhaps also colored the narrative. Historical hindsight brought a retrospective resentment of the English, which Goncharov might have further exaggerated to soothe his country's wounded national pride. The opening chapter of *The Frigate Pallada,* which describes Goncharov's stay in England, from November 1852 to January 1853, is actually the last chapter he wrote. It is shaped not only by the outcome of the Crimean debacle, but also by the completed journey. As such, it combines the functions of introduction and conclusion, proposing a certain baseline attitude toward the English that aggregates, and sometimes belies, Goncharov's impressions from various stages of the voyage.

Russia's imperial rivalry with Britain, later known as the Great Game, also colored the travelogue's affect and its politics. Known to nineteenth-century Russians as "the tournament of shadows," this game, too, was galvanized by the Crimean War. As one Russian general put it, Britain "threw down the gauntlet under the walls of Sebastopol"—a site of protracted battles in the Crimea—and Russia "accepted the challenge." Contrary to British propaganda, the Russian empire was far from incompetent in this contest.[6] As the Crimean War unfolded, the *Pallada*'s elite crew watched it intensify from the Britain-dominated coastal rim of Asia. Yet they set out on their voyage in 1852 already inclined to perceive the global dynamic of power in terms of a Russo-British rivalry. As far as Goncharov was concerned, Russia had much catching up to do. Curiously, this included, in his view, devolution of power and other humanitarian arrangements for the benefit of colonies.

On a purely personal level, Gocharov was well disposed toward the English. After Russia, England was apparently the writer's "second love," according to Goncharov scholar Vladimir Melnik, even though this love had its "well-defined limits." Goncharov's appreciation for things English—including Dickens as a favorite author, English breakfast, and, quite likely, constitutionalism—was well known to his family and acquaintances.[7] It brought him closer to his boss Yevfimy Putiatin, an enthusiastic Anglophile. The writer may have inherited admiration for England from the sentimentalist Russian writer Nikolai Karamzin, whom he avidly read, and from his uncle and surrogate father, the naval officer Nikolai Tregubov, whom he remembered as "an English gentleman." Tregubov taught the future writer about geography and navigation and inspired his interest in voyages of exploration.[8] So it is not surprising that Goncharov's letters from England lack any noticeable negativity toward the English. Though aghast at London's horrible air pollution, Goncharov the traveler seemed to enjoy its mild climate, cheap oysters, and elegant shops. He voiced sharper comments in these private letters about the conduct of drunken Russian sailors than about any deficiencies in the English character.[9] It was in his public capacity, as the author of *The Frigate Pallada*, that Goncharov mixed condescension and critique in his initial description of London and the English.

Still, whatever flaws the English have in the opening of *The Frigate Pallada*, they seem to outgrow them in the chapter on Africa and beyond. Indeed, some of those very flaws begin appearing as valuable imperial aptitudes. Goncharov's account of southern Africa is his paean to Britain's colonizing prowess. He emphasizes the superiority of the British colonial model over the Portuguese and Dutch ones, echoing British travelers to Africa, ever eager to discredit the continent's other colonial traditions.[10] Solidly grounded in a Eurocentric vision of human progress and the racial hierarchy it authorized, Goncharov emphatically endorses the idea of total European colonization of Africa—an endorsement ignored by the Soviet proponents of seeing *The Frigate Pallada* as an anti-colonial text. He supports Britain's colonial rule in the Cape Colony and its brutal wars against indigenous Africans. The grievances of the latter never rise to the level of legitimate arguments against colonial rule. Africa is merely a backdrop for the instructive lessons that the writer hopes to glean from British colonial management. Rather than an African locus in its own right, the Cape Colony is for him no less—and no more—than a flourishing "corner of England."

Journeying through foreign countries brings up parallels with one's own, Goncharov writes. Looking at the world around him, Goncharov had Russia at the forefront of his mind.[11] Thinking about a typical Englishman led him to think about a typical Russian. The homing beacon for Goncharov's observations about other empires was ultimately the Russian one. How did Russia compare with its competitors and what could it learn? A rosy image of Britain's successes in Africa was ultimately meant to inspire progress in Russia's own vast imperial domains.

London as Nexus of the Colonial World

Goncharov visited London a few times while the frigate was being repaired in Portsmouth. He was giddy to find himself in this bustling metropolis of two million, "seething with life and activity" and bathed in "an ocean of light."[12] He took note of the tens of thousands of carriages that traversed the city and the gigantic sums of capital traded daily on the stock exchange. He marveled at clean taverns and found English food, while heavy and unsophisticated, tasty enough and cheap. Like Karamzin, he raved about the beauty of Englishwomen, and was particularly pleased with their habit of lifting their skirts rather high. He communicated in English, in which he was less fluent than in French and German.

London becomes a symbolic place in the travelogue. Already in 1790, Nikolai Karamzin had proclaimed it in his popular travelogue *Letters of a Russian Traveler* as "the center of world commerce."[13] Yet Karamzin described it as just one of Europe's capitals, however more brilliant than Paris. Goncharov, by contrast, describes London as the capital of the colonial world and the nest of an entrepreneurial British bourgeoisie that holds the entire world in its grip. This global imperial frame of reference connects for Goncharov the bustling English metropolis to the colony on the southern tip of Africa, to the newly opened ports in China, and to the formidable Royal Navy that chased the *Pallada* along Asia's eastern shores.

London also emerges in the travelogue as the center of nineteenth-century modernity and its consumer culture. Elegant London shops are veritable "museums of merchandise": even shopping can be educational in London. Thrilled by novel sales techniques such as home deliveries and displaying of prices, the writer shares consumer tips with his readers. The affordability of shopping in London leaves Goncharov powerless to resist the acquisition of useless knick-knacks: a book he'll never read, a pair of pistols he'll never use, a cigarette case, a dagger. Admiral Putiatin also went on a shopping spree in England, purchasing such military necessities and diplomatic sweeteners as a steam schooner that, appropriately for his mission to the Orient, he renamed the Vostok ("the East"), several cannon, sixty Lancaster and Wilkinson carbines (samples were dispatched to St. Petersburg, presumably for copying), and assorted souvenirs for Japanese dignitaries.[14]

Goncharov scoffed at sightseeing with a guidebook in hand, eager to distance himself from mere tourists bound to conventional itineraries.[15] And yet he visited most standard sites, from the National Gallery and the British Museum to St. Paul's Cathedral and Westminster Abbey. With the exception of the abbey's soaring Gothic arches, however, London landmarks left Goncharov unimpressed. The exhibits in the British Museum appeared to him indistinguishable from those in the museums of St. Petersburg, Vienna, or Madrid. He compared the National Gallery, whose collection he deemed trifling, to a mere vestibule of the St. Petersburg Hermitage.

He was also ostentatiously unmoved by Londoners' excitement surrounding the sumptuous state funeral in November 1852 of a British hero, the Duke of Wellington. The celebrated commander of the Allied forces in the Battle of Waterloo, whom the British, in a narrative contested by the Russians, credited with ending Napoleon's rule, Wellington had also vastly expanded Britain's imperial dominions in India.[16] But watching the public pay its respects, Goncharov finds a similarity to the curious crowds flocking to see novelties such as the steam-powered incubators on display nearby. His comparison is clearly meant to deflate both Wellington and the English:

> I summoned patience to look over various curiosities, such as chicks hatched by steam, or American locks that cannot be picked, etc. Judging by the fact that the English have been fussing about their dead duke for three weeks now, it would seem that they hatched out this rarity as well. He is dead and buried, and they still throng to gaze at—guess what?—the stands erected in the Church of St. Paul for the funeral! For this reason I still have been unable to peek into the church's interior: I'm not an Englishman so stands don't interest me. It is impossible to make a step without running into the duke—his portrait or his bust or an engraving of his hearse. . . . "Did you come for the Duke's funeral?" I was asked by a shopkeeper who recognized me as a foreigner. "Yes, oh yes!" I replied. For the life of me I could not tie together into one knot all the merits of the

> deceased duke, which is why (to my shame), his demise left me cold and even (may the Lord God forgive me!) annoyed that by his solemn procession through the streets, and, worse of all, by his stands, he prevented me from seeing what I wanted to see. Do not think that I disapprove of the respect for the innumerable merits of the British Agamemnon—not at all! I even bought from some boy a medallion of the hero. Intending to pay a fourpence, I mistakenly took out from my purse a Russian ten- or fifteen-kopeck coin. The boy chased me down, poked me in the back with the coin, and hollered like someone being slaughtered "No use, no use!"[17]

Goncharov reduces the state funeral of "the British Agamemnon," whose claims to fame supposedly elude him, to mere "fuss" that brought city life to a standstill, complicating his sightseeing plans. The extent of Goncharov's homage for Wellington is the purchase of a trivial knick-knack. These flippant comments about the English military hero must have been received like a restorative tonic by a post-Crimean Russian audience.

What most fascinates the writer is not state pomp, however, but the life of the street. Observations of it give rise to humorous vignettes of the English, such as a glimpse of two Englishmen who nearly "rip each other's arms out" in a handshake, their faces beaming with "comical self-importance." He chuckles when his servant Faddeev smirks at the sight of kilt-clad Scots or rudely barks orders in Russian at an uncomprehending shop assistant. A misuse of the English language becomes an occasion to poke fun at the English rather than the Russians' limited command of foreign languages. Goncharov gleefully reports Faddeev's name for the English—"asei"—which picks up on their constant repetition of "I say."[18]

Though Goncharov seeks out the life of the street, he claims to find little of it in London, where all life is concentrated in commerce. Prudence and order reign: "The city, like an animal, holds its breath and pulse. There's no purposeless shout, no needless movement. Singing, jumping, or pranks are rare even among children. Everything seems counted, weighed, and evaluated, as if taxes were levied not only on windows and wheels but on facial expressions and human sounds." By naming what is missing—the passers-by do *not* jostle, carriage drivers do *not* holler, pedestrians do *not* pause absentmindedly—Goncharov summons the obverse of this scene, the spontaneous and rambunctious Russian street life. It is a warm contrast to Britain's alienating modern urbanity, which, according to him, is all about business and comfort, governed by the clock.[19]

For the most part, Goncharov cultivates the persona of a bemused and aloof observer, too coolheaded for raptures. He nonetheless gives credit where credit is due, especially to England's arrangements in public life. Nowhere else, Goncharov surmises, can one acquire knowledge so cheaply and easily. Referring, without naming it, to the Royal Panopticon of Science and Art in Leicester Square, he writes: "Each step, the open doors of knowledge beckon. Everywhere there's something of interest to see: a machine, a rarity, a lecture on natural history. There's an institution that displays all contemporary inventions: uses of steam, a model of aeronautics, or operations of various machines." Goncharov's report on visiting a replica of the globe several stories high, which must have been Wyld's Great Globe, comes with a learned lecture on geography, natural history, and the political division of lands. At the British Museum and at a geography exhibit primarily devoted to England and its colonies, he finds detailed information and a wealth of resources provided to scholars and amateurs alike. Such institutions are countless, Goncharov informs his compatriots, and access to them is cheap.[20]

For Russia to be competitive in the imperial race, Goncharov implies, it needs similar educational institutions with easy public access. Having toured a zoo, he comments that any visitor "can rightfully delight in the awareness that he is a 'lord of creation'—and all that for just a shilling."[21] The geography exhibit on England and its colonies has presumably a similar effect on the Englishmen's sense of his own place in the hierarchy of peoples. The production and dissemination of knowledge, Goncharov suggests, powers British imperial enterprise and stokes Britons' imperial confidence.

The British avidly partake of such educational opportunities. They consider it a priority to learn about the larger world. Indeed, in post-Napoleonic Europe, which saw the emergence and rapid rise of tourism, the British earned a reputation as a "vagabondizing" nation.[22] Goncharov also marvels at incredible levels of domestic tourism that make the English akin to foreigners in their own country. On his travels to imperial frontiers, Goncharov will observe these same habits of close inspection of places and systematic gathering of information, the value of which may not be immediately apparent. The English learn at home how to be effective colonizers abroad. Goncharov intuits the connection between knowledge and power as he compares the attitudes toward knowledge typical of a Frenchman, a Russian, and an Englishman. Unlike Frenchmen's passion for knowledge or Russians' curiosity born of idleness, the information-gathering of the English reminds him of "taking an inventory of one's personal property."[23] Journeys along the coasts of Africa and Asia will reveal to Goncharov the literal truth of this metaphor. The English have a knack for turning information into property, in the form of imperial possession of territory and resources.

Tailcoated Gentlemen at Home and Abroad

This cold utilitarianism alienates the gregarious Russian traveler, yet he does not reject it out of hand. Describing the strict proprieties of the English in contrast to the relaxed social intercourse of the Russians, Goncharov concludes that "there's good and bad in this, but more of the good." The good seems to consist of respectful and polite social relations: on English trains, no one will prop his feet on a seat next to you. To a nation of polymaths and jacks-of-all-trades, as Goncharov views the Russians, English professionals and artisans may seem limited in their narrow specialization. Yet here, too, Goncharov warns against a rush to negative judgment: "an enormous talent and a strong mind often hide under this limitation." A conversation with such a person may be boring, he claims, but one will gladly give him business. In contrast to Dostoevsky, who in his *Winter Notes on Summer Impressions* would indict Western bourgeois capitalism for plunging millions of workers into destitution, Goncharov finds the English lower classes relatively prosperous. In sum, Goncharov balances some unsympathetic qualities of the English with others worthy of emulation, all the while remaining ready to take them down a notch.[24]

On the negative side, the vaunted practicality of the English has for Goncharov a dark, soulless quality: "Honesty, justice, and compassion appear to be extracted like coal, for the purpose of entering in the statistical tables, along with the steel products and delicate fabrics, that such-and-such law for this or that province or colony, has produced such-and-such quantity of justice." Good and evil are a matter of practical duty rather than profound moral need. Philanthropy is an aspect of social life, "but not of the human heart"; though it is widespread, "not only individuals and families, but entire countries perish under English rule." Goncharov allows that the "machine of social activity moves faultlessly," but finds it powerless to overcome the basic contradictions he sees in English life, such as the coexistence of severe laws and widespread criminality. This grim passage, over a page in length, is perhaps the sharpest critique of the English in the opening to *The Frigate Pallada*. Interestingly, it was only added with the publication of the

1858 book, and was not present in the original 1856 journal version. It was likely meant as a fitting postscript to the Crimean defeat of Russia orchestrated by the English. As such, it seems to respond to the realities of 1856 more than to Goncharov's impressions from 1852.[25]

Nevertheless, this machine-like quality does reappear in Goncharov's portrayals of the English beyond this fragment, especially in his day-in-the-life comparison of an Englishman and a Russian. This is an important passage to consider in detail because it proved one of Russian readers' favorites. It projected a memorable image of Russian national specificity, which Goncharov later developed in *Oblomov*. By and large, he pummels the English so as to bring Russian national virtues into sharp relief. Yet some aspects escape this neat contrast.[26]

The day of Goncharov's iconic Englishman is purposeful and efficiently scheduled. His is a quintessential modern life. Since, according to Goncharov, who may here be inaccurate, the use of servants is frowned upon in England, machines assist the Englishman in waking, washing, dressing, and cooking. His clock-bound routine starts with the perusal of newspapers and visits to a bank, the stock exchange, and the parliament. Steady activity fills the Englishman's day, with a calibrated balance of private business, public affairs of state, leisure, and educational activities both serious and trivial; a highbrow museum and a demonstration of the efficacy of rat poison interest him equally. The tone is tongue-in-cheek:

> He eats a chicken hatched from a steam-heated egg and donates a pound sterling for the benefit of the poor. Afterward, with calm assurance that he spent the day in requisite comforts, that he saw much that is useful, that he has the Duke [Wellington] and steam chickens, that he profitably sold a set of paper sheets on the stock market, and cast his vote in the Parliament, he sits down to dine.

Then "the whole machine falls asleep"—and this "machine" seems a metaphoric combination of the Englishman, his modern tools, and his social practices. Needless to say, this image is pure imagination and stereotype. Goncharov has earlier remarked that he has no acquaintances among the locals and no first-hand experience of the domestic life of the English. Though he claims to rely on personal observation and to shun blanket characterizations of other nations, already his image of the English belies both claims.[27]

The day of Goncharov's iconic Russian, just as stereotypical, replaces English efficiency with Russian sloth. The Russian landowner sleeps late and takes forever to get dressed. Servants, as "living machines," perform many tasks that real machines now facilitate in England. Sumptuous meals punctuate his day. His newspapers are hand-me-downs, a month old. In the time it takes him to stroll around his estate, the Englishman has visited three towns and the stock exchange. The homebound Russian, by contrast, leaves his estate only for market fairs and elections. While the Englishman turns surplus into investment capital, the Russian dissipates it on feeding countless live-in relatives.

This is a feudal life: backward, but touchingly homey to any Russian. It has its dignity and efficacy. Goncharov's lazy Russian landowner may miss a few wake-up calls, but he seems well informed about his estate and manages it wisely, neutralizing his steward's shenanigans. He may shun public charitable funds, but will never let an itinerant beggar or a neighbor in need go empty-handed. Here is philanthropy of the heart, not of the social machine. Russian readers have mostly judged this scene as a warm human antidote to the Englishman's mechanical efficiency.

This calls to mind life in Oblomovka, the rural birthplace of Goncharov's most famous literary character. His readers were already familiar with this locus of almost mythic seclusion from "Oblomov's Dream," a set piece Goncharov published on its own in 1849 and later incorporated into the novel. In *The Frigate Pallada,* Oblomovka becomes a paradigmatic Russian homeland. Its power seems unshakeable: "Back at home, our roots run so deep that wherever I go, and for however long I stay there, I will everywhere carry the soil of the native Oblomovka on my feet, and no oceans can wash it away![28]

Some have seen this as Goncharov's nostalgic idealization of the Oblomovka way of life, which is also a common interpretation of the novel *Oblomov.*[29] But this seems a rash conclusion—about either *Oblomov* or *The Frigate Pallada.* The characterization of Russian domestic serfs as "human machines" is an acerbic jibe at Russian serfdom, in force until 1861. It can hardly be seen as a morally superior counterpart to the machines assisting an Englishman. In the context of the rapidly modernizing world *The Frigate Pallada* portrays so vividly, the subsistence economy of the manor, for all its touching quaintness, persists as a relic that endangers Russia's national economy. Goncharov's point is that although the feudal life of the Russian manor may have no future, since the future, for better or worse, seems aligned with urban English modernity, it has had some redeeming aspects. A touch of nostalgia? Yes. Oblomovka as the Russian ideal? Not quite.

The indelible imprint of Oblomovka on every Russian is not a happy circumstance for Goncharov. Everything he tells his fellow Russians about the larger world, including Russian Siberia, points to a conclusion that Russian feudal ways have reached a historical dead end. By acknowledging Oblomovka's dust clinging stubbornly to his feet, Goncharov includes himself in Russian feudalism's lasting influence and speaks as a fellow Oblomovite. Yet we must not forget that he has, after all, managed to loosen the grip of Oblomovka's roots by venturing into the wide world. As Steve Clark reminds us, "on some level, even the most dyspeptic traveler has a preference for abroad through the mere fact of being there." Moreover, travel writers often employ complex rhetorical strategies to justify their severance from home culture and to negotiate their points of readmission. Goncharov's way of doing so is to stress abiding links to Russia and to eschew any suggestion that his voyages make him superior to his less well-traveled compatriots.[30]

Goncharov's stark contrast of nations ultimately falls short of a clear hierarchy. His satiric distance toward the English gradually melts away in imperial settings, replaced by respect tinged with jealousy. *The Frigate Pallada* shows Russian readers the world ruled by the understated British bourgeois merchant, with his obligatory black tailcoat, top hat, exquisite linen, clean shave, and umbrella in hand. They are everywhere in England, Goncharov writes: "on the streets, behind shop counters, in the parliament, and at the stock exchange." What these new-age figures lack in such conspicuous "attributes of power" as swords or crowns, they make up in ubiquity. In the opening chapter, as throughout the travelogue, Goncharov marvels at their confident presence and focused activity in every corner of the globe. The opening chapter's collective portrait of the tailcoated British merchant, written after the journey's completion, is an icon of British colonial might:

> With his cold and austere gaze he follows the crowds of swarthy natives of the South, who, bathed in sweat, extract the precious sap of their soil, roll barrels toward the shore, and dispatch them into the distance. The masters reward them by the right to eat bread in their own land. On the oceans, in brief encounters, the same person can be seen on the decks of ships, whistling though his teeth: "Rule, Britannia, upon the sea!" I saw him on the sands of Africa, supervising the work of Negros, on the plantations of India and China, amid

> bales of tea, commandeering nations, ships, cannons, and activating the immense powers of nature—all with just a gaze and a word, in his own native tongue. Everywhere, this image of the English merchant floats over the elements and over the labor of man, and triumphs over nature![31]

Fragments like this are precisely what led Soviet scholars to consider Goncharov's stance anti-colonial. Yet that interpretation does little to unravel such passages' affective and ideological complexity. It is true that Goncharov vividly captures the iniquities of Western imperialism. His British merchants at times resemble a plague unleashed on the world; there is something ominous about their infiltration of the globe. But classic *ressentiment,* an important ingredient of Russia's national identity, undergirds this description and the work as a whole. According to Leah Greenfeld, *ressentiment* meant that Russians accepted a Western model despite realizing their inability to surpass it, and at the same time rejected this model precisely due to this inability.[32] Goncharov's self-assured merchant of a nation that "rules the sea" is an image designed to goad the Russians back home, reminding them that their nation is losing imperialism's geopolitical race. Exploitative and smug though he may be, the British merchant has extended his nation's dominion over vast and fertile lands. It is the envy of the defeated that speaks loudest in this passage, not the moral outrage at the injustice of colonialism. Though likely galling to a Russian observer, the successes of British colonialism, including those that in Goncharov's view benefitted colonial subjects, receive a generous spotlight in his narrative.

As soon as the *Pallada* encounters non-European shores—none of which seem free of the British—it becomes clear that, although their mentality may appear unappealing, it gives Britons an edge in imperial settings. Goncharov reluctantly concedes this as he reminisces about his ten-hour stay on the Island of Madeira, a Portuguese colony teeming with British colonists about 360 miles off the coast of North Africa. Cold Europe finally left behind, Goncharov is giddy about the warm, balmy air—in January, no less. He is elated by the beauty of the mountainous island, its air fragrant with pineapple and clove. He gets his first taste of a banana and partakes of that paradigmatic pastime of a European colonist: getting carried around in a palanquin by the locals, just like an Oriental mandarin.

What mars the idyll is the familiar tailcoated figure of the British bourgeois. "They're here too?" the writer despairs, "as if we haven't seen enough of them already?" The British own the best houses, shops, and vineyards on the island. "Fine if they own," Goncharov exclaims in dismay, "but why must they stick around?" The English spoil Madeira's landscape for him, ruining its exotic charm: "How unpleasant it is to see these coarse apparitions in this soft air, under the tender sky, amid these magical colors!" Goncharov joined the expedition pining for the new worlds, anxious to leave Europe behind—but he learns that no new worlds are entirely free of the old one: "On the Hawaiian Islands, you will find everything: a German colony, French hotels, English porter—everything except savages."[33]

His thirst for exoticism unquenched, Goncharov is forced to admire the fruits of English industry during his trip to Madeira's hills. Agape at a sumptuous manor surrounded by vineyards and gardens of acacias and cypresses, he is dismayed to learn it belongs to—who else?—an Englishman. The gardens shade "houses of exquisite architecture, with galleries, verandahs, and all manner of seigneurial luxury." The prosperity of English vintners and merchants outshines that of the island's Portuguese masters. Goncharov concludes that "the English are masters here." This sets him to musing:

> It is certainly vexing [*dosadno*] that the English put down roots in all climes and soils. It is even more vexing that they proudly carry on like a hen with its egg and cackle about their achievements to the whole world. Finally, it is still more vexing that they do not discriminate in their methods of acquiring rights on foreign soil, taking what they can with the help of English industry or English law. If this fails, they resort to the medieval rule that might makes right [*Faustrecht,* literally "law of the fist"]. All of this could not be more vexing. But why not tell the truth? If they weren't on Madeira, the hills would not be so intensively cultivated, would not be covered with such exquisite villas, the road itself would not be so comfortable, the common people would not be so cleanly dressed on Sundays. No wonder they all speak English: without the prospect of gain an inhabitant of the South won't move his finger, but here he even moves his tongue, in English to boot. The English give these people unlimited employment and pay with a golden coin, which is scarce in Portugal.[34]

What opens with a deluge of *ressentiment,* "vexation" being a persistent refrain, concludes with a sober admission of the Britons' colonizing success, a sentiment Goncharov also voiced in his correspondence.[35] Without the British, he suggests, the Island of Madeira would be a fallow land with destitute population. He will soon say the same about Hong Kong. Goncharov now tempers his praise of British entrepreneurs by alluding to their greedy and unscrupulous opium trade in China, a critique that the Shanghai chapter will develop. Yet the due he grudgingly gives to the visible achievements of British colonization emerge as part of the bitter "truth" that Russians must hear about their imperial rival. Some did hear it, and resented being told, but pardoned the author in view of his passionate commitment to progress.[36] Goncharov would have found vainglorious Lord Palmerston's comments from this chapter's epigraph about Britain's leadership in the civilized world. Yet he would have also conceded their basis in reality.

Indeed, the *Pallada*'s next stop, in the Cape Verde Islands, also owned by Portugal, furthers for Goncharov the lessons of Madeira. While the ripples of English activity had enlivened Madeira, they had not yet transformed Cape Verde, an archipelago south of Madeira and about 350 miles off the Western coast of Africa, the latitude of today's Senegal. In Goncharov's bizarre imaginative geography, based on seeing so little of the African continent, these tiny, distant islands become symbols of quintessential Africa: lifeless and mute, in desperate need of Europe's civilizing mission. Endowing Cape Verde with this meaning also provides Goncharov with a useful contrast to this mission's successes in the Cape Colony, detailed in the very next chapter. A profusion of words denoting ways of lacking enhances this vision of Cape Verde as an icon of uncolonized Africa: lifeless, waterless, soundless.[37] In this domain of sleep, the sun-scorched "fairy-tale kingdom turned to stone," life subsists at the mercy of nature.

Yet Goncharov confidently prophesies the coming end of this grim fairy tale: "A hero will surely come. He will bring toil, art, and civilization. He will awaken from sleep this beautiful princess-Nature and shall give it life. The time is near." The sleep of nature will end and Cape Verde will awaken to civilized and prosperous life. Sure enough, the awakeners are already there: the English who busily tend their coffee plantations. Formerly labeled as "coarse apparitions," the industrious English now appear to Goncharov as *bogatyri*—the larger-than-life Russian folk heroes who will wake up the "sleeping princess."[38] Upon reaching the Cape of Good Hope, the writer will credit these heroes' civilizing miracles for transforming the life of southern Africa.

A Flourishing Corner of England

The topic of Goncharov and Africa neither begins nor ends with *The Frigate Pallada.* A translation of part of Eugène Sue's gruesome 1831 novel about an African slave sold to a Jamaican colonist, *Atar-Gull,* was the very first thing young Goncharov published, in 1832. His later protagonist, Oblomov, is addicted to travelogues, but as he descends into apathy, mold invades his copy of *A Journey to Africa.*[39] In the context of *The Frigate Pallada,* this image can only be seen as a visual emblem of Oblomov's regrettable avoidance of all purposeful activity.

A route around the African continent was not part of the *Pallada*'s original itinerary. It became one after the frigate's extensive repairs in Portsmouth caused the Russians to miss the favorable wind season. The easterly approach to Japan, around Africa's Cape of Good Hope, was also the route of Matthew Perry, who raced ahead of the Russians. Prior to the opening of the Suez Canal in 1869, this was the standard route to Asia from Europe. In March 1853, the *Pallada* dropped anchor on the Cape of Good Hope in Falsebay, south of Cape Town.

The first Russian expedition to circumnavigate the globe and to cross the equator, headed by the Baltic German Ivan Kruzenshtern (Adam Johann von Krusenstern), merely grazed the Cape's shores in 1803 without making a port call. Then, in 1806, the explorer Vasily Golovnin, who—like Kruzenshtern and Admiral Mikhail Lazarev, Putiatin's mentor—trained in the British Navy, arrived at the Cape of Good Hope. At that stage of Europe's Napoleonic Wars, England and Russia were enemy states. The British detained Golovnin as a prisoner of war, though they treated him well. In a spectacular caper that old anti-British Dutch Afrikaners gleefully recalled for the *Pallada* officers in 1853, Golovnin escaped after thirteen months of British captivity. The *Pallada* expedition, largely thanks to Goncharov's travelogue, created a milestone in Russia's emerging interest in the world of southern Africa. Future Russian navigators were known to follow in Goncharov's footsteps and to provide friendly updates on the sights and people that *The Frigate Pallada* had turned into household names in Russia.[40]

In the early decades of the nineteenth century, Russian ships—like most Asia-bound ships that sailed around Africa—often stopped at the Cape Colony on their way to East Siberia. This oceanic route from Kronstadt, the naval base near St. Petersburg, was then much faster than the overland journey through Siberia's challenging terrain. Goncharov met at the Cape a former Russian officer taken prisoner first by the French in 1814, and then by the British in the Battle of Waterloo. He was resettled to the Cape, married an African woman, and had six children with her. By the 1860s, the Russian community became sizeable enough to need its own Orthodox cemetery. During stopovers of ships bound for Siberia, Russian sailors occasionally escaped to join the Cape's European settlers. On the eve of World War I there were twenty-five thousand Russians living in South Africa.[41]

Before the arrival of white colonists, southern Africa was home to communities of hunter-gatherers, herders, and farmers. These communities were organized into chiefdoms, ranging from a thousand to a few tens of thousands of people, based primarily but not exclusively on kinship ties. Though hierarchical and intermittently at low-grade war, these chiefdoms relied heavily on cooperation and consent of the ruled both within and between communities, which alleviated the problem of scarce resources. Land was communally owned. The communities that combined herding and farming, such as the Xhosa community of the Eastern Cape, became most prosperous by the eighteenth century. By gaining increasing control over land and water, they eventually conquered or assimilated many communities of hunter-gatherers, such as the Khoisan. Ethnicity was far less important in this society than lifestyle and clan-allegiance; once admitted into the chiefdom, a member of a different ethnic group gained full rights. While contact with white people and their diseases decimated the Khoisan early in the colonial era, the Xhosa, who lived east of the Fish River boundary, were largely unaffected by white colonists until the early decades of the nineteenth century.

The first European visitors to the Cape of Good Hope were Portuguese sailors. A storm washed the explorer Bartholomeu Dias onto the peninsula in 1487. Vasco da Gama explored it three years later. In 1652 the Dutchman Jan van Riebeeck established the first settlement. It provided repairs and produce to Dutch ships headed for the center of the Dutch empire in Asia, in Batavia, Java (today Jakarta, Indonesia). The Cape of Good Hope was blessed with a salubrious climate free of tropical diseases, so Asia-bound troops could be kept there in good health. The settlement grew into a colony with a diverse population of Europeans (mostly Dutch, but also Germans and French Huguenots). These white settlers expanded their communities among the indigenous inhabitants of the Cape, such as the Khoisan and the Xhosa. The Dutch East India Company brought in slaves from the Malay Peninsula,

Indonesia, India, tropical Africa, and Madagascar. By the end of the eighteenth century, the colony was roughly the size of Spain. The British, in increasing need of their own stepping-stone to India, conquered the Cape Colony briefly in 1795, and then more permanently in 1806. Whoever controlled the Cape controlled the commercially lucrative and strategically vital route to Asia. In his *Wealth of Nations,* Adam Smith called the discoveries of America and of the passage to the East Indies around the Cape of Good Hope "the two greatest and most important events recorded in the history of mankind."[42]

But the settler colony the British gained in 1806 was at that time far from an imperial pearl. South Africa's vast gold and diamond deposits were unknown until the 1870s. At mid-century, the region's economy was relatively underdeveloped, with wool, ivory, and wine serving as main exports. It attracted few British immigrants. The British had to assume responsibility for the colony's debts and inherited a diverse and complex society of sharply clashing interests, with lots of determination on all sides to defend them. The volatile region was a challenge for London's imperial administration. At the time of Goncharov's visit, radical changes were afoot in its political status within the British empire, which he did not fail to appreciate.[43]

The chapter on the Cape of Good Hope is the longest in *The Frigate Pallada.* Unlike the classic and spectacularly popular travelogues of Mungo Park, which Goncharov read in childhood, or of David Livingstone, who was traveling in southern Africa at the same time as Goncharov, *The Frigate Pallada* summons an image less of Africa than of the European presence in Africa. The ethnography, anthropology, and natural history of Africa, so prominent in travelogues about voyages of exploration such as Park's and Livingstone's, are a distant background to Goncharov's focused story of how the Europeans were transforming the continent. The accusation that Nigerian writer Chinua Achebe leveled against Joseph Conrad's depiction of Africa applies equally to Goncharov: Africa is treated as mere "setting and backdrop" for European history, which eliminates the African "as a human factor." Indeed, Goncharov's true African heroes are the British.[44]

In the course of the nineteenth century, the question of effective methods of colonization increasingly preoccupied Russian intellectuals and administrators. Russians had long practiced settler colonialism in their vast continental empire, sending Slavic and German settlers to Siberia, the southeastern steppe regions, and Transcaucasia. What came to be called the "colonization question" was also factored into considerations of further territorial expansion in Central Asia and the Far East. The prominent nineteenth-century historian of Russia Vasily Klyuchevsky famously proclaimed colonization "the basic fact" of Russian history and a special destiny of a country straddling enormous open plains. Until the late nineteenth century, however, colonization was a fitful and fairly uncoordinated phenomenon with weak state support.

It was becoming, however, a topic of public debate and advocacy. What role should the state play in colonization? To what extent should it be encouraged? What rights, aid, and perks should be granted to settlers? Should penal labor be used for colonization? How should illegal migrants—those who resettled from European Russia without the state's permission—be dealt with?[45] These questions gained urgency in the 1880s, which saw a rapid upsurge of colonization. However, "colonization was on everyone's mind" since at least the early nineteenth century, according to historian Willard Sunderland. By the early 1860s, a widespread perception that the pace and success of Russian colonization were inadequate led the Imperial Russian Geographical Society, founded in 1845, to convene a forum of experts to debate reforms. Russia's colonists and pioneers were becoming a topic of popular fiction.[46]

Goncharov's comparison of Dutch and British colonization would therefore have resonated for Russian readers with the challenges facing their own empire. *The Frigate Pallada* unequivocally presents the Cape Colony as a testament to British colonizing competence, in sharp contrast to the dismal record of Dutch apathy and aimlessness. The colony's capital, Cape Town, which Goncharov describes as "a corner of England," shows how successfully the English have transplanted themselves in this new environment. This is no small feat, since the place appears to Goncharov so unfamiliar that even dogs seem to be barking in a foreign language. English institutions, English architecture, the English language, and English place names are in the ascendancy, displacing earlier Dutch models. An empire's assimilative potential counted for much among mid-nineteenth century Russians. Goncharov paints the decline of the Dutch and the rise of the English by describing two hotels. One, Dutch-owned, has dark rooms with cumbersome tables, uncomfortable chairs, and golden frames blackened with age. It greets the traveler like a kindly but "unshaven and unwashed person." The other features lacquered floors, wallpapered walls, sofas of fashionable design, and a grand piano. Of the second, Goncharov remarks: "it wasn't hard to conclude that the English were the masters."[47]

The dynamism of the colony, which Goncharov attributes to English rule, deeply struck him: "Things change here not by the day but by the hour."[48] Having subdued the wilderness, the English wield economic and political control not only over the aborigines, but also over the Dutch: both retreat to the interior, making room for them. As plantation owners, bankers, clerks, and engineers, the English employ Africans as farmhands, street cleaners, drivers, or servants. Goncharov occasionally winces at this transformation of the land's black African owners into a pool of low-skilled labor. Yet he also presents this as an inevitable and ultimately positive process: they will get civilized eventually.

The writer portrays Cape Town—with its population of twenty-five thousand made up half-and-half of white and "colored"[49]—as a well-run and thriving colonial capital. Local factories satisfy local needs. Taxes pay for excellent water supply. Even the most distant town he visits is clean "to the point of pedantry." As in the metropole, so also here, the British cannily combine brute force with cultural influence. Given the size of the population, the quantity of printing facilities and well-supplied bookstores is astounding. The magnificent local Botanical Garden catalogs and displays the colony's natural bounty: "what diversity, monstrosity, and beauty—all at once!" Cape Town's omnibus service extends to destinations fifty miles distant. On encountering such cutting-edge modernity in a colonial outpost, Goncharov wonders: "And is it long ago that one rode oxen, surrounded by a crowd of Hottentots, to hunt lions and tigers? Nowadays, one travels four hundred miles to reach lions, which were pushed out by towns, roads, hotels, omnibuses, noise, and bustle." For Goncharov, the British rule in southern Africa means head-spinning progress.[50]

This is further confirmed during a two-week excursion with an Afrikaner guide, Van Dyck. In the official government report Goncharov penned in Putiatin's name, this mission was billed as practice for exploring other little-known places the crew was about to visit. In *The Frigate Pallada,* Goncharov presents the trip as recreational sightseeing rather than a training mission, though with some on the trek having scholarly interests.[51] The itinerary led through the less volatile regions of old colonization, northeast of Cape Town, near the Slanghoek Mountains. Far from a rugged frontier, the land appears to Goncharov as an earthly paradise—and indeed this area of South Africa is very picturesque. Yet Goncharov stresses the landscape's manmade aspects. His account of colonial settlements and towns unfolds as

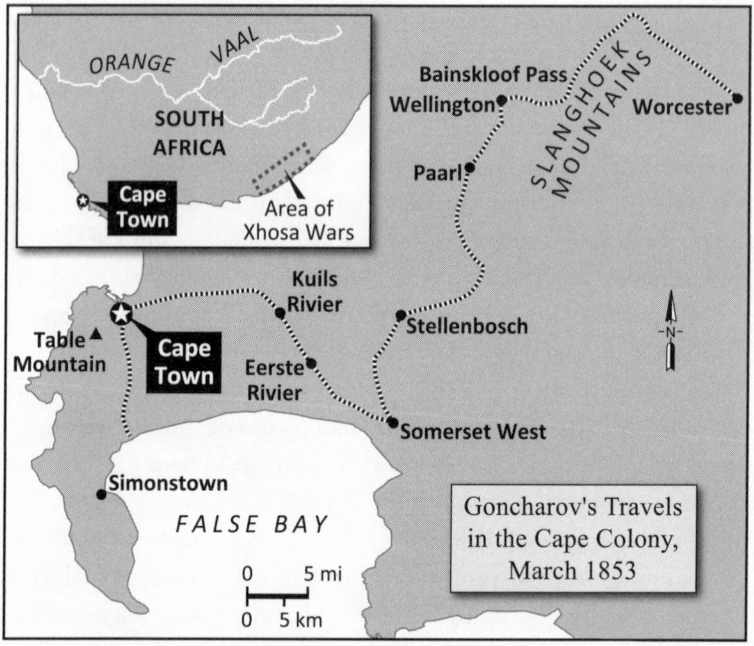

Map 2. Goncharov's excursion in the vicinity of Cape Town. The Russians were at a far remove from the area of the recent Xhosa wars.

a procession of idyllic spaces, a fortuitous merging of fecund nature with the industrious activities of the white settler.

The town of Stellenbosch drowns in green orchards. Although its population does not exceed five thousand, and only thirty years earlier the town had no road, Stellenbosch boasts the best classical education school in the colony. Goncharov wonders: Will Stellenbosch college become at some point "an African Göttingen or Oxford?" The town of Paarl, in a vineyard-draped valley graced by cascading waterfalls, is for Goncharov the iconic "pearl" of the colony. Its houses, shaded by picturesque oak trees and decorated by aloes and flowers, seem like "refuges of happiness, peaceful occupations, and home comforts!" The town has banks, thriving manufacturing, and public transport. Standards do not fall with distance from the center. The town of Worcester, Goncharov's most distant destination, strikes him as the best yet. Nestled amid lovely farms, vineyards, and hot springs, it commands an impressive mountain vista and is a model of modern comforts. Goncharov takes note of bridges that span remote mountain abysses ("marvels of engineering") and towns spaciously laid out to accommodate future colonists. A plan to build railroads awaits London's approval.[52]

It is important to keep in mind that Goncharov is reporting the achievements of a fairly new African colony to readers back in Russia. Often, travel writers' glowing descriptions of other places serve as veiled criticisms of one's home.[53] Indeed, the backwardness of transport infrastructure, education, manufacturing, and agriculture in the Russian core, not to mention its peripheries, were frequent topics of public debate and plans for reform. Such debates were invigorated by Russia's defeat in the Crimean War, a period that coincided with the publication of *The Frigate Pallada*. Goncharov's enticing images of a British colony that manages to flourish, in the face of considerable odds, on the tip of Africa, are meant to galvanize support for Russia's own post-Crimean modernization project.

Yet beyond supporting post-Crimean reforms, the image of Cape Colony's rich material life is meant to send a powerful message about the economic advantages of imperial ventures for those determined enough to undertake them. The fabulous prosperity of settler society astounds Goncharov. Every meal on the trek is a lavish affair, as evident in long lists of dishes, drinks, and fruits. The furnishings of homes and inns—sturdy and traditional among the Dutch, stylish and modern among the English—are inventoried with encyclopedic zeal. An affluent farmer in Stellenbosch, we are told, earns an annual income of 7,000–8,000 silver rubles. Even the meager salary of a doctor in British East India is the equivalent of 5,000–6,000 rubles. How would these figures strike readers in Russia, where ministerial salaries at the time ranged from 7,000–10,000 rubles? The annual income of a certain Dutch farmer and vintner, Goncharov learns, is 1,000 pounds sterling—roughly 80,000 pounds in 2010s purchasing power.[54] The cost to Putiatin of a cutting-edge piece of engineering, the steam schooner he bought in England, was 3,375 pounds sterling.[55] Excluding living expenses, the Dutch farmer could himself afford a steam schooner in roughly three years!

Visiting this farmer's huge, well-furnished, and comfortable house, Goncharov exclaims: "I could not believe my eyes: is he really a farmer, a peasant?" He also relishes an account of a bankrupted rich man who was reduced to subsisting on grapes, almond, pomegranates, and oranges from the trees he once planted, and on milk from his only cow. His sole remaining slave waits on him. "Here is African poverty for you: fresh milk daily, *les quatre mendiants,* straight from the tree, for dessert, and a Negro servant," Goncharov quips. "How much would such poverty cost in St. Petersburg?"[56]

Should we regret that the Dutch lost control of the colony to "the power-hungry, or rather, profit-hungry" British? Goncharov answers his own question firmly in the negative. If one compares the colony's development during two hundred years of Dutch rule and during less than four decades since the British takeover, then "not only will the violent English conquest appear justified, but one will be glad that it took place." In imperial settings, Goncharov's personal distaste for the pragmatic and soulless English recedes from view. Their missteps and unscrupulousness become mere peccadilloes in the face of their massive civilizing success. The Cape epitomizes for Goncharov an epochal struggle between "the all-powerful energy of man and a nearly unconquerable nature." To the extent that the present augurs the victory of humans, the English, in Goncharov's view, deserve the credit. Other members of his expeditions felt the same. Britons' restless energy impressed Russian travelers in other parts of the world as well.[57]

It is true Goncharov's visit coincided with the beginning of a cycle of boom in the colony.[58] Yet either he exaggerates the settlers' material prosperity or those he met were not representative. Eager to tantalize Russian readers with the economic potential of colonization, he seems oblivious to the class and economic stratification of the settler society. He mentions Britain's abolition of slavery in 1834 as a blow to the Dutch settlers' interests, but he frames it predominantly as a restriction on their autonomy rather than an economic hardship. In truth, the manumission of slaves deprived Dutch settlers of cheap labor and created a sizeable class of poor whites in the colony. This was a key impetus behind the Great Trek—an emigration of about fifteen thousand Boers, or Dutch-speaking farmers, from the British-administered colony in the 1830s and 1840s. Like European-American settlers, they set out in tented wagons to establish new settlements in the fertile northeastern regions of the Orange and Vaal Rivers.[59] So extravagant was Goncharov's praise of the colony and British successes there that some subsequent Russian visitors felt compelled to darken the image he created, by painting the landscape as less beautiful, the colonists as less affluent, and the public amenities as less impressive.[60]

Goncharov's assessment of the English colonizing success in *The Frigate Pallada* corresponds to the sentiments he expressed privately. Describing his impressions of the Cape Colony to his friend Avraam S. Norov, an Oriental philologist who worked in the Ministry of National Education and who recommended the writer for the position of Putiatin's secretary, Goncharov wrote:

> Most interesting, at least for me, was to see the victory of Englishmen over nature, ignorance, wild beasts, people of all colors, and, incidentally, the Dutch. If you evaluate what they accomplished in the Cape Colony during their short rule, and what the Dutch could have but did not accomplish in the two hundred years of their residence, you will not pity the latter. I am no Anglophile, but I must, sometimes against my will, give [the English] justice. Nowadays commerce and manufacturing flourishes in the Cape Colony, steamships dock in ports, excellent roads span cliffs, splendid bridges hang over abysses. These are not just empty phrases: I myself rode in the mountains on a beautiful, recently completed paved road, two thousand feet above sea level, across ravines that seemed hardly accessible to wild goats. There I looked down into precipices from bridges propped on stone pillars seventy feet high. They say that soon a railroad will be built to reach places where until recently only lions and tigers roamed.[61]

Goncharov's comparison between British and Dutch models of colonialism comes down to a contrast between the modernity, technological superiority, and infrastructure investments of the former, and the inactivity and backwardness of the latter. In *The Frigate Pallada,* he does give the Dutch credit for the very establishment of European settlement in the Cape and their unflappable determination. In that phase, what Goncharov calls their "Flemish phlegm" was in fact a unique asset: "Where others relied on warlike or administrative measures, [the Dutch] used [sang-froid] to get what they wanted. That is, they carved out their land, enslaved as many blacks as they needed, transplanted agriculture, managed to establish a decent market for their goods, and arranged the kind of lifestyle that they knew in Holland for centuries, neither restraining progress nor advancing it."[62]

In their patriarchal way of life, Goncharov's Dutchmen recall his Oblomovites.[63] And just like Oblomovites, the Dutch are becoming an anachronism in a rapidly modernizing world, where standing still means falling behind. Although he treats them with sympathy on a purely human level, as he does Oblomovites, Goncharov portrays Dutch Afrikaners as quaint relics. He scorns them for using the same cumbersome plow and harrow they used two hundred years ago. Crop rotations are unknown to them. Water shortages seem to be causing some of them to resort to nomadism.[64]

Nomadism carried a big stigma in nineteenth-century European social hierarchies. It ranked second lowest in the theory of the four stages of social development—a theory which had commanded formidable scholarly authority since the mid-eighteenth century and to which Goncharov subscribed. This theory held that all societies progressed through stages that corresponded to different modes of subsistence: hunting, pastoralist nomadism, agriculture, and commerce. As social scientist Ronald Meek explains, each stage was thought to be characterized by "different sets of ideas and institutions relating to law, property, and government, and also different sets of customs, manners, and morals." Whether in the Siberian tundra or African savanna, *The Frigate Pallada* treats nomadism as a "savage" lifestyle. For the Dutch to be reduced to nomadism thus signals a troubling plunge down the ladder of civilization.[65]

Indeed, in Goncharov's letter to Norov, quoted above, the Dutch appear alongside wild nature and the "colored" races that Europeans were supposed to tame and civilize. Such a slippage from the exalted calling of European to the level of slothful native, tied to nature rather than in control of it, was a frequent charge leveled against the Dutch in the period's travel writing, especially as authored by the British. This writing likely guided Goncharov. In fact, he mentions as his source a classic text of this kind, *An Account of Travels into the Interior of Southern Africa in the Years 1797 and 1798* (1801) by Sir John Barrow, who in 1830 cofounded what became Britain's Royal Geographical Society.[66]

Travel accounts such as Barrow's disparaged Dutch settlers in terms normally reserved for indigenous groups. Arguing for the restoration of British rule over the Cape, Barrow, naturally, judged the Boers harshly, describing them as "better fed [by which he meant obese], more indolent, more ignorant, and more brutal, than any set of men bearing the reputation of being civilized, upon the face of the earth." As South African critic and novelist J. M. Coetzee argued, "the true scandal of the nineteenth century was not the idleness of the Hottentots (by now seen as inherent in the race), but the idleness of the Boers." Their example showed "how European stock can regress after a few generations in Africa." This compromised the colonizing mission, which relied on the assumption that Europeans were better stewards of the land than indigenous people. Coetzee detects certain chauvinism in the contrast between "the diligent English yeoman and the listless Dutch boer." This is a chauvinism that Goncharov fully shared, which his reading in British sources likely encouraged.[67]

Another aspect that scandalized Europeans, especially the British, about the Afrikaner Dutch was their subsistence economy. This, too, typically appeared in attacks on "primitive" aboriginal societies considered more backward than surplus-oriented ones. This is precisely how Goncharov paints the Dutch: content to merely replicate the life they knew back in Holland, "neither restraining progress nor advancing it." As Mary Louise Pratt notes, Spanish-American creole society was similarly derided. Drawing on Coetzee's ideas, she emphasizes that the Afrikaner Boers "presented a particular challenge to European bourgeois values, precisely because as a colonial class with access to virtually unlimited land and free labor, they had the means to realize European values of accumulation, consumption, and enrichment through work, yet chose not to." Attacks on them evinced an anxiety that this choice might signal a preference for "an African way of life in which the fruits of the earth are enjoyed as they drop into the hand." Thus the specter was raised of Europeans going native, adopting the lifestyles of the very peoples they were meant to rule and uplift.[68]

Goncharov contrasts the colonial models of the Dutch and the British by painting the former as just such listless and indolent underachievers. He does this, we may note, despite his personal contacts with Afrikaner farmers he himself describes as fabulously rich. Consistency, as has been noted, is not a common feature of travel narratives. But Goncharov seems less troubled by the Dutch going native than by their not going British. His Afrikaners do not build bridges over abysses; they do not open ports or stimulate commerce; they do not run printing presses and banks. The British do all those things. In contrast to what he portrays as subsistence colonization of the Dutch, the British practice profit-driven colonization and make forward-looking changes. By Goncharov's scorecard, within less than five decades, they have added three new provinces, opened three new ports, built new towns, roads, bridges, and schools. They have enlivened and diversified the economy and trade.[69]

Stepping off the ladder of progress, for which Goncharov reviles the Dutch, also meant loss of imperial power and prestige. On his further travels in the Indian Ocean, the lackluster imperial performance of the Dutch strikes Goncharov in Anyer, on West Java. Having stopped there for provisioning, in order to avoid the dangerous fevers caused by Batavia's insalubrious climate, the Russians are nonetheless curious to visit the famous capital of the Dutch empire in Asia, distant by one day's travel only. This proves impossible because the Dutch, despite their presence on Java since the early seventeenth century, have neglected to develop any meaningful transport infrastructure. Everywhere, Goncharov perceives signs of imperial decline: the Dutch flag hangs "lazily" above the fortress, the military guards have the appearance of "sleepy flies," and on the street one can hear just about any language—including, of course, English—except Dutch.[70]

Back in the African chapter, against the backdrop of Dutch apathy, Goncharov clusters images of British success. Perhaps the most memorable of them is the character of Mr. Andrew Bain, a notable figure in the colony's history.[71] Bain is the resident geologist and engineer in the town of Wellington, who is esteemed in the colony. Goncharov reports that Bain has labored for fifteen years over a huge map of the entire colony and dispatched a copy to London for printing by a scholarly society. This map was indeed published in 1856 by the London Geological Society.[72] He supervises the building of local roads, bridges, and buildings using the labor of convicts, nearly all African, from prisons supervised by his sons. (Goncharov visited these prisons.) A colonial Renaissance man, he is also a naturalist, knowledgeable about local flora and fauna. Neither art nor music is beyond his ken. He has made four private expeditions beyond the colony's official boundaries—certainly a valuable experience in case of any future expansion.

"Bain is an amazing man of the colony," Goncharov sums up his portrait. He is the essence of the multiple imperial competencies of the English, a model of drive, resourcefulness, and efficacy. Married to a Dutch Afrikaner woman, in his private life he might also embody for Goncharov the prospect of an eventual healing of the Anglo-Dutch rift in southern Africa's white colonial society—before the brutal Boer Wars cast a pall over it.[73] Bain's national-imperial iconicity is underscored by the ceremonial portrait of Queen Victoria that adorns his living room. In Goncharov's characterization, Bain emerges as a hardy, restless, and undaunted doer, an African Stolz—the energetic hero of Goncharov's novel *Oblomov.* He is exactly what the colony, or any colony, needs: a man ready for a "heroic deed."[74]

European Settlers on Africa's Turbulent Frontier

Goncharov's travels in the Cape Colony led through regions of well-established white colonization: the lands of Khoikhoi and San pastoralists who were the first to be subdued by the European settler. White settlement was rapidly expanding, however, in many directions. The Great Trek led the Boers to the northeastern regions of the Orange and Vaal Rivers, beyond the control of British colonial administration. The fertile and water-rich region of the Eastern Cape, adjacent to the southern seaboard, was the theater of the colonists' protracted battles with the Bantu-speaking Xhosa people, who by the seventeenth century had migrated into the area from the north, pushed out by the expanding Zulu empire. When the Russians arrived in March 1853, the newly appointed Governor, Sir George Cathcart, was negotiating a peace treaty after the eighth British-Xhosa War of 1850–1853. These nine wars, which spanned a century from 1779 to 1879, pitted Dutch and British colonists, often assisted by African troops enlisted from subdued chiefdoms, against the Xhosa and their allies. This was the most protracted colonial conflict in South African history. Its source was the colonists' determination to remove the Xhosa from their land.[75]

The visiting Russians were at a safe distance from the recent theater of war, but Goncharov describes the conflict in a twenty-page subchapter on the colony's political and military history titled "The Cape Colony," prepared on Putiatin's order.[76] Despite having vowed, in the first chapter, not to dull his impressions with dull scholasticism, he decided to include this sketch in his book. Its key topic is the colonists' rivalry with the Xhosa, whom Goncharov, in conformance with British usage, calls the Kaffirs.[77] Goncharov researched books about the colony that he purchased in London and Cape Town. His main source, however, which he credits and in places incorporates almost verbatim, is a long and informative anonymous article about the Cape of Good Hope from a German Brockhaus encyclopedia, *Die Gegenwart*.[78] Perhaps due to its open support for a rough war of colonial conquest and extirpation, fully in tune with colonially minded European writing of the time, Goncharov's historical sketch was removed from some popular Soviet editions of *The Frigate Pallada*. It is missing from both English translations, which are based on those Soviet editions.[79]

Goncharov's descriptions of the colony affirm the ultimate prerogative and desirability of European rule in Africa. Yet the sketch diverges from the impressions that Goncharov generated during his trip with Van Dyck, which stress the colony's flourishing prosperity. In the sketch, instead of effortless abundance, we see dogged toil required to squeeze the harvest from the sun-scorched rock, in the face of formidable dangers, and for minimal profit margins. In contrast to the idyllic, and mostly white, spaces that Goncharov reports seeing on his trip, the historical sketch paints the colony as a volatile frontier peopled by truculent African tribes. Goncharov never brings the two perspectives into concordance, leaving his readers with something like a tale of two cities. The narrative tone shifts from an enticing account of the riches to be made through colonization to a celebration of the heroic deeds of idealistic whites, who, despite considerable odds and the uncertainty of success, bring progress and civilization to Africa:

> Each step forward in this scorched soil is bathed in blood. Each hill and shrub is an obstacle for whites and a hiding place for blacks. In the end, the European tries to incline the black man toward goodness by peaceful means: he extends a hand, gives him a plow, an axe, a nail—all that's useful. The black man, having exhausted foodstuffs and armaments, shakes the extended hand, repays the plow and axe with elephant tusks and animal hides, but only waits for an opportunity to steal cattle, slaughter his *enemies,* and after this tragic denouement, retreats to the interior. And so it goes, until a new comedy begins, that is, the conclusion of peace. How long will this last? How soon will Europeans lay a permanent road into the savages' distant hiding places? And how soon will the latter shake off this shameful name?[80]

Goncharov distills these questions about white-black relations into two key issues. The first is the likelihood of the whites receiving their "rightful" reward for their massive expenditures and efforts. Will these efforts remain a "profitless heroic deed accomplished for the good of mankind"? On this score, Goncharov corrects a misconception that "colonies in general, and the Cape Colony in particular, enrich the British treasury." In Africa, Goncharov now avers, the soil is poor, and winemaking keeps only a small number of farmers "from penury." Fishing and hunting "can barely feed" those who undertake them. Cattle herding and agriculture are still unprofitable. Few articles are fit for trade. Citing official statistics, Goncharov states that the expenses of running the colony, especially the infrastructure improvements and constant wars with the Xhosa, exceed any profit that Britain might gain from it. It is unclear what source Goncharov is using on this question, but he definitely no longer has his nose in the German encyclopedia.[81]

The colony as boon—with affluent farmers reportedly making 1,000 pounds a year—which Goncharov claims to have seen, is now replaced with a vision of the colony as idealistic sacrifice for the sake of progress, about which Goncharov apparently read. Both are exaggerations. Poverty and endemic underdevelopment overtake the picture of a flourishing colony. And yet the civilizing continues, despite the uncertainty of financial return. But even within the sketch, the question of profit is a slippery one, as can be seen from Goncharov's own, more positive assessments of the wealth of the vintners and the diversity of exports.[82]

The idea of disinterestedness clearly appeals to Goncharov, for he extends it to the European production of knowledge about southern Africa. He presents the voluminous writings of amateur missionaries and military men as "the most disinterested and fairest." With a level of naïveté that has been impossible since thinkers such as Michel Foucault and Edward Said shed light on the long history of collusion between knowledge and power, Goncharov crafts the metaphor of the sword and the cross, assisted on their colonial march by an innocent pen.[83]

Goncharov's second big question concerns the future of racial and political arrangements in African colonial society. Will whites remain masters and perpetuate, to use more current terminology, an apartheid regime? Or will blacks, "like the children of the same father, share with whites in the heritage of freedom, religion, and civilization, bequeathed also to them"? Goncharov soon rephrases this question in less innocuous terms: "How and for how long will the restless tribes get along under the ferule of European civilization and arms? Will they become closer to their conquerors and enlighteners?" The tool of European civilization is here likened to a ferule, or a ruler used for punishing pupils in the nineteenth century. In a rhetoric that will bloom later in the travelogue's Japanese chapters, where the metaphor of ferule reappears, civilization and violence, enlightening and conquering, appear as fully compatible. They are two sides of the same coin, rendered to the "savage" in need.[84]

On this question, according to the inserted sketch, all bets would seem to be off—though the British rule allows for greater hope than the Dutch one. In Goncharov's schema, the Africans' only hope for acquiring civic rights and transcending their current status as the colonists' "hirelings" is to shed "savagery" and Europeanize. The situation is complicated, however, by the Africans' stubborn noncompliance: "like children, they bite the hand that cares for them." Colonizing is hard here, we learn. Africans do not respond to preaching or acquire a taste for European conveniences. Though magnanimously liberated from slavery, "it hasn't entered their head" to enjoy their freedom and rights. "Limitless empty spaces"—this manipulative European fiction about homelands of pastoralist societies that did not erect fences—help the aborigines evade the force of European arms. In the case of some

Figure 1.1. A Xhosa chief, as depicted in the account of the Perry expedition.

warlike ethnic groups, like the Xhosa, their supposed inborn predilection for banditry complicates relations with settler society.[85]

Though historians today write about the Xhosa wars, lasting a century, as the most powerful anti-colonial challenge in South African history, Goncharov reduces them to pesky, if bloody and costly, encounters with unruly thieves. In his account, these are defensive wars of the settlers, who merely protect their livestock and land. He never considers the Europeans' colonial presence in Africa, or the policies of the colonial government, to be in any way problematic. The source of the problem is cattle raids and encroachments on settler territory by the unruly Xhosa. Goncharov will exhibit the same biases when writing about Siberia's indigenous people.

In this entirely one-sided account, the settlers' inexorable eastward advance into traditional Xhosa land—each war concludes with land appropriations for the settlers—plays no role in the genesis of hostilities.[86] According to *The Frigate Pallada,* wars begin because the Xhosa violate peace treaties and steal cattle. In a classic colonial fashion, Goncharov shifts the responsibility for the colonizer's actions on the colonized themselves. According to him, these wars do not begin because droughts and famines caused the Xhosa to seek, in their traditional nomadic ways, viable pastureland; or because the influx of refugees displaced by the violently expanding Zulu empire, such as the Mfengu, put a strain on their lands' resources; or because the Xhosa had legitimate grievances about continuous removals or the white man's broken promises. Historians have since confirmed these as the actual reasons, but Goncharov's German source also mentions some of them. He presents the creation of the province of British Kaffraria in 1847, under direct rule of the governor of the Cape, not as the ghettoizing of the Xhosa, but a generous bestowal of a well-defined residence: they were "granted the right to settle and live there." He brushes off as justified the 1829 expulsion of the Xhosa chief Maqoma along with 16,000 followers from the fertile Fish River area, which led to the sixth Xhosa war of 1834. Goncharov's German encyclopedia informed him that the Xhosa were expelled before they could harvest their crops and hence faced starvation in their new place, which according to one British officer, was "as bare as parade grounds."[87] Goncharov paraphrases the encyclopedia about this circumstance but does not entertain it as a justification of the Xhosa opposition to the expulsion.[88] While Goncharov's source, however biased in favor of settlers, rendered in excruciating detail the ravages of the Xhosa wars, Goncharov is mostly silent on this score. Presenting the British-Xhosa Wars within righteous narratives of colonial progress took some tinkering. David Livingstone, who barely missed the *Pallada* Russians when setting out from Cape Town in June 1852 for his last and longest trip to the interior, originally penned a twenty-page passage for his famous travelogue in which he supported Xhosa rights to the land and castigated the colonial government's injustices. Following consultations with his publisher, this text was excised from the travelogue's print version so as not to antagonize the Victorian public.[89]

Already in 1778, the Dutch colonial government made the Fish River the colony's official eastern border. This measure was aimed at restraining settlers from venturing into the Xhosa lands, which typically required costly military assistance. This had no effect on the settlers, whom successive governments had little choice but to defend. Each war with the Xhosa pushed the colony's boundary eastward. Goncharov thoroughly approves of this expansion. He triumphantly states that the ever-receding colonial border renders obsolete every map, book of geography, and travelogue the moment they are printed. To actually leave the colony is no small feat: "the border shifted far north and keeps moving farther and farther."[90] Goncharov's comments on the Cape Colony's evanescent colonial border would have resonated for Russian readers with Alexander Pushkin's quixotic quest to cross the Russian empire's southern border and step onto foreign soil. Pushkin recounts it in *The Journey to Erzurum*, an 1836 account of his journeys into a disputed frontier and war zone between the Russian and Ottoman empires. Elated to think he succeeded, he soon learns that what he assumed to be Ottoman territory has in fact already been conquered by the Russian army.

Goncharov's thinking about the Xhosa problem also resonated with Russia's own ongoing conquest of the Caucasus—the ethnically diverse mountainous region between the Black and Caspian Seas. The strategic importance of the Caucasus for Russia lay in the need to buffer the southern frontier from Persia and the Ottomans and secure safer trade routes. Furthermore, Russia's early nineteenth-century annexations of Georgia and Armenia, which lay beyond the Caucasus chain, increased the need to subdue the Caucasus in order to link up the empire's territories. Russia was not an empire that simply happened to be contiguous but one that made contiguity a strategic objective. In other words, contiguity was not merely a fact of geography but a factor of geopolitics. Lasting over a century and half, from Peter the Great's initial forays in the eighteenth century to the ultimate Russian victory in 1864, when Tsar Alexander II declared a cessation of hostilities, the Caucasian War was the longest conflict in the history of the Russian empire—just as the Xhosa war was in South African history. In various forms, it has continued to this day. In the post-Soviet period, the Russian Federation has fought two brutal Chechen Wars to keep its hold on the oil-rich region.

By Goncharov's time, the Caucasian War had become a quagmire for every single celebrated Russian general and a graveyard for tens of thousands of Russian soldiers. It swallowed up about a sixth of the state's income. The mountaineers waged spirited guerilla warfare against the numerically and technologically superior enemy. Since military victories failed to win the war, the Russians moved in the nineteenth century to strangling the rebels' sources of support. They razed villages and livestock and cleared forests that might be used for cover. As historian Charles King reminds us, Russia was using the techniques of conquest perfected by empires the world round: "wanton destruction of property, mass deportation, and indiscriminate killing." The Caucasians were unable to create a unified front due to a complex mosaic of confessional factions, political allegiances, and social traditions that overlay a landscape of unprecedented ethnic and linguistic diver-

Figure 1.2. Imam Shamil, a leader in the Caucasian War against Russian imperial encroachment. HIP / Art Resource, NY.

sity. Nor were they able to secure substantial and lasting support from other empires they courted as potential allies, whether Ottoman, Persian, or British.[91]

The Caucasians came closest to victory under the outstanding political, military, and administrative leadership of Shamil, a charismatic Avar imam and fierce fighter. Though still at large during Goncharov's work on *The Frigate Pallada,* Shamil was captured by the Russians in 1859. He lived out his days in "gilded captivity," as King puts it, paraded at court and throughout Russia like "a sideshow oddity." He died while on a pilgrimage to Medina.

But before his capture, he tied down the Russian army for twenty-five years, becoming, alongside Garibaldi, one of the century's most celebrated guerrilla fighters.[92]

Goncharov connects the dots for the Russian reader by saying that the Xhosa wars in Africa have "the same character as our wars in the Caucasus." In both cases, the dynamic includes the indigenous peoples' raids on imperial settlements, followed by retreats into the mountains, infighting among local ethnic groups, guerrilla warfare against the colonists and military outposts, and violations of peace treaties by the colonized at each opportune moment.[93] This is how Goncharov sees the Xhosa conflicts; this is how the Caucasian ones were widely perceived in Russia. "With them, nothing will be gained by force," Goncharov reasons, briefly losing enthusiasm for the persuasive power of arms: "they can be subjugated not by gunpowder, but by comfort." He is here quite forgetting his earlier gripe that modern conveniences hold little appeal to Africans. Bringing the natives into the imperial fold, he now claims, the Xhosa and the Chechen alike, is a matter of teaching them to enjoy life's comforts.[94]

As a policy recommendation for the Caucasus, this was unorthodox to say the least. Yet Goncharov did have a hawkish side. He appreciated that continual warfare propelled the British advance: they never retreated, only gained more land. His hero was Sir Harry Smith, the ruthless and arrogant "rogue governor" of the Cape from 1847 to 1853 who had earlier distinguished himself in India. Though treated by historians today as a cross between a buffoon and a psychopath, in his time he was hailed as "the first authentic military hero of the Victorian age." He kept this reputation despite what came to be regarded as his dismal failure in Africa.[95] Goncharov, here following his German encyclopedia, applauds Smith's tactic of sticks and carrots, or, as he put it: "severity and contempt, followed by gentleness and friendliness." He claims that Harry Smith was widely respected and loved by the colonists.[96]

He also revels in Smith's trademark demonstrations of power. All Smith does, Goncharov implies, is to speak the language that the primitive native will understand. He relays a well-known episode of Smith's public humiliation of the Xhosa chief Maqoma, a fearsome antagonist of the British and a foremost military leader. (Incidentally, readers unfamiliar with African history may be interested to know that the tradition of Xhosa leadership includes the first president of post-apartheid South Africa, Nelson Mandela.) In Goncharov's rendering of this episode, Smith made Maqoma kneel and placed his foot on the chief's neck, calling him a dog and proclaiming that "this is how henceforward he [Smith] will treat the enemies of the English queen." Neither Goncharov nor his source cite Maqoma's retort to the insult: "You are a dog and you behave like a dog. . . . I am of royal blood like [Victoria]." In Goncharov's retelling, such measures allow Smith to pacify the Xhosa people. Once that has been accomplished, Smith switched his tactics to exhorting the Xhosa about their path to civilization: "become friendly with Europeans, listen to missionaries, learn English, take up crafts, trade honestly, and get used to money." Goncharov calls Smith's measures "energetic and wise." The opinion of the British government, however, was different. Considering him inept and excessively violent, it ordered Smith replaced in 1852.[97]

Smith's strategy resembled those of Prince Mikhail Vorontsov, the hero of both Napoleonic and Caucasian wars and the first imperial viceroy in the Caucasus, in office until spring 1854. Born in England to a Russian ambassador, he attended Cambridge University. Like Smith, Vorontsov systematically pursued the twin goals of extirpation and civilization, perhaps inspired by the British methods about which he may have learned during his university years in England. He hounded anti-Russian rebels, but also built theaters and opera houses in Georgia, combining, in King's words, "military ruthlessness with what would now be called a hearts-and-minds campaign."[98] Goncharov's praise of Harry Smith may be an oblique endorsement of Vorontsov's methods and of Russia's own policy in the Caucasus. In either case, the shadow of the Caucasus hovers over the topic of the British-Xhosa Wars in *The Frigate Pallada.*

In a very real sense, Britain's global imperial projection connected the Cape Colony's British officers mentioned by Goncharov with another war back in Russia: the Crimean War. Commodore Sir Charles Talbot, who commanded a military squadron at the Cape during the *Pallada*'s visit and kindly assisted the Russians in procuring all necessities, was soon transferred to the Crimean front. He took part in the blockade of Sebastopol and the battle of Kerch, for which he was later promoted to Admiral. Much less fortunate was Sir George Cathcart (1791–1854), the governor of the Cape during the *Pallada*'s visit, who was killed in the Crimean War.[99]

Cathcart's Russian connection, however, had a very curious afterlife back in the Cape Colony. News of his death at the hands of some mysterious people called Russians spread like wildfire among the Xhosa. Could these Russians be black? When informed by the British that Russians were white and were losing the war, the Xhosa suspected trickery. According to Jeffrey Peires, who has studied this fascinating episode, the Xhosa became convinced that the Russians were a black nation resurrected from the spirits of the Xhosa warriors who fell in anti-colonial wars. Xhosa prophets claimed to be communing with them across the sea. Following Cathcart's death, an imminent return of the Xhosa-Russians was expected, so lookout points were set up to watch for Russian ships. The Xhosa hoped that the Russians would rid Africa of the British, repeating their Crimean triumph.[100] Who knows? Had the *Pallada* sailed in a bit later, and into a different bay, Goncharov and his mates might have received a very puzzling welcome.

A Progressive and Expansive Empire?

Neither for Goncharov nor for his contemporaries were the colonies' modernity, dynamism, and material prosperity the sole points of imperial comparisons. The political ideals animating colonial arrangements were such points, too. The age of imperialism, perhaps not coincidentally, also saw the birth of humanitarianism. Unlike age-old charity extended by individuals to those in one's immediate communities, humanitarianism denotes aid rendered to strangers in distant lands through institutions of organized society. Atonement has been an important motive for humanitarian actions. The violence and exploitation that assisted colonial expansion has bred a conviction in big and increasingly vocal sectors of metropolitan societies that they had much to atone for. As Michael Barnett puts it, "the international community has tended to rally around humanitarianism at precisely the moment when its humanity is most suspect." This is why the opposition to colonial slavery played a catalytic role in the emergence of humanitarianism. Adam Hochschild notes that the emergence of the anti-slavery movement "was the first time a large number of people became outraged, and stayed outraged for many years, over someone *else's* rights. And most startling of all, the rights of people of another color, on another continent."[101] By mid-century, the era of imperial humanitarianism was in full swing in Europe. The center of the most extensive global colonial system, London was also, since the late eighteenth century, the hub of international humanitarianism committed to remedying colonial abuses.[102]

Humanitarian activists, such as missionaries and anti-slavery advocates, typically sought to advance their agenda by lobbying governments to change or amend state policies. Yet humanitarianism also became part of imperial governance. As historians Alan Lester and Fae Dussart show, humanitarian ideals—such as various amelioration policies, or efforts to protect indigenous people, lessen settlers' violent impulses, or civilize benighted natives—became a central strategy of legitimating imperial rule. As such, humanitarian activities entered "the disciplinary apparatus of governance" in settler empires, including the mid-nineteenth-century Cape Colony.[103] This is the intellectual climate that produced the ideology of imperial trusteeship. This ideology held that Europeans were merely benevolent temporary trustees of the colonial lands and resources, which would be returned to their rightful owners once these owners proved capable of administering them wisely.

In the late eighteenth century, however, the central point on the humanitarian agenda was ending slavery. Britain abolished the slave trade in 1807 and slaveholding in the colonies in 1833. In the mix of factors leading to these moves, high-minded ideals coexisted with more pragmatic reasons, such as concerns with unproductive labor or the nightmare of slave rebellions.[104] From Goncharov's perspective, however, these were principled decisions for which the British should be applauded. He notes their price. In the Cape Colony, the pool of available labor drastically decreased. The Boers' hostility to the British increased proportionately, leading thousands to abandon the colony and venture north on their Great Trek.[105] As it happens, the question of slavery was also a burning domestic issue then in Russia, where it was abolished only in 1861. At the time of writing, Goncharov thus had to temper his enthusiasm about Britain's progressive choice to end it, though he clearly supported it. Later in the book, he proclaims the absence of slavery in Siberia as highly salutary. A reader inclined to draw parallels could conclude that Britain's colony in southern Africa had more humane laws than European Russia.

With evident relish, Goncharov also reports how the Cape colonists shooed off a British transport of prisoners that the London government dispatched to relieve the labor shortage. Determined to prevent the Cape from becoming another Australia, where the British government in the years between 1788 and 1868 resettled 160,000 convicts, the colonists thronged at the wharf threatening to stone the criminals rather than to accept them as fellow settlers. This story relates the arrival of the convicts at the Cape in 1849 and is based on Goncharov's German encyclopedia.[106] This, too, was a tidbit with domestic resonance for Russians. As was universally known, the Russian state used a system of penal servitude to turn Siberia into a dumping ground for the empire's undesirable and criminal elements, and this caused problems for Siberia's voluntary settlers. The Cape's colonial system, Goncharov suggests, was more wisely arranged than Russia's own largest colony.

The Cape Colony's political system, which at the time of the Russians' visit was undergoing a radical transition, also drew Goncharov's attention. He explains that the Cape was previously administered by a London-appointed governor, assisted by an Executive Council that enjoyed special powers. The Legislative Council was composed of top administrators and members appointed by the governor. Proposed legislation was brought before the Council and printed in newspapers. The laws that passed had to be ratified by London.[107]

But big changes were underway. The Cape was about to be granted a representative self-government and laws would no longer require London's ratification. The colony would begin to govern itself according to local needs and aspirations. "An English province" was about to gain independence. Though Goncharov does not mention it, by then Britain had also devolved power in Canada, Australia, and New Zealand (but not in India, or other territories where indigenous people vastly outnumbered colonists). In return, the Cape Colony was to assume financial responsibility for its defense and administration. At the time of writing, Goncharov noted that a "project" was being debated in the British Parliament. Its approval arrived at the Cape on the very day that the *Pallada* weighed anchor to set course for Asia.[108]

This approved "project" was the 1853 Constitution: the legal act that set forth the political changes outlined by Goncharov. He avoids using the word "constitution" because propagating constitutional ideals was at the time prohibited in Russia, and the term rarely appeared in print.[109] Goncharov does, however, mention "constitution" in his official report penned under Putiatin's name, which was delivered to the emperor, Alexander II, in March 1856. His fellow crew member Possiet managed to slip it into his *Naval Review* report about southern Africa.[110] What goes unmentioned in either Possiet's article, *The Frigate Pallada*, or Goncharov's official report is that this was a fairly liberal constitution. Though this did not radically redress the power imbalance between white colonists and Africans, any adult male inhabitant who owned merely twenty-five pounds' worth of property, irrespective of race, had the right to vote.[111] Given the importance of these developments to the life of the colony, this was likely known to Goncharov, so his skittishness on the topic likely reflected domestic Russian sensitivity about both constitutionalism and a devolution of power to the colonies. At any rate, for politically attuned readers of *The Frigate Pallada*, it was clear that under Britain's enlightened rule the Cape Colony was about to get a representative government and a meaningful measure of independence from London.

This, too, would have struck Goncharov's liberally minded Russian readers. The tsar's autocratic power in Russia was at that time unconstrained by any representative body. Elected local municipal councils (*dumy*) were introduced in Russia only in the 1860s as part of Alexander II's reforms. An elective state council with legislative powers was to become a reality only after the Revolution of 1905, which also gave birth to the first Russian constitution. The Russian empire never voluntarily devolved power to any of its colonies, though it sold Alaska to the US in 1867. In more ways than one, Goncharov's Cape Colony is thus an inspirational story for the Russian proponents of liberal reforms.

Goncharov believed, however, that for at least some period, progressive changes had to coexist with continued European expansion across the entire African continent. He realized that this process might not be completed in his lifetime, but was confident that eventually it would be. Europeans from Algeria and from Cape Town, he writes, "will meet somewhere in the [African] interior." He viewed this process as unstoppable, capturing its beginnings with characteristic lightheartedness: "Already now omnibuses traverse the colony, vodka is being distilled, there are hotels, shops, miladies with curls, and grand pianos—can complete victory be far off?" Deserts, wild animals, and Africa's fearsome anti-colonial warriors, such as Algeria's Abd al-Qādir or Cape Colony's Sandile, he wagers, would all prove powerless in the face of the unrelenting progress of modern European comforts. Only total European colonization of Africa, according to Goncharov, could mean "complete victory." All Soviet proponents of viewing this book as anti-colonial should have been stopped in their tracks by this passage.[112]

The audacity and precocity of Goncharov's vision must be given their due. Around 1850, it was not at all a foregone conclusion that Europeans would colonize Africa. Except for French Algeria in the north, the British Cape Colony in the south, and tiny, dispersed pockets of Europe's coastal footholds, the vast African continent was as yet uncolonized. Even as late as 1879, Europeans controlled only about ten percent of the continent. Only by 1912 did they gain nearly total control—and it took the notorious "Scramble for Africa" to get there. This scramble left Ethiopia, and in an unusual way Liberia (ruled by the freed or freeborn African-Americans resettled by the US), as the only autonomous political entities in Africa. Historians Jane Burbank and Frederick Cooper caution, moreover, against the false image of Africa as a supine continent populated with isolated tribes. Mid-nineteenth century Africa, they write, had commercially, politically, and militarily powerful kingdoms and empires, such as the Zulus'. The production of the continent's chief commercial articles—agricultural goods—remained firmly under Africans' control. Content for the time being with the imperialism of free trade, Europeans seriously considered "leaving the interior of Africa to Africans."[113]

In this context, Goncharov's expansive vision, tossed off so casually and yet with such assurance, is nothing short of breathtaking. And yet, as a Russian, Goncharov was a predictable forecaster for such visions. Perhaps it should be no surprise that conquering a vast continent would have appeared a realistic prospect to a citizen of an empire that in scarcely six decades extended itself from the Urals to the Pacific.

CHAPTER TWO

Pineapples in Petersburg, Cabbage Soup on the Equator

Parts of the world quickly get nearer one another: from Europe to America you practically shake hands. They say you'll soon be able to travel this distance in forty eight hours.

—Ivan Goncharov, *The Frigate Pallada*

Carriages in Australia's hinterland, Irish linen in China, French hotels on the Hawaiian Islands, a traditional Russian cabbage soup available on the equator: Goncharov opens his travelogue with such images of a rapidly interlocking world. Are there any ports, he wonders, without mail service to Europe? The *Pallada* encounters a commercial vessel filled to the brim with European migrants headed for Australia, then another one carrying Chinese coolies (or contract laborers) from Hong Kong to San Francisco. Manila's European street life strikes Goncharov as "the same as in Moscow, Petersburg, Berlin, and Paris" and the British Museum's antiquities the same as those in St. Petersburg, Vienna, or Madrid. British canned food sustains him in a remote corner of the frozen Siberian tundra. Thanks to the interconnections of Europe's imperial rule, a robber and kidnapper who committed his offences on the tiny Bonin Islands, south of Tokyo, is apprehended in New Zealand. Goncharov quips: "These days, you won't escape the police even on the Eastern Ocean!"[1]

This chapter examines Goncharov's perspective on this new global world order. What are its sources, structures, and prospects? How does Russia fit in? These questions are indelibly linked in *The Frigate Pallada* to the operations of European and American empires, and particularly their trade. The relation between economic forces and imperial regimes becomes especially evident for Goncharov through his visits to the European trading enclaves and colonies on Asia's southeastern seaboard, including Singapore, Manila, Hong Kong, and Shanghai. These visits cement his vision of a globalized world interlinked by the operations of modern European and American empires. At that time it would have been in Asia's port cities that the accelerating forces of modern globalizing processes were indeed most palpable. Even today, Goncharov's account of a globalized world reads as strikingly modern.

Goncharov is enthusiastic to discover what looks to him like an unprecedented level of global trade, which he portrays as an engine of prosperity for everyone involved. His attention is drawn not to the rivalry but to the collaboration and exchange of expertise among international imperial elites. He nonetheless confronts certain unappealing aspects of trade and, on this leg of the journey, becomes disenchanted with westerners' conduct in Asia. He is outraged by Europeans' and Americans' exploitative opium trade in China. Britons' demeaning treatment of the Chinese casts a shadow over his idealized images of the British from the Cape colony. Their moral and civilizational stature becomes diminished in the narrative, preparing the ground for Goncharov's articulation of Russia's own civilizing mission in Siberia. His portrayal of the Taiping Rebellion in China, critical of the rebels, reveals the degree to which trade concessions granted to westerners made the Qing empire vulnerable to foreign interference in its internal affairs. Yet Goncharov's critique of other empires' conduct does not extend to imperialism as such, which *The Frigate Pallada* consistently embraces.

Globalization, Empire, and Trade

Globalization used to be considered a fairly recent phenomenon, with beginnings in the aftermath of the fall of the Soviet Union in 1989 or, at the earliest, after the Second World War. It is now recognized to have a much longer history. The age of empires, especially between the mid-nineteenth century and the First World War, was vitally important to the genesis of the modern global world order. If globalization is a set of social processes that produce "tight global economic, political, cultural, and environmental interconnections and flows that make most of the currently existing borders and boundaries irrelevant," then the system of modern European empires greatly accelerated those processes.[2] Imperial trade in particular pushed globalization forward. At the end of the fifteenth century, according to historian Jonathan Israel, Western Europeans "forged a world-trade network which linked all the major zones of the globe, often via intermediary depots, with the great commercial and maritime emporia of the west, channeling wealth and resources from every quarter back to the European heartland." Sociologist Janet Abu-Lughod shows that a complex and sophisticated system of international trade, not inferior to the later one of Europeans, existed as early as the thirteenth century.[3]

The best way to think about globalization is in terms of degrees or relative rates of acceleration. Jürgen Osterhammel and Niels Petersson, who begin their history of globalization in the eighth century, claim that "we can only speak . . . about 'more' or 'less' globalization." They note that while the network of worldwide connections existing prior to the 1750s was impressive, it had many "holes." Local trade still predominated over long-distance trade, the world was still polycentric, and economic crises did not engulf whole continents. Over the course of the nineteenth century, the holes began to be filled in by the Industrial Revolution, the rise of capitalism and global finance, and the rapid extension of European imperialism. These were the forces that made the nineteenth century into "Europe's century," like no century before or after. "Never had changes originating in Europe," observe Osterhammel and Petersson, "achieved such impact on the rest of the world."[4]

Western European countries with their far-flung overseas empires receive all the attention in accounts of modern European imperialism. Yet this does not capture its full reality. John Darwin proposes instead a concept of "Greater Europe": a vast zone encompassing much of northern Eurasia and North America. An important advantage of this approach is the inclusion of Russia and the United States, countries that were integral to global imperialism's networks and ideologies but are typically omitted in historical accounts. Within this Greater Europe, Darwin writes, "political and cultural differences were moderated by a sense of shared 'Europeanness' . . . in the face of recalcitrant nature, hostile indigenes, or 'Asiatic' competitors." Just as Americanness was, according to Darwin, merely "a provincial variant," so, one might add, was Russianness. Calling the Americans "the indispensable sleeping partners of Europe's expansion into Afro-Asia," Darwin discounts their traditional declarations of anti-imperialism. This can to some extent be said of the Russians, too, even though in Asia, where the Russians saw their imperial destiny, cozy intimacy often turned to rougher play. Convinced of the universalist claim that its civilization was superior, this Greater Europe, flanked by Russia and the United States, set forth to dominate the Outer World (also Darwin's term) in the rest of Eurasia, Africa, South America, and the Pacific. By the 1830s, Darwin writes, "Europeans were assembling the means for the physical, commercial, and cultural domination of regions that had been beyond their reach only sixty years before, and whose civilizations had once seemed awesome and impregnable."[5]

Over the course of the century, Greater European networks and connections evolved into a global system that reached deeply into Outer World economies and societies. Darwin reports a twenty-five-fold increase in the volume of trade between 1820 and 1913, with the fastest rate of growth occurring between 1840 and 1870—the time of Goncharov's travels. Yet more than market penetration levels or the sheer volume of trade, Darwin points to key structural changes as the markers of a world economy's emergence. Europeans broke down the Outer World's mercantile hierarchies and its regional systems of exchange, pricing, and credit. By 1880, Darwin notes, the prices of basic commodities were set by world markets rather than by local supply and demand. Credit, investment capital, and insurance now operated globally. Flush with profits from the Industrial Revolution, Europeans and Americans became the main purveyors of investment capital and financial services to much of the non-European world.[6] The phenomenon of world economy emerged under the aegis of imperial free trade. Starting with the Long Depression following the financial crisis of 1873, economic busts and booms rippled across the entire globe.[7]

Migration and developments in communication technology also facilitated globalizing processes. No account of nineteenth-century globalization would be complete without mention of the railway, steamship, and telegraph—that "internet of the Victorian Age." More than sixty million people participated in the massive migrations of the second half of the nineteenth century—migrations that placed roughly forty-five million Europeans in the New World and displaced many indigenous peoples. About ten million Slavs set out for the Russian empire's Asian territories. Eleven million coolies, mainly from India and China, left their homes in search of work.[8] Gary Magee and Andrew Thompson argue that these global migrations led to rapid economic growth because they helped integrate labor and commodity markets and stimulate trade and capital markets. Emigration, as historian Asa Briggs reminds us, was an organized, profit-oriented industry in its own right, "with agents, shipping rebates, and propaganda offices." In the long run, global migrations meant that identities among diasporas and their host societies became less narrowly national and more cosmopolitan. Empire, which Magee and Thompson call "a species of global networking," played a major role in this globalization.[9]

Alongside such economic changes, Christopher Bayly traces many political and cultural trends toward uniformity in the nineteenth century facilitated by the worldwide expansion of Western European imperialism. Modern states, including imperial ones, forced diverse societies to adopt uniform administrative, legal, and educational structures. The boom in world trade made many popular commodities available around the globe. Western styles and practices took hold worldwide. Forms of art, architecture, and dress began to converge. The world was certainly not homogeneous, but differences were gradually being smoothed.[10]

It is precisely such imperial globalization—based on labor mobility, global capital, access to commodity markets, and vibrant trade—that *The Frigate Pallada*'s Asian sections perceptively diagnose. While, circa 1850, these globalizing processes were still tentative by comparison with the late nineteenth century, one would not know it from Goncharov's account, so vividly does he portray them. The Russians' desire to put their own imperial network more fully in global play—evident in the *Pallada*'s very mission—permeates Goncharov's descriptions.[11]

It was a time of rapid and radical changes in Asia's relations with Europe. China's Canton trade system, which operated from 1760 to 1834, strictly regulated foreign trade through the monopolies that enriched the Qing elites of merchants and local administrators. All trade with Europeans took place through the keyhole port of Canton. The Chinese officials held the upper hand and dictated cumbersome rules of the trade. Its balance was in China's favor: exports exceeded imports as Europeans flocked to bid for attractive Asian commodities. Here is the Qing emperor's famous reply to a British diplomat promoting his country's products in 1793: "We possess all things. I see no value in objects strange or ingenious, and have no use for your country's manufactures."[12]

As the Industrial Revolution gained momentum, however, Europeans selling locally managed to undercut the prices of goods produced in Asia. Over the course of the nineteenth century, improved transportation technologies, including steam power, lowered freight costs by as much as eighty percent.[13] Opening markets rather than securing raw materials became Britons' new objective. Others learned by their example that exporting more to global markets meant gaining imperial power. Briggs notes that "the whole world was the province of the British exporter, and in no single year of the nineteenth century did the Empire buy more than one-third of Britain's exports."[14] India and China, those former suppliers of textiles to Europe, become consumers of cheaply produced European cloth by the late nineteenth century. In consequence of the British victory against the Qing in the First Opium War, concluded by the Treaty of Nanjing of 1842, the Canton trade system was replaced by an "unequal treaty" or "treaty port" system. An assault on its sovereignty, this system forced China to open five ports to the European trade formerly restricted to Canton, to allow European settlement in those ports, to grant foreigners extraterritorial rights (excluding them from Chinese jurisdiction), to cede Hong Kong to Britain, and to accept a system of tariffs skewed in favor of European traders.[15]

The gates to China were thrown open. The commercial offensive of Greater Europeans had begun. Soon, the Second Opium War widened the scope of their privileges: more ports were opened, merchants and missionaries gained access to the Chinese interior, and diplomats were now to be permanently stationed in Beijing. Russia transacted its own unequal treaties with the Qing in addition to gaining huge territory. "China," Darwin writes, "had been forcibly integrated into the Europeans' international system, on humiliating terms, and as a second-rate power, at best."[16]

From the Europeans' perspective, all this was done under the banner of bestowing on backward Asians the modern European invention of free trade. The middle of the nineteenth century saw the demise of the old mercantilist system of international trade. Rooted in the assumption that the world's economic resources were finite, mercantilism promoted exports and restricted imports with the strategic intention of accumulating monetary resources in gold and silver. Each empire tried to operate as a closed circuit; inasmuch as possible, goods were to be traded, shipped, and produced within each empire's network. Unless they were buying, rival empires were ideally to be kept out. Economic policy was the province of the state.

Adam Smith offered a searing critique of mercantilism in *The Wealth of Nations,* claiming that it buttressed private greed and wasted resources without enhancing countries' overall economic development. He advocated instead for domestic laissez-faire capitalism and international free trade. Support for free trade ideas gained momentum during France's Continental Blockade of Britain in the Napoleonic Wars. These conflicts revealed mercantilism's endemic problems: wars, major disruptions of international trade, and the tendencies of monopolies—mercantilism's main economic instruments—to cause shortages, price increases, and fiscal crises. The example of the Americas showed how all of this could in turn lead to revolutions and territorial losses.[17]

In the 1840s, Britain unilaterally adopted free trade, which was a unique act. Led by Britain's example—or dragooned by its government—most European countries eventually followed suit. With the exception of Russia, Europe became a free-trade zone by 1870.[18] States and their militaries, however, continued to exert ancillary, and some claim fairly substantial, influence, especially in securing trade routes and opening new markets such as those in China and Japan. The tariff, seen as a more subtle negotiating tool, replaced the monopoly. Markets, at least in principle, were to be unregulated and open equally to all. It was widely assumed—and Goncharov shared this assumption—that free trade was the best guarantee of world peace. Open markets meant that no wars would be needed to gain access to them. Market protectionism reemerged during the end-of-century imperial scramble, but the mid-century, by and large, was a euphoric era of experiments in free trade.[19]

Russia participated in this worldwide trend. Free-trade ideas entered Russia quite early, mainly from England. To this day, a common Russian term for "free trade" is a calque from English: "fritrederstvo." The Russian translation of Adam Smith's *The Wealth of Nations* appeared between 1802 and 1806, sponsored by Emperor Alexander I.[20] During his rule, Russia violated the Continental Blockade of England, which was Russia's main export market; Napoleon cited this violation as his reason for invading Russia in 1812. The bold free-trade regime established by the Russian 1819 tariff, however, was mostly reversed in 1822. With duties on certain imports ranging from 100 percent to 250 percent of their value, the tariff of 1822 performed the basic function of a monopoly. These restrictions were lessened over time. Their most radical relaxation came with the tariff of 1850, enacted partly in response to Britain's 1846 repeal of its Corn Laws, which had previously restricted grain imports. However, a global crisis of the 1870s led to a fiscally motivated protectionist retrenchment in Russia and much of continental Europe that continued for the rest of the century.[21]

Russian society was divided on the subject of free trade. While economic liberalism was popular among the intelligentsia, many regarded Russia as unprepared for it. Early on, the proponents of liberal reforms known as the Decembrists warmly embraced Smith's ideas, especially his notion that political and economic freedoms tended to go hand in hand. Landed nobility, concerned about consumer prices and reliant on grain exports, tended to favor lower tariffs and duties. The manufacturers, industrialists, and merchants, however, tended to demand protections. Typical arguments against free trade claimed that unrestricted trade would cripple domestic manufacturing and trade and make Russia, in conditions of war or other emergencies, perilously reliant on foreign countries for essential commodities. Free trade might be all the rage, said its critics, but Russia had better proceed cautiously.[22]

Britain would have none of Russia's caution. Chafing at irksome Russian restrictions and tariffs on British imports, it campaigned vigorously to eliminate them, perceiving market protectionism as "an unacceptable civilizational deficit."[23] Like the Napoleonic Wars, the Crimean War had its economic underpinnings. Britain resented that its unrestricted right to buy goods in Russia was not balanced by an unrestricted right to sell its own goods there. When Russia rebuffed its demands for reciprocal free trade, Britain shifted much of its business to the Ottoman empire, which did agree—under duress—to trade with Britain on a free-trade basis in 1838. British wholesale customers for Russian wheat began shopping in the Ottoman empire. As a result, when Ottoman-Russian hostilities erupted in 1853, Britain's interests lay with its Ottoman trading partner, especially given the larger landscape of the British-Russian rivalry in Asia. According to Britain, Russia's protectionist stance required that the Black Sea be protected for free trade.[24]

On the other hand, Russia's resistance drew applause in some quarters in the United States, which, like Russia, upheld market protectionism domestically while clamoring for free trade abroad.[25] One vocal American defender of Russia in the Crimean conflict, historian Charles Brandon Boynton, lambasted Britain's free-trade agenda as hypocritical and credited Russia's tariff system for saving its empire in times of war. Boynton also drew a parallel between the Russian and the American overland empires in that they rose to economic prominence despite haughty British sneers, and both were unfairly checked in their expansion by the British behemoth.[26]

At his place of permanent employment, in the Ministry of Finances' Department of Trade, Goncharov had a ringside seat to such controversies. While understanding well the fears of Russian merchants, Goncharov, who worked as a translator, would have also been conversant with western arguments. When Goncharov set out on his voyage, the liberal new tariff of 1850 had just come into effect. In the imperial peripheries and key international trading zones toward which he was headed, free trade was more likely to be used in promoting economic growth. Free trade was also allowed along the Amur, the key river on the border with Manchuria that the *Pallada* later explored and that Russia would soon annex. The General-Governor of Eastern Siberia, Nikolai Muravev—who wined and dined Goncharov in Irkutsk, journeyed back to St. Petersburg with the writer, and was lionized in the pages of *The Frigate Pallada* and beyond—was a dauntless advocate of free trade. In the 1860s, Muravev even tried to transform the entire province of Eastern Siberia into a free-trade zone.[27]

Such new solutions held appeal to people like Muravev because, at mid-century, Russia's economic landscape looked bleak. In the 1840s, the total value of Russia's foreign trade stood at about thirty percent of France's and eighteen percent of England's.[28] Trade with Asia, so lucrative for Western Europeans, was to help lead Russia out of these doldrums. Reenergizing it was the chief objective of the *Pallada* expedition; it was never too distant from Goncharov's mind. Moreover, *The Frigate Pallada* was published in the aftermath of the Crimean War, which nearly plunged the state into bankruptcy. Stimulating foreign investment and developing overseas trade became urgent national priorities.[29] The popularity of *The Frigate Pallada* created a wide and receptive audience for its enthusiastic image of dynamic world trade and its profit windfalls, and raised anxieties that Russia might miss the boat.

Whatever pushback there was among Europe's metropolitan economies against free trade, there was much to recommend it as a trading platform with Africa and Asia. By the early nineteenth century, European empires had lost their American colonies. Slave-trading as a revenue stream was widely challenged domestically on ethical grounds. Moreover, as Jane Burbank and Frederick Cooper succinctly put it, "armed commerce is not cheap."[30] Huge overhead costs of administering colonies and maintaining armies to contain rival empires crippled imperial budgets. "These wretched colonies," British Prime Minister Benjamin Disraeli exclaimed in 1852, "are a millstone round our necks." Free trade offered European empires a more sustainable imperial model and reconfigured their relations. In the mercantilist system, the formal possession of colonies was essential to exploiting their supplies of precious metals and other resources. Free trade, by contrast, dispensed with the expense and bother of territorial control. In Anthony Pagden's phrase, commerce replaced conquest.[31] Territorial annexations became measures of last resort. Minimal means were preferred to maintain what in the British imperial idiom was elegantly termed "paramountcy."

Yet as John Gallagher and Ronald Robinson influentially argue, "refusals to annex are no proof of reluctance to control." Free trade was not the suspension of imperialism but its characteristic mid-century form. The "imperialism of free trade," whose routes were secured globally by the British Navy, was seen as simply a more cost-efficient way of securing profits. "To extend control informally if possible and formally if necessary" became the new mantra of British imperial policy. Its global success made the imitation of the British empire's new imperial repertoire—economic power backed by naval force—well worth considering by partners and competitors.[32]

Beyond promoting world peace, free trade was thought by its advocates to provide equitable access to prosperity. This fueled the moral fervor of its proponents, including Goncharov. Putiatin also presented the attractions of trade to the Japanese in terms of mutual benefit: Russians don't have salt in Kamchatka but have lots of fish. Sell us salt and we'll sell you salted fish. Why yoke all your labor to rice production? Buy it elsewhere and employ some people in mining for profitable metals. Only by trading do nations grow rich, Putiatin reportedly lectured the Japanese.[33]

For the Outer World, the reality proved less rosy. Much of this world was militarily coerced to accept free trade. Gunboat diplomacy—that is, the use of naval forces to shape foreign policy—enabled Britain to win the Opium Wars with China and Perry and Putiatin to "open" Japan.[34] The invisible hand of the market was not the only hand weighing in on free-trade transactions. Europeans found myriad ways to skew "free" trade in their favor. The treaties with China and Japan were, after all, "unequal." Moreover, instead of ushering in common prosperity, imperially run free trade led to major economic disparities between what later came to be called the First and Third Worlds; this was the phenomenon known as "the great divergence." African and Asian economies were largely reduced to supplying raw materials and cheap labor. They consumed Western manufactured goods instead of producing their own. However, recent studies in economic history show that in the eighteenth century non-European economies not only did not lag behind

European ones, they often surpassed them. The notion of Asian stagnation was a myth that Europeans concocted to validate their expansion. In 1800, of the ten most populous cities, seven were in Asia (Moscow ranked fifteenth). Contrary to the popular image of Europeans' modernizing influence on the backward economies of Asia and Africa, the advent of their control often arrested these economies' growth and homegrown processes of modernization.[35]

Circuits of Trade and Sociability

From its seaboard through the commercial arteries of its rivers, the face of Asia was rapidly changing. The trading depots of Dutch, British, French, American, and Portuguese empires grew into urban Western enclaves with a peculiar blend of Asian and European cultures. Canton in particular was a perfect example of "a raucous world of Portuguese, Spanish, Mandarin, Cantonese, pidgin English, Malay, and Indian languages, peppered with words from all of Europe and Oceania." By mid-century, when Goncharov visited, Shanghai's treaty port community included about two hundred firms and five hundred foreigners (not counting their families), with half coming from the British Isles.[36] After the Opium Wars, these European "concession areas," as they were called, enjoyed extraterritoriality, under which the Europeans there were governed by their own laws, not those of China.

Whereas they had been mere passersby in Africa, the Russians entered Asia as their own backyard. In the ports of the Indian Ocean, all the way to Japan, the imperial circuits of Europe and America started to overlap with Russia's. Singapore's Malay mosque did not strike Russian visitors as exotic; in Kazan they had seen one just like it. Kazan, in the lower Volga region (today's Republic of Tatarstan), was the 1552 conquest by Ivan the Terrible that launched Russia's imperial expansion into ethnically non-Slavic lands. Goncharov's fellow crewmember the archpriest Avvakum had served in the Russian ecclesiastical mission in Beijing. Whether in religion, trade, or diplomacy, Goncharov's Russians felt more at home in Asia than in Africa.[37]

At the time of Goncharov's travels, the enmities that had pitted Europeans against one another back on the old continent were softening on new imperial frontiers. Despite rivalries for profits and control, a remarkable cooperation characterized their joint venture. This was a recent development connected to the emergence of the informal imperialism of free trade. In contrast to the bloody wars for territorial control characteristic of mercantile empires, such as the Franco-British wars over India in the eighteenth century, the free-trade model helped save lives and money by lessening the need for military solutions—though never dispensing with them fully, as the Crimean War made clear. The costly and heavy-handed empire of the flag was superseded by an empire of commerce, with its lighter touch and potential for interimperial synergies. As David Igler argues, the Pacific maritime trade in particular exhibited "an internationalism that extended beyond the known geopolitical rivalries." These rivalries continued, but were channeled through what Mary Louise Pratt calls "new legitimating ideologies: the civilizing mission, scientific racism, and technology-based paradigms of progress and development." Yet the gods of mammon continued to demand their tribute. Paradoxically, it was precisely the competition of international capital that, in Pratt's words, "bound European powers together in finding new forms for Euro-imperial interventions."[38]

In the face of Asian governments, a united front was understood to be necessary for the greater cause of European dominance of Asia. This was especially so since Asian diplomacies' reflexive response to Europeans was to play the "barbarians" against one another—a strategy the Japanese considered in dealing with Perry and Putiatin. The race to open up ports was motivated by a desire to gain global prestige, or by a given market's priority for a particular European empire, or by the prospect of structuring trade relationships to one's own commercial advantage. At least in Japan and China (with the exception of Hong Kong), the goal was not to obtain exclusive trading rights. Both Perry and Putiatin negotiated with the Japanese fully aware that other European countries would demand similar trading privileges, which they did. The Japanese themselves expected multiple requests.[39] Both the American and the Russian trading contracts contained clauses that required Japan to automatically extend to the United States and to Russia any new trading privileges granted to other western countries. Once Britain won the right to trade opium in China, French and American suppliers were welcome to send in their boats, too.

When the first Russian circumnavigator of the globe, Ivan Kruzenshtern, visited China in 1805, while the Napoleonic wars were raging in Europe, he was struck that Europeans, "though their nations should be involved in wars at home, live here in the strictest bonds of friendship." Officials of the British East India Company advocated on behalf of Kruzenshtern's bid to make

Canton accessible to Russian maritime trade, claiming that as Europeans, Russians were entitled to the same privileges. (The Chinese authorities rejected the bid.)[40] Russians initially cheered the 1857 Sepoy Mutiny in India because it humbled the British empire, their chief antagonist in the Crimean conflict. But according to the nineteenth-century nationalist publicist and Moscow University professor Mikhail Pogodin, this military and political grievance quickly gave way to expressions of solidarity with the British as white, Christian Europeans who were threatened by "barbarians." Setbacks in the global imperial enterprise tended to suspend imperial rivalries. Capturing the mood of his countrymen, Pogodin claimed they wished the English—indeed, all European nations—success in establishing firm rule not only in India, but also in Asia, Africa, and America. In *The Frigate Pallada,* Goncharov derides the naïve assumption of the Japanese that one Western power might not know what another one is doing. He fulminates when the Nagasaki governor tries to prevent contact between the Russians and the Dutch: "how could an idea pop into the governor's head to interfere in the relations between two European vessels?" Free intercourse among Europeans was a sacred right on imperial frontiers, their community of interests a given.[41]

During the Crimean War, the amity between the British and the Russians operating in the Pacific understandably lessened. The French and British navies pursued Russian ships there and attacked, unsuccessfully, Kamchatka. In December 1854 the tsunami off the coast of Japan destroyed the *Pallada*'s replacement, the *Diana,* and Russian seamen intercepted then by the British found safe passage back to Russia after the war on board various British vessels, having been extended every courtesy.[42] The Russians and the Americans, for all the rivalry between Perry and Putiatin, and for all the Russians' displeasure at American whalers intruding into Siberian waterways, developed a close cooperation in Asia.

The American vice consul in Shanghai, Edward Cunningham, was an icon of such multinational diplomatic and business synergies. *The Frigate Pallada* notes Cunningham's double assignment: his work for the US diplomatic service and for a prominent American business firm, Russell & Co. But his assignment was in fact quadruple, since Cunningham simultaneously served as the consular agent of the French and Russian governments, in addition to the American one.[43] While in Shanghai, Putiatin lodged in Cunningham's mansion, where Goncharov was also entertained several times, and was ferried about on Cunningham's yacht. Against Perry's

Figure 2.1. The American consulate in Shanghai as it appeared to the Perry expedition in 1853.

prohibition, Cunningham sold Putiatin fifty tons of coal, a scarce commodity, from Perry's Shanghai stores.[44] Although the Russophobic Perry refused to cooperate with Putiatin, and was livid about the coal, the US officials who replaced Perry worked closely with the Russians. The American military and commercial vessels helped transport and outfit with various nautical necessities the Russian crew stranded in Japan after the tsunami. The American commander H. A. Adams took care of delivering to Russia the Treaty of Shimoda that Putiatin eventually transacted with Japan in 1855. The treaty traveled to St. Petersburg via Washington and Vienna.[45]

Thus, with only a partial exception of war conditions, Greater Europeans formed communities of common purpose and mutual support in imperial outposts. These communities developed their own circuits of sociability. In *The Frigate Pallada*, the ship's officers relish the social kaleidoscope of the dining hall at Cape Town's Welch Hotel, with its "company from all corners of the world." They rub shoulders with the global elite in transit between "Europe, China, the Philippines, and Australia"—administrators, doctors, pastors, officers, businessmen, and retiring nabobs from colonial posts. Goncharov's Manila accommodation sees a lively traffic of Spaniards, Americans, Frenchmen, and Englishmen. Global capital acquires for Goncharov a human face in Cape Town's English Club. He meets there a gentleman of unspecified nationality who has at his disposal enormous credit lines in the Cape Colony, in China, and in Australia. The man's promissory notes, Goncharov learns, "are honored just like bank-issued ones." The names of Goncharov's hotels—Singapore's "London Hotel," Shanghai's "Commercial House"—signal the linchpins connecting Greater Europeans to Asia.[46]

All this mixing of people fosters the cultural hybridity we now associate with globalization.[47] Britain's colonial cuisine, Goncharov notes, combines their simply prepared meats with Indian curries, "which are served daily everywhere, starting from the Cape of Good Hope all the way to China, and especially in India." Filipino musicians perform Verdi for the Manila governor and his guests. Perhaps most bizarrely, in the depths of Siberia, a Sakha (Yakut) aborigine offers to sell Goncharov a bust of a popular contemporary French actress, Eliza Rachel Félix, carved out of walrus tusk or mammoth bone, depending on the customer's taste. He patterns the busts on a gypsum model that by inexplicable circumstances reached eastern Siberia.[48]

Goncharov portrays the Cape of Good Hope as a nodal point in empires' business and military itineraries. Before the opening of the Suez Canal in 1869, all maritime traffic bound for Asia and the Pacific from Europe, the Americas' eastern seaboard, and Russia sailed via the Cape of Good Hope. Goncharov calls it "the crossroads of the world," where routes between Europe, India, China, the Philippine Islands, and Australia all converge. From the perspective of the Welch Hotel's diners, this means that "you dine in the company of twenty people, willy-nilly strike up acquaintance and sometimes, in the course of a few days, even bonds of affection. Each day, you hasten with ever greater pleasure to socialize, either at the table or during walks, with a new and unexpected friend." When these friends suddenly don't show up for dinner, their human trajectories become traceable only through local dailies' shipping news: "today such-and-such steamship, with such-and-such cargo and such-and-such passengers, departed for England, Australia, or Batavia [today's Jakarta]." In this evocative image of economy-driven global modernity, human paths are incidentals of worldwide trade. People are listed alongside cargo, with their routes shadowing business circuits and reported in mass print. To Goncharov's eyes, between the Cape of Good Hope and the Pacific Ocean, the entire world appears on the move.[49]

The circulation of labor and commodities thus coincides with the circulation of imperial elites, who gather in Europe's trading enclaves on the coastal rims of Asia to socialize, trade expertise, and collaborate on projects of imperial control. Upon his return from the trek to the Cape Colony's interior, Goncharov finds Simonstown's Russian and British crews in a flurry of reciprocal dinner parties and balls. The American Edward Cunningham throws a lavish dinner for the Russian officers and an assortment of British and American merchants in Shanghai. After several days there, Goncharov declares that "we know everyone and everyone knows us." Hong Kong's British officers invite Goncharov for a drink and a chat at their barracks. In each port, a stream of European visitors passes through the *Pallada*'s hospitable deck. One day in Hong Kong, the Russians are paid a visit by an international ecclesiastical delegation of sorts: an Italian bishop, a few Spanish monks and French missionaries, and a Rome-educated Chinese Catholic. Next arrives the English governor of Hong Kong, Sir Samuel George Bonham, greeted by music and cannon salutes. Matters of all-European importance are discussed—the Christianization of Asia, the progress of European civilization, the region's geopolitical challenges, and commerce—which implicitly acknowledges Russia's stake in these conversations.[50]

In colonial outposts, the Russians are extended courtesies as fellow Europeans that have often been denied them on Europe's home turf. Russia's modern identity, in the words of Susanna Soojung Lim, rested on a tension "between the effort to Occidentalize itself and the reality of being Orientalized; the desire to become a nation fully belonging to and accepted by Europe and the acute sense of self-consciousness or insecurity regarding European views of Russia."[51] *The Frigate Pallada* shows that this desire for acceptance was gratified on imperial frontiers in Africa and Asia. No longer eastern barbarians or demi-Europeans at best, the Russians are readily admitted to the club of civilized Europeans. Goncharov gets to experience what Dostoevsky, three decades later, will proclaim as the distinct benefit of Russians' embrace of their civilizing mission in Asia: the conferral upon them, at long last, of status as a European nation. Nowhere is their pride in this association more evident than in their mission to Japan. Putiatin's delegation presents itself to the Japanese primarily as a vanguard of Europe, and only secondarily of Russia.

In these colonial circuits of sociability, the interactions of rooted and transiting Europeans serve to grease the wheels of global imperial enterprise. Lively networking creates new social bonds and strengthens old ones, fosters exchanges of expertise and experience, and helps everyone refine their collective and national objectives and devise strategies of bargaining or coercion.[52] It is instructive to compare the visits of Putiatin's Russians with those of Perry's Americans on the northern hemisphere's vast imperial frontier. Evidently, by mid-century, such travelers' itineraries and social circuits had solidified into a sort of institutionally sponsored diplomatic-business tourism network—quite distinct from the private middle-class tourism of late Victorians. This network had standard routes, sights, and rounds of visits. Perry's and Putiatin's itineraries between the Cape of Good Hope and Japan mirrored each other almost exactly. They toured the same places, met for the most part the same people, and voiced remarkably similar opinions.

Just like Goncharov, for example, Perry made a trek into the Cape Colony's interior to admire the progress of colonization. It appears that a visit to the warlike Xhosa chief Siyolo, under house arrest, was a standard attraction for every high-level visitor to Cape Town, including Perry's and Putiatin's men. In Singapore, Perry met the same rich merchant Goncharov would soon meet, part of a showcase of successful Euro-Asian commercial synergies. Before extending his hospitality to Putiatin's officers, Vice Consul Cunningham had hosted in Shanghai those from Perry's squadron. The social whirlwind of the colonial frontier struck Perry in much the same way as it did Goncharov, leading him to comment on "great hospitality" extended to his officers and on "visits of ceremony, with a constant interchange of dinner parties and other courtesies."[53]

The Frigate Pallada also shows synergies between Greater Europe's business, diplomatic, and missionary elites. The book champions the so-called "three Cs" that commonly underpin nineteenth-century European travel writing: civilization, Christianity, and commerce.[54] These come to the fore in the wildly popular travelogues written by David Livingstone (*Missionary Travels and Researches in South Africa*), Henry Morton Stanley (*Through the Dark Continent*), and other famous explorers who became imperial-era celebrities. Like these authors, Goncharov treats Christianization and trade as a package deal. He notes their synergy in relation to China: "The Protestants began with trade and then shipped religion. The Chinese welcomed the first and are now accepting the second without even noticing." In Shanghai, Goncharov acquires three books in Chinese: the New Testament, a book on geography, and Aesop's Fables. All are fruits of Protestant missionaries' civilizing activities, printed in millions of copies in London, and distributed in China for free. Shanghai's customs office is housed in a former

Buddhist temple. This gives Goncharov's readers an evocative image of the changing fortunes of local religion and Western trade.[55]

On the Ryukyu Islands, southwest of Japan, both Perry's and Putiatin's men interact closely with the lay missionary Bettelheim, a Hungarian Jew who has converted to Christianity and works for an English mission—arguably an icon of ecclesiastical globalization. He supplies both crews with basic intelligence (not always reliable) about the islands' form of government, international alliances, and social institutions, as well as with practical details of navigation and geography. Sources indicate that the islanders, whom be treated horrendously, hated him and vigorously demanded his removal. He was later taken back to England by Perry.[56]

Bettelheim plans to bring a shipment of Bibles in the Ryukyu and Japanese languages, but Goncharov urges him to reconsider. Though an ardent supporter of missionary efforts, Goncharov believes in a deft balancing of multiple imperial objectives. Evidently this was consistent with the Russian government's approach; the archpriest Avvakum of the *Pallada* expedition was instructed to wear secular clothes while in Japan so as not to arouse fears of proselytizing.[57] Goncharov warns Bettelheim against flooding Japan with his Bibles too suddenly: "you will accomplish nothing for religion and will only spoil trade." Only after the Japanese "exchange their form of life for the European one," he says, will the conditions for proselytism become propitious. He advises Bettelheim: "You had better wait until European factories are established. They will surely secure the right to perform their own religious rites. You should first bring the holy books there, which is something that the Japanese even nowadays cannot prohibit. And from there, these books will imperceptibly pass on to Japanese hands." In Goncharov's opinion, Europeanization should precede Christianization, and religion should stealthily shadow trade—that great axis on which Goncharov's world turns.[58]

The Global Marketplace and the Democracy of Comfort

Goncharov is fascinated and not infrequently overwhelmed by the energy and diversity of Asia's Europeanized seaports, whose life revolves almost exclusively around global trade. In Singapore, a cosmopolitan free-trade port off the Malay Peninsula developed by the British East India Company, Goncharov is struck by the variegated crowds of Chinese, Malays, Indians, and

Europeans of all nations, the torrid heat, the pungent smells, and the exotic foods: "what life, what bustle, what noise!" All of this proves a little too much, having on Goncharov a "narcotic" effect. Here, too, as in southern Africa, the English have sniffed out commercial opportunities and prevailed over the Dutch. They have transformed Singapore into a thriving global warehouse and market. Impressed by the staggering volumes of trade and the economic boom, Goncharov nonetheless finds Singapore and other such ports to be somewhat joyless; they seem to be conglomerates of people gathered together by necessity rather than choice. Yet while the social life, especially of transplanted Europeans, leaves him unsatisfied, the lush nature nourished by the tropical sun leaves him positively breathless: "How much life lurks in this soft gentle warmth, to which one opens, trustingly, without fear, one's breast and throat, as one would trustingly open one's heart to endearments of kind people!"[59]

After a month of sailing amid showers of meteors and schools of frolicking whales, the *Pallada* sees its deck suddenly turned into a lively commercial hub. While still at a distance from shore, it is flooded with locals offering wares and services: "Crowds of Indians, Malays, the Chinese—tailors, washerwomen, and agents—started streaming into my cabin with business testimonials from the ships of various nations. On deck there's a veritable bazaar. Guests of all tribes have laid out their wares, each bawling in his own tongue to offer fabrics, shells, monkeys, birds, or corals." Goncharov gets his first taste of the business energies of Asia. Alongside legal trade, Singapore also accommodates a brisk trade in pirated commodities. Piracy on the eastern seas, historian Matt Matsuda observes, was "a phenomenon of global political economy." Pirates were known to both rob and collaborate with Europe's imperial trading fleets, although Goncharov credits them only for the former. From Goncharov's perspective, European arrangements—such as British-run free ports—interface seamlessly with traditional, homegrown commercial practices. The commercial dynamism of Singapore, Hong Kong, and Shanghai show him the economic potential of Asia that has been unlocked by Europe's imperial intervention.[60]

Though Singapore has lost some business to recently opened Hong Kong, Goncharov predicts it is unlikely to decline given its nodal position at the crossroads of "Europe, Asia, Australia, and the islands of the Indian archipelago." Another circumnavigator, the Danish travelogue writer Steen Bille of the 1845–1847 Galathea scientific expedition, declared that Singapore does not measure up to the republic of Venice, the former trade leader, in its global

Figure 2.2. Singapore, as drawn in 1842 by Charles Dyce ("The River from Monkey Bridge"). By permission of the National University of Singapore Museum Collection.

importance. Goncharov believes this assessment is wrong. In his view, Singapore has out-globalized Venice, whose feeble links to the puny "East and West of its time" were no match for Singapore's vast network of connections to "India, China, the Malay Peninsula, Australia, Siam, Cochin-China, and the Burmese empire." These countries route all their Europe-bound products, and receive all European imports, through Singapore. Free trade, Goncharov explains, is the force behind British Singapore's ascendancy. He compares it to a settlement the Dutch established nearby around the same time but, in their usual way, closed to other European traders. It has fallen while Singapore has flourished. Meanwhile, another memoir from the Russian expedition describes how free-trade Hong Kong has killed the nearby Portuguese port Macao.[61] These are the lessons in the value of free trade that the *Pallada* brought back to Russia.

Venice and Singapore also serve Goncharov as a contrast in patterns of consumption that produce vastly different economic structures. He resoundingly condemns the ideology of luxury, as one might call it, that drove Venice. More worthy is its modern replacement, the ideology of comfort, which he found in Singapore and the advantages of which he had been promoting since his first novel, *An Ordinary Story.* As Goncharov explains it, luxury is senseless because it creates artificial desires. It makes a person crave monstrous and rare status symbols, such as a dish made of birds' brains or supremely uncomfortable, jewel-studded clothing. Luxury ruins its addicts; poverty lurks in its shadow. As it ruined Venice, so it is now ruining Spain. Comfort, by contrast, is a balanced satisfaction of rational and legitimate human needs. While luxury requires riches, he writes, middling means suffice for comfort. One also hears in this an implicit critique of the Russian aristocracy's addiction to lavish lifestyles. Unlike mad rushes in pursuit of luxury fads, which Goncharov considers terrible for trade, a pursuit of comfort facilitates orderly waves of beneficial commercial exchange. Goncharov's evocations of fickle luxury (*roskosh'*), anthropomorphized as a female character (in keeping with the word's grammatical gender in Russian), and steady comfort (*komfort*), presented as a male character, underscore the point that, in a global world, comfort is a democratic and transnational equalizer:

> Luxury demands rare game or fruits out of season. Comfort will keep his regular table, but will require it wherever fate may bring a person: in Africa, on the Sandwich Islands [Hawaii], or on Norway's North Cape. Everywhere, he [comfort] will require fresh produce, tender beef, young chickens, and old wine. Everywhere, he will want to wear the same silk and cotton that he wears in Paris, London, or Petersburg. Everywhere, he will expect the services of a cobbler, a tailor, and a washerwoman. Luxury demands that I possess that which you cannot have. Comfort, by contrast, demands that you own what I'm used to seeing in my own home.[62]

To satisfy people's needs for comfort is thus to create a uniformly attired and fed world. Goncharov's choice of examples clarifies that this would be a pan-European and bourgeois world. "The need of a constantly expanding market for its products chases the bourgeoisie over the whole surface of the globe. It must nestle everywhere, settle everywhere, establish connections everywhere. Through its exploitation of the world-market, [it has] given a cosmopolitan character to production and consumption in every country. . . . The bourgeoisie, by the rapid improvement of all instruments of production, by the immensely facilitated means of communication, draws all, even the most barbarian nations into civilization. . . . In a word, it creates a world after its own image." These are the words of Karl Marx, who was sharply critical of this phenomenon.[63] But if we assign them a positive valence, Goncharov could not have put it better himself.

Trade, comfort, and civilization, are all tightly interwoven in Goncharov's schema. For him, "comfort and civilization are almost synonymous, or rather, the former is the inevitable and rational consequence of the latter." The "rational and just" goal of global trade, Goncharov concludes, is to make legitimate luxuries into cheap articles of comfort available to all. So long as it serves the needs of the majority, Goncharov assures his readers, rather than "the irrational whims of the few," trade will enjoy limitless prospects. Rarely do we witness such creature-comforts bourgeois ideology endorsed so emphatically and unapologetically by a major Russian writer. Far from the tawdry occupation demeaned routinely in Russian classics, trade emerges on the pages of *The Frigate Pallada* as no less than a handmaiden of civilization.[64]

Goncharov marvels at Singapore's cheap pineapples—luxury items back home—"piled up over here like turnips and potatoes are back in Russia." He reasons: "In the north, a pineapple costs five to ten rubles, while here—a mere kopeck. The goal of civilization is to quickly ship it to the north and drive down the price to five kopecks, so that you and I can treat ourselves to our heart's content." This is a juicy metaphor indeed. It pulls into a memorable nexus modern bourgeois comfort, a mercantile ethos, and the civilizing prerogatives of those who direct this traffic—Europeans. "Wherever a European sets his foot," Goncharov sings in tribute, "you will find the security, plenty, peace, and welfare to which you are used at home."[65]

This was a logical standpoint for Goncharov, given his merchant origin and his position at the Department of Trade. It is also a vision that fits remarkably well with our contemporary world. Today, Goncharov's paean to a globally traded pineapple would fit quite well in a press release by any price-cutting CEO of a corporation such as Walmart. As literary scholar Milton Ehre puts it:

> [Goncharov's] vision is of a world that has become perfectly tamed and domesticated, where all the wilderness and deserts are covered with tidy farms, comfortable homes, clean hotels, and well-provisioned restaurants, presumably moderately priced; where roads are plentiful and paved and seas offer few hazards to swift steamships; where strange peoples with names difficult to pronounce have become courteous and respectable burghers barely distinguishable

> from their European models. It is perhaps a pedestrian and narrow vision, certainly egocentric, but in some ways it foresees the actual shape of our modern world with its wide-spread industrialization, increasing uniformity, and almost universal desire for the "comforts" that in the past were luxuries of a few.[66]

It should be stressed, however, that Goncharov does not dismiss such desires as shallow. Ehre does.

Ehre sums up Goncharov's voyage in decidedly somber tones: "Except for Japan and a few other isolated spots, he found a world hopelessly similar to the Europe he had left behind, an Orient that under the rule of the several colonial powers had begun to achieve a pedestrian sameness, an East not of mystery and allure but of squalid ports, shabby hotels, and sullen natives." A disillusionment of Romantic expectations is Ehre's formula for *The Frigate Pallada.* Ingrid Kleespies similarly portrays the emotional tonality of the work as one of existential ennui and "agony of separation from home."[67] These characterizations distort the actual mood of the travelogue, which bubbles with excitement and giddiness at the sensory richness of the human and natural worlds. Far from always pining for home, Goncharov greedily welcomes the new. Confessing that travel makes life "beautiful," he reworks the Cartesian "I think therefore I am" into "I travel therefore I take delight."[68] To the extent that Goncharov evokes Romantic expectations, it is because he knows his readers hold them. He is not crushed or saddened by their frustration. He relishes showing their inapplicability to modern Asia.

This is not a journey of disenchantment with what we might see today as the dull uniformity of globalization. It is a journey of redefinition. Goncharov updates the East for his mid-nineteenth-century readers. With the exception of Japan, which is unlikely to remain anomalous if Europeans get their way, the East is not the exotic, romanticized Orient, stuck in a time warp, as some romantic Russian writers had portrayed it. The East is a vibrant global marketplace. One hears gleeful correction in Goncharov's tone, not nostalgia for the idyllic past. He energetically embraces imperialism and its corollaries: colonialism, globalism, commercialism, capitalism, and middle-class entrepreneurship. Globalization for him is a welcome sign of progress, not of dreary sameness:

> Progress has already won many victories. Read a description of any circumnavigation accomplished fifty years ago. What was it like?

> Sheer torture! A traveler had to suffer through a regime of privations. He fed on salted meat, stopped up his nose before drinking water, and fought with savages. And now? Scarcely do you show up at a port . . . when you are surrounded by boats, as we were here. A Chinese or an Indian washerwoman launders and starches your finest linen just like in Petersburg. A tailor with a long queue [a traditional Chinese braid], in a vest and wide trousers, shows you fabric patterns, takes measure, and sews a European suit. You come on shore, and the inhabitants don't run away, but greet you in a crowd—not to fight, but to offer a carriage, or a sedan-chair, or to direct you to a hotel. There you'll find the same tender beef steak, the same Lafite, sherry, and clean sheets, as in Europe.[69]

As he turns to presenting Russia's civilizing mission in Asia, in the last Japanese chapter of *The Frigate Pallada,* Goncharov will parrot classic Western European theories of Asia as somnolent, backward, and deprived of historical agency. These theories—popularized by Hegel, Marx, and Weber—have been refuted by recent scholarship, which prove the dynamism of Asia's economies, the sophistication of its financial systems, its vibrant domestic and external trade, and its innovative agriculture (how else would India and China feed their huge populations?).[70] Goncharov spouts the theories of Asia's backwardness to marshal support for the cause of European imperial expansion. But his eyewitness reporting of the effervescent daily life of Asia's bazaars and seaborne traders clash with these inherited mental schemas.[71] Hardly the sleepy Orient of European thinkers, Goncharov's Asia is a fortuitous merger of local business energies and the wise arrangements of European facilitators.

Goncharov is intent on showing, as are today's advocates of globalization, that the benefits of colonial trade trickle down. While European consumers get their cheap pineapples, the indigenous people get to earn a decent living. The rickety junks of Chinese and Indian traders streaming to Singapore only gain by comparison to Venetian golden galleys. Goncharov appreciates that the British transformed a strip of rocky wasteland, ceded to them by unsuspecting China in the Treaty of Nanjing, into the fabulously profitable port of Hong Kong that, he predicts, will secure Britain's trade with China for eternity. He imagines how impressed the Chinese must have been that the plucky "red-headed barbarians" erected opulent palaces on barren rock. But he also emphasizes that British employment saved from destitution thirty thousand Chinese who flocked there from the impoverished Portuguese

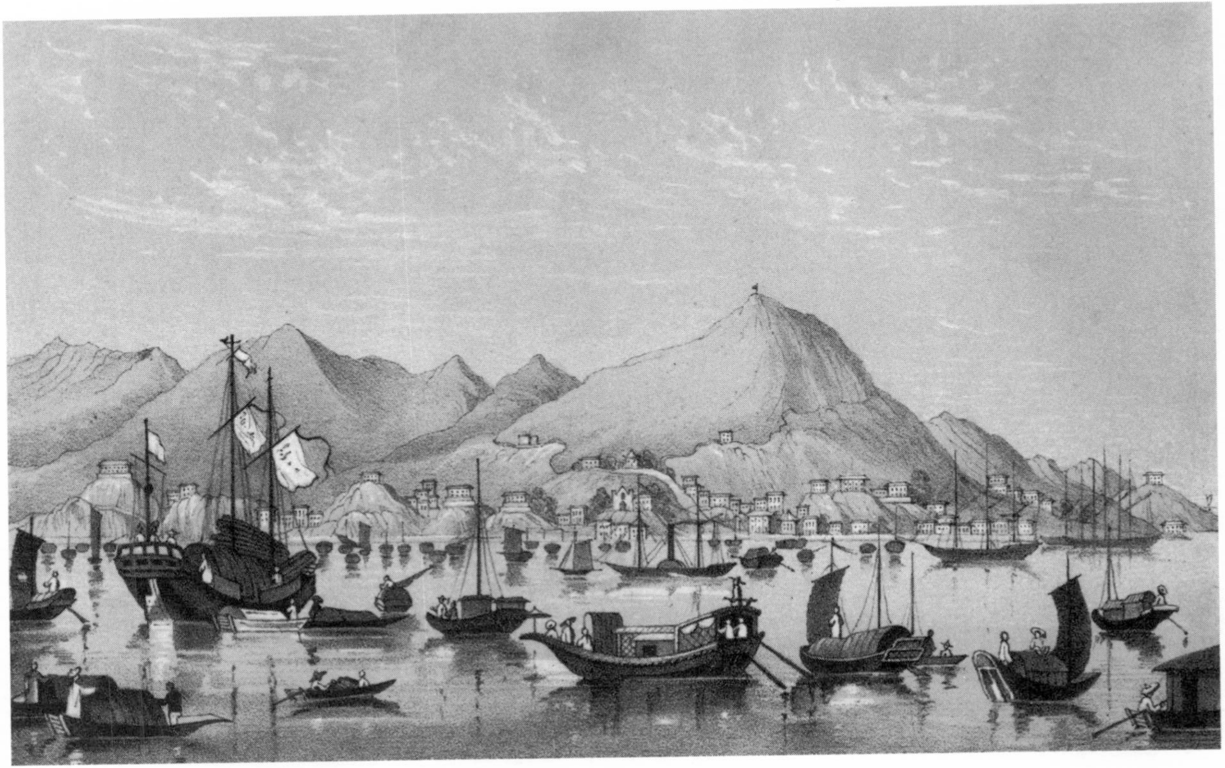

Figure 2.3. Victoria Town, Hong Kong island, 1847. HIP / Art Resource, NY.

colony of Macao to build the city: "work means bread and money." These masses of Chinese agricultural laborers, eager to retrain for whatever work paid money, evened out mountains and built huge commercial infrastructure for such British firms as Jardine, Matheson & Co. (This firm operates to this day in Asia, having transformed itself from a trader of tea and opium to a conglomerate of retail, automotive parts distribution, financial services, and real estate, including the Mandarin Oriental hotel chain.) According to Goncharov—although how he would know this remains unclear—the Chinese were happy to do so, grateful for the employment. Through such examples, Goncharov shows globalization bringing mutual benefit to foreigners and locals alike. "Reciprocity," as Pratt astringently notes, "has always been capitalism's ideology of itself."[72]

Moreover, unlike in Goncharov's Africa, where indigenous people could only aspire to low-skilled jobs, in Goncharov's Asia, British-run trade helps generate moneyed classes among Asians. When Goncharov visits an opulent suburban estate of a local Singapore merchant, Whampoa (this is also the name of an island near Canton), who had immigrated twenty years ago, he can hardly believe his eyes. The manicured gardens and orchards with tastefully laid-out alleys seem "like works of art." Amid this verdant "aristocracy of nature" nourished by the tropical sun, there roam peacocks and other rare birds. Whampoa's most prized possession is a purebred white Arabian horse, which also caught the eye of Matthew Perry, who a few weeks prior got the same tour of the estate. At the end of the evening, slightly tipsy on superb port wine and chilled ale, Goncharov is overcome with a visceral sense of wellbeing. As he watches a stupendous sunset and feels the plants exude the day's heat, he wonders: "Can this be the same sun that shines for us [back in Russia]?" Whampoa's palatial house, with galleries, finely wrought wooden furnishings, and gilded screens delights Goncharov with its felicitous blend of "European comfort and Oriental luxury." The merchant's impeccable English signals the business circuits on which his wealth rests.[73]

Turning Poison into Cash

This happy image of reciprocal benefits of trade between Europeans and Asians is tarnished five months later, during Goncharov's visit to Shanghai in November 1853, where he has an opportunity to observe the opium trade. It is galling to him that the British and the Americans made opium trade the lifeblood of their business in China, and then had the temerity to reproach the Chinese for addiction. Goncharov is shocked by the hypocrisy: westerners peddle the drug but blame the junkie, all the while professing lofty civilizing ideals. Seeking to secure the trade and its staggering profits, Britain fought the Opium Wars with the Qing. When the first of these ended with the 1842 Treaty of Nanjing, imposing on China the "unequal treaty" system that remained in force until 1942, China was reduced to semicolonial status and opened five ports to European trade, on European terms.

Britain's opium trade generated widespread opprobrium in Europe and America, and in Britain itself. Karl Marx scathingly denounced it, and praised the government of the Celestial Empire, as China was popularly called, for foregoing on principle multi-million dollar profits from duties on opium, since to accept them would mean legalizing the trade. Unlike the supposedly civilized English, who had no such moral qualms, "the Celestian barbarian"—here Marx invokes a smug western term for the Chinese—"declined laying tax sure to rise in proportion to the degradation of his people." Marx inverts here the typical contrast of Asian barbarity to western civilization.[74]

While opium was used medicinally in China for centuries, it became widespread only through the activity of European traders. China soon became the most important market for Britain's Indian-grown crop. Opium profits helped finance Britain's expensive colonization of India, which by the end of the eighteenth century had left a gaping hole of twenty-eight million pounds in the government's budget. The opium trade represented a silver bullet to eliminate Britain's deficit and reverse the Sino-British balance of trade. In the first half of the nineteenth century, China plunged from hefty surpluses to a trade deficit. The volume of opium trade increased exponentially, evidence of ever wider use. According to Immanuel Hsü, already in 1838 there were provinces in which nine out of ten people were addicts. They would go without food to acquire the drug and make their families destitute along with them. The Qing government, alarmed by the social effects of the epidemic and by the massive outflow of silver to pay for the drug, forbade the use and trade of opium. This ban proved ineffective. Britain's insistence on its right to sell opium in China also revealed the sham of its free-trade arguments, since such trade was not allowed in Britain. Historian Carl Trocki calls opium Asia's first mass-produced commodity, and finds the vast regional economic patterns it established still in operation to this day. He claims that "in a very real sense we can best understand the British Empire east of Suez as of 1800 as essentially a drug cartel."[75]

Figure 2.4. Chinese opium smokers, engraving by Thomas Allom, 1845. The Stapleton Collection / Art Resource, NY.

The Opium War also helped spark the Taiping Rebellion, which seriously destabilized the Qing empire. The French mission to Nanjing, a city controlled by anti-opium Taiping rebels, had ample opportunities to behold the severed heads of opium smokers garlanding the walls. Marx, too, credited the outbreak of the Taiping Rebellion to "the English cannon forcing upon China that soporific drug called opium." The opium revenues of the British East India Company in the 1850s approached four million pounds sterling. The trade intensified and continued, with some adjustments, until the 1940s. To this day, the trauma of the Opium Wars frames China's narrative of its modern national history, marking the beginning of China's "century of humiliations."[76]

Goncharov calls Shanghai "the warehouse of the poison." He reports that it has taken just two decades for the opium trade to rise as a proportion of China's total trade with Europe from one-fourth to four-fifths. To get opium, he notes, "the Chinese will give anything: their tea, silk, metals, medicines, sweat, blood, energy, mind, all life." Their trading partners have no qualms about this. "Unperturbed," he continues, and with full complicity of their governments, "the English and the Americans take all this and turn it into cash." Whereas before Goncharov praised the commercialism of the English, he now presents it as a blight: they don't hesitate to sell even poison. He sees the opium trade as inexcusable hypocrisy by an empire ostensibly bearing the banner of civilization and progress. He draws an analogy between Britain's opium trade in China and British entrepreneurs' sale of arms to the Xhosa, in the Cape Colony, at the height of the British government's war with them. In disregard of the eventual arms-trade ban, they smuggled the weapons in. "That's quite something," Goncharov jeers: "a trading nation indeed!" The dark side of Britain's spectacular commerce is revealed to Goncharov in Shanghai.[77]

His tirade about the opium trade, though certainly justified, might have lost some of its moral authority if his readers had been privy to a certain detail of which Goncharov, as Putiatin's secretary, must have been aware. It is true the Russians had no opium to sell, but because Putiatin was instructed by the Ministry of the Navy to establish sea trade with China's open ports, especially Shanghai, he did claim the same privileges the unscrupulous British had extracted from China through the Opium War—employing a strategy some have since called "hitchhiking imperialism." Qing officials had been refusing to extend these privileges to Russians since trade with them was already conducted over land. Although *The Frigate Pallada* is silent on this, other accounts reveal that Putiatin had earlier tried and failed in Canton to extract access for Russian ships, as had Kruzenshtern back in 1805.[78] Hitchhiking imperialism provided a way to reap the benefits of European imperialism while avoiding direct responsibility and any stigma that went with it. In fact, this was the preferred mode of operating in China both for the Russians and the Americans.[79] As will be seen later, the Russians eventually did catch a ride on Europe's free-port express in China in some measure thanks to Putiatin who, after the Pallada expedition ended, continued to pursue vigorous diplomacy to secure the same trade benefits for Russia the British enjoyed. Thus it is not that the Chinese were beset by Western Europeans while Russians stood by commiserating, as Goncharov makes it seem; rather, China was caught in what Hsü calls a "pincer movement," with pressures for trade concessions being applied simultaneously by Russians from the north and westerners from the sea.[80]

Shanghai certainly marks the low point in Goncharov's estimation of the British. How to make sense of his critique in the context of his overall praise for the British colonial project, especially in the Cape of Good Hope? A few partial answers and contextual clues present themselves. What Goncharov saw in Shanghai may have simply merited a tougher tone. A perception of lesser racial distance from Asians than from Africans may have made the Russian writer more sensitive to their plight. At this point in the narrative, Goncharov is also laying ground for the Siberian sections' argument that Russia treats aborigines better than Britain does. And Shanghai is where the Russians learn that the military phase of the Crimean conflict has begun. The war between Russia and Turkey is officially declared; the British and French entry into it is imminent.[81] For the British Navy, it will soon be open season for Russian ships not only in the Black Sea but also in the Pacific. This would certainly make the British less sympathetic to the *Pallada* Russians.

There was also a larger grievance on the subject of China. The British had broken the unique position in Chinese trade that Russia had enjoyed for two centuries. Regaining balance was part of the *Pallada*'s mission. Before the 1840s, by force of the Treaties of Nerchinsk (1689) and of Kiakhta (1727), Russia had been the sole foreign power to enjoy trade with China that was regularized by treaty, as opposed to ephemeral and restrictive imperial edicts that plagued the Europeans' Canton trade. Such recognition of equal partnership in trade was denied to western governments until 1842. Regular overland routes and cultural exchange between Russia and China were well established. Russia was allowed to maintain an ecclesiastical mission in Beijing, paid for by the Qing government. As the maritime trade of the Western Europeans grew, however, and the value of the Kiakhta trade declined, Russia twice sent ships to Shanghai in the late 1840s, and both times they were turned back. With half of Russia's manufacturing exports headed for China by 1851, according to Joseph Fletcher, "St. Petersburg had to take the China trade seriously." The British were jealous of Russia's overland trade routes, which might rival British maritime trade if Russia ever developed its railroads. The Russians in turn were jealous of Europe's seaborne trade, at the time a surer guarantee of speed, volume, and profitability. The very launching of the *Pallada* expedition was a response to the European and American activity in the region, and especially the alarm raised in Russia by Britain's victorious Opium Wars. Putiatin was directed to reenergize Russia's trade with China, which by mid-century was at a standstill. Goncharov could not have been working for the Department of Trade and Putiatin without being cognizant of these economic and geopolitical challenges.[82]

Trading at Gunpoint

The ongoing operation of "free" trade in China's open ports relied heavily on coercion and a constant threat of military force. This strikes Goncharov especially when he witnesses the Taiping Rebellion rocking the Qing empire at the time of his visit. He experiences the rebellion in Shanghai, which the Russians visit during a pause in diplomatic negotiations with Japan. In September 1853, two months before the Russians' arrival, the rebels of the Small Sword Society (named for short daggers used in close combat) seized control of Shanghai's walled old town, avoiding foreign concession areas. The rebels aligned themselves with the Taipings. Goncharov's key insight from this experience is that the defense of their trading rights emboldened Euro-Americans to interfere in China's internal politics to such an extent that China's sovereignty appeared a fiction.[83]

Between 1850 and 1864, the Taiping Rebellion swept through sixteen of the eighteen Chinese provinces and destroyed more than six hundred cities, leaving almost twenty million people dead. According to Stephen Platt, such casualties—thirty times greater than those of the American Civil War—made it "not only the most destructive war of the nineteenth century, but likely the bloodiest civil war of all time." The provinces most affected by the rebellion would not regain their former population levels until 1953.[84] This uprising mobilized vast sections of Chinese society with the promise of a social revolution based on new property, gender, ethnic, and civic relations. It aimed to overthrow the Manchu dynasty, the founders of the Qing empire who came from Manchuria. A ruling minority, the Manchus did not intermix with the majority Han, who perceived them as foreigners. The Han Chinese resented the Manchus' pliancy toward the European barbarians and blamed them for bungling the First Opium War and for attempting to enslave the Han people through opium addiction.

The Taiping leader and former schoolteacher Hong Xiuquan conceived of the cause in what he described as a religious vision, following his frustrated efforts to pass the notoriously difficult and ethnically discriminatory Qing civil service exams.[85] The movement Hong created combined several elements—millenarian Christian beliefs introduced to China by European missionaries, utopianism, the ideals of class and gender equality, and attacks on such vices as opium smoking and gambling—into a heady mix. The nineteenth century was rife with such movements, which reacted to the stresses, dislocations, and deprivations caused by accelerated social and cultural changes, especially in situations of colonial encounters.[86] As the self-proclaimed son of God and younger brother to Jesus, Hong took on the cause of converting China to Christianity. He concluded that the "Heavenly Kingdom" mentioned in the Bible stood for the Celestial Empire. The Biblical prophecies would therefore become realized in China, and he would help usher the chosen Chinese people into paradise. He declared himself the rightful emperor.[87]

Shanghai's community of European and American businessmen, missionaries, and the military remained unmolested by the Taipings. Early on, despite requests for assistance made by Qing officials, westerners by and large maintained neutrality—with the exception of those hired by each side as mercenaries. Western governments faced a dilemma: should they prop up China's old regime or welcome the prospect of it changing? Which party would prove friendlier to western commercial interests? At the time, British investments in Shanghai alone were estimated at twenty-five million pounds sterling.[88] American merchants, as reported by Perry, felt that their $1.2 million in investments entitled them to the US government's protection. Since US trade with China was second only to Britain's, and in some years even exceeded it, the stakes were high for the Americans. Perry was forced to cut his Japan-bound squadron by one warship, leaving it behind in Shanghai to defend American personnel and interests.[89]

During the Russians' visit to Shanghai, Europeans and Americans were weighing the odds that the Taipings would, in case of victory, extend the westerners' trading privileges. The Taipings kept them guessing. Between April 1853 and May 1854, the British, French, and Americans all sent delegations to the Taiping leaders in Nanjing. The American mission traveled on Perry's warship.[90] In the end, a known regime proved preferable. After the Russians' departure, in March 1855, European and American troops helped the Qing imperial forces suppress the Small Sword Society uprising in Shanghai; these troops also assisted the Qing government in putting down the rebellion elsewhere. In its later stages, the Taiping Rebellion overlapped with the onset of the American Civil War, in 1861. Faced with the prospect of losing its two key markets, Platt claims, Britain chose to intervene militarily in China rather than in the United States: "neutrality in the US came at the expense of abandoning it in China."[91]

Contrary to these grave historical realities, the Shanghai chapter of *The Frigate Pallada* portrays the bloody Taiping Rebellion as a comedy of errors. Goncharov reports that the cannon fire aimed at the insurgents by the imperial forces is "as harmless to the former as it is useless to the latter." He ridicules the impotence of the imperial forces in dislodging from the city a mere band of "tramps and ragamuffins." The local commander's largely fruitless efforts to recruit European mercenaries appear pitiful to Goncharov, as does the man's inept attempt to chase out the rebels by fire. (The imperial wind forecast was apparently off.)[92]

Goncharov's portrayal of the Taiping Rebellion becomes most comical in a lively scene of unimpeded trading between Shanghai merchants and insurgents who have occupied the walled Chinese town. Amid loud haggling between a thousand traders below and a thousand rebel-shoppers atop the fortress wall, commodities are briskly exchanged for money via buckets on ropes traveling up and down the walls. Seeing this raucous Oriental bazaar amply provisioning the rebels who have gained control of the old town is for Goncharov a rather surreal experience. Orders for pigs, cabbages, chicken, fruit, firewood, and clothing are shouted out and then, after querulous bargaining, trades are transacted. "An impossible hubbub!" exclaims Goncharov. He continues with a snide dig: "I became convinced that the traders besiege the town more energetically and successfully than the imperial troops." In this absurd situation, Goncharov writes, one party "attempts to annihilate the rebels, the other to prolong their existence." The result, predictably, is an impasse.[93]

The undercurrent of the Russian observer's irony seems to be confidence that in his own empire, rebellions—this familiar hazard of running empires—are dealt with more effectively. From the Ukrainian Cossacks at Poltava in 1709, to the Poles in 1794 and 1831, to the many rebellions in Siberia or the steppe regions, Russian imperial governments faced their own challenges in subduing the empire's restive fringes. More recently, at the Habsburgs' request, the Russian army expertly suppressed the 1848 Spring of Nations in Hungary, living up to its Western sobriquet as the gendarme of Europe.

Perhaps most analogous to the Taiping Rebellion was the rebellion led by the Yaik Cossack Emelian Pugachev. He was a lesser problem for the Romanovs than the Taipings were for the Qing, yet from 1773 to 1775, his forces nonetheless posed a serious threat to Empress Catherine the Great's reign. Alexander Pushkin imprinted this event in Russian national memory with his 1836 historical novel *The Captain's Daughter* which endows the villainous Pugachev with dark allure but ultimately celebrates the restoration of social order. The Pugachev Rebellion erupted in the empire's southeastern steppe peripheries, engulfing a huge area between the middle Volga River and the Urals. Like the Taiping Rebellion, it found a broad base of support among the peasants, to whom Pugachev promised the abolition of serfdom.

Pugachev's success, like that of the Taiping leaders, lay in harnessing the discontent of many different groups: religious sectarians, factory workers, the tsarist army, and a sizeable cohort of ethnic minorities, such as Tatars, Bashkirs, Kalmyks, and the Chuvash. The Pugachev Rebellion reached the outskirts of Goncharov's hometown, Simbirsk, on the Volga River. His grandfather described it in the family chronicle.[94] Catherine the Great suppressed the rebellion and, after exhibiting Pugachev in a cage, had him publicly executed in a Moscow square. Goncharov never makes any overt comparisons, but this historical parallel to the unrest within the Russian empire may well color his portrayal of the Taiping Rebellion.

As a potent symbol of the Russian interior's mutinous potential, the Pugachev Rebellion fed the darkest fears of Russia's Europeanized elite. It is therefore unsurprising that Vice-Admiral Putiatin's confidential reactions to the Taiping Rebellion were less sanguine than might be expected based on Goncharov's published travelogue. Far from condescending ridicule, Putiatin's private letter from Shanghai to the head of the Asian Department in St. Petersburg sounded a note of alarm. Having visited the imperial camp, Putiatin concluded that the Taiping forces were more numerous, had higher morale, and were better trained, disciplined, and equipped than the emperor's troops. He also summarized a report published in *The North China Herald* on the French minister M. de Bourboulon's visit to the Taipings' Nanjing camp. This French mission, like the British one before it and the American one after it, attempted to ascertain the Taipings' disposition toward the Europeans and to gather military intelligence. Though the Taipings claimed brotherhood with all Christians, they proposed to de Bourboulon so degrading a ritual for an audience with their leader that the Frenchman rejected it out of hand. Local foreigners, Putiatin reported, all agreed that the Qing dynasty was about to fall. Convincing the new Taiping regime of the necessity to maintain foreign privileges would require, in Putiatin's view, force of arms. The governor-general of Siberia, Nikolai Muravev, with whom the *Pallada* crew would soon meet, also watched the Taiping Rebellion with grave concern. He worried that the unrest would allow Britain and France to gain total control of China and to take Siberia away from Russia. He urged St. Petersburg authorities to start planning for a regime change in China.[95]

Russian government officials thus treated the Taiping Rebellion in their confidential correspondence more seriously than Goncharov did in his public text.[96] While Putiatin reads the rebels' diplomatic snub of the French as a worrying indication of their self-confidence, Goncharov dismisses it as hubris born of ignorance. Goncharov never confronts the possibility of the Qing empire's fall. The rebels' Christianity does not cloud his political vision. He scoffs: "All this irredentist scum call themselves Christians."[97] He voices no sympathy for the rebel cause and supports the reestablishment of the Qing rule. To be sure, if he felt any such sympathy, expressing it in print would be tricky. While a view of China as a moribund empire, much like Turkey, was popular in Russia, the countervailing domestic imperative was to assert the legitimacy of the geopolitical status quo and the imperviousness of imperial regimes to radical politics.

Given the parallel to Russia's own historical and political circumstances, describing the Taiping Rebellion to Russia's general public was a delicate matter. Addressing his compatriots back in a kindred continental empire that remained under constant threat of similar mutinies, Goncharov thus chooses to diminish the gravity of the Taiping Rebellion. While Putiatin privately described it as a geopolitical crisis, Goncharov publicly paints it as a misguided adventure leading to pointless violence. In his account, imperial soldiers eager to satisfy their superiors snatch random Chinese men off the street and present them as apprehended insurgents. As Goncharov learns from a local Englishman, these men are then executed and their impaled heads are put on display for gruesome deterrent effect. The insurgents, reportedly, are no better: they invite imperial envoys for talks, only to torture and murder them. In his travelogue, Goncharov calls such goings-on typical of internecine wars (*mezhdousobnye voiny*), a term strongly evocative of Russia's own period of social strife preceding the emergence, by the sixteenth century, of a centralized Muscovite state. In his official report of the expedition, he calls the Taiping Rebellion a "time of trouble" (*smuta*), a term used in Russian to denote the particular period of deep political and dynastic crisis from 1598 to 1613, when Muscovy nearly fell victim to foreign powers. The comedy of errors thus morphs into a cautionary tale with particular relevance for the Russian polity.[98]

Beyond the senseless loss of life, which he blames on the rebels, Goncharov also shows how protracted chaos harms business. While some trade continues, especially in opium, Goncharov declares the economic situation to be a "full-blown crisis." Consistent with his appreciation of global interconnections, he likens the crisis to an earthquake which will set off aftershocks in Hong Kong, Singapore, India, England, and the United States. He later discovers that unrest in China causes Siberian fur traders to feel the squeeze. The flight of Chinese merchants from Shanghai short-circuits the distribution networks linking the port to the Chinese interior. The Europeans have refused to remit customs duties in retaliation for the Qing government's failure to maintain peace and order. In Goncharov's portrayal, the western business community is a full-fledged participant in this domestic Chinese conflict, and must decide: At what point will their commercial losses compel them to intervene?[99]

Here, again, Goncharov's insight seems strikingly similar to the global approaches of current historians, like Stephen Platt, who regards the Taiping Rebellion not as an internal Chinese matter but an international war, in which foreigners played a decisive role. Platt shows that Western powers in the 1860s fought essentially an uncoordinated second front alongside the Qing army. In Goncharov's portrayal of the Shanghai conflict, the westerners' very presence hinders its resolution: the Qing soldiers who were besieging the old town fortress with the aim of dislodging rebels could perhaps prevent their provisioning "if they had more freedom than the besieged." While the insurgents freely stroll around the city, China's imperial forces dare not be conspicuous in foreign-dominated Shanghai. An English officer strikes a mounted Qing soldier off his horse for riding in an area restricted for Europeans. Shelling the city wall to disrupt the trade in comestibles might actually get the imperial troops in even greater trouble: "if but a single cannonball drops on the European quarter, then both the besieged and the besiegers won't manage to appease the consuls." Ultimately, Goncharov concludes, "the English and the Americans hold both [sides] in their grip."[100]

Eventually, the Europeans do feel their safety to be imperiled, and react in ways Goncharov foresaw. But as he writes about this, Goncharov turns his ire, in line with Shanghai's westerners, against the Qing army which has proven so spectacularly ineffective. "As I predicted, the Europeans' interference proved indispensable," he writes upon receiving news from Shanghai five months later, in April 1854, while sailing north along the Korean shore. Referring to the Battle of the Muddy Flat of April 4, 1854, Goncharov describes the united attack of Europeans and Americans on the Qing forces, which he deems utterly unprofessional. He calls them "a bunch of scoundrels without any discipline, brigands rather than soldiers." In his account, the incident that ignited the hostilities was the imperial soldiers' attempted abduction of an Englishwoman and an assault on her resisting husband. In retaliation, the Euro-American coalition (Russian forces did not intervene militarily against the Taipings) attack the imperial encampment and force it to relocate farther away from the European quarter. Shanghai has become a powder keg, with all parties, now including civilians and Europeans, armed to the teeth. "God only knows how this will end," Goncharov frets.[101]

Who Should Civilize Whom?

This final mention of the Taiping Rebellion crops up when Goncharov recounts the *Pallada*'s later northward progress from Korea toward Siberian shores, after the Russian mission to conclude a European-style trade treaty with Japan stalls. Compositionally, this fragment appears in the midst of Goncharov's argument about Asia's backwardness and its need for European revitalization, a project in which Russia aspires to play a role. One may see it as a moment when Goncharov's Russians pose for a group picture with European civilizers.

Yet some of the writer's observations show distance, ambivalence, or even outright critique, though this critique has firm political limits. The warm applause he gave earlier to British arrangements on the Cape of Good Hope falls silent as Goncharov depicts the strict separation guiding the arrangements of Asia's free port cities. Each one Goncharov visits has a rigidly defined European quarter, usually facing the sea, surrounded by the Asian city. This is true of Singapore, whose Asian sector features "everything offensive to sight and smell," while on the European side, "everything is different": spacious, clean, and beautiful. This is also true of Shanghai. Its Chinese side is abuzz with ant-like crowds engaging in busy economic activity. It starkly contrasts with the ritzy European embankment lined with columnated and balconied residences. A particularly lavish mansion, with an elegant park and a luxurious verandah, belongs to the American vice consul Cunningham. Flags of European nations dot the horizon. Goncharov recommends Shanghai as a model European city to a Japanese friend. He imagines that the Chinese, when they pass from their own quarter to the European one in Hong Kong, must feel like fish transported from a muddy river to a marble pool: the filth that felt cozy back in the river is suddenly exposed. On the streets of Shanghai, the Chinese humbly step aside to make room for Europeans. Only Spaniards are allowed to reside in the garrisoned city fortress of Manila. Such colonial cities featured what Osterhammel calls "urban apartheid along ethnic lines." Goncharov reports on these arrangements with distance but without discernible critique, perhaps viewing them as necessary. He has, after all, already reported with perfect equanimity on what will later become institutionalized as South Africa's system of apartheid.[102]

Visiting Asia's racially segregated cities, Goncharov wonders about the staying power of the European order. In Singapore he asks: "How do four hundred Europeans peacefully coexist with the local population of sixty thousand, given all the differences of faith, ideas, and civilization?" His French interlocutor's terse answer is: the British sepoy police (Indian soldiers in British service occasionally deployed outside of India) and the instinctive respect of the "colored tribes" for the whites. In Manila, Goncharov finds that Spanish rule rests on a garrison of Tagal soldiers under Spanish command numbering somewhere between six and nine thousand. Throughout *The Frigate Pallada,* "civilization" propped up by guns appears as the natural order of things. Goncharov speaks in one breath of the "civilization and war" exerting pressures on Africa's indigenous groups, with no pause to ponder the troubling relationship between the two. A British frigate in the Shanghai harbor has twenty-six cannon, and Russia's own civilization transporter (the *Pallada*), carries fifty-two—and makes sure its Japanese hosts take note. Cunningham's mansion has a cannon as well, aimed directly at the street. Cape Town's "Hottentot Square"—presumably a genteel European-style urban space whose name nods to local culture—is used for training British troops.[103]

Visiting Shanghai, however, Goncharov's support for this gun-propped European order does in fact falter. English brutality and cold contempt for the Chinese even cause Goncharov to doubt whether the Europeans' view of themselves as civilized is justified. His first important moment of dissatisfaction is his visit to Shanghai's "promenade." Not to be confused with today's waterfront, this promenade is an area for horseback riding just north of the city. "Shanghai Europeans" prance here on purebred horses to the stares of the locals. The place reminds Goncharov of "a circus arena." He highlights the performative aspect of this display of European power:

> A few pedestrians, naval officers, and we [Russians] comprised an audience, or rather, we all were dramatis personae. The real audience were the Chinese, the peaceable city or country dwellers, merchants, and farmers who had just ended a day's work. The clothing was mixed: a silk jacket and wide trousers of a merchant, a blue robe of a peasant, pantaloons and a vest of an imperial official, with em-

> broidered letters on the back. This whole public, without much enthusiasm but with curiosity, looked at the strangers who had forcibly torn into their land and, as if that weren't enough, freely cavorted amid their fields, and even put up signs prohibiting trespass to local masters. The Chinese watched each rider attentively and laughed. Female riders especially sparked their attention: an unheard-of phenomenon! Their own women are still more or less domestic property—a far cry from socialites.[104]

Goncharov quickly corrects his initial division between actors and audience—those who are riding and those who are watching—by juxtaposing all Europeans, including his own Russian party, against the Chinese. While including himself among the privileged actors, Goncharov adopts the Chinese point of view and imagines their humiliation. Yet despite his own indignation, a mood of protest does not materialize among the Chinese onlookers, who react merely with bemusement. In Goncharov's account at least, gender-based dissonance—women on horseback!—sets them wondering perhaps more than the absurdities or iniquities of imperialism.

Is this the travelogue's anti-colonial moment? It seems an enticing possibility, but to conclude so—as did critics in Soviet times—would be to discount the seven hundred pages that surround this passage. To assert that Goncharov opposes the right of Europeans to "tear into" lands other than their own is an untenable position. The entirety of *The Frigate Pallada* portrays this process as both inevitable and, in the long run, beneficial for all mankind. Instead, Goncharov's Shanghai musings serve the function of what critic Peter Hulme calls a "concessionary narrative." Like the story of Pocahontas or, to add a Russian example, Pushkin's narrative poem about cross-ethnic romance, *The Prisoner of the Caucasus,* a concessionary narrative "goes some way toward recognizing a native point of view and offering a critique of European behavior, but it can only do this by not addressing the central issue." The central issue is Europe's imperial intrusion into non-European worlds. Goncharov concedes the brutality of European conduct in China, but never questions Europe's imperial expansion as such. He does, however, begin to develop a rationale for why Russia needs to differentiate its imperial attitude from that of west Europeans. He will step up to this task in his description of Siberia.[105]

The promenade spectacle, moreover, does not exactly shock him to his core. In a short while, he rather effortlessly shifts his gaze to the riding

English socialites, appraising their sexual attractiveness and kinesthetic prowess with an eye of a connoisseur. His overall reaction to the spectacle of the colonizers' recreation is not outrage. It is distaste. What puts him off is the brazenness, the callousness with which the Europeans lord over the Chinese. It is the method of rule, not the right to rule, that is questioned here. Goncharov's Russian sensibility favors a more discreet exercise of imperial rule, in the Russian tradition of bringing into the fold rather than erecting unbridgeable divisions. The Russians placed a greater premium on shows of subjects' fealty than on shows of masters' superiority, especially when dealing with populations amenable or advanced enough to deserve a modicum of respect.

Nonetheless, the Shanghai chapter is where Goncharov finally takes the British to task. His former starry-eyed adulation (tinged with resentment) of British imperial successes, especially in southern Africa, here gives way to critique of their imperial methods. Strolling with a young British officer he has befriended—the English often serve the Russians as guides through Shanghai and the local "Asiatic" customs—Goncharov is aghast to see, when passersby do not step aside promptly enough, the Englishman grabbing Chinese men by their queues and shoving them away. Goncharov's Russian companion is scandalized when the English proprietor of their hotel, most likely a lowlife back home, mercilessly beats up a Chinese servant. Goncharov explains:

> In general, the way that the English treat the Chinese, and how they treat other subject nations, is—though not cruel—peremptory, vulgar, or coldly contemptible, so that it hurts one to look. They do not consider these nations as people but as some kind of beasts of burden. They do not beat them; they even care for them—meaning that they feed them and pay them generously and promptly. But they do not hide their contempt.[106]

Having pondered up until now the secrets of British success, Goncharov now brings to light its limitations: the material prosperity of British rule does not offset its dehumanizing indignities.

This mistreatment is needless, Goncharov writes, because "no nation is as meek, submissive, and courteous as the Chinese, with the exception of the ones from Canton." He earlier characterized the Chinese as industrious, resourceful, and decorous. A Chinese village, be it poor and muddy, shows signs of "a mind, order, exactness"; everything is clean and well thought-out, with not a straw out of place. But is Goncharov taking a principled or a pragmatic stand? Would he consider brusque measures acceptable toward the less deserving Cantonese, whose enmity toward Europeans was well known? In Africa, he certainly thought them appropriate for the Xhosa. A belief in flexibility and responsiveness to local conditions underlies Goncharov's critique of what he sees as Britons' rigid and indiscriminate contempt. Such bungling, Goncharov concludes, imperils the philosophical basis of the British imperial enterprise. In a passage made famous by critics in the Soviet era, Goncharov lambastes the English: "I don't know who should civilize whom: couldn't the Chinese, with their politeness, meekness, and, yes, their knowledge of trade, civilize the English?"[107]

This is a very pointed question. Yet though it threatens to invert the hierarchy on which Europe's imperial ideology stands, it does so for a polemical effect that falls short of the anti-colonial critique that Soviet scholars naively saw in it. On the contrary, such criticisms were part and parcel of imperial rivalries. Empires routinely found fault with other empires so as to cast in flattering relief one's own virtues. Indeed, Britain's barbarous opium trade frames Goncharov's argument in the upcoming Siberian chapters, about Russia's own superior civilizing credentials. (This despite the widely known fact that Russian alcohol devastated Siberia's indigenous communities.) An international outcry accompanied the treatment of Native Americans by the British and later the Americans. (As the French ranted against it, they themselves were butchering Arabs and Berbers in North Africa.) The British harangued the Spanish for the excesses of Catholic missionary zeal. The expansion of the tsars' rule was widely deplored for spreading despotism across huge swaths of the globe. And just about everyone accused everyone else of hypocrisy. More often than not, such tit-for-tat recriminations served to accentuate the prerogatives of one's own imperial model over a rival's, not to renounce imperialism as such. The point was not that running an empire was an immoral business, but that empires could be better run.

Goncharov does not push his challenge to civilizational hierarchies beyond the barb at the Britons' questionable civilizing credentials, swiftly moving to other topics. Yet readers today may well wonder at what point lapses of manners impinge on rights. In addition to attacking the hypocrisy of the British, made evident in their exploitative and inhumane opium trade, Goncharov also questions their civilizing credentials. For without these, what righteous vision could justify the brute English opening of China?

Besides, the Chinese village, with its stamp of an orderly and purposeful mind, appears "civilized" to Goncharov without any help from Europeans. Do the business-savvy Chinese really need any British lessons in trade?

The descriptions of the Europeans' equestrian cavorting in Shanghai and of the opium trade are the lowest points in Goncharov's estimation of the English. But as tense moments for *The Frigate Pallada*'s imperial propaganda, they may seem tense only for us. The Soviet reading of them as Goncharov's bitter crowning judgment on imperialism lacks support. The writer is back to defending the English a few chapters later. The Japanese section concludes with an affirmation and elaboration of Europe's civilizing mission in Asia. He later applauds Russia's signal virtues and achievements in colonizing Siberia. Goncharov's Shanghai crisis does not lead him to fundamentally question either empire or globalization.

This crisis remains a mere blip in his enthusiastic trade projections and figures. The Shanghai chapter overflows with detailed instructions for starting a business in China, including advice about Chinese consumer tastes and trading customs; information about prices, currencies, and rates of exchange; and descriptions of attractive Chinese products. Putiatin sent samples to Russia as instructed by his government.[108] If one were to settle on one guiding idea that captures Goncharov's impression of Asia—beyond the hot tropical sun—it would be the region's incredible economic dynamism and potential. Thick palisades of commercial boats lining the harbors, enterprising Asian artisans and traders accosting the Russians everywhere, a seemingly endless supply of labor—these are the images that shape Goncharov's Asia. The Chinese especially dominate the region economically. "Like peas from an overfilled sack," they spill out of China to fill all available economic niches, from Java all the way to California. In his less charitable moments, which couple anti-Chinese and anti-Semitic biases, he dubs them Asia's Jews, not meaning this as a compliment. Elsewhere he praises their industriousness and energy. He decrees that this nation of excellent traders, artisans, and workers is destined "to play a vital role in commerce, and perhaps not only in commerce."[109]

Tapping into this vibrant continent, the European and American business is so brisk that new harbors, wharfs, and warehouse complexes seem to crop up like mushrooms. The influx of attendant personnel is so precipitous that visitors sleep four to a bed in the Shanghai hotel during Goncharov's visit. Goncharov cites exponentially rising statistics on trade volume and profits. He eagerly contradicts naysayers who predict that these trends will go anywhere but up. The subtext here is that to miss this boat would constitute criminal negligence on the part of the Russians. Indeed, the same thinking drives the Russian public's surge of enthusiasm around this time for annexing the Amur region from China, a project to which the *Pallada* expedition will also contribute in a small way.[110]

Returning to a quite even keel after the Shanghai turbulence, Goncharov lets his enthusiasm carry him in Manila, the center of the Spanish empire in the East. He visits what is evidently a cigar-making sweatshop employing between eight and nine thousand Tagal women, aged fifteen and above, crammed seven hundred to a room. The plant is part of the diversified Asian portfolio of the US company Russell & Co., one of Cunningham's four employers. Goncharov gives an approving nod to the prohibition on laughter and conversation, and to the harem-style supervision by old men only. He uses this opportunity not to decry the exploitation but to create a comedic episode about the absurdity of being unable to buy cigars in a cigar factory. Impressed with the shiny machinery in a US rope factory in Manila—so gleaming and dandy it's fit for a living room, he writes—he seems content with a specious explanation of the good deal the workers are getting despite their starvation wages. Frequent double shifts, with workers sleeping and being fed in the factory, mean small expenses for "civilian" clothing and food, Goncharov learns. He reports without a hint of skepticism—neglecting to think back to his own visits to Manila's manufacturing facilities—that the Spaniards treat the Filipinos well and do not overwork them. Far from exploited colonial subjects, the Filipinos seem to Goncharov "the happiest people in the world." He appears sympathetic to the idea that if the Spanish masters weren't so lazy, more wealth could be squeezed from the colony.[111]

The work that Putiatin began during the *Pallada* expedition and later continued as the tsar's plenipotentiary in China eventually bore fruit in the 1858 Treaties of Tianjin (which Putiatin personally negotiated) and Aigun, and in the 1860 Treaty of Beijing. These treaties opened duty-free trade along China's entire northern border, and coastal trade through the treaty ports, while securing for Russia territorial gains in the Amur and the Ussuri region roughly equivalent to all of the United States east of the Mississippi. When the Qing emperor learned the details of the Tianjin Treaty, he ordered Putiatin's Chinese counterparts to commit suicide.[112] Indeed, Marx pronounced Russians, not the British, the real winners in

Britain's Opium Wars. Britain was apparently so incensed about Russia's deft Asian diplomacy that the London *Times* initially suppressed information about Russia's acquisition of the Amur.[113] Russian diplomats, Putiatin among them, hoodwinked both the Europeans and the Chinese, playing both sides for their own benefit. While posing to the Chinese as well-intentioned mediators hoping to dissuade the British from attacking Beijing, they turned to the British and advised them to do precisely that. Unbeknownst to the Europeans, the Russians used the wave of Anglo-French victory in the Second Opium War to propel the negotiations of their own treaties. In the end, they did hitch an imperial ride courtesy of the Europeans.

Today, Russian and Chinese views of this episode clash. Russian historians credit Russians for saving Beijing from Franco-British attack. They view the Amur affair as a mere settling of borders rather than an opportune land grab. And they portray the Russian government as high-minded and friendly toward China, in sharp contrast to rapacious Western powers. Chinese historians, for their part, regard this an important episode in tsarist Russia's long history of imperial conquest and aggression against China. In doing so, they echo their nineteenth-century forebears. Historian Sarah C. M. Paine argues that this episode "permanently changed Chinese perceptions of the Russians." After it, the "Chinese would consider them no longer to be barbarians of the traditional Central Asian variety but rather to be an unusually dangerous sub-species of the European genus." On imperial frontiers, the Russians were flattered to be regarded as fellows by other Europeans. For hardly flattering reasons, they seemed to be gaining this reputation also among Asians.[114]

CHAPTER THREE

Prying Open Japan, Prospecting Korea

Recently the loathsome Western barbarians, unmindful of their base position as the lower extremities of the world, have been scurrying impudently across the Four Seas, trampling other nations underfoot. Now they are audacious enough to challenge our exalted position in the world. What manner of insolence is this?

—Aizawa Yasushi (1782–1863),
Japanese intellectual and reformer

After ten months of sailing, in August 1853, the *Pallada* finally reached its goal: the kingdom of Japan. Prior to its arrival, the expedition's flagship rendezvoused on the nearby Bonin Islands with three smaller vessels: the steam-powered schooner *Vostok* ("the East"), purchased by Putiatin in England; the corvette *Olivutsa* of the Kamchatka fleet; and the Russian-American Company's transport *Knyaz Menshikov*, dispatched from Alaska. On the Bonins, Putiatin received additional instructions from the Ministry of Foreign Affairs, which had been sent from St. Petersburg on ships that sailed around South America. On initial approach to Nagasaki Bay, Japan appears to Goncharov like a magical place from Russian fairy tales—the never-never land of "the thirtieth kingdom." Referring to what the Europeans viewed as Japan's seclusion, lasting two hundred years since the seventeenth-century expulsion of Europeans, Goncharov calls Japan a "locked casket" whose key has been lost.[1] Finding this key is the *Pallada*'s mission. While the *Pallada* crew to this point has mostly observed other nations' imperial practices, in Japan the understudies become the actors.

Russian scholars have traditionally held up Goncharov's descriptions of Japan as evidence of the writer's humanistic and respectful attitude toward other ethnicities.[2] Such celebration either silences or exculpates the work's prejudices. While western scholars have been more forthright about them, neither critical tradition has sufficiently appreciated the political agenda of *The Frigate Pallada.* This agenda and the rhetoric used to advance it certainly temper, and may altogether compromise, the work's vaunted humanism.

Although suspended in colorful narration with lots of humorous episodes to brighten the mood, the political message of the travelogue's Japanese chapters is stridently imperial. Goncharov encourages Russia's bold posture in East Asian politics. He openly recommends not just trade links, but Russia's imperial control of the region, along the lines of the British model of informal imperialism (though this model is not named). As in China, trade is to be merely a gateway. Perhaps surprising for a jovial literary man, Goncharov embraces the option of military means for securing this control. At the same time, in the course of his stay, prejudices start to commingle in his account with moments of understanding and sympathy for the Japanese people. In this sense, *The Frigate Pallada* compares favorably to the arrogance and nearly pathologic sense of superiority found in the account of Perry's American expedition. Still, Goncharov finds in the end little worth saving in Japan's culture. Blending geopolitical and civilizational arguments, he advocates remaking Japan into a fully European country under foreign tutelage. However idyllic he finds the Ryukyu Islands, he likewise slates them for Europeanization. Intrusive Russian forays into Korean shore communities lead Goncharov to designate Korea as another attractive target of Russia's imperial expansion, which it indeed became a few decades hence.

How Japan Was "Opened"

Japan had been quite open to Europe in the mid-sixteenth century. However, the consolidation of the Tokugawa shogunate and rapacious activities of foreign traders and Christian missionaries changed that. In a series of 1630s edicts, the shoguns expelled foreigners, persecuted Christian converts, forbade the people of Japan to travel abroad (even refusing repatriation to castaways), banned the construction of ocean-crossing vessels, made teaching Japanese to foreigners and providing them with maps punishable by death, and generally sealed off their country from contact with the western world. The only exception was the Dutch, who were allowed to retain limited presence and trading privileges. It is from the Dutch that the Russians originally learned about Japan, in the seventeenth century. In 1853, the Japanese chose Dutch over Chinese as their language of diplomacy with the Russians.

Nonetheless, Japan's isolation was hardly as hermetic as it was made to seem by Europeans, including Goncharov. Japan was not cut off from the whole world, and even from Europe not completely. Throughout this period, it conducted active foreign policy and trade with its East Asian neighbors, especially China. Western ideas and technologies saw considerable dissemination. Marius Jansen argues that "the famous decrees that closed the country were more of a bamboo blind than they were a Berlin wall." William McOmie suggests that instead of "opening" we might do better to speak of "a broadening, liberalizing and modernizing of trade and intercourse with other nations," especially in the West. While even its critics often resign themselves for lack of a better alternative to using it, the flawed language of "opening" Japan reflects a mistaken, western view that Japan was previously closed.[3]

For two hundred years, the tiny artificial island of Deshima, near Nagasaki, where the Dutch resided, functioned as Japan's window onto the wider world. Through obligatory annual reports, the Dutch kept the Japanese apprised of world developments, including the impending American expedition.[4] "Dutch learning," in a list drawn up by Matt Matsuda, included European developments in geography, navigational science, cartography, mathematics, astronomy, botany, medicine, and hydrology. The Americans from Perry's squadron were impressed with the Japanese knowledge of astronomy, political geography, international affairs, and current events.[5]

The Dutch paid a price for the concessions they were granted. Deshima, to which they were strictly confined, was barely three acres in size. Little beyond sanctioned periodic visits from Japanese prostitutes distinguished this arrangement from incarceration. Exiting the compound through the narrow bridge connecting it with Nagasaki required treading on Christian images. The chief Dutch agent periodically had to perform ceremonial prostrations in front of the shogun in Edo (Tokyo). To a western sensibility this had the degrading appearance of crawling.

As historian George Lensen reminds us, it was Russia—whose empire once spanned the continents of Europe, Asia, and America—that "first and most persistently sought to reopen Japan."[6] In 1739 the Russians discovered the northeast passage to Japan, sailing from Kamchatka, along the Kurile Islands. (Westerners used a southern approach to Japan, around Africa). From the eighteenth century, state-sponsored exploration went hand in hand with commercial missions. Before the *Pallada* expedition, the most famous ones included Adam Laxman's 1792 mission, the 1804 mission of Nikolai Rezanov (then director of the Russian-American Company), and the 1811 mission of Vasily Golovnin. All such attempts to establish trade with Japan proved fruitless. Indeed, thanks to Rezanov's misdeeds, Golovnin and his crew were taken prisoner on their arrival and held captive in Japan for two years. Rezanov, having had his trade overtures rejected, had decided to vent his frustration by ordering the torching of Japanese settlements on Sakhalin and the Kurile Islands, neither of which belonged then to the Russian empire. Goncharov, keen to portray the Russians as always acting above board, makes no reference to this episode as he mentions Golovnin's imprisonment.[7]

Japan's seclusion policy, called *sakoku,* lasted for more than two centuries. Once it ended, the humiliation of western intrusion would create pressure for ongoing change in Japanese society. This ultimately would lead, in 1868, to the abolition of the Tokugawa shogunate and the reconfiguration of power in favor of a new generation of oligarchs, centered around the emperor Meiji. The Meiji Restoration would markedly increase the pace of Japan's modernization, ushering in rapid industrialization and the transition to a modern centralized state. One of the new government's first orders of business would be the attempt to renegotiate the "unequal treaties" Japan was forced to sign with the United States, Russia, and Western European powers in the 1850s.[8]

Russia sought such a treaty in order to restore its edge in the imperial contest for Asia. Having been reduced in China to hitchhiking on British gains, the Russians and the Americans were determined to lead the way in Japan. Both countries, by mid-century, had compelling interests there. For the United States, the development of California following the discovery of gold in 1848, and expansion into the Pacific Northwest, increased the importance of Asia's Pacific rim. American whalers and traders bound for Asia needed coal-refueling bases for their steamships. The safety of shipwrecks and crews was also a key concern. Russia, for its part, had colonies in eastern Siberia and Alaska that faced considerable provisioning problems, due to mostly impassable, frozen northern seas and the hardships of crossing Siberia. Trade with Japan could alleviate this problem. Political considerations added to the commercial imperatives. While Western Europe dominated the Atlantic, the Russians and the Americans increasingly felt that their respective manifest destinies bound them to the Pacific.[9] Britain's 1842 victory in the First Opium War had opened a new chapter in Russia's Asian politics. The Russian government resolved that Japan could not go the way of China—that is, become a sphere of British influence that would weaken Russia's position in East Asia. Conceived as early as 1843, the Russian expedition to Japan had been postponed. The widely publicized news of the Americans' impending expedition propelled the project.[10]

Commodore Perry's squadron reached Japan on July 14, 1853, and Putiatin arrived five weeks later, on August 22, 1853. Numerous and lengthy repairs to the rickety *Pallada,* required on most stopovers, had caused significant delays.[11] After a hurricane on the Indian Ocean loosened the main mast, Putiatin had requested a new frigate from St. Petersburg. The steam-powered American squadron also enjoyed a technological edge over the Russian sailing ships (with the one exception of the steam-engine schooner *Vostok,* purchased by Putiatin in England). A religious factor may have also disadvantaged the Russians. According to some reports not mentioned by Goncharov, Putiatin, known to be devout in his Russian Orthodox faith, chose the aging *Pallada* over available newer vessels because it contained a chapel.[12]

To this day, Putiatin's Russian mission is rarely mentioned in accounts of the "opening" of Japan, so eclipsed was it by Perry's mythogenic triumphs. When it is mentioned, the rivalry is discussed in terms of a "race." Yet did the Russians really race the Americans to Japan? Based on the Ministry of the Navy's "secret instructions" given to Putiatin before he set sail, Russian authorities did not consider this a race. Like the British, they simply aimed not to be excluded from any ports Perry might open. They knew that the negotiations about the disputed border, which was one of the mission's objectives, would take some time. They also recognized the United States' greater strategic interest in Japan and expressed no concern at the prospect of the Americans' reaching Japan first. Putiatin was instructed to let the Yankees do the heavy lifting and hover just close enough to profit from their actions, whether peaceful or violent. Should the Russians, contrary to expectations, overtake them, Putiatin was actually advised to postpone talks with the Japanese for as long as Perry's negotiations were in progress. The expectation that he would do so was reiterated in the "additional instructions" from the Ministry of Foreign Affairs delivered to Putiatin on the Bonin

Islands.[13] His task was simply to piggyback on the Americans' efforts. At the same time, Putiatin was given considerable leeway to adjust his course of action depending on the developing situation on the ground. He did not in fact wait for Perry to conclude a treaty before launching his own negotiations. Most likely, his perception of a growing risk of British and French attack due to the unfolding Crimean conflict made him act sooner. It was not uncommon for imperial agents to go beyond official mandates when they spotted a way to gain tactical advantage or when national prestige was at stake. As far as the Russian government was concerned, however, Perry was welcome to wedge the door to Japan open, so long as Russia could slip in as well.[14]

Perry used aggressive diplomacy backed by the threat of force. He arrived in Uraga's bay, near today's Tokyo, with a squadron of what the Japanese called "burning" or "black" ships. To the Japanese people, these were terrifying apparitions of enormous size—about twenty times larger than the biggest Japanese craft—that menacingly approached their shore against the wind, belching smoke (steam engines were then largely unknown in Japan). Mass panic erupted on the streets of Edo. The next year, Perry returned to receive the Japanese answer to his demands with an expanded fleet of nine ships and a quarter of the US Navy. He warned that any hostilities would make him return within twenty days with a fleet ten times the size. This was quite an undertaking for a young American nation of barely twenty-five million, less than Japan's population at the time.[15]

Yet sticks were counterbalanced with carrots, and the deployment of both allowed the Japanese to evaluate the two powers that pressured and courted them. While some sticks were scarier than others, some carrots may have tasted sweeter. Elaborate exchanges of gifts, always part of diplomatic protocol, showed off the assets of each of the three countries. As described in *The Frigate Pallada,* the Japanese presents included gold-incrusted inkstands, lacquer boxes, sabers, silk, pipes, chests of drawers, dolls, soy sauce, and sake. The Russian gifts included malachite clocks, pocket watches, crystal vases, liqueurs, sugar, mirrors, fabrics, rugs, lamps, thermometers, compasses, samovars, and drawings of St. Petersburg and London. From the account of Perry's expedition, we know that the American gifts for the Japanese, beyond agricultural tools, cordials, and clocks, included a telegraph and wires, a daguerreotype, a steam engine, rifles, and a scaled-down locomotive and tender along with a 370-foot circle of rails. Though the locomotive was sized to fit a small child, grown Japanese men delighted in taking rides: "it was a spectacle not a little ludicrous to behold a dignified mandarin whirling around the circular road at the rate of twenty miles an hour, with his loose robes flying in the wind."[16]

One wonders what role this state-of-the-art American hardware played in the Japanese decision to pick the American bid. Some Japanese diplomats contrasted the "extravagance" of the Americans to the Russians' "stinginess" and furthermore deemed the Russian firearms inferior to those of other foreigners.[17] In fact, contrary to Goncharov's depiction of the Russians' munificence as perfectly appropriate for the occasion, some members of the Russian expedition thought otherwise. Archpriest Avvakum complained that the Russian gifts not only did not impress the Japanese or offer an attractive image of the Russian empire, but scarcely amounted to the value of the tips that would be fair to pay for the extensive services of the Japanese personnel. He blamed this on Putiatin's miserliness: "it would befit an envoy of a great nation to be more generous."[18]

The sticks nonetheless proved decisive. The crushing defeat of the Celestial Empire in the Opium Wars was for Japan chilling to recall. As Lensen discovered, the Japanese initially considered offering the Russians exclusive trade, perceiving them to be the lesser of two evils, on the condition that they would fend off other foreigners. The outbreak of the Crimean War, however, raised doubts about Russia's ability to act as Japan's protector.[19] Meanwhile, Perry threatened to burn Edo to the ground if he were refused. Short of options in the face of American and Russian gunboat diplomacy, and possibly softened by the American gifts, which were exchanged on March 13, 1854, Japan agreed to the Treaty of Kanagawa with the United States on March 31, 1854, and with Britain a few months later.[20] The Kanagawa Treaty was merely an initial declaration of "friendship." It was followed by a detailed commercial treaty only in 1858.

Putiatin's first visits to Japan between 1853 and 1854, when Goncharov assisted him as secretary, failed to yield a treaty. Undaunted, Putiatin continued his efforts in the face of considerable setbacks such as, most notably, the Crimean War that made Russian vessels targets in Pacific waters, and a tsunami that eventually destroyed his ship. Proving himself a spectacularly effective diplomat, Putiatin reached his goal despite these obstacles, signing the Treaty of Shimoda with Japan on February 7, 1855. This diplomatic triumph, however, was deprived of its bard. His wanderlust sated, Goncharov by then had returned to St. Petersburg, after an arduous overland trek through Siberia.

Figure 3.1. The *Pallada* Russian delegation to the governor of Nagasaki, Japan, as seen by a Japanese artist. From *Dai Nihon komonjo. Bakumatsu gaikoku kankei monjo,* Vol. 3, 1911 (Tokyo: Tōkyō Teikoku Daigaku Bunka Daigaku Shiryō Hensangakari, 1910–present).

On the pages of *The Frigate Pallada,* Russia's Japanese business remains unfinished.

So who deserves "credit" for "opening" Japan? Lensen is right that Perry should share fame with Putiatin. The treaty that Putiatin eventually negotiated went beyond Japan's 1854 treaties with the United States and Britain. It demarcated the Russia-Japan borders across Sakhalin and the Kurile Islands, opened an extra port to Russian trade (Nagasaki), and provided for reciprocal extraterritoriality. In Lensen's measured assessment, Putiatin "assured Russia of a position of at least equal importance" to that of the Americans. In their effect, even if not in their design, the missions were symbiotic developments, which proves that inter-imperial rivalries in this period did not preclude important synergies. Though *The Frigate Pallada* does not mention this, Putiatin suggested cooperation to Perry. Suspicious that Russia's intention was to turn the Pacific into a Russian lake, Perry rejected the offer. But his hostility was not shared by other US officials operating in East Asia, many of whom closely cooperated with

Putiatin during his second expedition to Japan in 1858–1859. Indeed, at that time, Russia and the United States were natural geopolitical allies, both chafing at the British hegemony in world affairs.[21] William McOmie likewise concludes, having meticulously researched all parties to this historical drama, that the "opening" of Japan was a shared international effort in which not only Russian and American, but also British and Dutch contributions had their impacts.[22]

From the perspective of the Japanese themselves, however, their country was "opened" by the Russians. Curiously, their histories tend to designate not the *Pallada* expedition but the failed 1804 mission of Nikolai Rezanov as the watershed event. According to Kume Kunitake, writing in the 1870s, Rezanov's 1804 cannon salute "woke the Japanese up from their isolationist dreams." As late as 1916, in a remark that riled the American press, Japanese Prime Minister Okuma Shigenobu credited Rezanov, not Perry, with first convincing the Japanese that their seclusion policy was at a historical dead end. Moreover, as Lensen writes about the Russians, "theirs was the better part of the bargain, for not only did they receive all the concessions threats had bought, but also the good will of the people threats had alienated."[23] Today, the Shimoda History Museum devotes roughly equal exhibit space to Perry and Putiatin, and the Russian's more benign approach earns him the more favorable portrayal. Though the Japanese officials with whom Putiatin negotiated were irritated by escalating Russian demands, which seemed akin to "the eating habits of a silkworm," they ultimately came to regard him as a great leader and hero. In 1881, Putiatin was honored with Japan's Order of the Rising Sun.[24] His positive image is also evident in a recent Japanese anime film about the Russian expedition, which Prime Minister Hashimoto Ryutaro presented to Russian president Boris Yeltsin in 1997, and which aired on Russian television.[25]

It took no time, following Japan's "opening," for the contest between Perry and Putiatin to capture the popular imagination. Did the "Perry effect" buoy Putiatin's success, or did Putiatin's pressure on the Japanese help Perry? Accounts of both expeditions take up this question. When a Manila newspaper prints drawings of Edo homes purportedly made by Perry's men, which would indicate that Americans had been granted unprecedented freedom to roam around Japan's imperial capital, Goncharov quickly unmasks the hoax. The source of the drawings, he proves, is an 1820s travel book by German Japanologist Philipp Franz von Siebold. Resentful of the Americans' media spotlight, he also casts doubt on the newspaper's "cackle" about the United States' successes in Japan and report of US trade with Japan (which, Goncharov was right, was premature). "What if we loudly amplified our own successes in Japan," Goncharov peevishly asks, "and raised them to the square root? It would then appear that we've long been trading there, too."[26]

Meanwhile, the account of the Perry expedition, reflecting the Commodore's Russophobia, offers its own spin on the Russian co-presence in Japan. Perry feared that the Russians wanted to shut out all other nations from Japan so as to become "the controlling maritime power of the world." He was determined to prevent this from happening. In the American account, sneaky Russians lie in wait for Perry's misstep so as to foil him. Regarding Putiatin's proposal to join forces with the Americans, it smugly surmises that "this may have been prompted by an expectation of our success and a doubt of his own." The account indignantly refutes what many—most infamously von Siebold—alleged at the time: "For [our] success, we are not indebted in the slightest degree to Russia, by any direct act of hers to that effect." Of course, this legalistic language brackets off Russia's *indirect* effect, also injurious to American national pride.[27]

The gains guaranteed by the treaties were another focal point for competitive comparisons. The American account states that the Russian treaty "is copied from ours, with no change but that of the substitution of the port of Nagasaki for Napha in the Lew Chew [the Ryukyu Islands]." However, this is not quite true, as the Ryukyu Islands are not in fact mentioned in the Kanagawa treaty and were not formally part of Japan, but merely maintained a tribute-bearing relation to the Japanese lord of Satsuma and to the Chinese emperor. Hence the Russian treaty does indeed list an extra port (the others being Shimoda and Hakodate). Nonetheless, although some historians have disputed Hawks's allegation of treaty plagiarism, the two treaties do look very similar.[28] We know that Putiatin obtained a copy of the American treaty by bribing a Japanese interpreter. He also purchased in Shanghai, this time legally, copies of European treaties with China.[29] This seems a clear instance of a transfer to Russia of western imperial technology.

Against the Americans' classic gunboat diplomacy, the Russians could be said to have used gunboat diplomacy "lite." Guided by von Siebold's advice, they chose a more conciliatory path since friendly relations were important in view of the disputed frontier with Japan. Where it did not impinge on their national dignity, they followed the Japanese protocol for interaction with foreigners. Thus, unlike the bullying Americans, the Russians never threatened bombardment—much as they relished ignoring the prohibitions of the Japanese and scaring the wits out of them, or so they thought, with cannon salutes.[30] The Russians never entered the capital Edo, strictly off-limits to foreigners. They never addressed their demands directly to the emperor, at the time a puppet figurehead, but only to the Supreme Council (the Roju), as was proper. Entering Edo and addressing the emperor were actions they only threatened to take in moments of exasperation. Sources show that the Japanese appreciated the Russians' lesser arrogance, more orderly and considerate conduct, and greater respect for Japanese customs and cultural differences.[31]

However, the actual conduct of the Russians and how this episode of Russian diplomacy is couched in the ideology and rhetoric of Goncharov's book are two different things. This is an essential distinction to keep in mind. In addition to chronicling, not always reliably, events and conversations, Goncharov shares his inner thoughts. The fact that Russians treated the Japanese with less racism does not stop Goncharov from giving it looser rein in his travelogue. Relative restraint by the tsar's plenipotentiaries in bending Japan to submission does not mean he cannot imagine them acting more boldly, even violently. Though Russia's objective was to establish trade and demarcate borders, the writer indulges in grandiose thoughts of a Japan remade into a fully European country under foreign, ideally Russian, tutelage. Quite apart from the actual history of the Russo-Japanese encounter, *The Frigate Pallada* proffers condescending Eurocentric attitudes that helped shape Russian society's approach toward East Asia.

This was a wholly novel manner in which to write about Japan for the Russian audience. *The Frigate Pallada* supplanted the memoirs of Vasily Golovnin as the principal source of popular knowledge about Japan. Golovnin's captivity in Japan involved privation and occasional rough treatment, such as being tied up so tightly it caused nosebleeds. This gave him plenty of reasons to be resentful. Yet his sympathy for the people of Japan and his respectful portrayal of their customs, so free of European or Russian arrogance, make Golovnin's account a model of tolerance for his time. Indeed, his *Notes of Fleet Captain Golovnin about his Adventures in Japanese Captivity in the Years 1811, 1812, and 1813* take issue with the European accounts of Japanese "barbarity" and demeaning ethnic stereotypes in widespread circulation.[32] In Golovnin's view, the depredations of European missionaries and traders made Japan's seclusion policy eminently sensible. Japan's refusal to trade was not an affront to Europe but a choice within its rights to exercise. Golovnin portrayed Japan as a peaceful, prosperous, and happy country.

The Frigate Pallada differs starkly from Golovnin's account. Whereas Golovnin challenged Eurocentric stereotypes, Goncharov reinforces them. He makes Russian readers feel entitled to an attitude of confident European superiority. Flashes of sympathy and understanding do crop up, many of which Goncharov seems to import straight from Golovnin's account. Yet Japan's inferiority to Russia is never in doubt.

Goncharov's chapters about Japan were the first to be collected into a book, entitled *The Russians in Japan at the End of 1853 and Beginning of 1854*.[33] The relative dearth of information about Japan, the East's most elusive realm, and its strategic importance for Russia in the 1850s likely accounted for this. From this book and later from *The Frigate Pallada,* Russian readers gained information about Japan's quaint customs but also learned a certain way of thinking about Japan, and about the East more generally. *The Frigate Pallada* catered to a growing taste in Russia for Eurocentric depictions of the "Orient." It popularized a posture of imperial resolve, along with attendant cultural assumptions, political aspirations, forms of conduct and of speech, and perceptions of the rights of Russians and needs of "Orientals." This imperial resolve emanated less from the actual fine-grained history Goncharov recorded than from *how* he wrote about it—that is, to use Edward Said's phrase, from the "structure of attitude and reference" he employed as he spun his musings into an attractive yarn and put them into wide circulation.[34]

The Japanese chapters model for the Russian public how to embark on imperial ventures and feel good about them. Drawing on standard European rhetoric, these chapters make empire not only palatable but also righteous. Calling it a strategy of "anti-conquest," Mary Louise Pratt shows that Europeans used it to establish their "innocence" at the very moment of asserting their hegemony. To appear legitimate, acts of conquest or economic domination had to be masked as disinterested acts of humanitarianism or scientific pursuits.[35] And yet, what makes Goncharov's travelogue a fascinating cultural document is its pervasive slippage from the glossy surface of imperial humanitarianism to its sordid lower realms. Goncharov's justificatory and sanctimonious language is interleaved with aggressive stirrings and wholly self-interested considerations of power. The book professes best intentions only to lay bare the reasons to distrust them.

Pointing the Cannons at the Locked Casket

As soon as the *Pallada* approaches the first Nagasaki Bay roadstead (see Map 3), the Russians know that their fun-filled peregrinations through Asia's open ports are firmly behind them. Japan sends no sign of welcome. "We were not met here," Goncharov ruefully remarks, "with boats laden with fruits, shells, monkeys, and parrots, like on Java and in Singapore." Ferries offering to transport seaborne travelers to the shore—that vibrant service industry of Asia's open ports—are nowhere in sight. The Russian crew experiences "a heavy feeling of entering a prison."[36] Given Golovnin's fate, this is a fully justifiable anxiety.

The *Pallada* flies a white canvas with an inscription in Japanese: "Vessel of the Russian State." Japanese border guards who approach it deliver a note written in English, French, and Dutch requiring the Russians to stop at the harbor's third roadstead, most distant from Nagasaki. It warns of "great unpleasantness" if they do not. But this is quickly superseded by permission—for which the Russians did not ask—to move to the second roadstead. The Russians take this as a sign of their hosts' anxiety. In the course

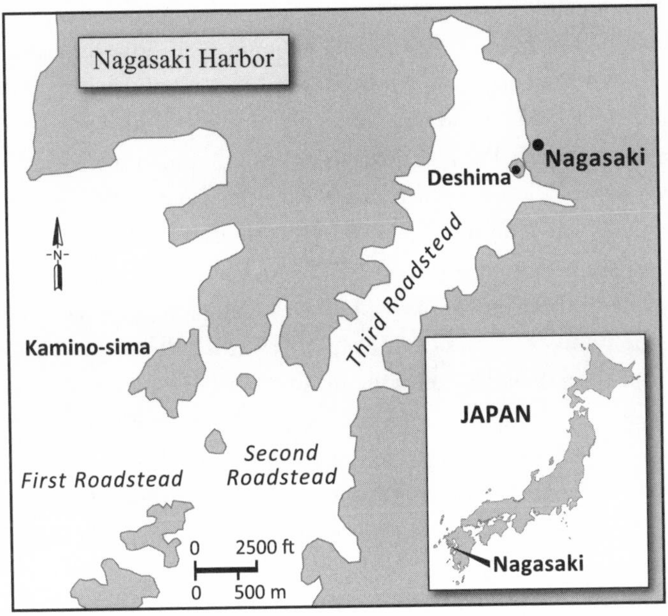

Map 3. Nagasaki Harbor. Reaching inner roadsteads was seen as an important sign of negotiating leverage. The *Pallada* was alotted a spot on the second roadstead, close to the border with the third.

of future interactions, Goncharov interprets such gestures as proof of Europe's power.[37]

Another party of guards, assisted by Dutch translators from the Deshima compound, delivers a lengthy list of questions. Endless interrogations of the Russians, who are not allowed to disembark, begin. These interrogations become the stuff of comedy for Goncharov, who paints Japan as a police state addicted to useless information, obtained through an elaborate system of "mutual spying."[38] Dates and ports of departure, the number of crew, by ship and by rank, the number of cannon—all such details are scrupulously entered in reports and passed on to superiors. Perry haughtily refused to answer such questions, but Putiatin acquiesces to local custom. An entire Japanese delegation is sent to investigate a discrepancy between two separate testimonies as to the date of a Russian ship's departure from Kamchatka and its exact route. The Russians become indignant: "How is it your business where we were? All that should matter to you is that we have arrived." For all their feeling of entitlement regarding the Russians' information, the Japanese jealously guard any about their own country. Goncharov is perplexed by his inability to find out the population of Nagasaki or the names of the Shogun and the Emperor.[39]

Although Goncharov never admits it, some of the guards' inquiries are incisive and pertinent, clearly aimed to assess what military threat the Russians pose to Japan. Russian assurances of peaceful intentions strike the Japanese as hypocritical. When Putiatin declares that his purpose in Japan is simply to deliver a letter to the Supreme Council from the Russian Minister of Foreign Affairs, Count Nesselrode, the Japanese are skeptical: "Why dispatch four ships to deliver one letter?" Goncharov detects the sarcasm but instantly neutralizes any impression that the Japanese ask smart questions. Rather, he points to this as evidence of "childish distrust . . . and suspicion about some hostile intentions on our part. We hastened to reassure them and answered all questions sincerely and openly, yet at the same time we could not restrain our smile, looking at their soft, smooth, white, effeminate faces, their sly and clever physiognomies, and their little braids and curtsies." Perceiving an accusation of hypocrisy, Goncharov thus parries by paternalistically belittling the Japanese as childish, effeminate, weak, and servile. (The Japanese custom of bowing is consistently so viewed in *The Frigate Pallada*.)[40]

From the start, Goncharov pairs his description of Japanese manners with hard-nosed political analysis that is anything but pacifist. The fairy-tale images that began with a "locked casket" quickly give way to sober realities of Europe's power play in Asia. Goncharov ushers his readers into the land of Japan with the following:

> Here is a populous part of the human family that slyly avoids the ferule of civilization, that dares to live by its own wit and rules, that bluntly rejects the friendship, religion, and trade of the foreigner, that laughs at our attempts to enlighten it, and that sets the inner, arbitrary laws of its anthill against the natural, national, and all manner of European laws, and against all untruth. 'How long will this last?' we wondered, our hands caressing our sixty-pound cannons.[41]

The indignation of a snubbed European suffuses this passage. How dare the Japanese live their own way? A European deems his laws both natural and universal, and certainly superior to those of some "anthill." Rather than benevolent and magnanimous, civilization appears as a disciplining force—the obsolete word "ferule" denotes a ruler used in schools to strike the hands of insubordinate children. In the Russian writer's hands—ungainly but perhaps less constrained than those of his Western European peers—the colonial rhetoric lavishly discloses what it is meant to hide: the almost sadistic underpinnings of this lesson in civilization. The sensuous stroking of the cannon perversely signals that if Japan does not open, the Russians are ready to pry it open. The sexual overtone gives this imperial venture the menacing air of rape. The "Orient" must be unveiled. As in the European writing about the opening of the Suez Canal that Edward Said discusses, the East's "cloistered intimacy *away* from the West, its perdurable exoticism" must be destroyed, its "resistant hostility" transformed into "obliging, and submissive, partnership."[42]

Curiously, Goncharov emphasizes in this passage Japan's belonging to "the human family," not its "otherness." Japan emerges as an estranged family member the Russians will bring back into the fold, by force if necessary. Imperial aggression is thus recast as the restoration of mankind's natural unity. The idea of a relatedness binding the imperial body is a common trope of the Russian imperial lexicon. In his influential poem "To the Slanderers of Russia," poet Alexander Pushkin famously used the term "family quarrel" to describe the Polish Uprising of 1831 that aimed to detach Poland from the Russian empire. Pushkin meant to dissuade Western Europeans from interfering in this purported domestic matter among kinsmen. Ukrainians have traditionally been denied autonomy or independence because they were seen as Russia's (little) "brothers," a sense that from the eighteenth century to the present day has shaped Russia's relation to Ukraine. In Soviet times, familial metaphors coded the Soviet empire, supposedly united by a "friendship of nations."[43] Russian colonial writing often invokes kinship as an argument against political defection, or as a license to punish it. This is not an imperialism built on the notion of irreconcilable difference, which was a dominant feature of western colonial writing. This is assimilationist imperialism, built on the enforcement of similarity.

Yet Goncharov also uses classic European devices to portray the Japanese as infantile and irrational, like all "Oriental" subjects. He expects that the irrational Japanese will require compulsion to do what's right for them, which is to adopt Europe's superior civilization: "to restore common sense to them can only be done with the use of force." According to him, external trade alone will not sweep aside the many restrictions on foreigners enshrined by the traditional Japanese order, such as forbidding the Europeans to roam freely in their cities, travel to the interior, or establish private relations with Japanese citizens. Only "external extraordinary circumstances"—as Goncharov euphemistically refers to belligerent tactics—can guarantee success. The solution is "to pit the threat posed by the Europeans against a desire for peace on the part of the Japanese."[44]

In other words, the solution is to act like Perry. This hope that Putiatin would abandon conciliatory measures and emulate the tactics of his bullying American rival was shared by some among the Russian squadron's elite crew. For example, the commander of the schooner *Vostok,* Voin Rimsky-Korsakov, favored this approach. Indeed, Putiatin reportedly did change his strategy toward "increased militancy" after reading in Shanghai newspapers about the efficacy of Perry's method. In McOmie's sarcastic quip, "This is indeed eloquent testimony to the 'Perry effect' on the Russian behavior towards the Japanese." As they circumnavigated the globe, the Russians learned the westerners' imperial tactics.[45]

It is nonetheless illuminating to reflect on Goncharov's pugnacious rhetoric in the context of the Russians' actual situation while in Japan. Perry sailed in, made his show of force, and swiftly left after barely a week, demanding that a reply be waiting for him upon his return. By contrast, the Japanese kept the Russians confined to their ships for three months. Granted, this was an improvement on how they had, half a century earlier, treated Kruzenshtern: he was confined for six months, his firearms confiscated.[46]

Still, in the course of three months, the *Pallada* Russians' only visit on land was to attend a ceremonial dinner at the residence of the governor of Nagasaki, Osawa Shitetsu, Lord of Bungo. They were shepherded to and from it. Religious idols were taken out of interiors, lest the gaze of red-haired "barbarians" defile them. (As late as the mid-nineteenth century, the Japanese and Chinese languages had no neutral term for "foreigners.") Buildings along their path were covered up lest they prove of reconnaissance value. Water and victuals were always brought to their ships. Hundreds of Japanese boats swarmed around to monitor their movements and prevent closer approach. Using a trick he learned from Perry, at some point Putiatin gave orders to shove them aside.[47]

The logistics of the Russians' presence in Nagasaki Bay were subject to endless negotiations as to which roadstead and which bay they would be allowed to use, and how close their ships could be to each other, to the shore, and to the Japanese boats. Just like Perry's obstreperous Americans, the Russians pushed for proximity but the Japanese vehemently denied it. Gorgeous, sun-drenched banks beckoned, but the Russians never set foot there. To appreciate the psychological effect of the Russians' sardines-in-a-can ordeal one need only note the contrast in the Ryukyu and Manila chapters, which describe the *Pallada*'s post-Japan course. There, Goncharov and his fellow Russians finally take a deep breath and relieve the accumulated stress by bushwhacking their way to picturesque picnic spots, hiking, sightseeing, and once again roaming freely.

But the reality of their Japanese sojourn was strict confinement and supervision. Goncharov compares his Nagasaki diary to "a prisoner's log." The monotony of the anchored existence even leads him at one low point to concede victory to Japan. A month into his stay, Goncharov takes stock of his paltry local knowledge. In his list, comestibles upstage the locals, and Japan as such is absent: "I know intimately Japanese pigs, elk, even crayfish, not to mention the Japanese themselves, but so far I have learned nothing about Japan." He makes a punning connection between the "Far" East—as East Asia in general and its Russian portion were called in Russia—and "extreme" boredom (using the Russian adjective *krainii* in both senses).[48]

On a psychological level, Goncharov's imperial swagger in the Japanese chapters might therefore be seen as a compensatory mechanism for relieving the pressures of his actual confinement. On the textual level, it masks the actual indignities the Russians were forced to suffer. Not that this excuses the swagger or lessens its social impact, but in this case, fantasies of projecting power were rooted in the reality of the Russians' relative powerlessness, or at least severe constraint, vis-à-vis both Japan and their stronger rival, the Americans. Often, the self-aggrandizement encountered in imperial travel writing provides, as literary scholar Steve Clark puts it, "aesthetic compensation for lack of actual political control."[49] Goncharov's forecast of a time when Europeans will go and do as they please in Japan springs from circumstances of their being manifestly unable to do so.

Clark uses this point to critique Edward Said's assumption of a strong link between imperial texts and the actual exercise of power. Indeed, Orientalism can be born of fear rather than confidence, an option Said does not consider. It can be a mask for insecurities or anxieties. However, such a mask can work, and likely did in this case. Though it may have been faked, the projection of European political mastery could still have a public life as a belief collectively held by readers. Whatever the psychological genesis of Orientalist poses, texts that projected them modeled for the public smug ways to think about and behave in the Orient.

Europeanization: Humanitarian Mission or Realpolitik?

Encounters with Japanese people time and again convince Goncharov of the European civilizing mission's excellent prospects. He emphasizes the powerful impression that the Russians' European customs make on the Japanese. Such imperial narcissism blossoms in much imperial travel writing, including accounts of the Perry expedition.[50] In Goncharov's travelogue, the Japanese "gape open-mouthed" at the wonders of the frigate. "A smile of delight and rapture" animates their faces at the sight of the Russian sailors' well-coordinated maneuvers. On Grand Prince Konstantin's birthday, when Russian crews on brightly decorated ships sing "God Save the Tsar," the Japanese onlookers, if we take Goncharov's word for it, stand a minute in astounded silence, then loudly express their "astonishment and rapture." Japanese rowers in boats encircling the *Pallada* "greedily grab" bread and money thrown to them from the deck.[51]

When a high-ranking Japanese delegation visits the *Pallada*, Goncharov assures his readers of the phenomenal impression the frigate and its European trappings make on the guests. Goncharov stresses the visitors' avid interest in all things Russian, which are clearly presented to them as European. In fact, their very ability to have such interest transforms the Japanese into Europeans in Goncharov's eyes: "One had to give them their due. They examined so thoroughly our ways that one could barely notice a difference between them and Europeans."[52]

Little did Goncharov know that some of the visitors found the frigate's interiors smelly and dank. One Japanese plenipotentiary compared meeting with Russian negotiators to "opening the door and receiving robbers." Goncharov was sure the Japanese loved Russian music played for their benefit, but some of them found it unbearable. Some Russian customs, such as shaking hands, appeared ludicrous to the Japanese. Later in Korea, Goncharov presumes it to be an awkward "Oriental compliment" when Koreans mistake Russians in their thirties and forties for sixty- or seventy-year-old men. In fact, to both the Japanese and the Koreans, the Russians simply look old. Though aware that the same thing may look different to different cultures, Goncharov does not always manage to keep this in mind.[53]

Goncharov's descriptions of social events paint a picture of friendly relations among Russian and Japanese elites. For an empire such as Russia that relied heavily on the coopting of peripheral elites, this transnational class amity augured well for the achievement of imperial objectives in Japan: the Russians and the Japanese could definitely do business together. Goncharov stresses the Japanese plenipotentiaries' thoroughly cultivated, "worldly" manners: politeness, dignified restraint, agreeable curiosity about their hosts. It is true that some eventually strike Goncharov as less polite, such as the supposedly "savage" Nakamura whose gruff bearings appear to the writer "animalistic," and the haughty translator Einosuke whom all the Russians seem to despise. But Goncharov gets along wonderfully with his favorite diplomatic counterpart, Kawaji. He appreciates Kawaji's pleasantries and aristocratic body language, so compatible with European manners. "And in what exactly is he not a European?" Goncharov asks, waving off the non-European habits he does indeed find in his favorite. He also respects the keen intelligence and perspicacity of the elderly Tsutsui—"even though he revealed his mind in artful dialectic aimed against us." Ultimately concluding that "intelligence is everywhere the same," Goncharov writes that "all smart people, just like all stupid people, are alike—irrespective of the differences in nationality, dress, language, religion, and even outlook on life."[54]

Treaty or no treaty, the Russians' display of Europeanness for the edification and pleasure of the Japanese is presented as already having a civilizing influence. At one point, Goncharov is captivated by a twenty-five-year-old youth, a symbol of the nation's future. Speaking halting English and sighing deeply, the young man confesses to an exultant Goncharov that "all he sees [of the Russians] leads him to raptures, and he would like to be a European, a Russian, to travel, and to take a peek at other places, if only at the Bonin Islands." The youth gratifyingly validates the Russians' cultural posture in Japan, which is to project Europeanness and Russianness as fundamentally the same.[55] As in Greater Europe's social circuits between Manila and Shanghai, the deep meaning of empire for Russia is a sense of belonging to Europe.

The episode with the precocious youth signals to Goncharov that Japan's Europeanization is a realistic goal. The Japanese themselves, if you only catch them off guard, admit to desiring it. "You poor thing," Goncharov muses to himself about the young man, "will you live to see the day when your compatriots, whether freely or compelled, let others come to them, or bring their own people to other places?"[56] According to the logic of this passage, even if compulsion proved necessary, making Japan European would not be a self-interested act of European aggression. It would merely correct a political aberration (Japan's senseless isolation), liberating Asians to pursue legitimate human needs, such as curiosity about the larger world.

On his way to dinner with the Nagasaki governor—in a passage deleted from some Soviet editions—Goncharov considers in detail the prospects for Japan's Europeanization. According to him, several obstacles bar the way. The first is the political impasse of Japan's decentralized rule, split among the shogun, the emperor, the Supreme Council, and lords (*daimyo*). The system makes any change unlikely, for all are afraid to take the first step. The second obstacle is the perpetuation of certain retrograde and barbaric customs such as hara-kiri, or ritual disembowelment. Goncharov is obsessed with hara-kiri just as the British were obsessed with the Indian practice of *sati* (widow self-immolation), or Russians with the Caucasians' blood feuds (*krovnaia mest'*). Such practices were seen as arresting social change and making "primitive" societies unviable, even as colonial rule often enshrined and widened their use. Japan's exposure to the Russians, Goncharov wagers, will help discontinue this brutal custom and teach the Japanese how to live "normally and rationally."[57] Primitive societies need Europe's help to save them from themselves. European intervention thus emerges as a humanitarian mission.

The greatest obstacle to Europeanization is the childishness of the Japanese, whom Goncharov infantilizes more than any other ethnicity in *The*

Figure 3.2. Goncharov among the Russian delegates in Nagasaki; he is the short figure dressed in light clothing. From *Dai Nihon komonjo. Bakumatsu gaikoku kankei monjo,* Vol. 2, 1910 (Tokyo: Tōkyō Teikoku Daigaku Bunka Daigaku Shiryō Hensangakari, 1910–present).

Frigate Pallada. Like children, he claims, they fear change, fail to comprehend their best interest, and rely on wishful thinking. He compares their seclusion policy to a schoolhouse prank: "it instantly crashed down at the appearance of the teacher. All that's left for them, helpless and alone, is to burst out crying and say, 'we are guilty, we're children!'—and to submit themselves, like children, to the grown-ups' direction."[58] Here, the humanitarianism of Europeanization shades into something like a punitive mission.

Indeed, the Russian bayonet, Goncharov writes, "though still peaceful and blameless, still a visitor, flashed in the rays of the Japanese sun, and the Japanese shores resounded with 'Forward! *Avis au Japon!*'" The persistent threat of violence implicit in the images of cannons and bayonets, layered onto images of children in need of a civilizing lesson, produces a most disquieting effect. The reference to the Russian bayonet ("*russkii shtyk*") likely echoes Pushkin's martial lines from his long narrative poem about the conquest of the Caucasus, "The Prisoner of the Caucasus." Goncharov thus menaces Japan with the fate of the Caucasus, which the Russian army was then in the process of subduing through bloody war.[59] The military cry that closes this passage—uttered in French, as if to highlight the Russian civilizers' European credentials—shows Goncharov to be more enthusiastic about militaristic imperialism than the average bureaucrat. As a literary man, he wasn't alone. In *A Writer's Diary* (a collection of pieces published between

1873 and 1881), Dostoevsky would later stoke fervor for the Russo-Turkish War of 1877–1878.

According to *The Frigate Pallada,* that Japan will be "opened" is beyond a doubt; it is merely a question of who will open it. The aura of inevitability, so characteristic of colonial writing, mitigates any ethical or political considerations. All that is left is to bolt for the finish line. Whoever does it, "it is fated that soon healthy sap will be poured into Japan's veins, which she suicidally let out of her body along with her own blood. And she grew decrepit in the debility and darkness of her pitiful childhood."[60] This gruesome allusion to hara-kiri suggests that loss of vital fluid has arrested Japan in perpetual childhood but has also made it into a kind of walking dead. Only an infusion of Europe's sap of life can animate the zombie country. Like any seductive metaphor, this is impossible to counter, for who would want a sick child to die? The pendulum swings back to the essential humanitarianism of the European intervention.

Who will provide these life-saving transfusions? Who will lead the Japanese from the error of their ways? It could be American industrialists, or—Goncharov impishly adds—"even . . . we!"[61] In volunteering Russia for this rescue mission, Goncharov assures his audience that it will be easy because the Japanese wish it. While the government dawdles, the people are ready; they are bored with the monotony of their self-enclosure. They crave novelty and contact with the outside world, ogle the Russian ships jealously, and swoop upon Russian trinkets. Under their mask of apathy, Goncharov detects talents, curiosity, and joy. All that's needed is to issue a call, and "the Japanese will run out of their prison." The conquest will thus liberate the Japanese from the fetters that hold them back. Goncharov is convinced that only the state's power prevents them from embracing Europe's material culture and its Christianity. He hopes that Russia will reintroduce Christianity to Japan, thus foiling the designs of western missionaries eyeing Japan from China, ready to pounce: "will God give us the chance to make the first modest step toward this?"[62]

But to combat the obstructionist state, military measures may be needed. As if to encourage them, Goncharov insistently points out Japan's weak defenses, such as poor fortifications, lack of large naval vessels, and laughably antiquated cannons. The American expedition judged these similarly. Goncharov stresses the deplorable condition of the Japanese army. Its soldiers are either effeminate or so old that "they can barely stand or see." He finds "almost not a single manly or energetic face, though there are plenty of intelligent and sly ones." Looking over the puny, sleepy-eyed, and poorly armed guards of Nagasaki, he wonders: "Can these really be soldiers?" He contrasts them with bayonet-bearing Russian soldiers, all vigor and discipline.[63]

Since it would take so little to get this mission accomplished, Goncharov explicitly calls for Russia's immediate forcible entry into Japan. On the path to humanitarian goals, violent means may apparently be necessary. Headed to an event meant to build bridges of amity—a ceremonial dinner with Japanese hosts in Nagasaki—the Russian guest contemplates a raid: "In the present moment [Japan] can be opened at once; it is so weak that it cannot withstand any war. But for that to happen, one should proceed the English way: enter Japanese ports, disembark without permission, and when they bar the way, start a brawl, then complain about the insult, and start a war. Or another way: bring opium, and when they try to restrict it, declare war just the same."[64] Despite his criticism of "the English way" in the Shanghai chapter, Goncharov here recommends it. Though his tongue-in-cheek tone shows he is not entirely serious about following the swashbuckling English too faithfully, Goncharov finds in their lack of squeamishness much to recommend.

The bold assault on Japan, Goncharov urges, must happen before Japan improves its army. Waiting any longer means letting the Japanese learn western military techniques. Should a military approach prove unworkable, Goncharov considers the range of other options. He settles on fomenting internecine conflict, that well-tested tactic of the Russian empire, as an effective Plan B. This is not the airy civilizing fantasy of a moony literary man, but hard, sinewy realpolitik.[65]

This approach perhaps seems necessary to Goncharov because Russia, as he argues in *The Frigate Pallada,* must regain its footing in imperialism's geopolitical race. What Susanna Soojung Lim calls an anxiety of lagging behind fills the travelogue. Goncharov thus applauds all instances when Putiatin takes a tough line with the Japanese officials—and he is not alone among Putiatin's high-ranking crew. Impatient with his admiral's strategy of "meekness and kindness," Goncharov prefers the occasional move "to scare them good and proper." Fed up with a tedious "comedy with the Japanese," as he terms the prolonged conciliatory strategy, he is euphoric when Putiatin finally decides to sail right to the seat of the shogunate in Edo, just as Perry did. His disappointment must have been equally strong when mollifying moves by the Japanese dissuaded Putiatin from carrying out this threat.[66]

Goncharov predicts that Japan will ultimately go the way of China, where Europe's plans have always been larger than just trade. The treaty ports, effectively Europe's domains within a decade, are the toeholds that will allow Europeans eventually to gain total control of Asia—making its future similar to the one Goncharov foresees for Africa in an earlier chapter. Such prognostication is meant to embolden Russia's imperialist resolve. Already in Shanghai the writer has been struck by the futility of China's efforts to restrain Europeans. Having expected limits on his movements, Goncharov delights that no one attempts to hinder his jaunts into the surrounding countryside, which soon becomes as familiar to him as St. Petersburg's environs. He mentions that Chinese law prohibits foreigners from venturing deeper into the Chinese hinterland than one day's round-trip from the ports. And yet he learns that the American consul (probably his Shanghai host Edward Cunningham), built a country home in the mountains eighty miles distant. The Chinese authorities apparently can do nothing about it. Nor are they able to enforce a prohibition on river trade with the interior, so the English are sending their opium ships directly to Beijing. The ultimate objective, as Goncharov understands it, is Europe's rule over all of China: "The Europeans increasingly do as they will, and Peking will learn about it only when the Europeans are at its walls, and when preventing the spread of foreign influence will be difficult."[67] For Goncharov, Russia's establishment of trade relations with Japan is, similarly, merely the first phase of a more ambitious imperial project.

Use It or Lose It

Artistic fantasy infuses Goncharov's first impressions of Japan. Of the graceful groupings of boats in Nagasaki's harbor and the wooded hills dappled with various shades of green, he writes: "All this was so harmonious, picturesque, and unlike reality that one wonders: Isn't this an image drawn from an enchanting ballet?" This passage blossoms into an extended landscape description, of a kind defined by Mary Louise Pratt as a "monarch-of-all-I-survey" scene, common in narratives of travelers' "discoveries."[68] A landscape so described is aestheticized and ordered spatially just like a painting (with details of background, foreground, and attention to size and symmetry). Rich materiality and dense semantic meaning, summoned through various artistic tropes, suffuse such passages. The scene tends to be a "broad panorama anchored in the seer" who projects a sense of mastery over the landscape, inherent in his ability to appraise it and, it is suggested, to possess it. As these seers tended to be men, Pratt considers the monarch-of-all-I-survey a gendered trope. Everything in such a scene is subordinated to the traveler's vantage point, with the implication being that he sees all there is to see. In short, such visions claim completeness of their spatial inventories, authoritativeness, and interpretive competence.[69] Here is Goncharov in his monarch-of-all-I-survey mode:

> What coves, nooks, and cool refuges of languor pattern the shores of the sound! Over there, a hill cuts through a ravine, which is wooded, dark like a corridor, and so narrow that it threatens any minute to crush the little village that hid itself deep inside it. Here, a tiny bay encircled by trees, a tranquil retreat, always dark and cool, where even the strongest wind ruffles the waves only ever so slightly. A boat pulled on shore safely rests there, one end submerged in the water, the other in the sand.
>
> On the left, a wide, long, and twisty gulf. . . . On the right, a tall hill with a sloping shore, that beckons one (*manit*) to climb it, despite the prohibition of the Japanese, up the green steps of the terraces and ridges. Beyond it, a row of low, carelessly scattered hills, then rather tall mountains, which peek through earnestly and sullenly, having stepped back, like grown-ups behind their children. Further along, a strait disappearing into the sea, with black rocks scattered on its luminescent surface. On the farthest plane, Cape Nomo appears in the bluish distance. . . .
>
> Everywhere, spurs and little promontories jut out, or clods of earth overgrown with greenery or trees. In places, such groupings of greenery and trees clump on the edges of the ravines, like gigantic bouquets of flowers. Everywhere, one sees a perspective, a picture, just like an artistically contemplated whimsy![70]

Goncharov is fully in command of this panoramic vista, his focus zooming in on a lonely boat or the ripple of a wave, then swiftly zooming out to the distant Cape Nomo. The wide angle of vision coincides with considerable depth, with hills layered upon hills and then mountains receding into the distance. Such free movement of the eye simulates the free movement of the viewer, training readers to expect unhampered motion in imperial spaces. This is, of course, a seductive illusion in Goncharov's case, since, as mentioned, a whole month passes before he sets foot on Japanese soil, and when he finally does, it is for a highly supervised and choreographed march to the Nagasaki governor's mansion—not at all a carefree nature hike. And yet, from the *Pallada*'s distant deck, he confidently judges the coolness and tranquility of various places—judgments that simulate experience, where in truth there is none.

This richly aestheticized scene abounds in anthropomorphic descriptions of the landscape (villages that "hide," "sullen" mountains that "step back behind hills"). Chance arrangements of nature are endowed with artistic intentionality (trees arranged like bouquets, an "artistically contemplated" picture). The scene comes across as an artfully designed stage set one could find in an "enchanting ballet." There is an ethics that comes with such a way of viewing, which has subtle relevance for imperial encounters: one enters stage sets with more impunity than social spaces. Indeed, no people appear anywhere in sight. The Japanese prohibition to enter is acknowledged, but no actual human presence intrudes on the eye's direct intercourse with the pleasing scene.[71] What's more, the landscape itself lures one to enter, the mountain ridges conveniently composing themselves into stairs.

This welcoming gesture of nature overrides the political injunction of the people. Later, when describing a dramatic Nagasaki sunset, Goncharov concludes that "this was all a painting, poetry—except that the Japanese and their [defense] batteries weren't any of that. No sunrays can help them." Japan as a social space loses unity. Goncharov extracts people from their habitat, estranging them from culture and history. He pits the prohibitions of the people against the invitations of the landscape. He has similarly endowed the southern African interior with magnetic powers that draw white colonists inward. It would seem that to heed such calls means simply to act on an aesthetic impulse, following the stirrings of a sensitive and receptive soul.[72]

Goncharov dismisses the activities of the Japanese people as feeble and out of sync with the environment. The land is good, but the people are bad. The sleepy "lack of movement" makes the sight of the bounteous shores "unpleasant" to Goncharov: "People appear rarely. No animals to be seen; only once did I hear a dog bark. No human bustle; few signs of life." Rhetorical austerity captures here the semantics of scarcity. The ornate style of nature descriptions—saturated with artistic tropes and adorned with a heavy weave of relative clauses—contrasts with the spare, telegraphic style of descriptions of social life. This life appears inadequate, stunted to Goncharov: "Is this how these shores should be settled? Where did the inhabitants hide? Why don't they throng on these shores? Why can't one see labor, bustle, noise, din, shouts, songs—in a word, ebullient life? . . . Why don't steamships traverse these broad bays, but instead some clumsy big boat drags itself around?" The abundance of nature is juxtaposed with anemic social life. This life's only sign is the beat of the drums assisting the lords' surveying of their domains—an audible signal of Japan's feudal backwardness. The shore appears to Goncharov "empty and lifeless." "How soon will it come alive, become settled?" he wonders.[73]

Pratt writes that this approach of equating the civilizing mission with an aesthetic project is used in colonial writing as an argument for the West's "benign and beautifying intervention." Natives and their land are there to be disposed of in European betterment projects. While in western narratives this message tends to remain implicit, Goncharov comes close to spelling it out. The problem, as he sees it, is that Japan is improperly "settled" and developed. It needs modern technology (steamships) and robust growth, neither of which its feudal system (Goncharov's characterization) can provide. Goncharov openly designates Europeans as better trustees of the Japanese land. Admiring a particularly magnificent bay near the first roadstead, he exclaims: "what a splendid suburb would spread itself out here if only the bay were in the hands of Europeans! Well, it will come, and maybe even soon."[74]

Landscape descriptions in the account of Perry's expedition offer an instructive contrast. While commanding an equally "monarchic" visual hold on the terrain, they lack some of the Russian travelogue's ulterior equivocations. They do not divorce people (human encounters punctuate the landscape descriptions) or their labor from the land, but show both in a perfect harmony that rivals that apex of the civilized world: England. Perhaps because all that Americans truly wanted was trade and refueling bases, not to settle or Europeanize Japan, civilizing scenarios are not prominent in the description of Perry's visit to Japan. The seer seems perfectly contented. No mental upgrades are needed:

> Fertile fields, expanding parks, bounded with plantations, and varied here and there with carefully arranged clumps of tress . . . terraces lifting their smooth surfaces above the other, in the richest and greenest verdure, and retired groves of deep shade, showed upon the acclivities of the nearer range of hills all the marks of a long and most perfect cultivation and presented a beauty of landscape unrivalled even by the garden-like scenery of England when clothed in

> the fresh charms of a verdant spring. . . . The high cultivation of the land everywhere, the deep, rich green of all the vegetation, the innumerable thrifty villages embowered in groves of trees at the heads of the inlets which broke the uniformity of the bay, and the rivulets flowing down the green slopes of the hills and calmly winding through the meadows, combined to present a scene of beauty, abundance, and happiness, which everyone delighted to contemplate.[75]

Goncharov, too, sees plenty of beauty. But either he does not perceive, or he guardedly obscures, any indication that the Japanese may be content with their country just as it is.

On the contrary, *The Frigate Pallada* keeps diagnosing Japan's problems and views the Japanese as completely unfit to solve them. When confronted about them, the Japanese offer the kind of bureaucratic runaround familiar to the Russians from their diplomacy: "The officials say that one needs to ask the governor, and that the governor will send the question to Edo, to the shogun, and that the shogun will send it to the Mikado in Miyako, and that the Mikado will send it to the Son of Heavens. There's no telling when we'll receive the answer!" The remedy for Oriental impasse is European efficiency. "This is practically a prison," Goncharov later complains about Japan, whose people in the meantime have slightly risen in his estimation. Still, "although the nature is gorgeous, and man is clever, adroit, and strong, so far he does not know how to live normally and rationally." The remedy for Oriental irrationality is European reason and norm.[76]

Arguments about the land's inadequate use or the ineptness of the Japanese contradict other facets of Goncharov's own portrayal of Japan. While viewing picturesque vistas, Goncharov repeatedly notes signs of intensive agriculture, such as "cultivated terraces that, like a gigantic green ladder, climb the entire mountain, from the sea waves to the clouds." Consistent with the strategy of minimizing human presence, residents appear only as "traces on the landscape," to use Pratt's term. "Entire mountains," Goncharov writes, "are sliced through with furrows running from top to bottom." As in China, he is impressed that "not an inch of uncultivated soil can be found." Feats of engineering have stemmed erosion and provided the water necessary for growing rice. A reader might understandably wonder: In this supposedly depopulated, dysfunctional country, bereft of active stirrings of life, who did all *this*?[77]

Just as his image of Asia is bifurcated—in precipitous decline, as European thinkers taught him, yet marvelously vibrant in his own experience of it—Goncharov's image of Japan is split. As always, he either does not perceive or does not acknowledge the contradiction. Thus on the one hand, his depiction of Japan is consistent with the classic colonial rhetoric of *terra nullius,* or empty land. A magical lubricant of colonial logic, this rhetoric encouraged projects of peopling these "empty" lands with Europeans. On the other hand, the abundant evidence Goncharov offers of busy human labor gives the lie to the *terra nullius* trope. If anything, this labor suggests *over*-population, since there would be no need to till mountains unless there were lots of hungry people determined to wrest food from any soil. But since, at that moment, the peasants and those they feed do not present themselves for Goncharov's gaze, they may as well not exist at all. Rhetorically, the space is open for European settlement. This time, imperial intrusion is recast as the righting of a balance between demography and environment.

Equally noteworthy are moments when Goncharov plummets from the pedestal of an aesthete to the perch of a grabby intruder. His fiery talk of the "ferule" of civilization in the first Japanese chapter, and the suggestive "stroking" of the Russian cannons, show the power intoxication that comes with contemplating a bending of Japan to Europe's will. This passage seamlessly segues to an analysis of Japan's natural resources, making for an unholy alliance of lofty cultural schemas and down-to-earth, pragmatic concerns. Goncharov introduces the mineral survey of Japan as a topic of disinterested, scholarly concern. As the last remaining blank space on the "geographical and statistical" map, Japan must, it seems, reveal its riches for the full accounting of the globe's resources.

Regardless of this scholarly rationale, the greed of a resource-hungry European laces the passage: "[Japan's] mountains—we already know—contain the best copper in the world. But we do not yet know if these mountains contain the best diamonds, silver, gold, topaz—and finally, that which is more precious than gold, the best coal, that most precious mineral of the nineteenth century." What began as innocent science shades into the pursuit of material gain. One can give the writer the full benefit of the doubt that in his mind the mining profits should increase the prosperity of Japan. Yet his breathless hope that these resources' likely extractors, Europeans, would also share in these riches is unmistakable. This sets *The Frigate Pallada* apart from the travel account of Kruzenshtern, who reported about various lands' natural resources in terms of provisioning ships rather than profitable extraction.[78] We also know—although Goncharov's readers didn't—that prospecting for resources indeed figured in the *Pallada* expedition's objectives. The schooner *Vostok* undertook a secret reconnaissance mission to Sakhalin, then an object of unreconciled Russian and Japanese territorial claims, where the Russian sailors found coal deposits and mined thirty tons of it.[79]

Goncharov often appraises Japan, and the colonial world in general, from the perspective of an imperial prospector. Nature is to be exploited, resources monetized. In that, *The Frigate Pallada* summons the "extractive vision" of the European "capitalist vanguard" that Pratt identifies in nineteenth-century travel writing about South America. In one 1820s British account of Colombia, for example, we read: "In that country there is every facility for enterprise, and every prospect of success: man alone is wanting to set the whole machine in motion, which is now inactive but which, with capital and industry, may be rendered productive of certain advantage and ultimate wealth." Like his British predecessor, Goncharov contrasts the land's value with the locals' sloth and views the Japanese landscape, to use Pratt's fitting phrase, as "a dormant machine waiting to be cranked into activity."[80]

Indeed, Goncharov presents imperial conquest as simply realizing the potentialities that would otherwise remain underutilized. His "landscanning European eye" detects "resources to be developed, surpluses to be traded, towns to be built."[81] Approaching Nagasaki, Goncharov can barely suppress his "vexation" that "nature, for its part, has done everything to enable man's creative hand to accomplish miracles, but man has done nothing." The ingenuity, intelligence, and civilizational advancement that went into establishing agriculture on steep mountains do impress Goncharov, but imperfectly:

> Here's a hill. However green and cozy, it lacks something. It should be crowned with a white colonnade with a portico, or a villa with balconies, a park, and paths trailing down. And there, a road leading down to the sea would be good, and a pier, where steamships would dock and people mingle. Here, on this high mountain, there should be a monastery with towers, cupolas, and a golden cross peeking from across the cedars. And there warehouses would fit nicely, with a forest of masts crowding in front of them. . . . "And what if we took Nagasaki from the Japanese?" I asked aloud, mesmerized by the idea of masts. Some laughed. "They don't know how to use this potential (*kak pol'zovat'sia*)" I continued, "What could this port

> be if others owned it? Look around! All the Eastern Ocean would liven up with trade." . . . I wanted to develop my idea of how Japan could link up its trade routes, through China and Korea, with Europe and Siberia, but we approached the shore.[82]

This is the classic Victorian ideology of improvement, which Goncharov would have imbibed in his English reading. Rooted in the Enlightenment idea of progress, by the early nineteenth century this ideology pervaded many spheres of human endeavor, from urban development, estate management, manufacturing, organization of labor, and schemes to eradicate poverty, to agriculture, transport, and landscape design. It held that it was everyone's moral duty to work on improving the social and material conditions of life through rational design and prudent care. As Sarah Tarlow explains, "improvement required active, directed effort: historical Progress was to be realized through the accumulation of numerous acts of Improvement." In the economic sphere, improvement assisted the rise of capitalism. In England's rural economy, for example, estates began to be viewed not simply as inheritances with a fixed income, but as investment opportunities.[83]

Improvement fever also ran high in zones of imperial activity. Daniel Defoe's *Robinson Crusoe*, for example, showed a remote non-European island "improved" by the rational and practical activities of a western castaway. The very idea of a civilizing mission is fundamentally one of improvement. Backward natives were to be uplifted; imperial peripheries were to be "developed" so as to generate profits. Convinced of the native inhabitants' incapacity or unwillingness to properly dispose of their own land, the Europeans felt entitled to expropriate it. *The Frigate Pallada* assures its readers that the Japanese don't know how to use their land. The Russians will come to the rescue.

To demonstrate the benefits of such stewardship of Japan, Goncharov's imagination builds up the landscape with modern structures and conveniences, European but also distinctively Russian (the monastery with golden cupolas and a cross). Christianization, technology, trade—Japan lacks what Europe can provide. In "improving" Japanese hills with European villas and imagining Japanese harbors as enlivened by trade, Goncharov indulges in the well-established trope of colonial writing Pratt describes as "industrial reveries." He thus participates in the tradition that produced, for example, this British vision of the Andes: "Gazing on the nearest chain and its towering summits, Don Thomas and myself erected airy castles on their huge sides. We excavated rich veins of ore, we erected furnaces for smelting, we saw in imagination a crowd of workmen moving like busy insects along the eminences, and fancied the wild and vast region peopled by the energies of Britons." In the same tradition, an American prospector, Perry McDonough Collins, gazed at Russia's landscape near Siberia's Lake Baikal and envisioned American steamers on the Amur River: "The scenery is picturesque, and nothing is wanting but an occasional steamboat puffing along, with more cultivation, scattered farm-houses, and pretty villages, to give it a strong resemblance to some portions of the Upper Mississippi."[84]

The aesthetics of the monarch-of-all-I-survey visions thus typically shade into the pragmatics of industrial reveries that make European presence indispensable. This is precisely how Goncharov justifies Russia's presence in Japan. Yet while his British counterpart speaks vaguely of the Andes someday animated by the "energies of the Britons," not specifying what this would mean politically, Goncharov blurts out that the Russians should actually take over Nagasaki. This leaves no doubt as to the political wellspring of his reverie. As he did in mentioning cannons as tools of civilization, Goncharov says more than is proper for glib colonial discourse. The images of superior arrangements thinly veil an intoxication with power. Though his comrades balk, what could be more natural in the context of Manila, Singapore, or Hong Kong? If the English can run Shanghai, why shouldn't the Russians run Nagasaki?

Goncharov finds these visions irresistible. Revisiting the same site later, he can only perceive it through his rose-tinted binoculars of progress: "I busied myself as last time—that is, I mentally furnished these hills and copses with churches, dachas, gazebos, and statues, and filled the waters of the bay with steamships and a thicket of masts. I peopled the shores with Europeans; I could just see the lady Amazons riding horses. And close to the towns, I dreamed of factories—Russian, American, English . . ."[85] Goncharov's land-scanning eye can see Japan only as a field of dreams, a future home of a Russian, with all the conveniences of European life. His rhapsody upgrades Japan at the same time that it upgrades Russia, finally in a respectable lineup of industrialized nations with enviable, thriving imperial outposts.

Far from idle fancy, such visions from travel literature had a way of becoming reality. Russian explorer Kruzenshtern mused in his travelogue about the annexation of southern Sakhalin from Japan, and it did indeed take place in 1875. Noting that region's abundant timber, arable land, and game, and the seafood of its Aniva Bay, he assessed its strategic importance. In nineteenth-century travel accounts, it mattered not only what a place was, but also what it could become: "If any safe harbor exists here, this bay would be extremely well calculated for an establishment of any active European nation, and might serve as a depot of European goods; as it would be perfectly easy to open a trade from hence with the Japanese, [Koreans], or Chinese. . . . Even Kamchatka may easily be supplied from thence with European articles." Kruzenshtern estimated the insignificant military resources that would be needed to chase the Japanese off the island. The American traveler Perry Collins, a fervid proponent of Russia's expansion in East Asia, argued that China's neglect of the Amur region, abandoned in "a wild state," gave Russia the moral and political right to annex it from China—the same principle that, in his view, justified European conquest and settlement of North America.[86]

Interestingly, Europeans themselves were at risk of expropriation if they did not exploit their imperial holdings robustly enough. "Use it or lose it" seemed to be the underlying principle of global imperial order. Kruzenshtern criticized the unprofitable colonial management of the Portuguese, especially in Macao, and recommended that some other European nation take it over lest it fall into Chinese hands. When the French similarly floundered on Mauritius, the English took possession of the sugar island. As far as Charles Darwin could see, this resulted in greater prosperity, excellent roads, and a seventy-five percent increase in sugar exports.[87] In *The Frigate Pallada,* the Britons' improvements in the life, infrastructure, and profitability of the Cape Colony prove to Goncharov that they deserved to own southern Africa more than the Dutch.

Manila also emerges in the travelogue as an underutilized resource, emblematic of Spain's imperial decline. Though sugar cane is abundant, no refineries have been built. Despite excellent soil and climate, much farmland remains uncultivated. While Spaniards lie about on their siesta, American capitalists rev up manufacturing in Manila. Goncharov is frustrated by the lack of basic amenities and the local administration's red tape. Today we would use the term Kafkaesque to describe the barriers he encounters to purchasing Manila cigars in the place identified as their global production center. Spain's neglect of the colony renders its proprietary claim precarious. Indeed, Goncharov reports that Spanish rule has been repeatedly challenged by the Chinese, Dutch, English, and even by Japanese pirates. He lends a sympathetic ear to a local Frenchman's wistful comment: "Ah, if only the Philippine Islands were in different hands! . . . What treasures one could derive from them." It may be that the prospect of European "improvements" posed a greater existential threat to the Japanese regime, but the Spanish one in the Philippines was not immune to it.[88]

Given Goncharov's high expectations of the benefits that could flow from the opening of Japan, it probably disappointed him later in life to see that Russia failed to use the country productively. George Lensen blames the dissolution of the Russian-American Company and the sale of Alaska to the United States in 1867 for the meager returns Russia realized. Russo-Japanese commercial relations, deemed by one Russian expert as late as 1883 to be "utterly insignificant," grew only in the early twentieth century. Since Russian businessmen did not flood into the recently opened "casket," in 1861 and 1878 the Japanese authorities, in an ironic reversal captured well by Lensen, sent their own western-style ships to gather nautical and geographical data along Siberian shores and to entice Russian customers with Japanese product samples. When they realized that the population of Vladivostok was less than forty-five hundred, their hopes for vibrant trade with Russian Siberia evaporated. Lensen reports that the Japanese were truly stumped that "the Russians, who more persistently than all others had clamored for trade, failed to take advantage of the opening of the country. . . . Above all, the inability of Russia to develop the much-vaunted commercial relations revealed to the Japanese Russia's backwardness and vulnerability in the Far East." The recognition of this vulnerability likely emboldened Japan's imperial designs, as Russia's ability to counteract them appeared weak. The risk of war with Russia lost its deterrent value for Japan, and by 1905 Japan's assessment proved correct. Thus, by the principle of use it or lose it, Russia itself seems to have lost in the end.[89]

Improving the Paradise

The Russians visited Manila after their departure from Japan in January 1854 because they needed supplies and repairs. At that point in the escalating Crimean conflict, Manila's neutrality guaranteed relative safety from Franco-British attacks. En route, they stopped by a peculiar place: the Ryukyu Islands, between southern Japan and Taiwan. Ruled by a king, the islands had maintained tributary relations with both China and Japan since the seventeenth century. Administratively, they were under the control of the Japanese lord (*daimyo*) of Satsuma. Japan used the islands as their entrepôt for trade with East Asia. Goncharov's initial glimpses of the islands recall his gaze on Japan. He again makes use of the conventions of landscape painting, presenting the place as a stage set. He projects the authoritativeness and assurance of the imperial seers Pratt describes.

But while Japan had its drawbacks, the Ryukyu Islands figure in the travelogue as a nearly perfect place. Surrounded by coral reefs, so bountiful that even local roads are paved with coral, mottled with flowering meadows, and bathed in the moist and aromatic warmth of the tropics, the islands, again, seem to beckon visitors "faster, faster, to the shore!" According to *The Frigate Pallada,* such invitations of nature were spoiled in Japan by people's disinvitations. On the Ryukyu Islands, by contrast, the Russians' relative freedom of movement is marred only by rather harmless guardians, later revealed to be spies, who follow their every step. The Russians manage to turn this nuisance into a symbiosis, using them as guides. Goncharov leans his hefty frame on one of them during a steep ascent.[90]

The Russian writer sets foot on the Ryukyu shore expecting to be impressed. He has read of the islands in the British explorer Basil Hall's hugely popular *Account of a Voyage of Discovery to the West Coast of Corea and the Great Loo-Choo Island in the Japan Sea*, which presents an image of an idyllic patriarchal society with a whiff of the classical golden age about it. Hall closes his volume with a "Brief Memorandum upon the Religion, Manners, and Customs of Loo-choo," followed by "Advice to a Stranger Visiting this Island." Because travel accounts did double duty as sources of gripping narration and of practical, actionable knowledge about the world, such combinations of ethnographic synopses and travel tips were not uncommon. In his "Memorandum," Hall describes the Ryukyuans' "mild and liberal" manners, offering examples of harmonious and respectful intercourse between classes and individuals. He stresses their nonviolence, which is a historical fact: they knew neither war nor firearms. Concluding that they are "considerably civilized," Hall notes: "We saw nothing like poverty or distress of any kind, every person we met seemed contented and happy." The Ryukyuans' only source of distress appears to be the presence of foreigners. As shown in earlier parts of Hall's travelogue, they use every available means of persuasion to keep intruders off the islands and away from the villages.[91]

Skeptical nevertheless about Hall's utopian account, Goncharov sets out to verify it—and to his surprise, finds Hall's main claims to be basically correct. If anything, the islands' charms have defied Hall's powers of description. Goncharov is particularly delighted with the islands' patriarchal mode of life. The young show respect to venerable elders; modesty, decorum, and simplicity of manners reign supreme. In an erasure of history typical of colonial texts, Goncharov is sure that absolutely nothing has changed here "for two millennia." For Goncharov, the Ryukyuans are not heirs of history but "children of nature"—a reductive phrase that imperial ideologues are fond of applying to subsistence societies.[92] To Goncharov's eyes, this is indeed a timeless Utopia.

After meeting a local missionary, Dr. Bernard Jean Bettelheim, he tempers this hyperbole somewhat. Their conversation resembles one between the Pollyannish Chichikov and the malcontent Sobakevich from Nikolai Gogol's *Dead Souls*. While Goncharov finds Basil Hall's account "too modest" as checked against reality, Bettelheim discredits it with his own knowledge of pervasive spying, alcoholism, and gambling among the locals and his experience bearing the brunt of their violent tempers on his own skin. Though this torrent of criticism gives Goncharov pause, he ultimately distrusts Bettelheim, remembering that local men described him, in English, as a "bad man, very bad man!" (Perry likewise found Bettelheim to be inept and widely hated.) Any "sins" the Ryukyuans may have appear to Goncharov fairly "miniature." Though he ends up distrusting both Hall and Bettelheim, he continues to paint the islands in the best light. Utopia this may not be, but it looks to Goncharov like a gorgeous place with an enviably harmonious way of life and a perfectly content population. Such impressions were widely shared by nineteenth-century visitors to the islands.[93]

Goncharov also backs up Hall's observation that the one source of anguish for the islanders is the presence of foreigners. The Ryukyu people do not bar the way, as the Japanese did, nor do they hurl rocks, as the Russians will soon experience in Korea. They simply drop what they're doing and run. In vain do the Russians gently beckon. Shopkeepers abandon their wares at the approach of the Russians. Those suddenly accosted slink away or cover up their faces. When the Russians enter people's homes, feeling entitled to gratify their curiosity about private interiors, in line with the Europeans' custom, the inhabitants abandon them. The guards / spies shadowing the Russians send advance warnings to villages ahead. They are empty when the Russians enter, their temples shuttered against the desecration by nonbelievers. (The Ryukyuans shrank just as much from the Americans.) The Russians elicit, as Goncharov puts it, "a feeling of instinctive terror." So he struggles in the narrative to mitigate the resulting unpleasantness, searching for explanations for this extreme unsociability, and ultimately blaming it on Japan's pernicious influence.[94]

Nonetheless, Goncharov regards the inhabitants not as "savages," but as a people with "a fully developed conception of religion, of the duties of man, and of goodness." He applauds the absence of such signs of depravity as books and gunpowder.[95] Given that Greater Europeans who peeked into these islands were bringing both, would Goncharov advocate limiting such contacts, to save the enchanting islands from modernity? Or must the instinctive dread of foreigners be broken, to accustom the population to the leash of European progress? Given the islanders' contentment and their advanced material and social existence, what possible reason could there be to create needs that hinge on making them unhappy with the good things they do have? Must they be forced to abandon timeless Utopia and enter (European) history?

Predictably, for a writer whose mental templates linked progress to the spread of European civilization, Goncharov answers this question in the affirmative. Yet what would "progress" entail in the case of the Ryukyu people, with whose condition, unlike that of the Japanese, the Russian author seems rather satisfied? What do they stand to gain from Europeanization? Goncharov entertains this question while strolling through the Ryukyu capital, Naha:

> This is not the life of savages—filthy, vulgar, lazy, and wild—but neither is this the kingdom of spiritual life. Signs of enlightened existence are lacking. Well cultivated fields, clean abodes, orchards, an abundance of fruits and vegetables, a profound peace that reigns among people—all this proves that labor has brought life to the ultimate level of material well-being; that cares, passions, and interests do not transcend a few mundane needs; that the mind and the spirit are still frozen in a sweet youthful dream, like in ancient kingdoms of shepherds; that this life has reached the level at which the kingdom of spirit may begin, but hasn't yet. . . . But everything is ready; at one door stands religion, with the cross and the rays of light, gently awaiting the youths' awakening, at the other door stand the people of the United States, with paper and woolen fabrics, rifles, cannons, and other tools of the newest civilization.[96]

When observing the Japanese, Goncharov discerns, or perhaps concocts, their hidden desire for openness to Europe. When observing the Ryukyuans, he fails to detect, or concoct, any need for it. The Ryukyu shrink from the bearers of European enlightenment as from the plague. They must be *made* to need it, however, since, as a European, Goncharov considers it a natural and universal stage of human civilization. He relegates considerable evidence of Ryukyuan material prosperity and moral advancement—both of which cast in unflattering relief quite big sections of nineteenth-century Europe—to the mundane, material end of the spectrum. Its opposite end is a "spiritual" realm, into which the Ryukyuans have apparently not strayed, but which they must be helped along to reach, for the sake of the proper unfolding of Eurocentric conceptions of human history. And so, even a paradise may use improvement after all.

Such schemas used to get better traction when the focus was on societies more easily construed as "primitive." But Goncharov describes the Ryukyuans as a fairly advanced political and socially stratified society, a full-fledged "people" (*narod*), with developed forms of culture and religion. It is unclear on what basis Goncharov infers their lack of enlightenment. Nor is it easy to imagine how, not knowing the language and lacking access to obliging native informants, he can so confidently evaluate their spiritual condition. The problem appears to be that the Ryukyuans' spirituality and enlightenment are not of the European variety, the only one that truly matters. Admiring an elegant and solidly built arched bridge, Goncharov is baffled as to how these "children of nature" could construct this marvel of engineering with "no one" (read: no Europeans) having helped them.[97] How can a bridge that is impressive by European standards have been constructed without Europeans? This is a classic moment of Eurocentric universalism coming into collision with material evidence of its empirical constraints. As is typical of *The Frigate Pallada*, this collision does not lead to any intellectual, logically consistent resolution.

Equally typical, Goncharov muddies the water further by failing to project a coherent vision of European civilization's vaunted virtues. Colonial discourse waxes in his travelogue just as it shows signs of exhaustion, anticipating the more ambivalent, fractured approaches to empire of the late Victorians (among them Anton Chekhov, in the Russian context).[98] Goncharov's mention of US rifles and cannons subverts his claim of European civilization's wonderful "new tools." Do we sense resentment that the Ryukyuans might somehow evade the steamrolling progress of Europeanization? Or could this be a veiled complaint that certain less crass and materialistic empires (such as Russia) ceded the task of civilizing the world's unfortunates to peers with lesser spiritual resources (the Americans)? Either way, Europeanization is shown to be happening, and the Americans appear to be the most likely purveyors of their questionable civilizing product to the Ryukyuans.

The Russians missed Perry's Americans on the Ryukyu Islands by only two days. Along with a couple of sick sailors, the Americans left behind a piece of paper that nonchalantly announced to all the world's nations that might chance to come by that, in view of some concocted grievance against Japan, the United States took the Ryukyu under its "protection." Goncharov seems amused by the Americans' naive faith in such virtual ownership.[99]

Such claims of possession—typically as flimsy as a plaque nailed to a random tree, shrugged off by native inhabitants with perfect unconcern—were common imperial practice. Matthew Perry took "possession" of the Bonin Islands by affixing such a plaque and burying a bottle with a piece of paper proclaiming Peel Island a US colony. Needless to say, the inhabitants were neither consulted nor informed about becoming United States subjects. The British later politely informed Perry that the Bonin Islands already belonged to them. Perry did indeed find Britain's copper plate affixed to a different tree, but finding no signs of British colonization, he decided to claim the island anyway, putting into practice the use-it-or-lose-it rule of empires. Perry reports that Captain Lutke of the Russian Navy made similar acts of "possession." Indeed, since the late eighteenth century, Russian ships plying the North Pacific planted metal plaques with inscriptions "Land under Russian Rule" on "virtually every attractive cove they came across."[100] Although Goncharov presents the Americans' chutzpah sarcastically, these "blessed islands" are so lovely that at one point he declares the Americans "absolutely right" to take them in possession.

Moreover, much as he likes to expatiate on the blessings of European spirituality, Goncharov again plummets from his lofty pedestal to the kind of crass materialism he derides in the Americans. As elsewhere in the travelogue, economic interests lurk just behind altruistic pronouncements. Goncharov reports that the king of Ryukyu delivers to its Japanese lord a tribute in kind worth 200,000 rubles (note the helpful currency conversion). Goncharov assures his readers that these fertile islands can bring income five times that amount. He lists attractive crops and products: rice (far superior to the Japanese kind), tobacco, amber, fabrics, and sake. According to Goncharov, the Ryukyuan king tried to renounce his Japanese overlord but failed. Goncharov stops short of recommending that Russians take over the islands. Yet he models a way of thinking about them as a resource to be utilized—or what Edward Said calls a "realm of possibility"—and a staging ground for "fortune enhancing" activities. Indeed, Putiatin asked the Ryukyuans to open trade with Russia. Like his proposals to the Chinese in Canton, this offer was summarily rejected.[101]

Goncharov claims not to be sorry to leave the Ryukyu Islands. One wonders if seeing the Russians' commercial and social overtures shunned plays any role in that. Climbing back onto his pedestal, he ponders the reasons for his ultimate disinterest in the place: "Nature alone, and animalistic, if original, forms of life will not fulfill a person or absorb one's attention. A great emptiness remains. In order to experience deeply the new that is thoroughly dissimilar from anything that is one's own, it is necessary that, for comparison, a parallel developed life be in existence." This is a put-down of the Ryukyuans, to be sure. But viewed in light of the travel-writing conventions of the time, it is also a rare admission of the incomplete knowability of societies very different from one's own, and of the writer's imperfect resources to bridge such gaps. This is not the first time Goncharov reflects upon such limitations. "However great one's knowledge of the human heart or experience," he writes in an earlier passage on Japan, "it is difficult to operate according to customary laws of logic where a key to a nation's worldview, morality, and customs is missing—just as it is difficult to speak its language while lacking access to grammar and lexicon." Had he only taken these scattered insights as his guiding principles, *The Frigate Pallada* would be a very different book.[102]

A Clash of Cultures and Its Perils

High political stakes depended on the Russians' ability to bridge such gaps in Japan. How did the cultural divide figure in Russo-Japanese interactions and diplomatic protocols? To what extent did it shape political outcomes?

According to *The Frigate Pallada,* the Russians were stymied by Japan's pomp, Byzantine bureaucracy, and red tape. No gift can be accepted without a superior's permission—not even an empty bottle. Without the imperial capital's authorization, the governor of Nagasaki will not accept official Russian correspondence that communicates even so much as the purpose of their visit. "The reply from Edo has not been received" is the maddening response

Figure 3.3. The Russians were puzzled by the Japanese tradition of presenting official documents in several boxes of decreasing size and silk wrappings. From *Dai Nihon komonjo. Bakumatsu gaikoku kankei monjo,* Vol. 3, 1911 (Tokyo: Tōkyō Teikoku Daigaku Bunka Daigaku Shiryō Hensangakari, 1910–present).

to the most mundane of questions, to the point of becoming a comedic device. Important correspondence is locked in six boxes of graduated size and, for reasons inscrutable to the Russians, wrapped in swathes of silk. (The Russians must have been unfamiliar with the Japanese tradition of *furoshiki,* or ceremonial cloth-wrapping.) To prevent the Russians from setting up a chronometer on a rock sticking out of the water, the Japanese sneakily prop up a tree there, so it resembles the shore which the Russians promised not to trespass. Goncharov is amused by this "farce."[103] Tedious negotiations about procedure and etiquette delay the simplest of tasks. These are mostly described with wry humor, enlivening what comes off as dry ethnography in travelogues written with less flair.

Although Goncharov does not discuss it, mutually agreed-upon fakery was an integral part of diplomatic maneuvers. Lensen notes that "the Japanese officials feared their own government more than they feared the Russians. They were less afraid of opening their country than of being suspected of not having exerted enough effort to prevent it." The Japanese translators "would purposefully distort, modify, and soften" many of the Russians' statements for the official reports.[104] The Russians protected their Japanese hosts by making it seem that Russian concessions were hard won. The two sides would sometimes prearrange questions and answers in such a way as to absolve the Japanese negotiators of any dereliction of duty. Records of these staged "negotiations" would then be passed on to Japan's higher authorities. Professional solidarities coalesced transnationally. This was a diplomatic tango with quite ingenious lunges.

At the same time, the Russians realized quickly that the Japanese did not negotiate from a position of strength. "They are ashamed," Goncharov writes, that Japan's people should see their government as too weak to enforce its own orders. "It is impossible to deal with them," he complains. "They procrastinate, act cunningly, lie, and then refuse. One pities them too much to beat them." He describes as pathetically touching the Nagasaki governor's efforts to puff himself up in a full display of Oriental self-importance, only to have his carefully assembled pose deflated by the news that, contrary to his injunction, the Russians will sail right into Edo to deliver their letters should he decline to accept them. The interactions painted in *The Frigate Pallada* show Russian pity for Japanese weakness and condescension to the face-saving needs of a cornered adversary.[105]

Although the Russians knew to expect the formality of Japanese ceremonies, they seem poorly prepared for its extreme degree. It takes two days to reconcile Japanese etiquette with Russian customs before the meeting at the Nagasaki governor's mansion, a task for which Goncharov was personally responsible. The Russians grow thoroughly exasperated; the Japanese envoy breaks into a sweat. The Russians refuse to sit on their heels during the visit, as is Japanese custom, because their limbs are not flexible enough and their clothes are too constraining. When the Japanese suggest putting legs off to the side, the Russians lose patience: "And maybe we leave our legs behind on the frigate?" They fulminate about having to specify the precise place where Japanese officials will be seated while on the Russian frigate: "they can sit where they please . . . they may climb the tables if they so like." Unperturbed, the Japanese translator demands that a drawing be prepared.[106]

Chafing under his official burden, Goncharov exclaims: "Well, be so good as to say how is one to deal with such people? Serious matters await discussion, after all. Lord give us patience! This is what comes from seclusion. You fall to utter childishness without meaning to." Goncharov begs his

Russian readers to commiserate. "You in Europe worry about whether to be or not to be," he notes, "and over here we struggled whole days with the question of whether to sit or not to sit, to stand or not to stand." In the end, the ceremony's minutiae are set forth in a written scroll. Goncharov could not have guessed that, in just six years, Japan would open its first European hotel, furnished with a wine cellar and a billiard table. In 1889, it would become the first constitutional state in Asia. In 1905, it would militarily defeat the Russian empire.[107]

Although Japanese customs are the target of Goncharov's ridicule, some of the Russians' behaviors may appear equally comical today. Their insistence on using chairs proves a big sticking point in the logistics of this diplomacy. Having firmly rejected sitting on tatami mats, the Russians bring their own chairs from the frigate to the Nagasaki governor's mansion. This forces the Japanese to erect platforms on which to sit, so as not to be placed too low vis-à-vis the Russians. Far from entirely comfortable in their chairs and tight parade uniforms, the Russians have trouble reaching the refreshments placed on the floor in front of them. During the most active phase of negotiations, in January 1854, the Russians ferry chairs to and from the frigate for each meeting. The Japanese refuse to store the chairs, in case damage by fire or rats makes them responsible for these exotic items. The Russians solemnly release their hosts of such liability, to no avail. During the initial reception at the governor's, the Russians also refuse to take off their footgear, as is proper in Japanese interiors—but in order not to offend their hosts, they place specially sewn calico covers over their shoes. As he shuffles through the corridors of the governor's palace, Goncharov keeps losing his shoe covers, thus imperiling the success of Russian state diplomacy with his clumsiness.[108]

While regaling his readers with such slapstick, Goncharov is at the same time noticeably reticent about the actual content of the discussions with the Japanese. He refers to a "matter" at hand often enough, which clearly involves trade, but he discloses neither specifics nor the full array of Russian demands. Much ado is made of Nesselrode's letter to the Council of Shoguns, but its contents are not revealed. Goncharov chatters about his interactions with Japanese plenipotentiaries, but keeps the discussions' political cards close to his chest. As Putiatin's secretary, he knew well what was on these cards. Indeed, his active role in the negotiations led the Japanese to suppose that he was Putiatin's main adviser. But Goncharov's readers learned little about the political goals that took the Russians to Japan, drowned as they were in amusing scenes of social interactions.[109]

Figure 3.4. To the puzzlement of the Japanese, the Russians carry chairs to an official meeting. From *Dai Nihon komonjo. Bakumatsu gaikoku kankei monjo,* Vol. 2, 1910 (Tokyo: Tōkyō Teikoku Daigaku Bunka Daigaku Shiryō Hensangakari, 1910–present).

Mutual entertaining supplied useful material for this sort of amusement. Upon the *Pallada*'s return from Shanghai, on January 12, 1854, the Japanese again host a reception in honor of the Russians. Goncharov is one of only three people assisting Putiatin in a separate dining room with two top Japanese officials. As he confesses in his travelogue, he experiences a minor crisis when handed chopsticks: "Oh well, I guess no dinner for me." His desperation is shared by the ship captain, Unkovsky, who gloomily inspects his chopsticks. Noticing their consternation, the Japanese hosts have a good laugh. Fortunately, spoons and forks, borrowed from the Dutch, are brought to the rescue. Unsweetened tea, unsalted rice, and lack of bread are notable hardships for the Russian diners, but ultimately bearable ones. However, Possiet is unnerved at realizing he has just consumed "raw fish" (sashimi). The scene recalls the first feast at the Nagasaki governor's, where Goncharov is similarly taken aback by candied carrots, a vegetable not put to confectionery use in Russia. Open-minded gourmand that he is, he tastes them, guided by a Russian folk proverb according to which, if sugared, even a shoe sole can be eaten.[110]

At the banquet in January 1854, having cautiously inspected and nibbled the first three dishes, Goncharov abandons all "analysis" and wolfs down the remaining ones. While they welcome hot sake in conclusion to the meal, the Russians balk at hot water that follows. What persuades Goncharov not to abstain from so plain a drink is a disinclination to mar the authenticity of dining in Japanese style. But when tea finally comes with a clove at the bottom of a teacup, this proves too great a violation of the well-developed Russian tea protocol, and prompts Goncharov's mental remark: "what barbarity, and in a country of tea at that!" Unbeknownst to him, his Japanese counterpart is similarly unimpressed with the Russian tea served on the *Pallada:* "The leaves are coarse and boiled dark, and [taste] like medicine." However, the Japanese rave about the excellent quality of sugar the Russians serve with their tea. Barring the clove-flavored tea, the Russians are pleased with the experience (though small Japanese portions tended to leave them, just like Perry's men, still hungry).[111]

The Japanese hosts serve the Russians traditional Japanese fare. However, when planning a reciprocal dinner for the four Japanese plenipotentiaries, to take place three days later on the well-scrubbed frigate, the Russians conclude that traditional European fare would be too much of a shock to the Japanese system. They hybridize their menu with Japanese culinary customs they have observed during their own visit. They lay out chopsticks instead of forks and knives, replace bread with all-you-can-eat rice, and—most comically—serve soup in teacups. The menu leans heavily on fish, but, to the Russians' surprise, the guests—clearly more venturesome than their hosts gave them credit for being—request meat. They seem to find lamb pilaf very tasty. Lower-class guests receive parting gifts meant to solidify their appreciation of Russia's and Europe's attractions: elegant boxes of confections, pictures of Moscow, St. Petersburg, and Russian troops, and images purchased in London of European women's heads. "New sighs of pleasure and astonishment!" reports a self-satisfied Goncharov. How surprised the Russians would have been to learn that the Japanese delegation spent its entire visit in a cold sweat, fearing that at any minute they might be abducted or attacked by the Russians.[112]

These moments of meaningful cultural contact—so lacking on the Ryukyu—do leave Goncharov with important insights about Japan. In the course of his work, he develops friendly relations with some of the translators. The positive progress in negotiations also improves Goncharov's disposition. Official functions, for all their ceremonious pomp, seem to warm both sides to each other. Genial toasts are raised, flattering compliments exchanged. The senior plenipotentiary Tsutsui welcomes the rapprochement between the peoples of Russia and Japan, formerly so alien and distant. Grateful for his expressing so well the friendly sentiments they also share, the Russians say they consider Japan to be East Asia's most highly developed nation. "We parted the best of friends," Goncharov writes. The Japanese negotiators also draw up warm accounts of these interactions, being pleasantly surprised to find a common humanity with the Russians.[113]

The typical engine of Goncharov comedy is to reduce Japanese customs to sheer nonsense. Yet to his credit, he also exhibits tolerance and understanding. He eventually admits that suspending "European logic" in favor of its "Far Eastern" variant helps make comprehensible much that had seemed nonsensical. He at times recognizes that the Japanese possess a form of rationality rooted in the particularities of their historical experience and geographical location. Their frustrating habit of temporizing and extreme caution, he concedes, does make sense in dealings with Europeans, from whom the Japanese had after all seen "much evil." Chairs are called for in cold Europe, whereas the custom of sitting on mats, he comes around to admitting, is understandable in Japanese homes designed as refuges from heat. And given that food is laid out on the floor, it makes sense to remove shoes to keep it clean.[114]

Goncharov typically uses the ritual of Japanese ceremonies, which he finds ludicrously pompous, as proof of the general silliness of the Japanese. Yet in more generous moments, he resists his own urge to condemn an entire culture on this account. Rather than an expression of fear or groveling, respect for elders and superiors sometimes strikes him as admirable and sincere. Regarding the "prostrations" of Japanese subordinates, Goncharov interprets them as "an Oriental ballet, or at any rate a spectacle enacted for our sake." As such, this choreographed display is not indicative of normal daily interactions between Japanese people. Nor is this ceremony devoid of a certain beauty. The formal attire of Japanese plenipotentiaries may be utterly impractical, designed only to "sit and look important" (*vazhnichat'*), yet it possesses its own statuesque grandeur, and thus serves its purpose.[115]

Moreover, Goncharov eventually needs no recourse to "Far Eastern logic" to surmise that delaying the Russians, far from Oriental thick-headedness, is a sensible tactic to prevent them from encountering the Americans, then present in Edo. Although this was not known to Goncharov, the delays also had other reasons. Unprecedented and time-consuming consultations among different classes, clans, and professions preceded Japan's decision to appease, rather than oppose, the foreigners. Incidentally, this hardly fit the stereotype of Oriental despotism, to which the traditions of Russian autocracy were in fact closer.[116]

On occasion, Goncharov presents cultural difference as a matter of cultural gradient. He reminds his readers that Europeans of yore also rejected everything new, burning astronomers at the stake. Some of Asia's current customs resemble Russia's own from times past. Goncharov knows that his compatriots are shocked to see the Japanese share food from their plates with servants and openly pack leftovers to take home to kinsmen and domestics. But he reminds his readers that only a few decades earlier, Russian gentry did the same. Such customs, Goncharov claims, entered Russia from its "Asian cradle" and still persist among lower classes. Observing his hosts, he thinks of Russian proverbs that must have been born in Asia. In his view, the notion of a cultural gradient carries a comforting message for the Japanese. Ultimately, the wrenching process of westernization they now face is what Russia, as a more mature historic entity, went through itself, beginning in the time of Peter the Great, Russia's tsar westernizer. With paternal solicitude, Goncharov advises that the pain will pass and the gain will be worth it.[117]

But Goncharov is reckless about the implications of this parallel. He does not foresee that westernized Japan will rise to the status of an imperial rival in the way that westernized Russia has come to rival its European teachers. He thus paints what is clearly Japan's military reconnaissance as the naive curiosity of children, which the Russians are only too glad to satisfy. The Russians happily answer their hosts' questions about the frigate and its armaments, and about navigation, sailing times, itinerary, the size and composition of the crew, and Russian ranks. They brag about cannons, rifles, and the new English aiming equipment, untroubled by Japanese scribes taking feverish notes and making detailed sketches. "Their curiosity had much that is childish and naive," Goncharov himself naively concludes.[118]

In a sketch written twenty years later, Goncharov describes how the Japanese helped build a new schooner for Putiatin after a ship-destroying tsunami stranded him in Japan. Putiatin based it on plans he found in an issue of *The Naval Review* (*Morskoi sbornik*) salvaged from the shipwreck. (The same journal, produced by the Ministry of the Navy, would later print numerous sketches from *The Frigate Pallada*.) This was Japan's first exposure to modern western shipbuilding techniques. The Russians essentially trained some two hundred Japanese carpenters and artisans, who kept detailed technical records of the construction. They went on to produce six exact copies of the Russian schooner by the order of the Japanese government, and later joined the Shogun's navy. Lensen calls them "the fathers of the shipbuilding industry in modern Japan." The Russians were also forced to leave in Japan the cannons salvaged from the shipwreck. The Russian emperor later formally bequeathed them to the Japanese government in appreciation for the help rendered to the stranded Russian crew.[119]

The historic irony for the Russians is that, just half a century later, Japan, whose fleet did not exist in 1854, would sink the Russian fleet in the 1905 Battle of Tsushima. The Russo-Japanese war earned Russia the ignominious distinction of being the first European power to lose to a modern Asian one. Among the war trophies won by Japan was the cruiser *Pallada*—a younger cousin of Putiatin's *Pallada*—which the Japanese torpedoed and sank in 1904.[120] Lensen goes so far as to suggest that Goncharov's travelogue played a role in this defeat. Portraying the Japanese as "childish, effeminate, and militarily incompetent," he writes, created an impression that Japan's military prowess was negligible. Lensen concludes that the writer's mocking and patronizing attitude, amplified by the travelogue's popularity, "contributed no doubt to the unfortunate failure of the Russians in later years to take the Japanese seriously." *The Frigate Pallada,* he argues, fed the pernicious stereotype of the Japanese popular at the turn of the century, according to which they could be sunk merely by having "hats thrown on top of them" (*shapkami zakidat'*). Indeed, a simple Russian sailor's wisdom that Goncharov put through the loudspeaker of *The Frigate Pallada* was that no rifles were needed to defeat the Japanese—"a thick piece of rope would be enough."[121]

Following the Meiji Restoration, Japan played well the cards it had been dealt from the European deck, and extended its imperial reach over much of East Asia and the Pacific. Forcing Korea, in 1876, to open its ports to Japan and accept a trade treaty at gunpoint was one such Perry-like tactic. While initially focused on trade, Japan soon revealed its expansionist ambitions, establishing colonial enclaves in Korea, Taiwan, and China. Trade as a prelude to colonization was a conceptual schema as presented in *The Frigate Pallada*; Japan implemented it as a strategy. It annexed in quick succession the Kurile, Bonin, and idyllic Ryukyu Islands, and extended its "protectorate" over Taiwan. After the Sino-Japanese War of 1894–1895, Japan wrested control over Korea from the Qing empire. It installed formal colonial rule in 1895 in Taiwan, and in 1910 in Korea. Resurgent Japan emulated European styles of colonial rule in those newly acquired dominions, systematically exploiting their human and material resources to soon rival the western empires themselves. The "locked casket" with the lost key would become, as Lensen put it, "a Pandora's box" for Perry's and Putiatin's descendants. A target of Greater Europe's patronizing imperial nations, Japan soon became their *enfant terrible*.[122]

Prospecting Korea

Just as he was prescient in his comments on globalization, Goncharov identified Korea, which the Pallada visited in the spring of 1854, as the arena of imperial activity it was to become two decades later. Historically linked through a tributary system to China's emperors, Korea became a target of resurgent Japan in the 1870s and of Russia two decades later. Their conflict over Korea became a leading cause of the 1904–1905 Russo-Japanese War. But already in the 1850s we see *The Frigate Pallada* urging Russians to stake their claim. Indeed, although Goncharov does not mention it, Putiatin sent an official letter to Korean authorities proposing trade with Russia. In the course of his later diplomacy in East Asia, he made several visits to Korea.[123]

Headed north to Siberia, the *Pallada* briefly surveyed the Korean shore. As Susanna Lim argues, Russians mentally divided Asia into three parts: the Orient controlled by Western Europeans (*their* Orient), Russian Siberia (*our* Orient), and the as-yet-unclaimed Orient, to which East Asia then belonged. As part of that unclaimed third category, Korea appears to Goncharov ripe for the picking. His recommendation to annex Korea is accompanied by assurances of easy success. He emphasizes that although Korea observes rituals connected to its nominal status as China's vassal, it effectively operates as an independent state. Previous incidents make Goncharov confident that the Qing government would not lift a finger to defend Korea in the event of European intervention. This is meant to allay the perpetual worry of Russian foreign policy in Asia: the risk of antagonizing China.[124]

When the Russians disembark, the Koreans—whose seclusion policy ended only in 1876—flee in horror, just like the Ryukyuans. They ask if the Russians are northern or southern "barbarians"; the Russians ignore the question. Goncharov finds the Koreans to be less advanced than the Ryukyuans or the Japanese, although he is aware that the coastal communities the Russians visit are mostly populated by lower classes. Curious

Koreans touch the Russians' hair, white skin, and clothes, and reportedly fall prostrate at the sound of a piano. Like the Ryukyuans, they desperately try to keep the Russians away from their villages.[125]

But the Russians, armed with hunting guns, are not to be deterred in their sightseeing. As on the Ryukyu Islands, they barge into Korean homes as if they were open-access museums. These disturbing scenes resemble intrusions described in Alexander Pushkin's travelogue about the Russian empire's southern frontier, *A Journey to Erzurum*. When Pushkin enters a Turk's hut uninvited, the master of the house pushes him out, cursing. "I replied to his welcome with a whip," Pushkin writes. Two decades later, the Russians seem comfortable dispensing with invitations also in Korea. The Americans on the Ryukyu did the same. Goncharov writes that the Koreans "even held us back by our coats, and sometimes shoved us quite rudely. We would then beat their hands, and they would instantly quiet down and cower like dogs running after passersby: eager to bite but not daring." They calm down only when the Russians are at a distance from their village.[126]

The Russians also encounter spirited pushback from Japan's lower classes, as when some locals hurl a log at a Russian officer. In Korea, this happens more often, and the Russians counteract it more confidently and aggressively. At one point, an angry crowd of Koreans abducts a Russian sailor and starts pummeling him. He is rescued by his comrades, but a shower of rocks leaves several Russians bloodied, whereupon they blast the Koreans with bird shot. To head off any diplomatic repercussions from the incident, Putiatin sends a report to the Korean capital describing the clash and denying any Russian responsibility for it. In another episode, billed by Goncharov as "a tiny unpleasantness," Koreans bar Russians from disembarking and rudely shove them into ditches. The Russians return accompanied by armed sailors, which does the trick; a village elder offers profuse apology. They enter a spacious bay and start measuring it, and this time when "savage" Koreans commence rock-throwing, the Russians respond by firing blank cartridges. With perfect imperial superciliousness, the Russians behave as if it is their God-given right to measure anything anywhere, just as Perry acted in Edo Bay. *The Frigate Pallada* holds up violent intrusions into Korean spaces as successful applications of the Russians' strong-arm approach. In sharp contrast to their behavior in Japan, the Russians ignore all constraints placed on them in Korea. In the absence of rivals and diplomatic protocol, the Russians act with restrained but sure-footed aggressiveness. Was this a rehearsal of Perry's lesson? Did it model behavior in imperial settings for Goncharov's readers?[127]

According to a pattern established by voyages of exploration, it was the explorer's prerogative to rename "discovered" landmarks with western appellations. These places would often be so known only in western circuits. The British explorer Frederick Beechey's renaming of some of the Bonin Islands as Buckland and Stapleton Islands did not deter the natives from continuing to call them the Goat and Hog Islands. Commodore Perry graced Edo Bay with names such as Perry Island and Mississippi Bay. Indigenous claims to sovereignty seemed no obstacle in this staking of claims. American whalers contemporary to Perry had renamed Russia's Siberian landmarks with such names as Bowhead Bay or Cape Thaddeus. The Russians enjoy such an "explorer" moment in Korea. They name one bay in honor of recently deceased Admiral Mikhail Lazarev, under whom Putiatin served, and another one in honor of expedition member Possiet. Though *The Frigate Pallada* does not mention it, Goncharov himself serves as eponym for an island off the coast of Korea. Today known as Mayang-do Island, it happens to be a North Korean missile base. Goncharov's descriptions of Russians' conduct in Korea model replicable behaviors providing blueprints for Russia's New Conquest and New World.[128]

Russia's Civilizing Mission in Asia

Off the shores of "unclaimed" Korea, reflecting on the *Pallada*'s Japanese mission, and headed toward Russia's Siberian colonies—this is the symbolic crossroads at which Goncharov articulates his most systematic statement of Europe's and Russia's imperial mission in Asia. Goncharov, the harsh critic of Britain's imperial superciliousness in China; Goncharov, the keen observer of lively Asian bazaars; Goncharov, the open-minded traveler capable of discerning commendable Japanese customs—all are under wraps in this passage. Goncharov speaks here with the stentorian voice of a civilizer and geopolitical expert.

As befits a major pronouncement, he begins with a state-of-civilization statement. While he is "comforted" by the condition of Africa, that of Asia fills him with "deep despondency." Africa is virgin land awaiting seed, but Asia is a "depleted, impassably choked field." A phase of vigorous youth has been followed by senile decrepitude, skipping maturity. Asia has fallen off the path of history. Enervation, stagnation, and paralysis have ensued. It is with precisely these characteristics of Asia that Goncharov associates his famous fictional protagonist, Oblomov. In the novel, an iconic "Oriental dressing gown" drapes Oblomov whenever he is in his natural, slothful state. This is a roomy, indolence-inducing garment "without the slightest hint of Europe about it." It signals the Asian provenance of Russia's chief failing, according to post-*Pallada* Goncharov: a propensity for apathetic aimlessness.[129]

In suggesting solutions to Asia's impasse in *The Frigate Pallada,* Goncharov relies on organic metaphors that come bundled with seemingly incontrovertible political conclusions. Asia is a field overgrown with weeds, which now requires new seed and labor to make it fertile again. Or it requires fresh blood to replace its vitiated sap. In both cases, the order of biological life on earth is coopted for a political point: someone must clear the weeds and plant new seed, drain old sap and infuse new blood. The example of India and Egypt prove to Goncharov that renewal can only come from outside, in a process as beneficial as crop rotation. "We," by which Goncharov means Europe's imperial nations including Russia, can revive Asia by destroying old rot and creating new life. Goncharov thus attenuates Europe's imperial thrust into Asia with the imagery of methodical, prudent farm work and life-saving transfusions. Consistent with patterns of Eurocentric historiography, Goncharov portrays Asia as residing in what Dipesh Chakrabarty calls the "imaginary waiting room of history." Only Europe can usher it into history's splendid halls.[130]

Goncharov foregrounds the need for such Europe-facilitated renewal in his depressing snapshot of Asia's contemporary condition. Political ideas must be rooted, as intertwined traditions of nineteenth-century realism and nationalism required, in a study of a people's "physiognomy." A civilizational assessment of potential subjects must precede and sanction an argument for domination. Taking the pulse of China's political and social life, Goncharov detects the "death rattle." To this day, he claims, China's "senile" civilization is paralyzing the rest of East Asia. China lacks strong central rule, religiosity, and patriotism, proving to Goncharov its unviability; "the body" lacks "inner warmth." He writes that "there are Chinese people, but no Chinese nation." Goncharov learns from a Russian sinologist that the Chinese language even lacks a word for "fatherland." (The sinologist, incidentally, was wrong.) The individual's link to state and society is weak.[131]

Surprisingly, the contrary situation of Japan—its superior development and strong centralized state—does not prevent Goncharov from also diagnosing it as a patient in need of European transfusion. Our fastidious analyst finds other drawbacks. Japan's central system is strong, but propped by fear only; it functions effectively, but in service of the wrong goal, that is, to maintain Japan's isolation. This system must therefore fall, the author decrees. The Japanese—among whom he has made many friends, one might note—will then "become human" (*ochelovechatsia*). Goncharov believes that two decades will suffice for the Ryukyu islanders, whose pacific patriarchal ways he so appreciated, "to exchange their bamboo sticks and fans for firearms and sabers and thus to become human (*stat' liud'mi*) like everyone else."[132] By this point, questioning the humanity of Asians and Africans is a well-established trope in *The Frigate Pallada*. So much for Goncharov's vaunted humanism. Contrary to praise by Soviet critics, Goncharov fails to see un-Europeanized Asians as fully human. Equally disturbing, complete humanity seems inseparable to him from a strategic use of violence—hence his call to replace bamboo sticks with firearms.

And replace they did. Japan soon evolved from a country that on the eve of Perry's arrival had enjoyed over two hundred and fifty years of relative peace (though some of it was enforced by the ruling Tokugawa elite) into a militarized empire that menaced its neighbors. From a medieval principality that had never found use for war, the Ryukyu Islands became militarized upon their annexation by Japan. The main island became the site of the bloody Battle of Okinawa during World War II known as the "typhoon of steel," in which a quarter of the civilian population perished.[133] Of course, Goncharov could not have wished for such a future. Yet he ignores its obvious likelihood if firearms really come to replace bamboo sticks.

In Goncharov's metaphor, Europe's "seeing man" joins hands with Asia's "blind man," inclining the latter toward the light of Christ. The Taiping Rebellion proves to him that Asians themselves understand that "success" is only possible within the framework of Christianity. But—yet again—this transition to humanity must ultimately be effected by European cannons. Goncharov thus finds himself agreeing with a Manila bishop who says Japan will only open "*Á coups de canons.*" This underside of European humanitarianism always clings to its shiny surface in *The Frigate Pallada;* the mission of salvation twines with the punitive mission. Goncharov now suggests, for example, that the forcible opening of Japan is a just comeuppance for "having regarded us, Europeans, as worse than dogs." In what seems like a plan for revenge through infrastructure, Goncharov prophesies that a place where the Japanese once slaughtered Spaniards and burned their ships will one day become the site of "a nice pavilion." Once again, we hear the familiar dissonance of lofty and aggressive sentiments.[134]

Interestingly, Goncharov earlier imagined rather astutely why the Japanese might not welcome Europeanization. How "scared and distressed" they must be by the sudden appearance of foreigners who do not heed their prohibitions! To let the Europeans in, Goncharov saw, meant to lose peaceful and quiet traditional ways of life, but not to let them in meant provoking the use of force. After all, he reasoned, seclusion was a logical reaction to the "evil" Japan suffered from Europeans. He could easily fathom why Japanese officials, their careers hanging in the balance, might be "mentally sending the Russians to the devil." A Russian proverb, harking back to the Mongol invasions of medieval Muscovy, advises that an uninvited guest is worse than a Tatar. The Russians' inopportune intrusion indeed made them "worse than the Tatars" to the Japanese, the writer supposed.[135]

Goncharov went to the effort of imagining the Japanese perspective, however, not to legitimate their wish to be left alone, but to expose the reasons for their folly in opposing Europeanization. He dissected these reasons in order to explain Japanese hostility, not to question the Russians' actions. In the end, realpolitik trumps all else yet again. The Japanese are naive to suppose, Goncharov writes, "that wishing alone will spare them from being touched." On the contrary, one must possess the means—an allusion to a militarily strong state—to make such wishes a reality. Ultimately, Japan will be opened simply because it cannot prevent it.[136]

Interrupting his statement of the civilizing mission in Asia, Goncharov learns that the Japanese are still withholding their response to Putiatin's embassy, and that Manila newspapers have reported on Perry's triumph. At this moment, the writer's solicitude toward the Japanese visibly contracts. Korea, with its trade potential and spacious easy-access bays, once more fires Goncharov's imagination. He now compares Koreans favorably to other Asians, raising their civilizational capital as potential subjects. Back when he still cherished hopes for establishing Russian influence in Japan, Goncharov had compared the Japanese favorably to the Chinese, appreciating their livelier and less pedantic minds and their hidden wellsprings of joy and playfulness. They were, in a sense, a resource lying fallow, like cultivatable land. "Without a doubt, in these parts, the Japanese are the French, while the Chinese are the Germans," Goncharov wrote, hoping that the Russians would help the Japanese realize their inner Frenchness.[137]

Now that these hopes have dimmed, the Koreans move up in the writer's civilizational ranking. Though he reads—or, rather, skims—Koreans like a book too boring for pauses, he appreciates the qualities that will make them good subjects. Their athleticism will make them perfect soldiers. Their venerable poetic tradition shows their culture and, in turn, will boost the cultural capital of the empire that engulfs them. Unlike the Ryukyuans, they are not fearful. Unlike the Chinese, they are not crafty. Unlike the Japanese, they are not effeminate or sly. While the Japanese prevaricate, the Koreans share true information about their country of value to an imperially minded European: geography, topography, traveling distances, trading centers, articles of trade. Rather than appreciate the honesty, Goncharov concludes that Koreans have not yet managed to "develop politics." But, he hastens to add, "it is better if they don't, so as to sooner and faster make the inevitable step toward the rapprochement with the Europeans."[138]

All in all, Goncharov suggests that if Japan proves a disappointment for Russia, Korea offers good prospects. Just as Goncharov's imagination erected gazebos in Japanese landscapes, so in one remote Korean location it fills the bay with huge military and trading fleets. Korea is a blank slate on which Europe should confidently inscribe the story of its own progress: "Korea is still a huge, almost untouched virgin soil for seafarers, merchants, missionaries, and scholars." Goncharov sees the enormous benefits from trade that Europe's "seafaring nations" could gain in Korea due to its proximity to Japan and Shanghai: "how life would stir here!"[139] But the time to act is now:

> It seems to me that it would be best to establish relations with [the Koreans] now, before they harden in their mistrust of Europeans and lock themselves away, and before their government takes strong measures against foreigners and trade. The people are sympathetic to change. How they swooped upon glass tableware, copper buttons, porcelain—on all they saw! Their eyes glittered at the sight of our tailcoats.[140]

Resentful, in the voyage's earlier stages, of the infiltration of the globe by English tailcoats, Goncharov finally finds a welcoming shore for Russian ones.

JAPAN MAY HAVE BEEN the object of Europeans' evaluative gaze, unceremoniously slotted into biased civilizational hierarchies, but it was quick to learn. It soon reciprocated by ranking its would-be civilizers. In 1871, the

Japanese government sent an unprecedented mission of fifty officials on a two-year expedition to circle the globe and compare western forms of government, industrial development, educational systems, and trade. The goal was to study models that Japan might imitate in its own modernization. Paying visits to twelve countries, including the United States, Britain, Prussia, France, and Russia, the Iwakura Embassy, named after its head statesman, produced voluminous documents that show Europe through Japanese eyes.[141] The tables are here fully turned. Japan would now survey the Greater Europeans, so full of the highest opinions of themselves, and say how their civilizational achievements stacked up.

Models it would ultimately select included American education, British industrialization, French jurisprudence, and German representative institutions. Russia was not chosen for emulation. The impressions of Russia gathered by the Iwakura Embassy resembled the critical images made famous three decades earlier by Marquis de Custine, though they were free of the Frenchman's condescension. The sumptuous capital of St. Petersburg dazzled the envoys, but they judged it "a single fine city" amid desolate and dilapidated countryside. They commented on Russia's widespread illiteracy and inadequate schooling, the debilitating social effects of contrasts between the rich and the poor, and the lack of provincial assemblies. Russia's absolutist government appeared to them as a European anomaly. All in all, they found Russia to be the most backward of Europe's powerful nations. Even sooner, in the ranking of civilized nations made popular in 1869 by the Japanese monthly *Meiji gekkan,* Russia did not make it to the top rung where England, France, and the United States were placed.[142] The account of the Iwakura Embassy mentions that visiting Russian ships and crews had presented Japan with an image of Russia that made the Japanese fear the country more than they feared Britain or France. Seen up close, Russia's greatness was dubious. The account closes by voicing perplexity at how such a "delusion" would have found its way into Japanese minds at all.[143]

CHAPTER FOUR

Eastward Ho!

The world is small, but Russia is great.
(Svet mal, a Rossiia velika.)

—Russian saying, recalled by Goncharov
as he travels across Siberia

As he sets foot on the Pacific coast of Siberia, Goncharov marvels at the space that separates him from his home in St. Petersburg:

> How vast is this Ithaca, and how are our Ulysseses to reach their Penelopes? Ten thousand versts [to St. Petersburg] and what don't we have here! Huge oceans of snow, swamps, arid abysses and wet rapids, our own forty-degree tropics, the eternal verdure of pines, savages of all kinds, beasts, beginning with black and white bears all the way up to bedbugs and fleas, instead of being tossed by the waves—you get jolted by the road, instead of the boredom of the sea—that of the land, all climates and all seasons, just as on a round-the-world voyage.[1]

Siberia, which the writer visits for the first time, emerges here as a world all its own, possessed of vastness and diversity that match, or perhaps even dwarf, those of any imperial domain Goncharov has seen on his voyage.

After London, the Cape of Good Hope, Singapore, China, Japan, Manila, and Korea, how does Siberia appear to Goncharov? He has visited a settler colony before, on the southern tip of Africa. Does Siberia seem similar to him? On what terms is this region integrated into the spatial, cultural, and political tapestry of *The Frigate Pallada?* Having keenly observed the operations of European and American empires on global frontiers, what does Goncharov have to say about the Russian one? Critics have tended to view Goncharov's chapters on Siberia as simply an enthusiastic account of Russian-sponsored "progress" in the wild expanses of northern Asia. To read this progress outside of imperial and colonial categories is to miss the point. Goncharov's Siberia functions as the Russian piece in *Frigate Pallada*'s mosaic of the global imperial world order. Though a world apart, it is part of that world.

Describing his own empire, especially in the midst of the Crimean War, is a sensitive matter for the writer. His nationalist fervor heightened by the historical moment, Goncharov mixes keen observations with a healthy dose of wishful thinking, desirous to project Siberia as Russia's success story. The governments of some of those kindly Europeans who have hosted the *Pallada* elite crew in various ports of call now wage war on Russia, posing a very real danger to the crew's survival. Though he has admired their imperial achievements, Goncharov now feels the need to differentiate the Russian empire from its suddenly hostile rivals, especially after witnessing their unscrupulousness toward the Chinese. So he champions Russia's unique colonial mission in Siberia, and along with it, a great deal of boosterist propaganda. Charles Kingsley's 1855 bestseller, *Westward Ho!* glorified the British empire's Elizabethan-era victory over the Spanish and cast muscular imperial adventure as a patriotic feat. Goncharov summons Russians to Siberia to accomplish a similar feat.

And yet Goncharov delivers this message while managing not to discuss Siberia in explicitly imperial terms. As with other corners of the world, he devotes a considerable degree of ideological shaping to his presentation of Siberia. This becomes evident when we compare the travelogue against other records of the expedition and Goncharov's private correspondence. While he studiously avoids acknowledging Siberia as a colonial site, Goncharov presents it in ways that are recognizably colonial, especially in the context of his own book's preceding chapters. His Siberia is nothing like a European colony and at the same time a morally superior example of it. In Siberia, Goncharov's Russians seem to accomplish Europe's greatest civilizing feats. However, unlike Europeans in their overseas colonies, they do so supposedly without stepping outside Russia's own national territory. Siberia's indigenous peoples, subjugated by Russia through military conquest, undeniably populate the landscape of Goncharov's Siberia. Yet this matters as little in his scheme as the presence of Native Americans mattered to proponents of the United States' continental expansion. A belief in manifest destiny—or the "natural" growth of a nation into its predestined contours—far from unique to the US, was common to a vast majority of Goncharov's compatriots, and is also stamped on his book.[2]

The sun of Goncharov's nationalism does much to warm Siberia's frozen expanses in *The Frigate Pallada*. He cheers any signs of Russian culture displacing indigenous traditions, not hesitating to press the scale to tip the balance. Though he records striking examples of cultural hybridity, these mark for him only a temporary stage on the path to a culturally Russian Siberia. *The Frigate Pallada* offers impassioned praise for Russia's civilizing accomplishments and a rallying cry for a new commitment to develop the region. Reflecting the tangled imperial and national ideologies common to nineteenth-century European empires, the book shows progress on the periphery augmenting the national glory of its imperial sponsor. This is a vision of total and irrevocable absorption of the imperial periphery into the national body.

Yet in one evocative passage, Goncharov gestures toward a future in which Siberia is released from the imperial trust, as a region vastly improved by Russian colonizing activities, with a well-earned right to stand independent on the world stage. Surprisingly to us today, in a text that overflows with a desire to bind Siberia closely to Russia, Goncharov also muses about the distant prospect of some form of decolonization. This, too, was in keeping with the times, when imperial expansion was often justified by a notion that "backward" peoples, upon becoming sufficiently "civilized," would eventually regain control over their lands.[3]

In this, as in other aspects of his portrayal of Siberia, Goncharov engages with contemporaneous ideas and debates about Siberia—Russia's eventual imperial pearl, crucial to this day to the country's economic and geopolitical power. Siberia acquired new significance in the mid-nineteenth century as the Russians pivoted to Asia, responding to Western Europeans' increasing political, economic, and military reach into the continent; to the rippling energy of United States activity in the Pacific; and to the impediments to Russia's southern expansion in the Black Sea region, made painfully tangible in the Crimean War. Goncharov tries to shape that significance in *The Frigate Pallada*.

The Road Back Home

For some of Goncharov's contemporaries, his description of the Far East, as the region of Siberia east of Lake Baikal has been known administratively in Russia, was even more revelatory than his images of Japan, so unfamiliar was it to metropolitan audiences. Like the Cape of Good Hope, Siberia was not part of Goncharov's itinerary when he signed on for the expedition. After its secret mission to Japan, the *Pallada* was to complete its official mission to inspect Russia's North American possessions. The outbreak of the Crimean War, the unfinished negotiations with Japan, and the poor condition of the frigate short-circuited that plan. The *Pallada* had to be on high alert. As a sailing frigate, it stood no chance against British and French steam-powered warships. Putiatin's bold plan in case of attack, which he revealed in secret to his senior staff, was to sidle up to the assailant and blow up the frigate along with the crew. Due to its decrepit condition, the *Pallada* would not withstand a transpacific journey to seek refuge in a neutral port such as San Francisco. The closer neutral Spanish port of Manila, where the Russians received a cold welcome, proved unreliable. The coasts of California and southeast Asia were well policed by the British and French navies. The relative proximity of the Russian base in Kamchatka was inconsequential, since it had insufficient food reserves and sleeping facilities to accommodate a crew of nearly five hundred.[4]

The squadron therefore sailed north along the shores of Korea, toward the Russian territories on the Sea of Okhotsk. Having transferred from the rickety *Pallada* to its replacement, the *Diana,* Putiatin evaded the British, by then in full attack mode, by exploiting their mistaken belief that Sakhalin Island was joined to the Asian continent. In the Tatar Strait, between Sakhalin and the mainland, a military clash was narrowly averted when an unmarked ship at which the Russians were about to fire, suspecting it to be British, turned out to be one of the many US whaling ships that actively fished and traded along Siberia's Pacific shores.

His thirst for adventure satisfied, Goncharov requested to return to Russia, restless about the indefinite hold the Crimean War might place on the negotiations with Japan. Putiatin granted permission, adding a complimentary assessment of Goncharov's service.[5] Putiatin continued his diplomatic mission, returning to Japan in the fall of 1854 on the *Diana,* without his litterateur-secretary.

In August 1854, the schooner *Vostok* transported Goncharov from the Amur region to the Russian port of Ayan, newly established on the Sea of Okhotsk by the Russian-American Company, a joint-stock company established by an imperial charter for the purpose of conducting trade and colonization in Russian North America. Then the most arduous part of Goncharov's journey began: an overland trek of almost 7,000 miles from the shores of the Pacific, across the mountains, swamps, forests, and snows of Siberia, back to St. Petersburg. From this new perspective, being tossed around in a leaky frigate's closet-sized cabin appeared to the writer the height of luxury. Goncharov made a short stopover in his hometown of Simbirsk, and arrived in St. Petersburg six months later, in February 1855, one week before the death of Tsar Nicholas I and six months before the surrender of Sebastopol, which ended the Crimean War. To set out from Simbirsk from the right bank of the Volga and to return, having circumnavigated the globe, to the Volga's left bank, had been Goncharov's childhood dream.[6] Though the circumnavigation proved to be a semi-circumnavigation, the wish was as good as granted.

On the westward journey from Ayan, Goncharov's traveling party, led by indigenous guides, crosses the formidable Dzhugdzhur Mountains running along the coast of the Sea of Okhotsk. Not one for roughing it, Goncharov despairs at having to mount a horse, since vehicle travel is impossible. He reaches his first Siberian town, Yakutsk, on the Lena River, by a notoriously difficult stretch of the trans-Siberian route, opened only a decade earlier, leading from the port of Ayan along the Maya River.[7] This leg of the journey winds through sparsely populated terrain with only rudimentary travel infrastructure. As horses sink up to their bellies in mud, crossing swamps proves more formidable than forging rivers or climbing mountains. Goncharov arrives in Yakutsk late in the season, in November 1854, where he is heartily wined and dined by local society. After healing his legs, which swelled painfully during the cold journey, he decides to press ahead, against the locals' advice to wait until spring. Just as he couldn't purchase Manila cigars in Manila, however, he has no luck procuring fur in Yakutsk, an important center of the Siberian fur trade. With the summer trading season over, Goncharov must buy the fur he needs for Siberian winter travel from a private person rather than a merchant. Covered head to toe in all manner of animal hides, from ermine and rabbit to deer and bear, the writer jokingly frets that animal spirits may crowd out his human spirit.[8]

The route to Irkutsk, then the capital of Eastern Siberia, on the western shore of the Lake Baikal, leads along the Lena—Siberia's major river which empties into the Arctic Sea, powered by a thousand tributaries. Expecting the Lena to be an august spectacle of nature, Goncharov instead finds its vast network of crisscrossing rivulets more of a muddy flat. (He is told that this changes after the springtime floods.) The area is more densely populated, both by Russian settlers and native populations. The Russian presence in this part of eastern Siberia consists of a network of post stations (*stantsii*), or clusters of dwellings separated by a day's journey, where travelers can find refuge from the elements and sometimes fresh horses and a meal. With cold reaching −40 degrees Celsius, cabbage soup is chopped into rations with an ax for heating. On Christmas Day in 1854, Goncharov reaches Irkutsk, with a swollen, frostbitten face, but in fairly good spirits. Though his journey will continue another 3,500 miles, Goncharov abruptly breaks off his travelogue at this point, never describing Eastern Siberia's capital or the journey beyond it.[9]

A Colony without Colonialism?

The boundaries of what has been considered Siberia have changed over time, but it is today understood to be a vast stretch of the northern Asian continent that extends eastward from the Ural Mountains to the Pacific Ocean, and from the Arctic Ocean in the north to the steppes of Kazakhstan and Mongolia in the south. It encompasses about one-twelfth of the world's landmass, across eight time zones, and today is home to about thirty million people. Siberia is a region of enormous climactic and geographical extremes: from some of the world's coldest temperatures to very hot, if brief, summers, from the sparse tundra of the permafrost to fertile farmland and grassland, from swampland to steep mountains and even active volcanoes and hot springs. It boasts mighty rivers and the world's deepest lake, the Baikal, containing one-fifth of the world's fresh water. By now, Siberia's vast underground natural resources are widely known. It is a place where one can mine, in the colorful phrase of Soviet Siberians, all of Mendeleev's Periodic Table. This has historically been an incredibly diverse region, inhabited by Turkic, Mongolian, Tungusic, and Paleoasiatic ethnic groups, professing Shamanistic, Islamic, and Buddhist faiths. Aboriginal Siberian societies tended to be organized by kinship, and most people were semi-nomadic herders, fishermen, or hunters-gatherers. Though sparsely populated on the eve of the Russian conquest, Siberia was by no means "empty," as apologists of Russian expansion later claimed. It was home to over two hundred thousand people speaking at least a hundred and twenty languages, of which thirty-five remain officially recognized today.[10]

In the thirteenth century, parts of Siberia and the medieval East Slavic principality of Kievan Rus were both conquered by Genghis Khan, the founder of the largest continental empire in world history. After his Mongol empire, and later its west Asian successor, the Golden Horde, disintegrated, several Eurasian states continued the Mongols' political traditions. These included the Siberian Khanate, which emerged in the fifteenth century, centered in present-day Tiumen on the Irtysh River, and the Grand Duchy of Moscow, which emerged in the fourteenth century and remained the Golden Horde's vassal until 1480. By the fifteenth century, the Great Duchy consolidated its power over the predominantly Orthodox East Slavic lands and entered the rivalry for the inheritance of the Golden Horde by conquering, in the 1550s, the Khanates of Kazan and Astrakhan on the lower Volga River. These conquests of non-Slavic, Turkic khanates launched Russia's imperial course proper. Thus, as Andreas Kappeler argues, having gathered the lands of Rus (or East Slavdom), Muscovites began "the gathering of the lands of the Golden Horde," a task that kept them busy until the end of the eighteenth century.[11]

Donning the mantle of the Golden Horde meant inheriting its tribute entitlements. Alarmed by the fate of Kazan, the Siberian khan began paying tribute to the Muscovite tsar in 1555. The historical record is spotty, but according to a widely accepted account, when the next khan, Kuchum, ceased payments and became belligerent, Tsar Ivan the Terrible decided to retaliate. To minimize cost to his treasury, he granted royal charters to the Stroganov family, owners of a hunting and trading emporium. The Stroganovs equipped the Cossack freebooter Yermak for an expedition against Kuchum. Yermak and his detachment of a few hundred Cossacks won a swift victory in 1582, an event that came to symbolize Russia's conquest of Siberia, even though Yermak conquered only a small part. According to Russia's first official historiographer, Nikolai Karamzin, "the conquest of Siberia was in many ways similar to the conquest of Mexico and Peru: a handful of people, shooting fire, overwhelmed thousands wielding arrows and spears." In fact, Kuchum's Tatars were no strangers to firearms. The Cossacks' decisive technological advantage was, specifically, the rifle.[12]

Figure 4.1. Beginning of the Russian conquest of Siberia, 1582. In this painting by Vasily Surikov, "The Conquest of Siberia by Yermak" (1895), Cossacks under Yermak won a victory over the army of Khan Kuchum on the Irtysh River. HIP / Art Resource, NY.

Despite fierce resistance by Siberia's indigenous groups—Yermak himself perished in their ambush—initial conquest was followed by rapid expansion. The pursuit of fur, Siberia's first lucrative commodity, stretched Russian rule all the way to the Pacific. In 1639, Ivan Moskvitin reached the Pacific and founded the port of Okhotsk. Within just fifty-seven years, the Russian empire acquired about forty percent of the entire Asian continent, an area about one-and-a-half-times larger than the United States.[13] Today the region is known to contain between eighty and ninety percent of the Russian Federation's natural resources.[14] Historian Alan Wood writes that "at least in terms of territorial aggrandizement," it was the conquest of Siberia that "transformed the land-locked medieval Tsardom of Muscovy into the mighty Russian Empire."[15]

Although now indelibly connected in the world's imagination with Russia, Siberia was—in the words of historian Mark Bassin—the Russian empire's "oldest, largest, and in many senses most important colony" (though the plural term "colonies" would better capture the region's diversity). Wood argues that already in the seventeenth century Siberia was "regarded, and plundered, by Moscow as a 'colony' in the classic sense of the word." It was "an alien land invaded and occupied by an imperial, expansionist power that exploited the conquered territory's natural resources, [cheated] the indigenous inhabitants and settled her own people on the occupied territory, claiming it to be her own, imposing her own values, language and religion, and looting its material products and human stock for the benefit of the metropolitan center."[16]

Fur, which supplied Western European markets (and later, Chinese ones), was obtained by private hunters or through a rapacious system of tribute (*yasak*) imposed on the aboriginal groups. This "soft gold," which accounted for a large share of the state budget, solidified Russian rule in Siberia, financed further expansion across the continent, and helped establish the Romanov dynasty that ruled the empire from 1613 to 1917. It financed Peter the Great's westernization of Russia at the beginning of the eighteenth century and the subsequent development of Russian arts. As Alexander Etkind puts it, "to a certain extent, the collections of the Hermitage were financed from the revenue that came from Siberian pelts." Fur trade also exerted, according to Ilya Vinkovetsky, "a powerful globalizing influence on Russian economy and society." After fur profits declined, agriculture and the forging of metals became important sectors of the economy. The ironworks in southwestern Siberia transformed Russia within fifty years from an iron importer into one of the world's largest exporters. After the Siberian Gold Rush of 1830–1840, Russia's gold accounted for forty percent of global production in 1850.[17]

Starting in the eighteenth century, this rich "resource pantry" of the empire also became a settler colony. European colonization was of both a voluntary and involuntary type. Voluntary settlers, about eighty-five percent of the total by mid-nineteenth century, were mostly peasants to whom the state gave loans and tax exemptions. Involuntary settlers were mostly soldiers and exiles. To the legal settlers' ranks were added fortune-seekers and illegal refugees escaping serfdom or religious persecution. In the late eighteenth century, the government began using Siberia as a place of exile (*ssylka*) and of penal servitude (*katorga*), the second of which combined incarceration with forced labor. Often, convicts were required to remain in Siberia as settlers or administrators after their prison terms were served. They included criminals, political opponents, religious dissidents, prisoners of war, and national liberation activists, such as Poles, Ukrainians, and Caucasians. As a pressure valve for relieving domestic social and political conflicts, Siberia helped stabilize the autocratic core; its role was comparable to that played by other overseas colonies of Western European empires. Spontaneous migration became a state-directed affair by mid-century, and then a massive government operation that moved millions of Slavic peasants to Siberia. It relieved land shortages, poverty, and overcrowding in European Russia.[18]

While profits flowed to the capital or to Siberia's colonial masters, Siberia's aboriginal populations suffered a precipitous decline. The demographic balance shifted inexorably toward European settlers. Within a century after Yermak's conquest, the settlers roughly drew even in number with the indigenous inhabitants. By 1911, the aborigines' share of Siberia's population fell to 11.5 percent. In the face of European influx, many indigenous ethnic groups were either exterminated or sharply diminished, due to nearly genocidal military campaigns, European diseases like smallpox, the loss of land to Slavic or other European settlers, and the tribute system and barter exchanges that were scarcely distinguishable from robbery. However, many Russians also intermixed with indigenous Siberians, whose culture they sometimes adopted.[19]

The late nineteenth-century regionalist historians of Siberia rang alarm bells about "the dying out of aliens," as the empire's aborigines of non-Slavic origin, mostly in Asia, were then legally categorized (*inorodtsy*). Nikolai Yadrintsev, for example, drew attention to the plight of Siberia's aborigines in his study of Siberia as a colony and in a separate book he devoted to this topic, blaming it on the deleterious effects of their contact with Russian civilization. Echoing Yadrintsev's assessment, historian James Forsyth stresses that "there was no class or institution that did not exploit the natives, and trade in conformity with normal concepts of fair exchange and honest dealing simply did not exist." The Russian historian of Siberia Anatoly Remnev tersely sums up Siberian trade as "unconcealed robbery of the local population."[20]

The seventeenth century was certainly a dark age of Russian rule for the indigenous populations, with torture, mutilations, and enslavement common. Forms of indigenous non-accommodation to the Russian rule included sieges of Cossack forts, assassinations of tribute-collectors, countless uprisings, and when those failed, sometimes mass suicide. Well into the nineteenth century, the government's tribute-collectors extorted bribes above official pelt quotas. Starting in the eighteenth century, Russia's enlightened monarchs made attempts to improve the administration of Siberia, eliminate abuses, and improve the welfare of aborigines. The 1822 reforms of the energetic bureaucrat Mikhail Speransky recognized the natives' legal right to own land and encouraged their transition from nomadic to settler lifestyle, though they failed to eradicate the abuses. Moreover, in a region where imperial decrees might take months to arrive, and possibly never reach implementation, official policy and facts on the ground diverged widely. Siberia was a severely "under-governed" part of the Russian empire, its imperial bureaucracy perennially understaffed. However well-intentioned the government, it could not rectify the misrule.[21]

Rampant abuse and lawlessness thus became part of Siberia's public image and remained so throughout the imperial period. Carpetbagger bureaucrats who administered the distant and inaccessible region with almost limitless authority made fabulous fortunes through graft, misappropriation of public resources, nepotism, and the predatory treatment of local populations. The legendary profiteering of these "Siberian satraps," as they came to be known, led, in the words of historian Igor Naumov, to "a stupendous misappropriation even by Russian standards." To evade Speransky's scrutiny, one official put all ink, pens, and paper in his district under lock and key to prevent citizens from writing complaints. Before Speransky, almost all Siberian high-ranking bureaucrats were dismissed or imprisoned for corruption. Some were even executed, such as Siberia's first governor, Matvei P. Gagarin, whom Goncharov invokes in one of his late Siberian sketches. One plenipotentiary of Catherine the Great who was tasked with rooting out corruption traveled to Siberia with two blank orders of commuted death sentence signed by the empress, which shows both the weak communications of the time and Catherine's alarm about the goings-on in her Siberian domains. Russian merchants, various joint-stock companies, and speculators, made huge fortunes, whether by legal or illegal means, often thanks to monopolies granted by the state. Although by the nineteenth century the imperial treasury lacked confidence about Siberia's profitability, huge fortunes were made and huge profits derived by the multitude of imperial Russia's agents, beneficiaries, and institutions.[22]

The Siberia that Goncharov encountered in 1854 was thus shaped by several factors: the conquest of a land inhabited by an ethnically distinct population; the center's instrumental rule, perceived as foreign by the original inhabitants; economic exploitation; establishment of settler colonies on native land; and its separate legal status within the state. Anyone familiar with European colonialism will recognize its features here. And yet this has not been the consensus view of Siberia in Russian historiography or its accepted cultural image, either in Russia or in the West. As Willard Sunderland has shown, Russians intellectuals and administrators found reasons to view Russia as an "empire without imperialism"—similar enough to its

European peers to be recognized as an empire, yet sufficiently different to disavow the label when expedient. The differences in question included the blurred line between the metropole and the colonies, religious tolerance, and the ability of subjugated elites to join the imperial ones.[23] Similarly, Siberia came to be perceived by Russians as a colony without colonialism (though the latter term was not yet in use then). It certainly seems to have become that for Goncharov.

Nineteenth-century historians of Siberia who were actually from Siberia, such as Nikolai Yadrintsev or Mikhail Veniukov, had no doubt about its colonial status and the metropole's exploitative practices toward both aborigines and settlers. Anger at these helped propel Siberia's regionalist movement, which stirred in the 1860s and which Yadrintsev helped found. It advocated for Siberia's autonomy and, in more radical visions, its transition toward something like a United States of Siberia. (The notion of outright independence from Russia never became prominent.) Siberian regionalism never spread beyond a small group of the Siberian colonial elite, and the mass migrations of the early twentieth century weakened it further, but regionalist ideas resurfaced in the revolutions of 1905 and 1917.[24] From autonomist leanings to defiant regional pride, Siberia remains imperfectly assimilated into Russia, whose federal government remains vigilant about any hints of separatism.[25]

Colonization and empire lacked negative connotations in nineteenth-century Europe. However, the gathering forces of Russian nationalism discouraged viewing Russian expansion in the same light as the European colonial experience. More appealing by far was the mentality of manifest destiny. Only a "foreign" land can be "colonized." Russians, by contrast, believed they simply spilled over into a homeland they were predestined to fill—a contiguous, practically empty space with no seaborne passage required. Unlike in Western European colonial empires, the boundary between the Russian core and imperial peripheries was never clearly demarcated: the two spaces blended into each other, their zone of transition always in flux. The Russian empire's territorial contiguity would thus seem to have exempted Siberia from colonial categories.

However, for all practical purposes, Siberia's natural terrain functioned in much the same way oceans did for Western European empires. Goncharov himself draws a parallel of this kind in *The Frigate Pallada.* In fact, the travails and perils of overland transport in Siberia rivaled those of maritime passages. As late as the 1880s, it took about thirty days for mail to reach Irkutsk from St. Petersburg—about the same time a letter traveled from London to Calcutta around 1850. Goncharov reports mail reaching Yakutsk only once a month. By mid-century, a sea voyage on a steamship from London to the Cape Colony took about three weeks, while crossing Siberia by land took a few months. Indeed, it was easier for Russians to reach their Pacific shores by sailing around Africa and China than by traveling through their own contiguous overland empire. Moreover, according to Vinkovetsky, "the Russian empire's *contiguous* space was arguably more culturally differentiated and diverse than most colonial empires' overseas space." Wood is right that Siberia's territorial contiguity to this day blurs its colonial experience for both western and Russian scholars.[26]

In popular perception, Russia's development of the region did not fit into colonial categories. Siberia was not "exploited"; its dormant resources simply became utilized. Russians harnessed the region's economic potential, modernized it, and dragged its obstreperous natives up the ladder of civilization. The claim of Russian benevolence and tolerance—not without merit, but routinely exaggerated—in contrast to Europeans' exploitation and rapacity, convinced many Russians that their empire did not engage in colonial practices. The validity of such arguments is limited. All European empires had some such version of their own moral righteousness, superiority over rival empires, and claims of "development." There was a time when the French did not consider Algeria to be a colony.[27]

Finally, Siberia's colonial question also invited pure political rhetoric. The specter of separatism and decolonization dissuaded many administrators and intellectuals from adopting colonial vocabulary in reference to Siberia, though they did not necessarily dispute its empirical validity. Britain's loss of its North American colonies served as a particularly stern warning. If it is the natural course of history that colonies eventually detach from the metropole—as was commonly assumed already in the nineteenth century—then best not to talk about Siberia as a colony, even if it worked like one. While the administration of Siberia in real terms became more colonial in the mid-nineteenth century, referring to Siberia as a colony was seen as weakening Russian rule there. Throughout the nineteenth century, imperial administrators lost much sleep over real and imagined signs of Siberian separatism.[28]

Deep-seated traditions and novel rhetorical makeovers of Russian conquest and rule in Siberia depicted the region as an inalienable part of Russia's national space. For this to work, the act of conquest and expansion had to be disguised. "Conquest" (*zavoevanie*), with its clear military ring, was replaced in the nineteenth century—"uniting" and "conjoining" (*prisoedinenie*), in the sense of adding to a larger whole. Goncharov speaks of the "taking" of Siberia (*zaniatie Sibiri*), or of "uniting" (*prisoedinenie*) the Amur with Russia, or of "subduing of Kamchatka" (*pokorenie*)—this last term connotes bringing in line anyone acting uppity or rowdy. While initially Russia's Asian subjects were called *inozemtsy,* or people of a different land, by the early nineteenth century they become *inorodtsy,* or people of a different birth. The plurality of "lands" was incompatible with the ascendant notion of a single, unified "Russian" land. By the 1880s, Russian metropolitan journals were switching their word for Siberia from "country" (*strana*) to "borderland" (*okraina*).[29] The very name of Siberia was being expunged from the empire's administrative maps and replaced by "Asiatic Russia." So vigilant was one Irkutsk governor about the vaguest suggestion of Siberia's separateness that he censored from local journals the phrase "Siberia and Russia," ordering it replaced with "Siberia and European Russia," which cast Siberia as Russia's subordinate, non-European part.[30] Such word choices mattered, since they encapsulated a political theory and a vision of history, and in public parlance shaped how Russians thought about Siberia.

David Collins, who has traced the evolving views of Siberia in Russian and Soviet historiography, finds that nineteenth-century justifications of colonial rule in Siberia were fully in the mainstream of European colonial writing. Though nineteenth-century historiography acknowledged the conquest's negative aspects, it also stressed the overall benefits of Russian colonization, such as the transition from nomadism to agriculture. This changed in the early Soviet period, according to Collins, when Soviet scholars exposed the military and exploitative aspects of tsarist imperialism and colonialism. They tended to treat Siberia as a typical colony, subjugated for profit and strategic value, and ruled to the detriment of both indigenous populations and settlers. After the 1930s, however, authorities worried that tsarist-Soviet parallels might be drawn, and began promoting a brighter image of Russian presence in Siberia. Progressive and benign Russian rule and its civilizing triumphs in Asia became the new history of the region. The applicability of the term "colony" to Siberia was questioned. In what Collins calls "an antiseptic Soviet version of events," the late Soviet Union favored the rhetoric of the peaceful coming together of all ethnic groups (*sblizhenie*), their assimilation or taming (*osvoenie*), and their gradual fusing into a harmonious Soviet people (*sliianie*). *Pax Russica,* or "Russian peace," it was argued—a competing analogy to *Pax Britannica*—sheltered peoples from "falling into the rapacious hands" of the United States, Japan, or Britain.[31]

Western historians and post-Soviet Russian historians have been more willing to treat Siberia as an imperial space. However, a disinclination to view Siberia's colonization as enmeshed with colonialism persists, as if the processes involved could be narrowed down to agrarian settlement or the reshuffling of people, and were not predicated in the first place on the foisting of foreign and exploitative rule over someone else's land. Sunderland explains that "the tsarist empire was undeniably an empire in the European mold, but the imperialism that built and sustained it was highly ambiguous and all its own." Its key quirk was viewing Russian colonization as a matter of both external expansion and internal development such as agriculture. This lack of distinction, Sunderland writes, "helped to turn the Russians into a people who ended up with an enormous empire but a somewhat less developed sense of imperialist identity." The "imperialist dimensions" of the Russian colonization of Siberia became "easy to forget, or at least to omit from the picture."[32]

The sense of Russian exceptionalism in this matter has its roots in the belief that Russian colonization was fundamentally dissimilar from what is considered the "classic" European model. But rather than embrace this exceptionalism, we may do better to question the model itself—a model that enshrines the west as the European norm and fails to account for the Russian experience, or anyone else's. Likewise, we should not overestimate the tidiness of the Western European experience itself. Just as we should not lump together all of imperialism's subjects, so we should not conflate imperialisms. There are good reasons to speak of plural colonizations and colonialisms in the English-speaking world alone, to say nothing of the whole entity called "Europe." What "colonist" meant in the French context was as varied as what "colonization" meant in the Russian one. Meanwhile, although Siberia's colonization might have looked utterly unlike colonialism to many tsarist-era Russians, that should not constrain our assessment of it today. Despite the "epic proportion" that James Forsyth rightly assigns to Russia's conquest of Siberia, that event has yet to be incorporated into the histories of European imperialism. Today's popular perception is that Siberia is an integral part of "Russia" rather than a (former) colony, a notion that has gained empirical plausibility thanks to a long history of integrative and assimilative policies that are still ongoing. This has taken a lot of cultural work to achieve, and it was work that Goncharov energetically took up in *The Frigate Pallada.*[33]

What instantly strikes a reader of the Siberian chapters is Goncharov's scrupulous avoidance of the term "colony" (*koloniia*) or its derivations ("colonist," "colonization"). While throughout the travelogue, in reference to the rest of the colonial world, the vocabulary of colonialism is used in a neutral, classically European manner, it vanishes from the Siberian chapters.[34] Instead, Goncharov calls Siberia "our possessions" (*nashi vladeniia*) or simply "*krai,*" which means country, territory, or simply land.[35] Instead of "colonization," he opts for "settling" or "resettling" (*zaselenie, pereselenie*). This was clearly a meaningful difference for Goncharov. He calls European settlers in the Cape of Good Hope *kolonisty,* but never *pereselentsy;* he calls European settlers in Siberia *pereselentsy,* but never *kolonisty.* According to Sunderland, up to the mid-nineteenth century, the term "resettlement" was primarily used for agriculture-related activities within a contiguous state, while "colonization" was used for external colonies where extraction of resources or trade, for example, were also practiced. The term "colony" was mainly used for Europe's overseas possessions and, within Russia, for territories operated by foreigners; for distant Russian commercial or military outposts; and for such regions as Transcaucasia that were not intended for full integration with the rest of empire. As the century progressed, the two terms began to be used interchangeably and the usage of "colony" in reference to Russian imperial regions, including Siberia, started to rise.[36]

Beyond reflecting linguistic practice of the time, however, Goncharov's avoidance of the term "colonization" seems ideologically motivated. He uses the platform of Siberia to contrast a superior Russian colonial model to its Western European equivalent, enthusiastically praised before but now proclaimed inferior. Reserving the term "colonization" for Europe's possessions sharpens this contrast. Furthermore, eager to Russify Siberia's image, Goncharov treats its land, irrespective of its demography or history, as simply Russian, a vast arena in which Russia's national destiny is unfolding. "Colony" connotes an artificial grafting onto a foreign space. "Resettlement," by contrast, evokes a nonhierarchical reshuffling of people within a unified national space; the term "settlement" (*zaselenie*) goes further to empty this space of indigenous populations. That that this bifurcated terminology is Goncharov's deliberate choice is proved by the fact that, outside the pages of *The Frigate Pallada*, in his correspondence from the voyage and his official report of the expedition, he does refer to Siberia as "our colonies."[37] It isn't that he fails to see the coloniality of Siberia; he simply chooses not to mention it in a publication meant for a popular audience. This distinction is important to keep in mind, lest we too readily assume that Goncharov's representations of Siberia reflect his perceptions of it.

And so, in harmony with the Russian intellectual tradition of viewing Russia as a non-imperialistic empire, Goncharov's Siberia emerges as what might be called a non-colonial colony. The processes Goncharov describes as taking place in Siberia are clearly colonial: the rule of a distant metropolitan government representing interests of an imperial elite; the colonization of Siberian lands by Slavic settlers; extraction of resources; the overhaul of indigenous political, social, economic, religious, and cultural traditions and their replacement by Russian ones. At some point he even explicitly compares Siberia's patterns of settlement and trade to those of Australia and California.[38] A reader skipping from Goncharov's chapter about Britain's settler colony on the southern tip of Africa to his descriptions of Russian rule in Siberia would be hard-pressed to find substantial differences. There is merely a difference of degree, given Siberia's comparative underdevelopment. (This may be a reason why some post-Soviet editions of *The Frigate Pallada* omit the Siberian chapters altogether.)

Goncharov feels justified in presenting the Russian presence in Siberia within the frame of global human progress rather than colonial management because he shared—or felt compelled to project—a conviction that Russia's civilizing activities were marked by disinterestedness, benevolence, and peacefulness. This notion does not withstand historical scrutiny. Nor is it unique to Russia. All colonial empires viewed their civilizing missions in terms of progress. A sense of their own exceptionalism and superiority was common to them all.

An Ascending Gradient of Russianness

Apart from an imperial region, Siberia has also been an idea. Like Siberia's climate, this idea tends toward extremes. In the words of historian Yuri Slezkine, Siberia has been seen as "both the frightening heart of darkness and a fabulous land of plenty."[39] It has been both a notorious place of fetters and a refuge of freedom, both a den of corruption and a haven of prosperity, both a storage for the rejects of society and the cradle of a self-reliant, egalitarian new society. Russian images of Siberia were forged in the clashing of such antinomies.

Mark Bassin argues that Siberia's territorial contiguity to European Russia made it meaningful in much the same way that the moving continental frontier was to Americans: less as a foreign realm than as a place that revealed something crucial about a nation's own identity. He identifies four main approaches to Siberia in the Russian culture of the first half of the nineteenth century. The most popular view of Siberia was that of a foreign mercantile colony, a repository of exploitable economic resources, not unlike those of Western European colonies. When profits were high, it was referred to as "our Peru" or "our Mexico." When fur trade declined, it came to stand for a barren Asiatic icebox, useful only as a place of exile. The exiled Decembrists, who had rebelled in 1825 against the accession of Nicholas I, drew a parallel with the vigorous New World republic: the United States. In this second view noted by Bassin, the absence of serfdom and landed aristocracy in Siberia made it a democratic and egalitarian beacon for a European Russia fettered by feudal bonds. Decembrists conceived of Siberia as a place where liberal European values could be allowed to flourish. The third, nationalist, vision treated Russian exploration and colonization of Siberia as the nation's humanitarian achievement and a world-historical event that rivaled western empires' successes in the New World. The eighteenth-century image of Yermak as a lawless brigand was readjusted to that of a national hero. Finally, Bassin finds a fourth view in political dissident Alexander Herzen's vision of Siberia as de-Europeanized embryo of future Russia: a fiercely independent, self-reliant, anti-autocratic, and egalitarian society that would not tolerate any tyranny. Reserving the first approach for his private correspondence, and unsympathetic to Herzen's anti-European fourth way, Goncharov combines in *The Frigate Pallada* the Decembrist and the nationalist approaches to Siberia.[40]

Siberia's Russianness, so iconic today, remained controversial for most of the nineteenth century. "No one could really decide," writes Slezkine, "whether [Siberia] was part of Russia or not." When the Russian writer, historian, and journalist Nikolai Polevoi asserted in 1827 that "Siberia is just the same as Russia," he did so in the spirit of contradicting the widespread view that it was not. His lesser-known contemporary, Siberian writer Nikolai Shchukin, viewed Siberia as a unique Asian country. In the nation's capitals, the cultural transformation of Siberia into Russia under the ideological banner of Russia's manifest destiny had great currency. In the second half of the nineteenth century, an effort to create an image of Siberia as an inalienable part of Russia united journals of all ideological bents. The popular play by Slavophile writer Aleksei Khomiakov, *Yermak,* which portrays the celebrated conqueror of Siberia as a national hero, concludes by erasing Siberia and overwriting it with Russia: "Siberia is no more: from here on this is Russia!" Such erasure also characterized the mental habits of bureaucrats. "As Siberia shrinks, Russia grows," wrote one of them. It was only in the mid-1880s, when the project of the Trans-Siberian Railway gathered steam, that Siberia's essential Russianness became a widely shared perception of the Russian public. Today, Siberia is central to ethnic Russian identity, declares Sergey Glebov, its incorporation in the Russian national myth "almost total." Yet this incorporation emerged gradually, through the work of nationalistic artists and intellectuals of various political stripes, including Goncharov.[41]

Prior to the twentieth-century wave of decolonizations, imperialism lacked the kind of stigma we attach to it now. The possession of large territories was seen as augmenting the imperial nation's grandeur, serving as proof of its vigor and even racial superiority. In the Russian context, to make the dynastic empire congruent with the nation was a long-standing goal of the ruling elites. According to Remnev, "the Russian imperial project envisaged the gradual absorption of the periphery by the imperial core." Russian nationalism perceived no contradiction between national and imperial projects. As Bassin argues, their fusion was seen as natural, symbiotic, desirable, and even necessary by nationalist intellectuals of all political factions. Indeed, nationalists were "among Russia's most enthusiastic and determined empire-builders." Imperial expansion was meant to compensate for Russian nationalism's perennial sense of inadequacy with regard to the west by furnishing proof of Russia's superior national qualities. Olga Maiorova similarly finds that most Russians treated empire as "an attribute of the nation," unable to conceive of separating the two.[42]

Both overt swagger and concealed insecurity figure in Goncharov's image of Siberia as a maturing embryo of Russianness. His progress through Siberian space ultimately tells the story that, just as the Cape Colony grew to become a quite cozy "corner of England," Siberia is bound to become a prosperous and vibrant part of Russia.

Figure 4.2. The lonely outpost of Ayan, Siberia, where Goncharov was dropped off to begin his trek back home. Lithograph by P. Smirnov, 1857.

As he finds on his trek, this is work in progress. The "shore of the fatherland" that welcomes Goncharov shows only rudimentary signs of Russian presence. The port of Ayan, then only ten years old, is a disorderly scattering of ten huts, a few Cossack tents and Evenki (Tungus) yurts, a church, and the warehouses of the Russian-American Company. At a total population of two hundred, Ayan is only a very modest "corner of Russia" where Goncharov and his fellow travelers barely manage to find a roof over their heads. So distant are Siberia's "cities and civilization" that Goncharov and his French-speaking companions confess feeling like Robinson Crusoe on his foreign, uninhabited island. The trek's initial leg strikes Goncharov as depressingly desolate—just thin paths across primeval forests, swamps, and mountains. "There is nothing terrifying in these savage landscapes, but much that is sad," he sighs. "Anguish grips the heart, when one traverses these mute deserts," he confesses. "Oh, the faster to leave these uninhabited, silent places."[43]

Like his descriptions of Africa, Goncharov's portraits of Siberia empty it of indigenous populations or marginalize their presence. As befits a place where territorial control is key, the *terra nullius* formula remains in force. To those readers who might wonder why he does not describe meeting anyone, Goncharov explains: "No one lives here, from the Arctic Sea to the

Chinese borders, except the nomadic Tungus, scattered here and there on these vast spaces." In point of fact, the Far East of Siberia *was* very sparsely populated. For Goncharov, moreover, as for many of his contemporaries, to "live" in a place meant not to move, so nomadism didn't really count as a form of habitation. Asked whom he encountered on his journeys north, a local Russian missionary replies: "No one lives there, only Yakuts, Tungus, and Chukchi roam around (*kochuiut*)." Yet even in areas more densely populated by aborigines, including those relatively settled, Goncharov perceives no contradiction in reporting that he "constantly meets the Yakuts," while claiming only a few lines down that "almost no one lives here." Meaningful human presence clearly means both settled and Russian presence for Goncharov.[44]

Westward movement toward European Russia summons ever more optimistic images of a properly human—that is, Russian—presence. These include cleared forests and cultivated fields, better roads and transportation methods, and more prosperous settlers and aborigines. Goncharov's spirits rise along with this ascending line of progress. The network of post stations becomes denser the farther west one travels toward Yakutsk. Signs of development rapidly multiply. This civilizational gradient is for Goncharov also a gradient of Russianness. One settlement of Christianized Sakha (Yakuts), who are said to live not in yurts but in half-Russian, "half-Yakut" huts, illustrates the ascendant power of Russian culture, itself an emissary of the European one. Decorated traditional tables underneath Russian icons in those abodes of the natives signal to Goncharov "Europe and civilization."[45]

It is precisely through its ability to Russianize the Sakha—through religious conversion and inculcating the Russian way of life—that Russia fulfills its European calling to spread enlightenment. As Slezkine notes, while in the seventeenth century enlightenment meant merely baptism, in the nineteenth it meant Russification, with "the door theoretically open to all." Yet as Vinkovetsky remarks, the point of opening that door was to make natives into "submissive imperial subjects, culturally as well as politically."[46] Assimilation, whatever its motives, may appear morally superior to western colonialisms' regimes of exclusion. However, refusing to recognize someone's sense of being different is also a traumatic form of colonial oppression. Goncharov's insistence on the settlers' Russianizing potential, moreover, tensely coexists with his many examples of their instead "going native" and adopting the Sakha language and culture.

After two years of wanderings, Goncharov yearns to behold the first proper Russian town and has his sights set on Yakutsk. Yet Yakutsk initially disappoints him:

> Despite Russian churches, Russian houses, Russian officials and merchants, how naked it all was! How would it be possible in Russia (*na Rusi*) to have not a single little orchard or hedge shading homes and fences, no greenery, if not apple or pear trees, then at least acacias? Are these slanted-eyed, flat-nosed people really Russian? When I drove up to town, I kept running into Yakut men and women on oxen, horses, carts, and on horseback.

Goncharov quickly moderates this displeasure. Although he can do without the Sakha residents and would wish for greater splendor, the town of Yakutsk cheers Goncharov up precisely because of its discernible Russianness: "after all, this is Russia (*Rus'*), even if only Siberian Russia." Despite its unique social, cultural, and linguistic hybridity, he claims, Yakutsk has "its own grand, if a bit stern, physiognomy."[47]

Siberia's hybrid Russianness strikes Goncharov especially in the sphere of language. Fascinated by non-standard usages, phonemic shifts, and phraseological innovations of Siberia's pidgin Russian, he at some point unceremoniously pulls out a notebook and starts documenting the live speech of one of his Russian interlocutors. Though Goncharov does not make this connection for his readers, Siberia's pidgin Russian is partly a consequence of its diversity. From the myopic distance of European Russia, people who looked like "Russian" colonists were in fact a motley crew of Ukrainians, Belarusians, Poles, and Czechs—that is, Slavs of varied cultural and linguistic traditions, who moreover mingled with Germans, Jews, Tatars, and other ethnic groups summoned by various monarchs to settle Siberia.[48]

As Goncharov travels further, he applauds both the signs of rye and barley, favored in the Slavic settler's diet, and the decreasing use of the Sakha (Yakut) language. As he draws closer to Irkutsk, he notes that "almost no one speaks the Yakut language, and the stations began to be all Russian." Painting a gregarious scene of village life that would be familiar to any Russian, he exclaims, relieved:

> Thank God! Everything started to resemble Russia: frequent settlements, little villages. . . . Horses roaming in the streets play with ours or, frightened by the sound of bells, rush headlong to the side, along with pink piglets. Sparrows and rooks fly about, roosters crow,

> little boys whistle and wave at passing carriages, and smoke rises in solid vertical columns from a multitude of chimneys—the smoke of the fatherland! The pictures of Russia (*Rus'*) that would be familiar to all! The only thing missing is the manor house, a lackey opening shutters, and a sleepy master in the window. . . . This has never existed in Siberia, and this—that is, the absence of serfdom—represents the most remarkable feature of its physiognomy.[49]

Though the term *Rus'* also has other historically specific meanings, it signals here an ancient, traditional Russian community, the essential national core beyond tsars' and bureaucrats' reach. "The smoke of the fatherland" is a well-known trope with which Russian writers evoke warm patriotic associations; in their poetry this smoke appears "sweet and pleasant." To speak of colonies here would spoil the effect. Goncharov envelops Siberia for his readers in a rich and cozy blanket of nationalist allusions. What he identifies as lacking in this picture—landowners and serfdom—proves in fact Siberia's advantage. Goncharov believed, like many Decembrists, that this contributed to greater egalitarianism and individual initiative among Siberians.[50]

In imperfectly Russian Yakutsk, Goncharov consoles himself that all that is non-Russian in Siberia "will in time become Russian." Through his own descriptions of Siberia in *The Frigate Pallada,* he does his part to bring this to pass.[51]

Siberian Aborigines under Russian Rule

Detailed ethnographies of the kind encountered in many explorers' travel accounts are not part of the mix of *The Frigate Pallada*. Moreover, Goncharov seems less curious about the aboriginal people of Siberia than he was about their counterparts in southern Africa.[52] He focuses his narrative lens on Russians and Cossacks, marginalizing both the presence and significance of indigenous populations. Yet when we shift the focus to those margins, what do we learn about Goncharov's view of Siberia's aborigines as social groups and about their place in the imperial polity? How does he portray the impact of the Russian conquest on Siberia's indigenous peoples?

The first Siberian native Goncharov encounters is a classic creature of the borderlands. He is an Evenki (Tungus) man, an itinerant trapper from the Manchurian shores of the Ussuri River basin, who goes by the Russian name Afonka. Afonka hunts game for the Russians, far preferring his makeshift shooting contraption to the newfangled modern rifle the Russians offer

Figure 4.3. An ethnographic portrait of the Sakha (Yakuts), a Siberian native people. Goncharov sees in a Christianized Sakha settlement the ascendant power of Russian culture.

him as a gift. He is said to be the only local brave enough to have dealings with the Russians. In his hunting, he effortlessly traverses the Sino-Russian borderland "speaking all languages a little, including the savages' dialects, and mostly using a mixture of them all." He seems a prototype of Dersu Uzala, a Nanai trapper immortalized by a 1923 memoir by the Russian explorer of the Ussuri region, Vladimir Arsenyev, and by Akira Kurosawa's film adaptation of that book, *Dersu Uzala.*[53]

The Sakha (Yakuts) are Goncharov's favorite Siberian ethnic group. Given the writer's many interactions with them, they acquire special prominence in *The Frigate Pallada.* The largest of Siberia's Turkic-speaking populations, the Sakha were the most advanced and culturally dominant in central and eastern Siberia. Given their ancient links to the Arctic, Chinese, and nomadic steppe civilizations, Glebov describes these cattle and horse pastoralists as "a remarkable case of pre-European cosmopolitanism." They practiced shamanism and had a well-developed oral epic tradition.[54] The Cossacks, who reached the Lena basin in pursuit of sable pelts in the early seventeenth century, imposed fur tribute on the Sakha but met with resistance, which they systematically and ruthlessly crushed. The Cossacks and their fortified wooden garrisons (*ostrogi*) were followed by settlers who competed for the Sakha land. Many Sakha eventually interbred with Russians and after nearly a century of resistance, adapted to the ways of the colonial regime, often to the detriment of their communities.[55]

Goncharov portrays the Sakha as kind, competent, friendly, and exceedingly obliging toward the Russians. A vibrant presence amounting to about two hundred thousand people in the Yakutsk district alone, they have their own administrative units based on clans. The writer disagrees with Speransky's classifying of the Sakha as nomads. If moving between winter and summer yurts is a sign of nomadism, he scoffs, then Petersburgers are also nomads, given their summer migrations to countryside dachas. Expecting grimy hovels, Goncharov finds Sakha yurts surprisingly comfortable and—something a traveler in central Russia would envy—free of vermin (this later proves less than universally true). Yet not everything about the Sakha delights him. Few Sakha women appear fetching to Goncharov, who finds them distinguishable from men by earrings only. (Mercifully, he later removes an offensive comparison to cows standing on hind legs.) Few Sakha speak Russian, moreover, forcing Goncharov to learn some of their phrases. This is no small feat, since in Goncharov's judgment, the challenges of pronouncing English pale in comparison: "not only throat, tongue, teeth, and cheeks, but also eyebrows, forehead wrinkles and even, it seems, hair" are harnessed in the elocution of Siberia's local languages.[56]

Given that until recently, as Goncharov harshly puts it, the Sakha were "half-human, half-animal," he is impressed with the strides toward civilization they have made since the Russians' arrival. Goncharov's demeaning racial attitudes toward them remain confined to his correspondence. Though he calls them the land's "natural masters," he suggests that they owe their welfare and prosperity to the Russians. Thanks to Russian employment and care, they are clean, well clothed, and well fed. He claims that all are Christian, drawing an overly hasty conclusion from their copper cross pendants.[57]

His experience with Sakha guides confirms for Goncharov the prevailing view of them as smart, capable, hard workers. Heavily employed in transport, less so in agriculture, they also excel in fashioning objects from walrus tusk and bone, which Goncharov can imagine becoming fashionable St. Petersburg knick-knacks. Their biggest fault is a propensity for larceny; in their canniness as thieves, Goncharov writes, they match the industry's leaders in London. A stolen cow is shod in human footwear to disguise the trail in the snow. Though he judged the Xhosa harshly for stealing cattle, Goncharov is more lenient toward the Sakha, perhaps disarmed and amused by the "subtlety" of their craft.[58]

Exploited and downtrodden colonials the Sakha are not, by Goncharov's account. Their resourcefulness, spirit of enterprise, and cultural resilience impress him throughout. Dashing urban Sakha in Yakutsk sport beautifully ornamented fur attire; some Sakha are more affluent than the Russians. The writer is astounded to meet a Russian by the name of Bushkov who hires himself as a driver to a Sakha master. The Russian driver and his family live in the yurt of their enterprising employer. Bushkov's monolingual Sakha-speaking daughter finds no need for the Russian language. Goncharov can only shake his head: "Why Egor Petrovich Bushkov lives in the Inguchaia-Muranskaia station, why he hires himself out to a Yakut and lives in the same yurt with him—these are mysteries for which I have yet to find the key." The cultural hybridity and economic patterns of the Siberian frontier violate Goncharov's expectations of a colonial situation. Accustomed to seeing the white European always in the position of authority, in both his reading and voyaging, Goncharov is perplexed to see this hierarchy reversed. No Dutchman tended a vineyard owned by an African in the Cape Colony, but in the colony of Siberia—and indeed in many parts of the Romanov empire—such "anomalies" were relatively common.[59]

Describing eastern Siberia, Goncharov devotes barely six lines of text to its conquest. He fleetingly mentions Sakha attacks on the Cossack fortress in the 1830s. Eventually, infighting among the Cossacks "forced our government to take this land in its hands." Earlier he presumed the British government in the Cape Colony to be similarly "forced." Though Goncharov is silent on this, the Sakha raids were unsuccessful attempts to drive out the Russians and end their ruinous extraction of tribute. The writer does not consider the very presence of a Cossack fortress a reason for Cossack-Sakha discord, just as he did not see the presence of European intruders as the reason for the British-Xhosa Wars. As in the African chapter, the historical memory of colonial encounters extends only as far as is convenient for the colonizer. The prehistory of the conquest may as well not exist. The clock of Siberian history started ticking with the coming of the Russians. Goncharov would likely agree with the nineteenth-century Russian historian who memorably claimed that "Siberia did not emerge from the diapers of oblivion until the Khan's turban fell from Kuchum's head."[60]

Contrary to the impression created by *The Frigate Pallada,* the 1630 imperial takeover of the Sakha land did not restore peace and order but merely aggravated the depredations. According to historian John Stephan, refusals to provide fur tribute resulted in hostage-taking and the torching of villages. Between 1638 and 1642, the military governor of Yakutsk succeeded in collecting over a hundred thousand sable pelts "by hanging recalcitrants from meat hooks." This brutality led to a Sakha rebellion in 1642. The Cossack response was a campaign of terror involving torture and the butchering of hundreds of men, women, and children. Stephan reports that the Sakha population fell by seventy percent over the next four decades. It is unclear how much of this Goncharov actually knows. He does know that the Cossacks were far from blameless—he mentions their abuse of the local population in a private letter.[61]

At the time of his visit, not all of Siberia's ethnic groups are as amenable to Russian rule as the Sakha, but in mentioning them, the writer masks their anti-colonial challenge. He presents the strained relations between the Russians and the Luoravetlans (Chukchi) as arising from mutually irrational suspicions of hostile intentions. Goncharov does not disclose that the Luoravetlans waged a successful military challenge to the Russians. They secured autonomy and a ban on Russian settlement on their territory. Officially declared by the tsarist government as "not completely subdued," they remained unsubdued well into the twentieth century. As Goncharov may have read in Ferdinand Vrangel's travelogue, they were better connected to the American economy than the Russian one. Nor does Goncharov's reader learn that in 1742 the imperial Senate ordered their "total extirpation." The Russian military simply proved unable to carry out the genocidal order. Instead, Goncharov stresses the Luoravetlans' destitution, hence worthlessness as subjects, almost as face-saving insurance against the Russians' continued failure to conquer them. This argument had other flexible uses. Were the Russians to emerge victorious, the poverty of the Luoravetlans would help demonstrate that profit was never a motive. According to *The Frigate Pallada,* not armies, but government officials and missionaries were sent to the Luoravetlans, in order to "lead them out of savagery and to make their lives human. All that is done for free, unselfishly: there's nothing to take from them."[62]

Whether Goncharov is knowingly untruthful or evasive is beside the point. After all, what imperial travelogue and what travel writer is objective or truthful? But the social impact of *The Frigate Pallada* makes its relation to historical reality worth pondering. This extremely popular book has purveyed to the Russian reading public, from the mid-nineteenth century to today, an idealized picture of the Russian conquest and rule in Siberia. Ignoring the brutality of conquest, the book summons a vision of indigenous

Figure 4.4. An ethnographic portrait of Siberia's Luoravetlans (Chukchi). A perception of them as more "savage" likely stemmed from their staunch resistance to Russian rule.

Siberians as thriving under benevolent Russian rule, sometimes surpassing Russian settlers. Goncharov portrays the Sakha as successful businessmen, merchants, and even farmers. It is quite likely that he met many such Sakha—other contemporary travelers did, too. Yet as an iconic image of Siberia, his depiction is one-sided: it exaggerates the indigenous populations' colonial-era prosperity and leaves important problems in its shadow. This is what Mary Louise Pratt calls a strategy of anti-conquest, whereby "European bourgeois subjects seek to secure their innocence in the same moment as they assert European hegemony." The victim of colonialism is transformed into the object of paternalistic care.[63]

Public Booster, Private Skeptic: Russia's Civilizing Mission in Siberia

The Frigate Pallada was written and published at a time of important changes in Russia's imperial politics. This was a period of accelerated modernization, increasing power of Russian nationalism, and traumatic rebuff in the Crimea. According to Remnev, between the 1850s and 1860s, the imperial state departed from its former strategies of flexibility, pragmatism, and relative ethnic and confessional tolerance. It adopted a new lexicon in which national objectives and colonial aspirations came to the fore. Remnev credits in particular travelers and navy men for familiarizing Russia with western colonial management. Vinkovetsky similarly stresses that the lessons learned on voyages of circumnavigation helped modernize Russian colonial management, bringing it more in line with European models. "While demonstratively stressing a difference of Russia's Asian politics from the colonial politics of other states," Remnev writes, "Russian imperial ideologues carefully imitated their ideological and administrative experience." This experience was a subject of systematic study and observation by the Russian imperial government.[64]

The Frigate Pallada illuminates this transition, especially in its vision of Russia's civilizing mission in Siberia. Any self-respecting European empire was bound to articulate such a mission. Goncharov has outlined one for East Asia, especially Korea and Japan. This was a broad regional vision, which outlined a common European agenda, provided its philosophical justification, and volunteered Russia as a partner. And what of Russia's own civilizing mission in its biggest Asian region already under its control? What was Goncharov's local vision for Siberia?

Goncharov's thinking about this question was indelibly linked to the character and prospects of Siberia's colonization. Though it did not become a full-blown, vexed social question until the last two decades of the nineteenth century, colonization was on its way to becoming one by mid-century. By then, the state's interest in colonization grew. No longer content to fitfully regulate the outflow of migrants into the colonies, the imperial state became more involved in managing and directing colonization in areas such as infrastructure, legal framework, selection of locations, and public incentives.[65]

Apart from moving real people into real places, colonization was also a "cultural construction," as Sunderland stresses. As such, it attracted writers, poets, historians, explorers, ethnographers, and travelers who endowed it with special significance:

> Just about everywhere the colonization-watchers looked, they found "empty" lands that seemed to cry out for settlement, backward "aliens" (*inorodtsy*) who seemed to cry out for "civilization," and wondrous feats of pioneering that seemed to symbolize Russia's vast imperial potential. Colonization was becoming a grand event associated with grand connotations. . . . As educated Russians looked out on the settlement horizon of the early-to-mid 1800s, they . . . saw the march of progress, "civilization," utility, imperial destiny, and a whole range of other phenomena that arguably did not have much to do with "objective" circumstances of peasant settlement. The Russian colonizing vision, in other words, took place somewhere between fact and fiction. Much like the Russian representations of other aspects of the imperial experience, the representation of colonization in the early nineteenth century amounted to a mix of what educated Russians saw, what they wanted to see, and what they thought they should be seeing.[66]

This happens to describe Goncharov's attitude perfectly: colonization of Siberia as "a grand event with grand connotations." His descriptions of it in *The Frigate Pallada* are based on actual experience mixed with the heavy dose of wishful thinking that stemmed from having to present Russia's own imperial region in the double context of the Crimean War and the other empires' possessions depicted in his travelogue. Comparing Goncharov's travelogue to his other writings makes the disjunction between the writer's perceptions and representations visible. Like his educated peers, Goncharov combined what he saw, wanted to see, and thought he should be seeing. What he wanted *his readers* to see is also a compelling question in the present context.

For Goncharov, as for his contemporaries, civilization began with sedentary lifestyle and agriculture. Lack of either meant "savagery." By tilling Siberia's virgin land and teaching natives to farm, the Russian settler was seen as the main vehicle of progress. This also made him the main vehicle of Russianization due to a widely shared conviction that only the land tilled by the Russian plow could be regarded as "Russian."[67] The ascending gradient of Russianness that Goncharov experiences in his travel through Siberia is therefore tied to signs of agriculture. As he moves westward, the landscape is increasingly saturated with stacks of grain (signs of receding nomadism) and with haystacks (signs of increasing connectivity, since hay meant feed for horses that made transport possible). These are for Goncharov the visual markers of the civilizational progress achieved by the Russian agricultural settler, the fundamental engine of Russian colonization. Intrepid merchants and gold-seekers are mentioned but play a secondary role in the narrative. Undaunted explorers and government officials receive brief praise. Exiles make only a cameo appearance. It is the peasants who occupy the spotlight in the Siberian chapters.[68]

Throughout, Goncharov combats the widespread perception of the government as an inept manager of colonization. While a few settlers complain of poor soil and lack of necessary means, most are pleased with their harvests and the government's assistance. They report that the treasury sponsors the initial stock of horses and cattle and sometimes supports them with regular provisions of bread. One settler battling a particularly troublesome mice infestation claims that the only thing he lacks is a cat. Goncharov never calls Russian farmers in Siberia "colonists," even though what they are doing in Siberia—settling on a land originally not their own and employing indigenous people as laborers—is not in any qualitative sense different from what the Dutch do in the Cape Colony.

The settlers portrayed in *The Frigate Pallada* are hardworking, self-reliant, and resourceful. One sixteen-year-old female settler on the Maya River, a tributary in the Lena basin, uncomplainingly does man's work such as plowing and chopping wood. Her family resettled without a penny but now they own livestock and are building a stone house with high ceilings and big windows—hardly a typical peasant abode in European Russia. "These are free and easy parts," she explains. "Just work hard and don't be lazy; rye grows well, especially the winter variety, and hemp, too."[69] This vignette seems an invitation for others like this family to follow.

Though personal prosperity is a worthy goal, selfless sacrifice appears even more heroic to Goncharov. His real Russian hero is the settler Sorokin. A former sailor, he settled along the Maya River, hired the Evenki, sowed virgin land with no guarantee of harvest, and now boasts a profitable farm with excellent cattle. To Goncharov, one bull looks impressive enough to win prizes at English agricultural exhibits. Sorokin feeds his guests sumptuously, almost like an Afrikaner farmer. A moral imperative rather than a prospect of self-enrichment motivates Sorokin. Not content to rest on his laurels and enjoy his hard-won prosperity, he donates his property to the church and sets out for new territories to repeat his colonizing feat. Just like the settlers who arrive at the Lena region from older colonies west of Lake Baikal, Sorokin's movement charts the rippling course of Russian colonization of Siberia. While selfless, Sorokin is also humble. He displays government officials' letters of appreciation on his walls, but not prominently. Goncharov calls Sorokin "a little Titan" and prognosticates: "and how many such heroes will follow! Their name is legion."[70]

While the peasant binds Siberian land to the Russian economy, the missionary is the mainstay of Russia's spiritual and cultural power. The dauntless Orthodox priests who traverse mind-boggling expanses in any weather are also imperial transmitters of culture in *The Frigate Pallada*. Goncharov lavishes special accolades on the Kamchatka, Kurile, and Aleut Archibishop, Innokenty Veniaminov, whom he met in Irkutsk. He went on to become the Metropolitan of Moscow and has since become an Orthodox saint. His early spectacular successes in Russian America were later transplanted in eastern Siberia. His proselytism bound indigenous communities to Russian culture and empire. Largely thanks to him, Orthodoxy remains the main religion among many native and creole communities in Alaska. Innokenty actively fostered synergies between the church, colonial administration, and the business interests of the Russian-American Company, becoming, in Vinkovetsky's words, an "empire booster."[71]

Goncharov has the utmost respect for Innokenty's accomplishments and dauntlessness. Baptizing the distant Aleutians was no easy task, he writes, as Innokenty had to learn the Aleut language, which then had no written form, before translating the New Testament into it. Innokenty also laid the foundation for impressive scholarly studies of ethnography, geography, topography, and the natural history of the Aleut region. Goncharov deems Innokenty's publications about Russia's American colonies the best histories of the region available. According to Vinkovetsky, by contrast, they read like "a booster guide to improving the Russian colonial effort," with their cataloguing of the region's natural resources and comments on politics and economy. At once a missionary, a scholar, and a politician, Innokenty Veniaminov becomes in the travelogue the Siberian equivalent of southern Africa's geologist, engineer, and explorer, Mr. Bain: an exemplar of the varied competencies and unique virtues of the Russian colonial intelligentsia. With the passing of time, Goncharov's respect for Innokenty only grew. In the 1891 sketch "From Eastern Siberia," he claims that Innokenty's "apostolic" stature increases over the years, in proportion to the degree to which Siberia "becomes settled, enlivened, and humanized."[72]

Like farming, Christianization also meant Russification, even if conducted in the language of the convert. The missionaries transcribed the Siberian languages into Russian Cyrillic script. Innokenty and his followers, Goncharov reports, compiled Russian grammars and dictionaries of Siberian "dialects." At the time of Goncharov's visit, they were translating the Bible into the Sakha language. To illustrate the fruit of the local Orthodox clergy's missionary and linguistic labor, Goncharov reproduces "The Lord's Prayer" spelled phonetically in the Sakha, Evenki, and Tlingit languages. In his letters from Siberia, Goncharov pictured Innokenty as an ardent patriot: "Russian face, Russian mind, and living Russian speech." Innokenty reportedly trembled with excitement at the news of Russian military victories at Crimea. Incidentally, his belief that the Bible should be made available in the language of the convert would become controversial in the 1870s, when the famous Nikolai Ilminsky, a missionary and a professor of Turkic languages at Kazan University, had to wage battles with Russian nationalists to do the same for the steppe region's Tatars.[73]

Beyond agriculture and religion, trade plays a role in Goncharov's vision of Siberia's future. He and his fellow travelers make a point of buying up all the produce and game offered for sale by both the Russian settlers and the Sakha, generously paying without bargaining. So weighed down with comestibles is their river boat that it reminds Goncharov of a Chinese junk. As in his visits to Asian ports, Goncharov firmly believes that trade is a force consolidating the European presence in imperial settings. Not unlike certain straitened western economies of our own time, Goncharov presents consumerism as a patriotic duty, in this case needed to buttress the colonization effort. Speaking of the settlers' hope to find markets for their products, he decrees: "It is desirable that all travelers should, within their means, support this hope." The settlers should be reinforced in their decision to people the peripheries, and the natives should be made happy with the Russian rule. "With each year, everything improves," Goncharov confidently proclaims, recalling "mountains that have been plowed" and "impassable swamps that have been made passable." He eulogizes the work and patience that made these feats possible.[74]

Boosterism suffuses this section of *The Frigate Pallada*.[75] Though not exactly a glossy brochure, the work serves as an inspirational invitation for

Russians to come to Siberia and participate in a heroic feat. Goncharov's positive accounts of the government's assistance and the settlers' prosperity function within this framework. He rejects Siberia's popular disreputable image by disputing printed sources that disparage the region. He reassures his readers that legendary corruption, brigandage, and criminal impunity are problems of the past. To lessen common fears about extreme isolation in Siberia, justified especially with regard to its northeastern regions, Goncharov presents Russian settlers as ubiquitous while relegating the indigenous people to mere background. This was a demographic fantasy, to be sure. Readers of *The Frigate Pallada* would have been shocked to learn that fully three decades after Goncharov's visit Russians still constituted only two percent of Yakutia's population. Indigenous *terra nullius* this certainly was not. Goncharov also minimizes colonizing challenges, especially eastern Siberia's daunting climatic conditions. Thus in revising the book in 1879, he edits out information about the permafrost that never thaws deeper than two feet, and even then only briefly in August. He never mentions in his book that near the Amur, an area Russians were preparing to annex, he found the climate on shore so insalubrious that he refused to disembark from the frigate.[76]

While his correspondence contains images that might curb the enthusiasm of potential settlers or their advocates, Goncharov keeps these images out of his book. In one despondent letter, Goncharov describes Russian settlements as places "where nothing has yet been established except for a cemetery. Last winter thirty people who died of scurvy managed to find repose there." This did indeed happen to one isolated Russian garrison stationed in the Ussuri region in 1853–1854.[77] The narrative's boosterist momentum, its inoffensiveness to the censor, and Goncharov's own status as a government official would all suffer by the mention of a cemetery as the sole Russian colonial institution in some outposts, especially since scurvy is a disease of malnutrition.

In the relaxed censorship atmosphere of the early twentieth century, with Goncharov dead and buried, another veteran of the *Pallada* expedition exposed Goncharov's boosterist bluster. The former navy officer A. M. Linden took exception to Goncharov's description of the status of Russian colonization on the Maya River. Goncharov claimed to have obtained there with ease such produce as bread, cabbage, carrots, potatoes, and even beef and milk (cows were then a rarity in the Far East). The Maya River area was also home to some of Goncharov's iconic colonization success stories: the formerly penniless family building a spacious stone house, the "Titan" Sorokin and his prizeworthy cattle.

Following in Goncharov's footsteps three months later, Linden gathered quite different impressions of the Maya settlers' condition. Tasked with maintaining the mail service from Yakutsk to Ayan, the settlers suffered harsh privations according to Linden. Neither grains nor vegetables would grow; the cold was fierce, mortality and sickness high. Though he claimed to love Goncharov's book, just as everyone did, Linden nonetheless confessed:

> It was a bit strange to read Goncharov and his *Frigate Pallada* where he wrote, presumably to do Muravev a favor, that the settlers on the Maya River faced a radiant future once river transport develops and life stirs up. It is truly difficult to suppose that Goncharov could have seriously contemplated some sort of flourishing trade and manufacturing activity in the tundra, where unbearable frosts keep it frozen for ten months out of the year, and where soil never thaws. Luckily, the long-suffering Maya settlers were resettled to the southern Ussuri region in the early 1860s, and the Maya region again became a desert, which by virtue of its geographical location it should remain.

Linden implied that Goncharov volunteered to act as a propagandist for the General Governor of Siberia, Muravyev, who was intent on showcasing eastern Siberia's colonizing potential back in European Russia.[78]

Goncharov also seems to have given a facelift to the up-and-coming frontier town of Yakutsk, on the Lena River. As noted above, happy to see the first approximately "Russian" town, Goncharov nonetheless complains about its lack of a hotel and of greenery, both *de rigueur* in truly Russian towns. A reader inclined to make connections will wistfully contrast the bare-bones Yakutsk with the flourishing towns on Goncharov's excursion in southern Africa. Nonetheless, the people in Yakutsk are friendly enough, and rudimentary amenities exist. Though cultural Sakha-Russian hybridity currently prevails, Goncharov is confident that everything non-Russian "will with time become Russian."[79]

Such cautious optimism is absent in his epistolary impressions of Yakutsk. "The Yakut capital is so pitiful and poor that it pains one to look," he confesses in one letter, noting teetering houses, scarcity of females (a perennial problem of Russian colonization in Siberia), and an incident of apparently being propositioned by revolting Sakha prostitutes. He worries that depression and

Figure 4.5. "On the Road. Death of a Migrant," painting by Sergei Ivanov, 1889. By contrast to Goncharov's boosterism, late nineteenth-century artists stressed the challenges and perils faced by Russian settlers. Scala/Art Resource.

rheumatism will "eat him alive" if he remains here long. In a letter to the editor of the prestigious journal *Notes of the Fatherland,* Andrei Kraevsky, Goncharov's tone changes to black humor. The Sakha women apparently like to loiter in the ruins of the Cossack fortress "either crying over their lost Jericho or with a more practical aim," by which he implies the natives' use of this dilapidated symbol of Cossack power as an open-air bathroom. Phlegm coats the local store, giving it an "antique greenish hue." All homes, including the governor's residence, resemble that of Baba Yaga, the classic witch of Russian fairy tales. The staying power of Russian culture is shockingly low. The Russians, even government officials, have gone entirely native, having adopted the Sakha language and customs.[80] Such contrasts between the travelogue and other accounts of Goncharov's experience further demonstrate that *The Frigate Pallada* is not a collection of carefree impressions, but an ideologically shaped argument.

Nowhere is this more obvious than in the innocuous description of the efforts to steer the *Pallada* up the Amur River. Since all other major Siberian rivers flow into the Arctic Ocean, the Amur was seen as Russia's only chance for a meaningful egress to the Pacific, deemed as crucial for the eastern part of the empire as the Baltic Sea was for the western. To acquire and colonize the region would close the Russian frontier in the East.[81] In order for

Russia to establish a military and economic presence on the Pacific, control of the Amur was widely seen as critical. At the time, this control belonged to China. In the seventeenth century, the Cossacks attempted to establish a Russian presence in the Amur region, then China's vassal territory. Despite initial successes, they were routed by the Qing army, forcing them to cede the territory in the 1689 Treaty of Nerchinsk.[82] Using the opportunity of China's weakness during the Opium Wars and the Taiping Rebellion, the Russians annexed the Amur and the Ussuri Rivers region. To this day, the Chinese and the Russians have competing historical narratives about this event. The Chinese consider it an unjust land seizure orchestrated through a classic European "unequal treaty." The Russians consider it a "return" of territory that rightfully belonged to them, a claim in which the initial unsuccessful conquest by the seventeenth-century Cossacks serves as proof of original possession. Goncharov unquestioningly subscribed to the latter view.

The person who made the annexation of the Amur his personal mission was the General-Governor of Eastern Siberia, Nikolai Muravev. Appointed to the post following his imperial service in Poland and the Caucaus, he was the quintessence of bold geopolitical ambition and single-minded determination. The regionalist Siberian historian Mikhail Veniukov, with just a touch of self-confessed hyperbole, appraised Muravev's importance for Siberia as comparable to that of Catherine the Great for Russia or of Louis XIV for France. As governor general, Muravev enjoyed extraordinary powers, including such atypical foreign-policy prerogatives as the right to negotiate borders with China in the name of the tsar. He was the single most important driving force for annexing the Amur. He treated Siberia as the place where Russia could take revenge "for all that the West made her suffer." His dogged efforts ultimately secured the grudging approval of the St. Petersburg government, which had been wary of antagonizing China.[83]

In his gripping account of what he terms the "Amur euphoria" of 1840–1865, Mark Bassin explores the intense public advocacy surrounding the cause of annexation. Its proponents argued that the Amur was of key strategic significance for Russian rule in Asia. The grassroots support for the annexation not only defied a stubborn government but also ignored the vast evidence furnished by explorers about the river's dim navigational and economic prospects. The Amur's navigability for large vessels was of particular importance, in view of its intended uses as a military base and a shipping route. Almost single-mindedly, and deaf to any opposition, Muravev achieved his goal through the 1858 Treaty of Aigun, in which China ceded the region to Russia. This gain was confirmed by the 1860 Treaty of Beijing. Almost overnight, the region then fell back into the obscurity from which it had emerged, its vaunted potential proving illusory. Muravev had to resort to forced resettlement. Voluntary colonization saw an increase only in the last two decades of the nineteenth century, spurred by the discovery of gold.[84]

One will vainly attempt to glean from *The Frigate Pallada* these high political stakes of the *Pallada*'s exploration of the Amur estuary. In two brief paragraphs, Goncharov portrays it as a frivolous, if bumpy, jaunt. He placidly mentions the ever-changing topography of the shallows that obstructed navigation. He admits that a few times the ship scraped the sandy bottom, but uses this fact to create comic relief, describing the quizzical glances of diners when their table started hopping. Once, he writes, the frigate leaned so heavily to the side that it had to be propped—"but, thank God, we emerged from the estuary and, having successfully slid between the Asian continent and Sakhalin Island, we entered the Sea of Okhotsk."[85]

Not only does Goncharov silence the politically charged purpose of the *Pallada*'s Amur exploration, he also spectacularly diminishes the hardships. According to records reviewed by literary scholar Engelgardt, sailing up the Amur was the most dangerous phase of the entire expedition. No storms on the high seas matched this adventure with a Siberian river. Rather than a brief exploratory foray, it took two and a half months. The *Pallada* nearly crashed several times. Human losses were tremendous. Engelgardt states that during the Amur phase, "the *Pallada* lost more crewmembers than during its entire voyage, the overall mortality being already very high in comparison to other expeditions." Anxious about his *cause célèbre,* Muravev had prematurely sent a triumphant report to St. Petersburg that the *Pallada* proved Amur's navigability. In order to cover his lie, Muravev relentlessly forced the ship's captain, Unkovsky, to keep trying. All this was to no avail. In the end, Putiatin had to disobey Muravev's order. Only the smaller and swifter *Diana* was capable of navigating further up the Amur, but Goncharov was by then transported by schooner to Ayan. Muravev later denigrated Unkovsky and Putiatin to the St. Petersburg authorities, attributing failure to their feeble efforts. Though it involved occasional starvation, Putiatin nonetheless journeyed on the Amur back to European Russia after his Japanese and Chinese diplomatic missions, a highly symbolic journey given Russia's recent imperial gains in Asia.[86]

The reason for Goncharov's glaring misrepresentation of this episode is his own enthusiastic support of the Amur's annexation, in line with the sentiments of the nationalist aficionados described by Bassin. He thus never divulges in *The Frigate Pallada* that the expedition concluded the Amur was *not* navigable for large vessels. Goncharov loved Muravev's bravado and thought the Russian government overly timid in territorial expansion—hence Goncharov's own coaxing policy recommendations about Korea. Muravev no doubt also had Goncharov's sympathetic ear when the two men journeyed together from the Amur to Ayan, and later from Irkutsk to St. Petersburg. In a letter from Irkutsk of January 1855, Goncharov mentions Siberia's two true patriots: Archbishop Innokenty, who Christianized Siberian tribes, and Muravev, who despite the diktat of the Ministry of the Interior "returned" to Russia a huge fertile chunk of Siberia including the Amur River, and who spectacularly repulsed the British attack on Kamchatka during the Crimean War. In other writings, echoing the customary sobriquets of the Amur euphoria, Goncharov called the Amur "our Mississippi" and Muravev "a brave, enterprising Yankee." He raved about Muravev: "What energy! What breadth of horizons, quickness of imagination, unquenchable fire in his whole constitution, what will to fight obstacles!"[87]

Goncharov's vision of the Russian civilizing mission in Siberia, in sum, is one of successful improvement. It rests on the colonization of the land, the Christianization of the indigenous people, and—somewhat more distant—the development of trade. In this, it is similar to the Spanish mission in Latin America and the French one in Canada. Russian peasant and missionary are the main vehicles of this progress for Goncharov. Their civilizing activities double as Russianizing ones, ensuring the spread of Russian culture, customs, and economic patterns, thus binding Siberia ever closer to Russia. They may experience setbacks, but Goncharov has no doubt about the eventual trajectory of this process. Assimilating indigenous people is implicitly treated as the best guarantee of securing Russia's imperial control. In promoting this vision, Goncharov creates a positive image of the civilizing efforts undertaken so far—the relative prosperity of farmers, the successes of missionaries, the improvements in infrastructure—and argues that those who would take up this cause in the future would be performing a patriotic feat. The national and imperial goals work in tandem. Goncharov's boosterism makes him deemphasize the challenges so as to avoid dampening the prospects and merits of further territorial expansion, as in the Amur.

The colonization of Siberia may be said to be ongoing. President Putin made Siberia's development a twenty-first-century priority. Summons to modern-day pioneers to head out for the eastern frontier have recently resounded from the Russian Federation's halls of power. In 2016, the Ministry for the Development of the Far East designated nine Far Eastern regions for a settlement program, offering free land in exchange for its development in a program similar to the US 1862 Homestead Act. Revanchist sentiments among the Chinese, many of whom consider the Amur-Ussuri region to rightfully belong to China, make Russians nervous. Might China one day demand restitution of the lands seized in tsarist times? Such questions and tensions keep this chapter of Russian history open.[88]

Russian Answer to the British

Other nineteenth-century European empires were, of course, also annexing, settling, Christianizing, trading, uplifting natives, and spreading their languages and cultures across the globe. Some, like the British, enjoyed a considerably greater reputation of being successful. But Goncharov is no different from his like-minded Russian nationalists: to catch up with the West was not enough. Was there any way in which Russia as an imperial power was different or superior to its rivals?

This question arose for Goncharov in Irkutsk, where he received mail with political news about the Crimean War, by then in full swing, from his St. Petersburg friend, the painter Nikolai Maikov. The letter exuded the patriotic fervor that gripped St. Petersburg society. Appended to it was a feuilleton full of patriotic and anti-English sentiments, published in a St. Petersburg daily by Maikov's son Apollon. Goncharov described both the feuilleton and his own response to it in the text of *The Frigate Pallada.* In the part he omitted from the travelogue, Apollon Maikov railed against the Europeans' slanderous images of the Russian empire as a "colossus that suppresses nations, a Saturn that devours its children." The presence of many Finnish, Baltic, Polish, Georgian, Armenian, and even Muslim soldiers on the battlefields of the Crimea, he claimed, proved this false. Try finding, Maikov challenged his correspondent, "even one Indian name in English history, of the 100,000,000 Indians subjugated by England." What the Europeans failed to understand about the Russian empire's constituent minorities, Maikov argued, was that "having joined the great family of nations comprising the Russian empire, each of them acquired the right and the opportunity, as it were, to participate in world events and to inscribe their name in the annals of the history of mankind! Russia opens for them the door to glory, a grand path for their descendants."[89] In a classic trope of Russian imperial imagery, the Russian empire for Maikov was not a structure of subjugation or oppression, but a harmonious family of nations. Inclusion in the imperial polity bequeathed to its members a world-historical significance, one that could purportedly become available to them only by riding Russia's coattails.

Goncharov imports to the travelogue Maikov's subsequent rejection of the Europeans' view of Russians as "barbarians." A glance at Russia's colonizing successes, Maikov writes, easily proves them wrong: "could barbarians, in less than half a century, lead to such flourishing in the erstwhile wilderness now known as New Russia, the Crimea, the Astrakhan and Orenburg districts, and southern Siberia? And Transcaucasia? And Georgia? . . . No, barbarians did not do all that. On the contrary, a civilized nation, or—what's still more important, more lofty—a civilizing nation did this. A Cossack picket in the Kirghiz steppe: that's an embryo of Europe in Asia (*zarodysh Evropy v Azii*)." The formula stresses Russia's contribution to Europe's common mission in Asia. Yet the passage also illuminates the imperial stakes of Russian identity: Europeanness comes with the possession of an empire one can civilize. Dostoevsky would advance this formula three decades later by proclaiming that it is *only* in Asia where a Russian can confidently feel European. Maikov's outburst also testifies to a certain "grandeur and chic," as Sunderland aptly catches this psychological nuance, that was felt by Russia's imperial elites by virtue of "ruling over non-Russian peoples." Goncharov was so enthused by Maikov's ideas that he claimed to have started an article in which his own Siberian experience would corroborate Maikov's insight that "Russia opens up for its subjugated peoples a wide field of activity and of rational application of effort."[90]

The article was never finished, but its ideas entered *The Frigate Pallada*.[91] In particular, Goncharov bolsters Maikov's vision of a civilizing empire by highlighting the material progress of Siberia's domestication. He reports this in the second person plural, placing his readers rhetorically in his own vantage point, inviting everyone to share in his experience. These days, uninterrupted travel is available in places that don't yet have geographical names. The Sakha guides helpfully guide "you," solicitous of "your" comfort, "modest and meek," as it should be. They are usefully occupied "clearing land, smoothing roads, and building bridges." Ample provisions are available everywhere—"all in a country until recently known as a wilderness." "You" are safe everywhere, just as on Petersburg streets. To be sure, one encounters difficulties, but harsh nature alone is responsible for those.[92]

Goncharov also supports Maikov's ideas by more decisively calling Siberia's indigenous people the objects of Russians' civilizing efforts. This exchange between two Russian intellectuals shows how theories of "civilizing" imperial minorities emerge in the context of imperial rivalries. Imperial humanitarianism was one of these rivalries' platforms. Potent theories of uplifting "savages" (or lesser nations) were an important way of keeping up with the imperial Joneses.

Civilizing is absolutely what Russia has been and should be doing in Siberia, according to Goncharov. He reveals this conviction in a sharp polemic with an earlier traveler to Siberia, Matvei Gedenshtrom. Goncharov rejects the fatalism of Gedenshtrom, who argued that no attempts should be made to civilize Siberia's native peoples. In Goncharov's paraphrase of Gedenshtrom, to do so would mean to force them to realize the wretchedness of their condition and their inability to remedy it. Goncharov considers this a hopelessly outdated apostasy. He argues that the ability to alleviate wretchedness hinges on recognizing it. Gedenshtrom's disavowal of the Russian civilizing mission in Siberia also stemmed from a concern that the infantile savage would necessarily gravitate to civilization's superficial glitter. If that is so, Goncharov counters, this only proves that more spiritual care is needed. According to Goncharov, the progress in Siberian affairs, such as the subsiding of natives' vices, proves the defeatist Gedenshtrom wrong: "Like a fire, enlightenment spreads over the entire earthly globe."[93]

But since the Russian empire was not alone in spreading enlightenment, this wasn't enough to differentiate it from its rivals. In responding to Maikov's feuilleton, Goncharov identifies a better platform. Maikov claimed that the Cossack picket in Asia was an "embryo of Europe." Goncharov ups his friend's ante by claiming that Russia's remake of Siberia inculcates not merely (corrupt) European ways, but uniquely Russian ones. His cardinal evidence is the prohibition on the sale of alcohol, in force from the shores of the Okhotsk Sea all the way to Yakutsk. When their crate of liquor breaks during the passage across the Dzhugdzhur Mountains, Goncharov and his companions must wait until their arrival in Yakutsk to drink again. Goncharov credits this prohibition for Siberia's colonial and economic miracle. Having just seen the ravages caused by the Europeans' opium sale in China, he embraces this fact as proof of the moral superiority of Russian colonialism. Sale of alcohol may be well and good in more densely populated areas, he writes,

> but here—in this young country, where all measures and actions of the government aim to fuse with the huge Russian family a handful

> of alien-tribe children (*inoplemennye deti*), mankind's wild youths, for whom systematic labor is an excruciating, unnecessary novelty, and who require careful and gradual education—here alcohol would cause this handful of people to perish, as it led the American natives to perish. . . . This governmental measure reveals a profound calculation, but it is *an embryo not of Europe in Asia*, but a uniquely Russian example of civilization. It wouldn't be bad if some European vessels shuttling between East India and the ports of China took a lesson.[94]

Given the prominence of alcohol-related revenues in the state budget, the Russian government's prohibition shows the priority of principle over economic interest. Goncharov contrasts Russia's moral authority with the unscrupulous opium trade of the British, heedless of the Asians' welfare, and with the American colonists' use of alcohol as a tool of expansion, which decimated Native American peoples. Western colonialists should be taking lessons from the Russians, Goncharov claims. He is gratified to reverse the roles between teachers and students from his earlier survey of the imperial world. While a member of Europe's civilizing cohort in Asia, Russia simultaneously implants the "embryo" of its own superior civilization.

Unfortunately, as regards alcohol at least, this was misleading. The prohibition on the sale of alcohol to native people had little effect, as traders commonly used it to extract lower prices for pelts. In Slezkine's sober assessment, "the liquor trade was theoretically illegal but practically universal"; without vodka "no commercial transaction could ever take place." Stephan concurs that the prohibition on the sale of alcohol to natives was as "unenforceable" as another well-intentioned legal measure: a ban on the sale of native women to Russian military men. Beside epidemic diseases, alcohol addiction contributed greatly to the "demoralization and near-destitution" of Siberian peoples.[95] Chekhov would later discuss rampant alcoholism among both natives and Russians in Siberia in his travelogue *Sakhalin Island*. Moreover, if the official sale of alcohol was banned east of Yakutsk, the vast majority of Siberia was not exactly a dry county. Yakutsk emerges in Goncharov's travelogue as well supplied with a wide assortment of liquor. In fact, in a late sketch about eastern Siberia, Goncharov described the life of the Russian society in Yakutsk as revolving around alcohol, drunk in huge quantities. Even by the evidence of *The Frigate Pallada*, there are reasons to doubt the effectiveness of this ban. Goncharov mentions, for example, that the Sakha prefer to be paid in vodka, which would indicate this to be a common enough practice. He himself used alcohol as barter to obtain necessities from an addicted native—the trapper Afonka, though this was outside the then official borders of the Russian empire.[96]

Nonetheless, Goncharov did have a point about a qualitative difference between the Russian empire's ineffective alcohol ban in Siberia and the British empire's government-sponsored drug-pushing in China. That Goncharov feels compelled to make this argument as an answer to the Europeans shows his awareness of Russia operating on a global imperial chessboard. Not merely the possession of territory, but one's conduct in it became in the nineteenth century an important measure of an empire's worth. The stakes seemed high enough for Goncharov to omit some facts and embroider others a bit, though he may simply have been unaware of many. Concerns about censorship may have also played a role, but up to a point. While he took the opportunity under a more relaxed censorship regime to fill in some such blanks of *The Frigate Pallada,* key among them his meetings with the exiled Decembrists, recanting boosterism was not among them.[97] A comparison with his private writings and other sources allows us to catch Goncharov with his hands in the cookie jar: he certainly fudged *some* of what he knew to be true. He did that because he wished to propagandize the empire's benevolent guardianship of the natives' welfare and a vision of Siberia as the pinnacle of Russia's civilizing achievement. *The Frigate Pallada* thus helped create a popular mythology of Russian Siberia. It inculcated in its readers national pride about their empire's colonial ventures and a belief in their government's probity and effectiveness, myths Chekhov would later try to dislodge.

Purity of motives reigns supreme in Goncharov's separate public effort to inculcate in Russia's youth the virtues and duties of Russia's colonizing mission in Siberia. He champions this cause in an 1858 youth magazine article based on the *Pallada* voyage. Drawing on the travelogue, he contrasts for his young readers the profit-oriented western model and the disinterested Russian one. According to him, scientific and humanitarian ideals are a mere mask for the true driver of the English and American expansion: greed for natural resources. Throughout *The Frigate Pallada,* Goncharov unapologetically gives profit a positive value in his comments on global trade and on the British rule in the Cape Colony; he himself greedily eyed Japan's natural resources from the deck of the *Pallada.* But now he chastises such vices and presents Russian imperialism, at least in Siberia, as innocent of crass motivations.

Why are we in Siberia? Goncharov's answer for his young Russian audience is: a pure neighborly feeling and the Russian man's burden. He lectures: "These places are contiguous to our possessions and those savages are our neighbors. It behooved us more than others to learn about these places, describe them so as to make this information universally available, and, perhaps, to settle them. Colonization—which means a settlement and cultivation of empty spaces—has been considered since deep antiquity a duty of enlightened nations."[98] Young Russians, in other words, should espouse Russia's colonizing mission, which is their duty as citizens of an enlightened nation. Their very espousal of this duty, conversely, confers the status of the enlightened nation on Russia. The "empty" land of Siberia awaits them.

Siberia and Africa under Imperial Trusteeship

Troubled by such pessimistic assessments of Russia's contribution to human progress as Petr Chaadaev's famous "Philosophical Letter," which gauged this contribution to be negligible, Goncharov casts the colonization of underdeveloped lands as Russia's signal contribution to the global progress of mankind. He writes: "I am now an actual witness of a chemical-historical process, in which deserts are turning into human habitations, savages are promoted to the calling of man, religion and civilization combat savagery and awaken dormant forces to life."[99] It is a "chemical" process because cultivation was thought to warm the soil and thus change the very structure of the earth. This "laboratory" is run by the Russian "Titans"—people of all walks of life who took up the challenge of awakening Siberia to life. Goncharov prophesies that the end result of these processes will be nothing short of monumental. As reviewers would remark, Goncharov narrates his travelogue with commendable calm; his pulse rarely quickens. The following passage is one of the few exceptions:

> And when a completely ready, settled, and enlightened country—once dark and unknown—rises up in front of amazed mankind, demanding name and rights, let history then enquire who erected this edifice. This question will remain as unanswered as the one about those who built the pyramids in the desert. History will only remark that those same people who called for an abolition of slave trade in one corner of the globe, in another corner taught Aleuts and

> Kurilians how to live and pray. These people created and thought up Siberia, settled and enlightened it, and now they wish to return to the Creator the fruit of the seed He sowed.[100]

Siberia's Christianization and colonization crop up here in the context of imperial humanitarianism—in particular, the British empire's 1833 ban on slave trade. The heroic toilers in Siberia are here put on a par with the nameless builders of the Egyptian pyramids, projects of presumably comparable grandeur. Strikingly, Goncharov's compliment to Britain comes at a point when Britain and Russia are actually warring nations. This further proves the deep-rooted commonality of purpose among Euro-American imperialists that trumped any rivalries. Goncharov ignores the ongoing Crimean War to stress instead Britain and Russia's common toil for the benefit for the benighted "savage." He puts aside the two empires' differences and highlights the noble, disinterested goals they supposedly share.

Most strikingly, Goncharov basically implies through his metaphoric language that the logical conclusion of the colonial process is what sounds like decolonization. The work of Russian colonizers completed, Siberia will rise up and "demand name and rights." This idea is endowed with the dignity of Christian ethic: to "return to the Creator the fruit of the seed He sowed." This fruit's ripeness to be presumably determined by the Europeans, this would follow the achievement of prosperity, enlightenment, and progress, all gifts of European colonizers to their backward subjects. The passage frames colonial rule as the fulfillment of the divine mandate and merely altruistic temporary stewardship.

How to make sense of Goncharov's sudden pathos? Could he have honestly believed that Siberia's future held a release from imperial control? Was it the extremely distant prospect of this future that made him so sanguine? Or did he work himself up to such a solemn frenzy that the moment simply called for some grand idea, however provisory or inauthentic? Or, given the international stage on which Goncharov climbs in this pronouncement, was this merely a way to assert the nobility of the Russian colonial project in a manner consistent with that of Russia's European, especially British, peers? There is no sure way to know the answer. However, the presence of this idea in a text that otherwise overflows with evidence of more crass concerns of imperial profit, metropolitan benefit, and cultural and racial arrogance is not unusual. Perhaps the most iconic expression of colonial racism and Eurocentric hubris, Rudyard Kipling's poem "The White Man's Burden," also frames colonial rule as a high moral obligation to assume a thankless toil for the benefit of non-white people. And despite its jingoism, the poem's ambiguous closing opens up the possibility of colonial subjects transcending their subservience and becoming the white man's "peers."

Though not available for public discussion due to censorship, the prospect of Siberia's separation was on many Russians' mind. Imperial administrators were certainly less sanguine about it than Goncharov was. As mentioned above, the disinclination to call Siberia a colony was partly due to what Remnev calls "the American syndrome," or the anxious expectation that colonies will separate from the metropole. According to an influential survey of colonial systems published in *The Notes of the Fatherland,* a major journal, while all colonies naturally tend toward secession, agricultural colonies are especially apt to secede because they can become self-sufficient for foodstuffs. The possibility of Siberia's separation from Russia figured prominently in the government's strategic planning for the region. On the one hand, Siberia's underdevelopment could lead other countries (Britain, the Unites States, or even China) to snatch it from Russia. Pouring resources to develop it, on the other hand, could result in Siberia gaining the confidence and the material wherewithal to separate itself from the imperial core. In his advocacy to gain support for the annexation of the Amur, Muravev expertly manipulated the authorities' fear of separatism, arguing that Russia's ability to hold on to Siberia hinged on preventing the British takeover of the Amur. To Russian anarchist and Siberian exile Mikhail Bakunin, by contrast, the Amur annexation allowed Siberia to establish links with the larger world through the Pacific, only increasing its chances to separate from Russia.[101]

Some, though they were a minority, considered the specter of Siberian separatism with greater equanimity, pointing to Britain's ability to derive economic gains from its relationship with its former colonies. Remnev argues that "Russian policy makers and intellectuals were convinced that in the future all colonies would separate themselves from the metropolis." Many European political thinkers argued publicly that the best empire was one that, its civilizing objectives met, eventually put itself out of business.[102] This would not have been a novel notion for Goncharov, who was after all a government official well acquainted with western colonial literature. Highly attuned to the sensitivities of censorship, his future profession, he knew better than to be explicit; instead, in his book, he wrapped this idea in the requisite understatement and figurative dressing.

That Goncharov may have viewed decolonization as the logical terminus of the colonial process also appears likely in view of another passage, in the Cape Colony chapter of *The Frigate Pallada.* A plausible and desirable development that Goncharov foresees for the indigenous people of Africa is that, "like lawful children of the same father" they will "share with whites in the heritage of freedom, religion, and civilization, bequeathed also to them." Future freedom and parity with the white colonial suzerains certainly sounds like the end of colonial dependency and racial subordination. Goncharov's German encyclopedia, his key source on the Cape of Good Hope, predicts this future unambiguously and in politically universal terms. A withdrawal of "European guardianship," it intones, is a point to which "all great colonies are headed in the end."[103]

While this certainly seems a nobler sentiment than an indefinite perpetuation of colonialism, it has its darker side. For Goncharov as for European intellectual elites, eventual leveling of disparities—in material or social development or in civilizational "level" of various peoples—was a powerful opiate of imperial thinking. As this thinking went, the colonizers were not changing the world, but merely repairing its malfunction: inequality. Of course, colonial subjects were not consulted either about the desirability or the means of leveling this inequality. Nor were they allowed to judge its attainment. Commenting on imperial guardians' reliance on postponements and deferrals, Ann Laura Stoler calls such statements "promissory notes on eventual release from subjugation." Dangling that carrot forever out of reach justified dismissing any political grievance. It also made it easier to ignore the intervening iniquities. It certainly sounds a worthy goal to allow colonized peoples to share with their colonial masters "in the heritage of freedom, religion, and civilization, bequeathed also to them." With this as one's shining ideal, it may be tempting to acquiesce to the cruelties of the Harry Smiths of this world (the British Cape administrator eulogized by Goncharov) along with his Siberian counterparts, all purportedly working to bring this ideal about.[104]

Imperial humanitarianism was an important platform for imperial rivalries. Territories and profits weren't all. The notion of a civilizing mission itself was a humanitarian ideal, rooted in the idea of mankind's perfectibility, with Europe serving as the standard of perfection. It often functioned as imperialism's "window dressing" to rationalize imperial expansion and conquest for domestic publics. However, it sometimes also set constraints, however flexible, on government conduct in the colonies.[105] In the nineteenth century, an empire's self-regard depended to some extent on its perceived ability to colonize better than its peers. This is why Goncharov feels compelled to articulate Russian civilizing mission in Siberia in comparative terms.

The notion of imperial trusteeship was an aspect of imperial humanitarianism. According to Michael Barnett, beginning in the eighteenth century, questions about the purpose and legitimate use of colonial power gained prominence in European political philosophy. Edmund Burke's ideas about the relationship between rulers and ruled in the context of colonialism stimulated the ideology of imperial trusteeship. Addressing the British House of Parliament in 1783 during a debate about the East India Bill, Burke asserted that, given the natural condition of mankind's equality, all political power was in a sense "artificial," justified only when exercised for the benefit of the ruled. It follows, therefore, Burke said, "that such rights or privileges, or whatever else you choose to call them, are all in the strictest sense a trust; and it is of the very essence of every trust to be rendered accountable, and even totally to cease, when it substantially varies from the purpose for which it alone could have lawful existence." Such benevolent stewardship was to prepare the colonized people for political sovereignty. As Barnett argues, Burke "was not opposed to colonialism but rather objected to a colonialism that was irredeemably exploitative." The legitimacy of an empire, Barnett writes, "depended on acting as a public trustee and for the benefit of the ruled."[106]

The option of "ceasing" imperial trust could not be as openly discussed in Russia, but it clearly captivated more worldly members of the Russian elite. Inspired, or perhaps galled, by Britain's example, another member of the *Pallada* expedition—Goncharov's friend Voin Rimsky-Korsakov, the commander of the English-made schooner *Vostok*—expressed quite vocally his eagerness to see Russia join the global devolution trend. England's bestowal of autonomy on Australia and the Cape Colony made Rimsky-Korsakov fret:

> Will England hover over the entire world, magnifying itself tenfold through the states it created, or will the progeny crush the mother (*ili pridaviat detki matushku*)? Lord only knows. But if England herself keeps freeing the colonies it had created, hardly anyone will overshadow its historical legacy and fame. What mark will our Russia leave in the history of humanity?! It would be honorable if we competed with England in this. It will be as God wills, but we

> shouldn't despair: there are resources in our character, perhaps just as powerful as in the Anglo-Saxon one, which are better than their unquenchable thirst for acquisition.[107]

This shows that freeing the colonies could be thought of as fully compatible with imperial nationalism, indeed with the furtherance of imperial power. England surrounded by former colonies appears to this *Pallada* officer as England magnified, not diminished. He thinks of a decision to renounce imperial control as a test of national character. Goncharov is even more radical, intimating some form of autonomy for the indigenous people in both Africa and Siberia. All in all, while prestige accrues to those who conquer, an even greater prestige accrues to those who know when to let go. The Russian Argonauts seemed to have shared a belief that the arc of a truly glorious empire ends in decolonization.

CHAPTER FIVE

Russians Confront Human Diversity

I have no curiosity. I've never wanted to know. I have only wanted to see and to verify the pictures of my imagination: merely to erase a bit, and to add a bit.

—Goncharov writing from Hong Kong to a friend, July 1853

In Singapore, Ivan Goncharov strikes up a conversation with a person he describes as a French-speaking Indian. He asks the man (presumably in French, though the book has it in Russian), "Where do you come from?" The word uttered in response by the "Indian" (*indiets*) is unrecognizable to Goncharov as a place name. "So, you're an Indian, right?" he attempts to verify. His interlocutor shakes his head. Asked whether he is a Malay, in that case, he denies the suggestion even more vigorously. "Then who are you? From which country?" Goncharov presses. "Islam, Muslim," comes the reply. Goncharov corrects the local—that would indicate religion and not a place of origin—but the answer remains unchanged. Undeterred, Goncharov hones his quizzing: "What city are you from?" The "Indian" names the town Pondicherry (today Puducherry), in French East India. "Ah! Then why are you saying you're not Indian?" the writer protests. At this point, the exasperated interviewee points at another group of people nearby, whom Goncharov describes as looking "exactly the same." He says: "That's a Hindu [*indus*], and I am Islam." Goncharov finally gets it: "I see, these people are of the Brahmin faith." The local confirms it—"yes, yes"—relieved to finally get his point across. "Brahma, Hindu," he keeps repeating.[1]

In this episode, Goncharov reacts to the world of difference his voyage reveals to him with the same penchant for typology and classification that Europeans have brought to their encounters with non-Europeans since at least the Age of Reason. Slotting diversity into recognizable rubrics was part of the job of traveling. The episode also highlights that the templates of human difference Goncharov brings with him to faraway lands sometimes clash with how the people he encounters self-identify. His interlocutor refuses to accept that he is "Indian" because it is religion and not place of origin that structures his identity. This wasn't much different from common people in Russia at the time declaring their nationality to be Orthodox. In his interaction with the Pondicherry native, as with others he meets on his voyage, Goncharov is negotiating categories of human difference. The rough-and-tumble of experience creates potential for new knowledge.

Since Goncharov, however, conversed in languages not native to him or in many cases to his interlocutors, miscommunication was always a real possibility. Judging by the travelogue's record, such interviews, moreover, were rare. For the most part, Goncharov passively fell back on the assumptions he brought with him, or relied—often to his peril—on preparatory reading in Russian and European sources, which purveyed a predictable diet of Eurocentric concepts and hierarchies. As this chapter's epigraph makes clear, openness to radically new knowledge was not Goncharov's guiding principle. Instead of paradigm shifts, he sought basic confirmation of what he thought he already knew. And yet he also endeavored to fulfill what he considered to be a modern travel writer's chief task: "to merge one's life, if only briefly, with the life of a different people."[2]

Goncharov encountered a bewildering variety of people on his journeys across Africa and Asia. The diversity and intensity of these cross-cultural contacts left a vivid imprint on his book. Whether describing Africans, Asians, Jews, or Siberian aborigines, Goncharov typically deploys Orientalist, Eurocentric, and racial rhetoric characteristic of contemporary European writing. His travel narrative exudes the palpable sense of superiority that, as a "civilized" white-skinned European, he felt over the differently hued people Europeans ruled or aspired to rule. Yet, just as important, Goncharov's perceptions of "others," far from a coherent system, reveal ambivalence and inconsistency. Logic and a stable view of human variety are hard to come by in *The Frigate Pallada,* as in many colonial classics. One gleans instead a record of impressions rooted in specific circumstances that tell us about psychological mechanisms of confronting human difference and about triggers of prejudice.

For all the book's humor and gregariousness, this racial and ethnic prejudice is likely to alienate modern-day readers. Indeed, the American publisher of the only relatively complete English-language translation of *The Frigate Pallada* felt it necessary to include a disclaimer that dissociates the press and the translator from "any offensive racial-ethnic attitudes" of Goncharov's book. Significantly, the most offensive of those passages had already been expurgated from the Russian edition that is the basis of the American translation. This gives one a sense of how much the original text diverges from the current standards of the thinkable and the sayable.[3]

The glaring prejudices of *The Frigate Pallada* have not received much attention in critical commentaries on the book.[4] And so Goncharov tends to be praised, especially in Soviet scholarship, for his openness to other cultures and for his humane and sympathetic characterization of various ethnicities. Incredibly, this gung-ho imperialist has been described as Russia's bleeding-heart anti-colonial conscience. Not prejudice but tolerance has struck most commentators on *The Frigate Pallada.*[5] While benign sentiments and moments of understanding do crop up in *The Frigate Pallada,* and while the annals of colonial writing, both Russian and European, have seen more malevolent commentators than Goncharov, this position is untenable given the record of the full text. That the sensibilities of Goncharov's time were different is no reason to set aside how they appear to us today. Only by analyzing racial and ethnic stereotypes in the texts that gave them currency can we understand these stereotypes' legacies.

Ethnicity and nationalism have long featured in explorations of the Russian social imagination. Race has seldom been considered, largely due to the fact that it was not a category of institutionalized social practice in tsarist-era continental Russia.[6] Yet nineteenth-century Russians did think in racial terms, which *The Frigate Pallada* amply evidences. Before exploring the representations of human diversity, it is therefore important to understand the concept of race and its place in Russian culture.

Classification was evaluation in imperial settings. Bodily typologies that claimed to reflect internal characteristics and aptitudes gave rise to racial hierarchies. Goncharov's implicit version of such a hierarchy, ascending from black, to yellow, to white, maps onto his civilizational hierarchy ascending from Africa, to Asia, to Europe (with Americans treated as resettled Europeans). That Goncharov speaks of East Asian nations but never African ones, which were mere tribes to him, reflects his ranking of these populations' relative development. As he scans bodies and reflects on customs and social practices, Goncharov's hierarchies, however, prove unstable. They are modulated by political considerations. For example, the writer racializes East Asians living beyond the Russian empire's borders, but restrains such impulses when speaking about those living within those borders. Miscegenation between black and white races in Africa repulses him, but he views it more permissively when it involves Russians and Siberian aborigines.

While exotic difference tends to steal the critics' spotlight, it is equally important to examine how travelogues deploy the rhetoric of similarity. Familiarizing the new, or presenting aspects of foreign cultures as merely variants of elements in the traveler's home culture, is a common device of travelogues. The lines between familiar and unfamiliar, however, do not always form a predictable pattern in Goncharov's book. In his ethnographic musings, he often treats fellow Russians of a different class as exotic subjects. From his elite vantage point as a Europeanized, educated Russian, he observes the customs and habits of mind of lower-class, uneducated Russians as if they were imperial minorities. How the Russian sailors and servants make sense of the world of difference on the voyage, Goncharov learns, does not exactly align with his own manner of doing so.

Indeed, Russianness is also an enigma that captivates Goncharov in *The Frigate Pallada.* To confront the amazing human diversity on the coastal frontiers of Africa and Asia means for Goncharov not only to confront how other people are different, but also to reflect on his own identity: white, European, Russian. The voyage gives him a chance to ponder in unique circumstances the plural identities of Russian society. The "Russianness" of Russians comes into sharper focus for Goncharov under foreign skies. On occasion, it becomes a conundrum for those who meet the Russians. The *Pallada* officers are sometimes apprehended as exotic rarities by African and Asian aborigines and by their European colonial masters, many of whom have never seen a Russian before. Studies of imperial travel narratives tend to focus on the perceptions of what have been termed "travelees," or those "traveled upon," which may create a sense of them as inert objects of imperial travelers' racial and cultural constructions.[7] This one-sided picture can be enriched by *Frigate Pallada*'s record of how Goncharov and his fellow Russians thought they were being perceived by those they met on their journeys. In the expedition's Japanese stage, moreover, Goncharov's statements can be juxtaposed with independent sources that reveal the travelees' actual perceptions of the Russians. In particular, the historical record of one specific interaction between the Russian crew and the Japanese, when contrasted with Goncharov's realm of representations, throws overboard customary scenarios of imperial conquest and its power dynamics.

As we have seen, it is beyond question that the sentiments of *The Frigate Pallada* are pro-imperial. This chapter shows the book's racialized outlook and various other prejudices. Yet, in order to render a fine-grained image of the mindset reflected in Goncharov's book, one must also explore anxieties and ambivalences, not just the full-throated imperialist cant. Despite its stridency, *The Frigate Pallada* is a text with its own fissures, anxieties, and discontinuities. Comparisons with Goncharov's private statements, when available, help put these in relief. Goncharov's colonial discourse has moments of instability and sometimes subverts itself. If we focus less on its bottom-line "messages" than on the imagination, frames of reference, underlying assumptions, ideological matrices, rhetorical strategies, and contexts in which these messages have been crafted, the imperial path they jointly chart is not without pitfalls, detours, and blind alleys.

Culture versus Nature

The Frigate Pallada both reflected and propagated racialized understandings of human difference. But what exactly did race mean to a mid-nineteenth-century European, as Goncharov emphatically saw himself to be? While in the eighteenth century, race was linked to cultural and geographic factors, the nineteenth century saw increasing focus on the human body. Populations were thought to be divisible into groups on the basis of somatic traits that determined behaviors, mental aptitudes, and levels of development. By and large, these were thought to be inborn and heritable. Propelled by the taxonomical projects of the Enlightenment, the rise of natural sciences, and colonial slavery, racial thinking gradually biologized conceptions of human diversity and behavior. As historian Nancy Stepan explains, the first half of the nineteenth century saw a shift from a sense of people as primarily social beings "governed by social laws and standing apart from nature" to a sense of them as primarily biological beings "embedded in nature and governed by biological laws." Racial commonalities were thought to trigger or prevent civilized behavior. The notion of racial hierarchies, which invariably placed

Europeans on top, caught the popular imagination. This was part of a larger nineteenth-century trend of treating non-western societies as "control groups" of sorts, in historian Philip Curtin's phrase, "against which Europeans could measure their own achievement."[8]

Philosophically, ideologically, and logistically, imperialism fostered the emergence and growth of racial research. To justify expansion, theories of white supremacy had to be developed. Race as a legal definition emerged in seventeenth-century slavery laws. The presence of large populations of African slaves in the midst of European societies sharpened interest in human difference. Siberian colonies became a laboratory of ideas about the "Russian race." Large collections of "exotic" skulls made available by Captain Cook's South Seas voyages were linked to early research in phrenology.[9] Religious considerations limited the supply of European cadavers for research purposes. The opening of Australia as a penal colony reduced this supply even further: those sentenced to capital punishment, whose corpses would typically be used for dissection, could now instead start new lives on a new continent. African corpses were therefore a boon to a British pioneer of racial biology, Robert Knox, who collected them while serving as a surgeon during the British-Xhosa Wars in the Cape Colony. Skulls and skeletons were extracted, brains and sexual organs preserved, and off they went to museums. Live racialized bodies were brought in from the colonies and put on display in ethnic shows, world fairs, colonial exhibitions, freak shows, and circuses. Such displays helped disseminate to the general public "a new visual culture of the 'races.'"[10]

Travel literature, which first proffered accounts to the European public of the New Worlds' exotic peoples, contributed to the emergence of racial thinking. Early pioneers of racial science, such as Georges Buffon (Georges-Louis Leclerc), James Cowles Prichard, and Johann Blumenbach, were "voracious consumers of travel literature." Travel accounts also popularized their theories. The symbiosis of travel writing and racialization is evident in the case of English explorer and polymath Francis Galton, to take one high-profile example, who wrote travel books on Africa before moving on to coin the term "eugenics" in 1883. As Robert Young put it, "racism knows no division between the sciences and the arts." It was the symbiosis of the two that gave racial ideas prominent status in the modern world. Culture provided material for many scientific intuitions about race and also propagated theories developed by science. What was ultimately at stake in this process was the self-definition of European culture.[11]

Though Goncharov subsequently showed no passion for racial science, *The Frigate Pallada* served such a popularizing function. Racialized descriptions of various populations and hierarchies based on race are prominent in the full version known to nineteenth-century readers. No Soviet abridgement could fully erase them. This is particularly true of Goncharov's comments on Africans, who typically occupied, along with Australian Aborigines and occasionally Russia's Kalmyks (a Mongol ethnic group from the north Caucasus), the bottom of European racial hierarchies. The sundry prejudices in *The Frigate Pallada* are based not only on culture or ethnicity but also on the corporeality of Africans and Asians. What we see in *The Frigate Pallada* is in fact a creeping racialization of ethnic groups and nations, Goncharov's principal categories.[12]

Goncharov operated within a racial discourse typical of his time. Recent work by historians of Russia has dispelled the myth that race was only a marginal concern in imperial Russia. These scholars have found that racial ideas and debates reached Russia as early as the 1830s and 1840s and spread into the public sphere. By 1840, the Russian intellectual Petr Chaadaev proclaimed there was no doubting the existence of races, even as he hoped that they would eventually unite into one nation of brothers. As historian Vera Tolz shows, by the 1860s the word "race" (*rasa*) entered Russian dictionaries. *The Frigate Pallada* adds evidence to these findings. The multilingual Goncharov had free access, moreover, to ideas about race in original German, French, and English sources, which made their way into his travelogue.[13]

Biological determinism, which claimed race as a fixed, heritable template and was later to dominate European racial discourse, was alien to Goncharov. Around mid-century, racial traits were still considered modifiable by education or geographical displacement, and this view persisted in Russia. Both fixity and fluidity were central to how racial discourse operated. Ann Laura Stoler has stressed that "nineteenth-century racism was not built on the surefooted classification of science but on a potent set of [malleable] cultural and affective criteria."[14] Goncharov, for example, considered it plausible that Europeanization might elevate Africa's "blacks" to equality with the "whites," so that, "like the children of the same father, [the blacks] will share with the whites in the heritage of freedom, religion, and civilization, bequeathed also to them." This sentiment seems to echo early nineteenth-century British abolitionist literature. By the 1860s, this attitude was becoming displaced by what Patrick Brantlinger calls the myth of the Dark Continent, according to which Africans were only suited to be a laboring class in the whites' civilizing projects. In Goncharov's interactions with black Africans, this new, harsher attitude also reverberated.[15]

The notion of black-white consanguinity and potential equality ("children of the same father") signals another key race debate of the era: between adherents of monogenesis and polygenesis. Monogenesists, among whom were most Russians and Britons, considered all people to belong to the same biological species. The supporters of polygenesis held that the human genus was divided into different species—as many as fifteen of them—which gave rise to different races. Though his encounter with the San ("Bushman") tested him severely, Goncharov remained a loyal monogenesist. In both this loyalty and his belief in the malleability of races, Goncharov reflected enduring trends that distinguished the Russian tradition of racial thought.[16]

Race-ing *The Frigate Pallada*

Goncharov sets the racial tone of *The Frigate Pallada* in its opening pages. Among other signs of progress, such as the availability of comfortable European hotels in recently "wild" places, he approvingly mentions that black Africans have grown ashamed of their own skin and begun wearing white gloves. Throughout the travelogue, Goncharov uses categories such as "blacks," whites," "colored" (*tsvetnye*), and black or yellow "tribes" (*plemia*)—a term frequently used at the time to connote race, both in Russia and in Goncharov's foreign sources. He applies the label "savages" (*dikie*) to native Africans and, less often, Asians—essentially, all those who in his view aren't Europeanized or civilized enough.[17] More than that, he frequently animalizes non-white people. By Goncharov's time, a racial variation on the Great Chain of Being became commonplace. By measuring things such as facial angles or skulls, eighteenth-century racial science organized living organisms in ascending developmental order, from lower organisms, like apes, all the way to white Europeans. Black Africans typically occupied in these schemas, often visually rendered through drawings, an intermediate status between animals and humans.[18]

Apparently in tune with such thinking, Goncharov claims to be unable to distinguish a Khoikhoi boy from a monkey, just as he later compares a Ryukyu islander to an orangutan. He finds the places for African and Siberian natives on his seamless animal-human continuum. Lions and rhinoceroses are mentioned in the same breath as African anti-colonial leaders; the

Xhosa and wild beasts seem united in the common enterprise of stealing cattle from white settlers. A Siberian road, Goncharov reports hearing, is free from wolves and bears; one encounters on it "only Yakuts, and also lots of rabbits." In his private letter from the voyage, Goncharov even demotes the indigenous people of Africa and Asia in his naturalist's ranking to a slot below tropical fruit. He calls "bananas, palms, and pineapples"—"the aristocracy of nature." As for "Negroes, Malays, Indians, and the Chinese," these are "nature's plebeians." Racial bigotry is part of the book's humor: it is supposed to be funny that an African boy is hard to tell from a monkey. Of course, to make such attitudes humorous means to stamp them as permissible.[19]

With the curiosity that might drive one in search of a two-headed monster, Goncharov seeks out a "Bushman." Known today by the neutral designation "San," these were hunter-gatherers living in the north and east of southern Africa. Along with the pastoralist Khoikhoi, they were the first indigenous group to be colonized by white settlers. Race scholars viewed the San as humans of the lowest order, the last representatives of the Stone Age. Their bodies were therefore sought after as specimens for science and exhibits for ethnic shows, a huge commercial enterprise in nineteenth-century Europe. One German collector went so far as to preserve an entire San corpse in brine and ship it to Berlin. Had he visited London only six months later, Goncharov could have seen natives of southern Africa, including the San, at one of the city's popular ethnic exhibits—the kind of spectacle that led Charles Dickens to conclude, infamously, that such ignoble savages should be "civilized off the face of the earth."[20] This wider European fascination likely fed Goncharov's curiosity and conditioned him to expect a freak of nature. In fact, before he met a San, he had read an anthropological account by a fellow travel writer, Thornley Smith, who likened the San to troglodytes who fed on vipers and lived in holes in the ground.[21]

Yet when Goncharov finally locates and inspects a San prisoner during a visit to a Cape Colony jail, his revulsion feels visceral, and not just book-learned:

> In front of us there stood a creature that barely resembled the likeness of a human being, about the height of a monkey. The dark yellow old face had the shape of a triangle, with a sharp angle pointing upward, and was covered by deep wrinkles. A tiny nose on this tiny face was completely flat; thin and narrow lips were as if squashed. He resembled some kind of a deranged old man [*iuorodivyi starik*],

> hairless, toothless, one foot in the grave, demented. The head was the most remarkable: bold, just barely covered by sparse tufts of fur, so short that it would be impossible to grab them with the help of two fingers. "What is your name?" the prison guard asked. The Bushman was silent. His face bore a vacant expression devoid of all meaning. He seemed to have almost no awareness of where he was and what was being done to him.

Goncharov renders the San's improbable humanity through a grotesque description of his body: dark yellow skin, toothless triangular face, riven with deep wrinkles, flattened nose, "squashed" lips, and sparse tufts of "fur" on his head. His expression is dumb and insensate, animal-like. The classic racist slur used to demean non-whites—a monkey—proves of assistance as Goncharov searches for a fitting correlative to the San's body size. To verify what he has heard about the San's "inhuman," guttural language, Goncharov tests his specimen through an interpreter, asking about equivalents in the "Bushman language" of such basic words as "father" or "mother." The rumor proves correct: "A completely bestial [*zverinyi*] way of expressing oneself!" Incidentally, Goncharov is likely reacting to the use of implosive consonants ("clicks") common to languages of the Khoisan.[22]

The terminus of this racial and linguistic inquiry is Goncharov's perplexity that he and the San inmate belong to the same biological genus: "And this is my *brother,* my *kin* [*blizhnii*], thought I, painfully observing this unfinished, sorry creature." From Goncharov's perspective, the San's repulsive body and his "bestial" language make his humanity hard to fathom. He doubts the existence of normal human faculties in the San, telling the British prison guard accompanying him: "It seems that they are utterly devoid of reason, their mind appears to be completely undeveloped." Though the guard finds his own ways to dehumanize the San, his racism seems the lesser of the two. He reassures the Russian visitor about the San's status as humans and possessors of rational faculties, and explains their abject condition not by somatic traits but by their mode of life. They seem "savage and unsociable," he says, because they live in underground dugouts, but they are skilled as petty thieves and hunters. It is unclear to what extent this information modifies Goncharov's initial impression. He closes the episode in the following way: "They led out other Bushmen: old men—though they were barely thirty years old—just as small and exhausted, with senseless expressions on their faces."[23]

Doubts about the basic humanity of another person are not restricted to Africans or members of lower classes in *The Frigate Pallada*. Goncharov later experiences them when faced with Japan's elite diplomats. The situation appears to him palpably unreal:

> Who are they—with their shaven foreheads, cheeks smooth as those of mummies, hung heads, and half-lowered eyelids, all motionless, in their long and ample clothes, save for barely stirring lips, from behind of which there broke out muffled sounds, barely audible to our ears? Could these be corpses that arose from thousand-year old tombs and gathered for a summit? Can they walk? Can they smile, sing, or dance? Do they know our human life, our grief and joy, or did they lose all memory of how humans live?[24]

The Japanese functionaries are abased as the living dead. Alienated from normal coordinates of human life, such as smiling or feeling sadness, they display the torpor of the tomb. Shifting rapidly from Gothic horror to lowbrow comedy, Goncharov confesses that his stupefied vision came crashing down when the most venerable of the zombies blew his nose loudly into a handkerchief.

Alas, no such injection of what was meant to be humor lightens the Cape Town jail scene, where dehumanization is linked to bestiality rather than deadness. Postcolonial critic David Spurr argues that a rhetoric of debasement ultimately signals an anxious need of colonial agents—or their sympathizers, one might add—to starkly demarcate their own identity and valorize the established norm in stressful situations of cross-cultural contact.[25] Goncharov's discomfort at being lumped into the same species with the San makes him anxious and feeds his portrayal of them as abject creatures. For the narrator of Joseph Conrad's *Heart of Darkness,* similarly, the white person's relatedness to the African seems more unsettling than the possibility of the African's "inhumanity."[26] Goncharov's other strategy for rationalizing the prejudice he knows he feels is to paint it as shared by other Africans. He writes that other inmates picked on the San, holding him in utter contempt. If the San's inferiority is a matter of Africans' own consensus, can a white visitor be blamed for merely concurring? This long passage about the San—perhaps the nadir of the book's racism—is missing from both English translations and some popular Soviet and post-Soviet editions.[27]

Goncharov was not alone in struggling to reconcile a belief in a common humanity with what appeared to him to be radical human differences.

Charles Darwin, sailing in the 1830s on the *Beagle*, was initially equally incredulous about the humanity of the Fuegians who inhabited an especially inhospitable southern region of South America called Tierra del Fuego. The Fuegians appeared to Darwin as abject savages who possessed an inarticulate language and in fact resembled the devil. He reported that they slept on naked ground coiled up like snakes, failed to protect their bodies from fierce elements, and practiced cannibalism in times of famine and war, eating old women before moving on to dogs. To ascertain their humanity, Darwin devised experiments testing their grasp of rudimentary human concepts, such as barter, truth and falsehood, and private property. He was much relieved when the Fuegians passed these tests.[28]

It is deeply significant that Goncharov's racial analysis of southern Africans takes place in the midst of a colonial jail. Though not a panoptical but a face-to-face institution, the Cape Colony jail nonetheless operates through what Michel Foucault terms a "machinery of dissymmetry" that imparts power to the observer and entraps the observed.[29] As an opportunity to produce (fake) knowledge, the Russians' visit to the jail derives from the fact of white colonial rule in Africa (that is, the privilege of imprisoning Africans) and at the same time produces insights that endorse this rule. The colonial jail not only disciplines indigenous inhabitants by white men's law, but also functions as a laboratory where whites get to study African people for the purpose of constructing racial hierarchies useful for colonial rule. Black bodies are made available for examination, classification, and buttressing of white hegemony.

Goncharov's "landscanning eye" prospected Japanese territory for capitalist prospects. Yet in this and other colonial texts, bodies are scanned for prospects much like territory, since labor can be extracted from bodies that possess skills. Goncharov's "bodyscapes," as Mary Louise Pratt calls such descriptions, are thus supplemented with a listing of skills. The Khoikhoi, for example, are "wonderful farmers and shepherds, and good servants, drivers, and unskilled workers." The combined effect is that Goncharov's jail scene ultimately reduces Africans to bodies with labor value.[30]

The jail appears to Goncharov as "a full collection of all tribes inhabiting the colony" in the same way that the Cape Town botanical garden appeared to him as a collection of its vegetation. In the cataloging of life forms, both kinds of institutions function as inventories of imperial possessions. Goncharov, the armchair ethnographer, in an uncharacteristically dry, "scientific" language, offers a racial typology of the jail's population, based on head shapes, facial features, body sizes, and gradations in skin color.[31] "Black color," he writes, "from the blackest-velvety with gloss, like lacquered leather, went through gradations in hue all the way to dark yellow." The Russian word for "gloss" (*s gliantsem*) is typically used in reference to inanimate objects, like shined shoes. Indeed, elsewhere Goncharov compares black skin to "a well-polished boot." Though today we may gasp at this taxidermic analogy, the skin of black corpses headed for research was then often repurposed for leather. What appears to be a shocking metaphor was in fact correlated with widespread practices.[32]

Goncharov the comparative anatomist spans his spectrum of blackness from the darkest "tribes," such as the Zulu and Mfengu, to the lightest ones, such as the Khoikhoi. He praises the Xhosa's athletic bodies but considers their facial features inferior, due to flat foreheads and prominent cheekbones. This is not just a hierarchy of bodies, but of body parts. "Negros," whom Goncharov distinguished as a separate group, and who were likely slaves brought to the Cape Colony from other parts of Africa, impressed Goncharov by their well-proportioned and muscular bodies, so he compares them to "African Adonises." On all continents, Goncharov singles out old indigenous women as particularly monstrous, as did Francis Parkman in *The Oregon Trail* and Alexander Pushkin in *The Journey to Erzurum*. Yet he also regales his readers with sexualized images of young African and Tagal women.

Figure 5.1. From a later Russian expedition to the Cape Colony in 1857 came this depiction of a variety of racialized figures.

Repulsion and attraction—the latter evident in comments on the beauty and even desirability of other races—was often combined in European writing. It was not uncommon for a virulent treatise on the repugnance of Africans to mark out some of them as models for an Apollo.[33] One handsome Chilean "Indian" looked to Charles Darwin like none other than King James I. All in all, while some Africans are said to attain the classical beauty of Adonis, this lengthy rhetorical juggle of African body parts is ultimately as dehumanizing as Goncharov's anatomy of the San. Matthew Perry, who came through the Cape Colony a few weeks prior, similarly described races as if they were breeds.

This, then, is the unsettling record of Goncharov's thoughts, as recorded in *The Frigate Pallada.* Aside from his treating the San as a human curio, however, the book records the author's actions as mild-mannered and generous. He asked for permission to give African inmates money, in line with the Russian tradition of offering alms to prisoners; British law, unfortunately, forbade it. He always claimed to treat his black servants kindly. However, *The Frigate Pallada* is not an entirely reliable account on this score. Its readers would not know, as we now do from Goncharov's correspondence, that he could be rough with subordinates, both Russian and non-European. He beat up an African guide who had, he claimed, cheated him. He had his own Russian servant flogged. Goncharov, who was overweight before the voyage and became increasingly so during it, did not seem particularly sympathetic to a Sakha guide who got a nosebleed from the strain of pushing him up a steep Siberian mountain.[34]

But such details do not mar the writer's public self-presentation in *The Frigate Pallada.* Respect with a touch of admiration resounds in Goncharov's account of the Xhosa chief and fearsome warrior Siyolo captured by the British in the most recent war, whom he visited under house arrest. (Somehow, Goncharov was able to have meaningful interactions only with incarcerated Africans.) Matthew Perry also met Siyolo, finding him to be a "remarkably fine-looking negro," as did Goncharov. Paraded by the British before foreign visitors passing through the Cape, sketched and photographed for souvenirs, Siyolo probably himself felt like a human curio. He was sullen but cordial with the Russians. Goncharov regretted that, due to the unavailability of a translator, he was unable to talk to him. But he presented the warrior with some tobacco and cigars, the best money could buy, and later gave his wife a photograph of Siyolo, which she reportedly appreciated. In sum, Goncharov's narrative never shows him acting on racial hatred. But it

Figure 5.2. Siyolo, the Xhosa chief with whom Goncharov spoke, as depicted in the account of the Perry expedition, 1856.

does show him viewing the world through racial conceptions and hierarchies, which his bestselling book validated and popularized in Russia.[35]

Asia's "Varicolored Bodies"

A journey from Europe to Africa means for Goncharov a departure from the domain of reason to that of uncultivated nature and her children. He views Asia differently: as a domain of ancient civilizations that have fallen dormant and now need to be reinvigorated by Europeans. Africans appear to Goncharov as bodies with labor value or as obstacles to European improvements of the continent. His Asians possess culture, society, economy, and sophisticated political organization, however inferior to European equivalents.[36]

This does not prevent Goncharov from racializing them. His physical descriptions of Asians, however, are additionally crowded with the kind of detail that is sparse in the African chapter: clothing, ornaments, hairstyle, language, diet, gestures, facial expressions, general bearing, body poses, and movements. These descriptions are layered onto classic nineteenth-century accounts of manners and customs. Asian racialized body types, in short, are aspects of broader ethnographic profiles. Furthermore, to an extent far surpassing the African chapters, and perhaps befitting a continent where Russia had trading ambitions, the Asian chapters are heavily weighted with rich materiality. The overwhelmingly long lists of objects and foods, such as the chronicles of endless gift exchanges with the Japanese, occasionally threaten to drown the narrative of travel.

It bears remembering that what from the modern perceptive may look like an unprincipled conflation of ethnic, national, linguistic, and properly "racial" groups was nothing unusual in the late eighteenth and nineteenth centuries. As Stepan notes, "at one time or another, the 'Jews,' the 'Celts,' the 'Irish,' the 'Negro,' the 'Hottentots,' the 'Border-Scots,' the 'Chinese,' the 'Anglo-Saxons,' the 'Europeans,' the 'Mediterraneans,' the 'Teutons,' the 'Aryans,' and the 'Spanish Americans,' were all 'races' according to scientists." Race has rarely been "about somatics alone," Stoler adds, but about "cultural competencies, moral civilities and affective sensibilities." Moreover, scientific, administrative, and popular European discourse about race "was no more an object of consensus than that about nation," as historians Jane Burbank and Frederick Cooper note.[37]

Ethnographic descriptions thus pad the rough racial packaging of Asians in *The Frigate Pallada,* who appear less debased than Africans. This also had to do with Russia's evolving attitudes toward Asia. Efforts to draw clear distinctions between Russians and Asians, which were needed to rebrand Europeanizing Russia, were increasingly rivaled by a sense of Russia's shared heritage with Asia, which may account for Goncharov's more sympathetic tone.[38] Indeed, he stresses the common origin of Russians and Asians, attributing cultural differences to Asia's developmental lag rather than any fundamental difference. Racial difference between Russians and East Asians sometimes appears to him relatively small. He claims that Chinese bodies are "almost the same as ours," with the exception of black eyes and hair. In fact, the "yellow" race was a relative newcomer in Europe's racial taxonomies. Until the end of the eighteenth century, most European travelers described the Chinese as white.[39]

Nonetheless, "diverse groups of varicolored bodies" instantly strike Goncharov in multiethnic Singapore. Along with these bodies' heterogeneity, he keeps remarking on their ample visibility—various degrees of "nakedness," so alien to buttoned-up Europeans, draw his attention throughout tropical Asia. Clearly addicted to hierarchies, he quickly establishes that the graceful bodies of Indians are superior to those of the Chinese, which in turn are superior to those of Malays. Having just drawn a merely insignificant contrast between Russian and Chinese bodies, Goncharov nonetheless claims to be repulsed by the soft "dark yellow bodies" of the Chinese, lacking "the expression of energy and manly physiognomy." The smell of Chinese cooking in a Singapore store that also sells opium is so revolting to the Russians that they run out without waiting for the opium to take effect.[40]

The assault of oppressive Chinese smells and scantily clad Asian bodies is briefly mollified back at Singapore's London Hotel by the therapeutic sight of an "inexcusably handsome" Englishman. In the context of the varicolored bodies of the Singapore streets, the Englishman emerges as a paragon of the white race. The onslaught of difference momentarily suspended, Goncharov takes refuge in racial kinship, describing the Englishman's beauty almost lyrically: "fine, delicate, matte-colored skin; blue eyes, vibrantly thoughtful; locks of hair, light and soft as flax, gracefully framing the delicate face. . . . This is a British type of beauty: delicate, pure, and intelligent, if one may call it so . . . rooted in the purity and harmony of lines and shades, as in a perfectly assembled bouquet."[41] Goncharov's adoration for this "bouquet" of whiteness seems integrally linked to his exertion in processing the Singapore streets' color rainbow.

Hotels for European clientele were often such places of refuge. In Cape Town, Goncharov charts his progress from the outside to the cozy domestic core of the Welch Hotel as an ascending gradient of whiteness among those who welcome him:

> At the entryway, on the lowest step, we were met by a completely black servant, followed by a Malay servant, not completely black, but not white either, his head covered by a red scarf. In the vestibule, we encountered an English servant woman, somewhat whiter, and beyond that, on the stairs, a beautiful girl of about twenty, decidedly white. And finally, an old woman, the hotel proprietress, *nec plus ultra* white—that is, gray-haired.

This miniature quest to the whitest inner sanctum of the Welch Hotel superimposes racial hierarchies on social ones. Class blurs the customary contrast between black and white. Not the type of color, but merely its degree distinguishes the Malay and English servants. Indeed, some environmental theories of race held that such factors as harsh living conditions, unremitting labor, and poor protections from nature were the cause of primitive societies' darkened complexion. To a lesser degree, this phenomenon was thought to be observable also among the laboring classes of the industrialized world. Class, in other words, produced race.[42]

Echoing such theories, the lowest and blackest servants guard the outside access to the Welch Hotel in Goncharov's image; the staff's whiteness increases as he progresses through the interior. The whiteness of the personnel inside is differentiated on the basis of social function and privilege. The English servant woman is described as less white than the lovely English twenty-year old, who is, we later learn, the proprietress's daughter. The daughter's nearly perfect whiteness corresponds with her spatially higher placement on the stairs. In a playful variation on his own metaphor, Goncharov marks the old proprietress's highest degree of whiteness by commenting on the color of her hair, rather than her skin, as if her excessive whiteness were spilling over and in fact shading into gray. She is the whitest person around in the combined senses of race, social status, property, and age. The passage is a perfect icon of a reigning nineteenth-century racial hierarchy and its social and economic correlatives. While race and class were often "covertly interchangeable or at least analogous" in British writing about Africa examined by Brantlinger, they appear overtly so in *The Frigate Pallada.* According to the critic, racism as a way of designating "inferior" people functioned as "a surrogate class system."[43]

Of all Asian nations, Goncharov finds the Japanese the most civilized and congenial, almost on a par with Europeans, and certainly not "savage," despite demeaning comments about them in various parts of the travelogue. In his mind, as in that of many nineteenth-century contemporaries, Japan occupied what Susanna Soojung Lim calls an "intermediary status in racial and civilizational classification schemes"—that is, "below the Europeans but above the people of Africa and the Americas (and even, among Asians, above China)." Moreover, Japan as Russia's "potential Orient" made its stock rise in Lim's view. That such evaluations were indeed linked to imperial prospects is also suggested by the fact that, when the negotiations with Japan turn sour, Goncharov portrays the Koreans, now seen as more likely imperial subjects, as superior to all East Asian nations, including the Japanese.[44]

The Japanese chapters offer an exhaustive ethnography of Japanese customs. Apart from "their dress and silly hair-do," the Japanese are portrayed in *The Frigate Pallada* as cultivated, pleasant, polite, and extremely clean—in which they surpass the Chinese, Goncharov is quick to add.[45] According to Goncharov, Asian "parrot-like" garishness is alien to the Japanese. Their pleasingly muted color schemes, which indicate a taste for simplicity, rather than "Oriental luxury," make Goncharov feel as if instead of the

Far East, as East Asia was called in Russia, he found himself in the "Far West." Nevertheless, some of the Japanese customs, such as hara-kiri, strike him as shockingly barbarous. Nor does he take, on aesthetic grounds, to married Japanese women's custom of blackening their teeth (*ohaguro*).[46]

In the course of frequent interactions, Goncharov develops friendly and respectful relations with many Japanese diplomats and officials. Yet this does not prevent him from portraying the Japanese as soft, effeminate, and mentally limited, like children. Their feminine bodies and clothes make their gender ambiguous, awakening discomfiting feelings in some Russians. Such gendering of "lower" races was frequently deployed to legitimize racial hierarchies. It also figured in Goncharov's overall image of the Japanese as easy military targets and potentially compliant subjects.[47]

In Goncharov's portrait, the faces of the Japanese reveal a grotesque lack of measure: too thick and fleshy or too thin and bird-like, often pockmarked and bucktoothed. He confidently reads lack of intelligence from their bodily appearance; the gaze of their eyes prompts his conclusions about "the stupidity of the head." Subsequent discovery of his Japanese hosts' intelligence fails to urge a revision of such statements. Like the Chinese, the Japanese in Goncharov's view lack manliness and vigor. He confesses seeing "unique" faces, but not many "beautiful ones." The sympathy Goncharov eventually develops for his Japanese colleagues does not erase the debased representations that pepper his descriptions. During the dinner at the Nagasaki governor's mansion—one of the Russian reading public's favorite scenes—Goncharov likens the expressionless Japanese faces to "shovels," or to porcelain dolls, seemingly competing with one another for which will look "stupider," or to zombies who "forgot to live like human beings." The running joke of the Japanese sections of *The Frigate Pallada* is the "crawling" of the prostrated Japanese interpreters, who are required by custom to bow low in the presence of superiors. Though by that time he was personally friendly with them, Goncharov compares the interpreters to setters, poodles, and snakes.[48]

At another social occasion, Goncharov complains of finding "nothing that according to our conceptions resembles human beauty." Granted, he deserves credit for at least conceding the very existence of other standards. Overall, however, he paints Japanese society on a spectrum running the gamut from dumb beastly creatures to the handsome new generation. When he finds it, Goncharov marks Japanese beauty with a European brush, a contrast to the typical Japanese face and body type rather than their quintessence. Describing one tall, erect, and well-proportioned youth, he writes: "His face was European, with regular features, thin lips, and jaws that were not prominent, as those of other Japanese tend to be. One sees in his facial expression neither obtuse self-satisfaction, nor comical self-importance, nor naïve, primitive gaiety, as is common among them. On the contrary, his eyes sparkled with a consciousness of his Japaneseness and of what he lacks, what he might desire. You see? Even a Japanese man can be interesting, but how rarely!" Another translator appears to him tolerably handsome, just because "he resembles a European, with an imprint of ideas and education on his face." Goncharov is clear throughout: only European civilization can correct infelicities of race. He affixes a European label to anything that might smack of beauty, "progress," or "enlightenment."[49]

Unlike their Russian counterparts, western scholars have given Goncharov a mixed scorecard on tolerance. They stress the mockery, sarcasm, and ethnic stereotyping that tend to overshadow Goncharov's understanding.[50] But on this question, perhaps the Japanese themselves deserve to be heard. While acknowledging Goncharov's colorful and good-natured accounts of Japan and its people, they also read condescension and unvarnished European arrogance in *The Frigate Pallada.* At one post-Soviet conference, anodyne analyses of Goncharov's ethnic tolerance brought by Russian scholars clashed with objections of the Japanese participants, who recognized in Goncharov's book a propagation of the "odious" vision of what came to be known as "the white man's burden."[51]

Russian Exotica

Not only non-Europeans but also Russia's own minorities are occasionally targets of prejudice in *The Frigate Pallada.* Whatever the shore, anti-Semitic sentiments burst to the surface. In Shanghai, Goncharov's fellow crewmember Goshkevich, the Russian from Ukraine, "smells Yids like a setter smells game." In Cape Town, one of the Russians—and in retrospect, this must have been the Semite-detective Goshkevich—spitefully denounces a British doctor, Mr. Wethered, with whom the Russians became friendly: "He's a Yid, gentlemen!" Goshkevich analyzes Wethered through a template of anti-Semitic physical stereotypes (pale face, red hair, big nose). This evokes the concept of "Jewish physiognomy," which coded the racialization of Jews in Russia well into the twentieth century. Though the obsession seems unique to Goshkevich, Goncharov finds it jocular enough to report it accordingly. It is "despite being Jewish" that the doctor appears to Goncharov to be a very amiable and educated person. Goncharov later compares a cockfight in Manila—with its shrieking and jostling, the goading of the cocks, the money changing hands—to the goings-on in Russia's synagogues. This racial recognition and debasement of foreign Jews signals practice with recognizing and debasing Russia's domestic ones.[52]

The episode with Dr. Wethered shows a curious interplay of anti-Semitic and anti-English sentiments. The doctor initially endears himself to the Russians by reviling the English in India as lazy gluttons and drunkards. Goncharov suspects that the doctor is not English because he does not mutter through set teeth, does not stare goggle-eyed, and speaks beautiful French. In other words, Goncharov praises the doctor by taking jabs at the English. Even after Goshkevich "outs" Dr. Wethered as a Jew, some remain incredulous. Yet all doubts vanish when the doctor asks about the condition of Russia's Jews, by which he "deal[s] himself a decisive blow." This phrasing assumes agreement that Jewishness is a shameful origin it would behoove a cultivated person to conceal. It is also noteworthy that the passage presents Jewishness and Englishness as mutually exclusive. Following the revelation of Wethered's Jewish identity, his critique of the English, formerly so congenial to his Russian listeners, comes to denote the stereotypical national unreliability of Jewish cosmopolites: "Would an Englishman betray his own drunkards?"[53]

As if tropical exotica were not enough, the Russian crew hold in reserve Russia's own imperial exotica to brighten a dull day. Cooped up on their ships for two months in Nagasaki Bay, they are entertained by eighteen Kamchadal boys—that is, aborigines of the Kamchatka Peninsula also known as the Itelmen. The boys were taught in their Petropavlovsk school to sing choral music and romances in excellent soprano and contralto, to dance traditional Russian dances, and to declaim popular fables by Russia's beloved fabulist, Ivan Krylov. To us today this has the whiff of a curiosity show, but Goncharov is exultant: "Just look where the spark of enlightenment and art has been lit!" Such were the Euro-American entertainment tastes of the day. US sailors performed in blackface for Japanese dignitaries, who according to Perry's report loved the "farcical antics" of "mock negroes." As recently as 2011, testifying to the limited progress on racial sensitivity in contemporary Russia, Russian sailors performed in blackface on the deck of the *Pallada*'s modern namesake, which in recent years has been making the rounds of the Pacific.[54]

Goncharov's attitudes to racial mixing are also a fascinating dimension of *The Frigate Pallada.* He describes with equanimity—or at least no offensive commentary—the Russian officer of Napoleonic campaigns who settled in the Cape Colony, married an African woman, and fathered six mixed-race children. This equanimity was by no means common in mid-nineteenth-century Europe, when creeping racialization of social conceptions, concomitant with the desire to maintain white European superiority, made racial mixing increasingly unpalatable. Charles Darwin expressed aversion to it in *The Voyage of the Beagle.* However, Goncharov is not entirely consistent on this score. He also expresses repulsion at racial mixing, especially in Africa. Upon meeting mulattoes on Cape Verde, he concludes: "If you are to be black, then be black like coal, so that your skin glistens like a well-polished boot." His tolerance of the Russian officer's Russian-African brood may be due to his not actually meeting the children.[55]

In the Siberian section, Goncharov shies away from mentioning the biologically mixed Russian-indigenous population. Such mixing was in fact quite extensive, especially in the Siberian north, and throughout the imperial period was treated permissively as long as the cultural outcome was Russian. But what made an outcome appear culturally Russian? In Siberia, legitimate children of mixed couples were considered Russian if they and the indigenous parent (usually the mother) became Orthodox. This was a flexible accommodation to an exigency of this particular colonial situation—in this case, the shortage of women in far-flung Siberian colonies.[56]

When the mixing produced the opposite outcome—Russians assimilating to indigenous societies—it was cause for regret, but not particular alarm. As the nineteenth century neared its end, however, it was increasingly viewed in terms of the Russians' racial and cultural degeneration, and hence a national disgrace. Ilya Vinkovetsky shows that round-the-world voyages with stopovers in Western European colonies exposed Russians to modern European ways of colonial management. This included viewing the world through a racialized prism and worrying about racial purity that needed shoring up. In the 1820s, this exposure to western colonial methods led to the introduction in Russian America (mainly present-day Alaska) of the social category of "creoles" (*kreoly,* Russian calque from Spanish *criollos*) to denote persons of mixed Russian-indigenous heritage. The term was first used in 1805 by the circumnavigator Nikolai Rezanov, who worked for the Russian-American Company. (This appears to have been a misapplication of the Spanish colonial terminology, which called such people *mestizos;* creoles were Spaniards born in the colonies.) In 1821 creoles became a separate estate with a defined legal place in Russian colonial society. This category was never used in Eurasian Russia.[57]

The globe-trotting Goncharov gained familiarity with western colonial practices regulating mixed populations and he popularized them in his travelogue. He explains that Manila's *mestizos* (in Russian *metisy*) are mixed-heritage descendants of "the Chinese, Spaniards, and other tribes with the Indians." He judges as doomed their pretensions to appear Spanish: "faces that are too dark and hair that is too black betray the non-Spanish blood on every step." An awareness of this reportedly "humbles" them. The distinctive headgear of *mestizo* women, we learn, distinguishes them publicly from "pure-blooded" Spanish women. Russian readers of this passage thus learned that their European peers were anxious about the purity of their "blood" and considered admixtures to it as corrupting and degrading. They also learned that, whatever the cultural outcome of mixing, its biology inexorably relegated bearers of such heritage to a lower rung of the social hierarchy in some parts of the world. The *mestizos'* humbled sense of self-worth, one can conclude from Goncharov's passage, merely internalized the existing hierarchy of the Spanish colonial system, about which Goncharov reports matter-of-factly, without critique, as something unique, but not necessarily reprehensible. Spaniards treasure so much the privilege of being born and educated in Spain, he writes, that the status of unmixed Spaniards born in the colonies is lower than that of Spaniards born in peninsular Spain.

His reading in western sources and observations of European practices in various imperial zones would have therefore taught Goncharov that permissive Russian attitudes about cross-ethnic interbreeding differed from popular western views of it as shameful and undesirable. One must resist assuming that Goncharov would have necessarily adopted western norms over Russian ones, but his awareness of the former may have played a role in the evolution of his own thinking. *The Frigate Pallada* in fact reflects a tension between traditional Russian tolerance of miscegenation and a creeping anxiety about it. Caught in these webs of ambivalence, Goncharov adamantly disapproves of the interbreeding of whites with darker-skinned peoples, especially in Africa, but appears unperturbed—at least publicly—about

Russians mixing with their empire's Asian ethnic groups. Views on miscegenation in general, especially between white and black "races," did not necessarily map onto views on miscegenation as a feature of Russian imperial life. Objections to one need not have connoted objections to the other. Still, in the travelogue, Goncharov is rather discreet about the interbreeding of Russians with indigenous Siberians. If he feels revulsion about indigenous people, he keeps it in check, merely wondering: "are these slanted-eyed, flat-nosed people really Russian?" Yet for the most part, he is careful not to indulge in the kind of abasement that runs unchecked in his portrayal of East Asian ethnic groups living beyond the Russian empire. By contrast, a German traveler through Siberia around the same time flat-out declared miscegenation between Russians and indigenous people to be a "contamination" of the former.[58]

Goncharov's restrained approach likely stemmed from a conscious decision to maintain decorous respectability in representing "our" empire's ethnicities. While Russian imperialism, like any other, devoted considerable energies to marking difference, it also featured a powerful current of enforcing confluence, whereby the entire multiethnic population of the Russian empire was in the process—fitful, but inevitable—of becoming Russianized (the term was *obrusenie*). This assimilating impetus discouraged "othering" or vilifying of minorities, since all were, in a sense, Russians in the making. In the town of Yakutsk, Goncharov finds Russian and Sakha elements coexisting, but reassuringly notes that the Sakha culture "is bound with time to also become Russian." Privately, however, he vents less open-armed attitudes about Siberia's indigenous people. This is how in one letter he reports concluding that an eleven-year-old girl he meets near Yakutsk is Russian: she is pretty and "very white," her cheekbones, thankfully, "do not resemble shafts [*oglobli*], and no bear fur replaces hair on her head—in a word, she's a Russian." Her Russianness hinges on her somatic difference from a bear-like Siberian aborigine.[59]

While avoiding the concept of race and racial mixing in describing Siberians in the travelogue, Goncharov vividly captures cultural hybridity. He is particularly struck by Russians adopting the language and culture of the Sakha (Yakuts). Historically, the phenomenon of Siberia's Russians going native was widespread in mid-century Yakutia, but also in Kamchatka and Buriatia.[60] Again, the contrast in the writer's handling of this topic in the book versus his private correspondence is revealing. The book portrays Russians going native as quaint, but not reprehensible. Levelheaded and neutral reporting accompanies representations of "Russian Yakuts"—people, that is, who are "Russians by birth, and Yakuts by language." That said, Goncharov's gut-level resistance to the idea of Russians stooping to speak Sakha reveals itself in a certain radicalism of demoting such a Russian to the designation of an actual "Yakut" (however qualified by "Russian"). Still, the use of the Sakha language by Russian settlers on the Lena River even among themselves is conveyed matter-of-factly. When a Russian official switches effortlessly to it, Goncharov confesses with a touch of humor that he was nervous about being asked "*Parlez-vous jacouth?*"—and having to reply, like a schoolboy, "*non, messieurs.*" The eleven-year-old Russian girl knows only Sakha, finding no need for Russian while living among the Sakha people. This is merely a cause for lightheartedness: "Ah, our passion for foreign ways remains strong: if not French or English, then make the children speak at least Yakut!"[61]

Such levity, however, is largely absent from the collective portraits of the Sakha or the Russians going native in Goncharov's correspondence from the voyage. In a letter to the editor of the prestigious journal *Notes of the Fatherland,* Andrei Kraevsky, Goncharov expressed shock at the low staying power of Russian culture in Siberia. He described the hybridization of Russians as disturbing slippage down the ladder of civilization. This judgment tapped into a widespread opinion of the Sakha and their northern neighbors as the most "primitive" people of the empire. The opposite of the expected colonial scenario unfolds: "Yakuts are not learning Russian, but Russians speak Yakut to an impermissible degree." Whole Russian settlements no longer even know the Russian language. This was no exaggeration. Travel accounts confirm that, from the middle of the nineteenth century until the early 1900s, Sakha language was a *lingua franca* in eastern Siberia. Far from promoters of Russianness, the settlers and even government officials Goncharov meets opt for the Sakha language and customs. Until recently, he writes to Kraevsky, Sakha was the language of Russian "high" society in Yakutsk. Goncharov is horrified that Sakha nannies care for Russian children and inculcate in them Sakha "mores"—and much else, he dubiously claims, most notably syphilis. Such racial fears were common among Europeans: the mere proximity of white children to "colored" nannies and servants seemed to threaten a degeneration of the white race. Goncharov tones down these racial prejudices and colonial anxieties as he recycles them into episodes of *The Frigate Pallada.* Whereas the pretty eleven-year-old Russian girl described in his letter, quoted above, is contrasted with an odious, ursine Siberian, for example, she becomes in his book simply "a very pretty girl, completely Russian." Judging by his correspondence later in life, the encounter with the Sakha-speaking Russians imprinted itself on his memory as an outrage.[62]

Goncharov's perceptions of human diversity and Russian identity exemplify the perspective of upper-class Russians. However, *The Frigate Pallada* also hints at the ways common Russians negotiated identity and difference on the voyage. Observers' different classes and educational levels contributed to differences in perception. The use of simile (for example, the Chinese are *like* the Russians) appears to be a practice of the educated in *The Frigate Pallada.* Simple Russian sailors use more hard-edged metaphors. They call dark-skinned Filipinos "Gypsies," and refer to the Malays on Java as either "Finns" (*chukhny;* an ethnic slur) or "Polish folk." They make sense of the unfamiliar through references to Russia's own ethnic "others." Their perfectly unified Russian viewpoint does not allow for a multiplicity of codes. Tipsy and bedraggled Korean traders inspire such comments from the Russian sailors as "worse than Polish folk [*litva*]" or "not just Polish folk, worse than Circassians—that's the kind of nation [*natsiia*] they are!" It is clear that the Russian sailors have pejorative associations with non-Russian ethnicities of the Russian empire, to whom they feel superior. For all the differences in perception, they are just as partial to hierarchies as their upper-class compatriots.[63]

The book's most individualized portrait of a lower-class Russian depicts Goncharov's servant Faddeev, born in the provincial town of Kostroma, about two hundred miles north of Moscow. A spunky, wily, and happy-go-lucky character, Faddeev became for Russian readers a favorite character of *The Frigate Pallada,* especially in the Soviet period, when there was a special premium placed on well-drawn lower-class characters. He resembles Jean Passepartout from Verne's *Around the World in Eighty Days*—a solid man of the people and unflappable servant who makes things work. Faddeev's condescending treatment of Goncharov as a gullible and helpless child was later reprised by the writer in his comical portrayal, in the novel *Oblomov*, of the protagonist's servant—another favorite among readers. Some Siberian Russians might be going native, but as for Faddeev, his Russianness is safe and sound in foreign lands. On the streets of London, he confidently elbows his way around. "He brought on foreign shore his Kostroma element," Goncharov jocularly notes, "and did not dilute it with even a drop of foreignness. He treated each custom or institution dissimilar to his own as a mistake, with hostility and even contempt."[64]

To Goncharov's amazement, Russian sailors do just fine on all foreign shores, without ever stepping outside their own culture. Not speaking English, they are canny enough to mimic it for necessary transactions in places like Singapore: they hold an object they wish to buy and ask "omatch," approximating the pronunciation of the English "how much." The midshipman Pavel A. Zelenyi, who after the voyage became the mayor of Odessa, keeps breaking into Russian folk songs in southern Africa's countryside. In the perception of any Slavic reader, for these songs to resound in such exotic landscape gives the narrative a decidedly surreal feel, as if Zelenyi were inadvertently Russifying Africa with his singing.[65]

The common Russians' lack of curiosity about the world can be disarmingly comical. Goncharov is flabbergasted that a Russian sailor on the *Pallada* cannot recall the itinerary that brought him to Japan. Faddeev is also badly in need of a geography lesson. When Goncharov asks him, at the Cape of Good Hope, if he knows where he is, the servant replies that he does not—and nor does he know why that matters. This is how Goncharov continues his lesson:

> "You'll return home. They'll ask you where you've been. How will you answer? All right, listen, I'll tell you, only pay attention and try to remember. From where did we arrive here?" He directed his stare at me, clearly intending to understand at all cost what I wanted from him and to please me. But I wanted to lead him to some form of understanding.
>
> "Where did we come from?" I repeated my question. "Well?"
>
> "From England."
>
> "And where is England?" He looked at me askance. I realized that my question was unclear to him.
>
> "Where is France, Italy?"
>
> "I don't know."
>
> "And where is Russia?"
>
> "In Kronstadt" he quickly answered [referring to the naval base near St. Petersburg from which the *Pallada* sailed].
>
> "In Europe," I corrected him. "And now we came to Africa, to its southern part, to the Cape of Good Hope."
>
> "Yes, sir."
>
> "Remember!"

Faddeev clearly has no conception of the continents or of geographical scale. For him, Russia is in Kronstadt, not the other way round; it's only the association between the two places that is of consequence. We might also note here Goncharov's own reflexive placement of Russia in Europe, not in Europe *and* Asia, by which he clearly taps into his cultural rather than physical geography.[66]

Russian commoners sometimes appear to Goncharov's Europeanized, educated sensibility just as foreign as Javanese Malays. He studies his servant Faddeev as an exotic native with thoroughly alien customs and ways of thinking. For example, he is repeatedly mystified by Faddeev's glee at another's misfortune and entertained when this Kostroma commoner is utterly unimpressed by a ceremonial Japanese dinner. Complaining that it left him queasy, Faddeev sums up the sophisticated Japanese menu as a list of plain Russian ingredients, minus the essential ones: "red and white groats [*kasha*], . . . fish served like mush [*kisel'*], no salt, no bread!" Unwilling to let a Chinese porter in Hong Kong carry his Russian master's basketful of purchases, Faddeev rips them out of the porter's hand and insists on carrying them himself. A protracted scuffle is resolved only once it becomes clear that the poor Chinese porter was merely trying to recover his basket. "Naked people came by and delivered some sort of paper on a stick" is how Faddeev reports to Goncharov that Japanese guards have delivered a list of questions to the *Pallada* on its arrival in Nagasaki Bay. In this very first encounter with Japanese officials, apprehensions about attack or imprisonment rife among the Russian crew don't ruffle Faddeev's characteristic sangfroid. A figure of comic relief, Faddeev possesses folksy, steadfast Russianness, which makes Europeanized Russians chuckle, but also gives them comfort. As members of the educated, cosmopolitan elite, for whom this sort of thing would be unbecoming, they vicariously relish the common folk's unabashed nationalist conviction in the superiority of everything Russian, which no foreign bauble or custom could ever put in doubt.[67]

In the course of his ethnographic analysis of Faddeev, Goncharov wishes to ascertain "the elements that make up a Russian." This work of analysis is actually mutual, but while it takes Goncharov three weeks to figure out Faddeev, the quick-witted servant accomplishes the study of his master in just three days. As Alexander Etkind argues, the Russian heartland could be as much a heart of darkness for a Europeanized Russian as Africa was, which makes colonial categories applicable to analyzing spaces and people in the Russian core. Goncharov likens his conversations with Faddeev to a dialogue between "European civilization" and "Kostroma simple-mindedness." While the educated and propertied Goncharov regards himself as a civilized European, he pegs the uneducated Faddeev as a Kostroma bumpkin, whose provincialism in fact trumps his Russianness. The island of Madeira appears to Goncharov as "a kind of Kostroma," in the sense that both are objects of a European civilizing mission.[68]

Yet while Goncharov's Europeanness may appear non-Russian in relation to his lower-class countrymen, he is certainly perceived as a Russian by foreigners he meets on the voyage. Identity is relative: it depends on where it is asserted and with respect to whom. While they view much of the world through an exotic lens, the *Pallada* officers realize that they are themselves apprehended as exotic rarities by not only Africans and Asians but also their European colonial masters, many of whom have never seen a Russian before. On occasion, the Russians' own identity thus becomes a conundrum for those who meet them. Londoners offer bearded Russians alms, taking them for beggars. In a parallel to Goncharov's and Faddeev's reciprocal analysis, the Russians and the Africans in the Cape Colony jail are locked in a mutually stupefied stare during Goncharov's visit. He writes of the African prisoners: "they looked at us with greater curiosity than we at them." Korean villagers are fascinated by the Russians' white skin and insist on touching it. Such self-exoticizing let-me-touch-your-skin scenes were common in accounts of exploration, but Goncharov mentions this only in passing. He is not offended that the Koreans never heard of Russians, since they are equally ignorant of the French and the English—a key test of international relevance. During Putiatin's second expedition to Japan, in 1858–1859, which is not described in *The Frigate Pallada,* throngs of Japanese onlookers touching and prodding the exotic Russian visitors made them actually feel unsafe. One Russian officer compared the curiosity of the Japanese to the way in which Russian peasants "look at a bear on a chain." The Russians' footwear apparently attracted much attention since the Japanese rumor had it that westerners lacked heels and therefore required boots to stand upright.[69]

In one scene of *The Frigate Pallada,* the local doctor in the Cape Colony, Mr. Verstfeld, runs over to the hotel where the Russians are staying because he has never seen a Russian before. He explains that his curiosity about "the Russian type" stems from interest in the natural sciences, geology, phrenology, and ethnography—the same sciences that buttressed white Europeans' epistemic projects of imperial domination and racial supremacy. Since ethnic purity is hard to come by among the *Pallada*'s crew of such Russified

Western Europeans as Baron Krüdener (Kridner), Dr. Weirich (Veirikh), and Possiet (Pos'et), this only makes these "Russians" laugh. The exoticizing and taxonomic gaze to which the Russians themselves are subjected, and which Goncharov ridicules, does not, however, prompt a reflection on his own essentializing of other ethnicities.[70]

Unlike the Africans Goncharov meets, the Russians are in a position to add nuance to Verstfeld's totalizing ethnocentrism. The naturalist Goshkevich, who spent ten years in China, is proclaimed by his Russian companions, to the increase of general hilarity, to resemble a Chinese person more than a Russian. As "pure Russians" among the higher-class crew, Goncharov can count only himself and one other person. This shows that "Russianness" in Goncharov's view resides in something deeper and more visceral than culture. He later calls a Baltic German who migrated from the Russian empire to the Cape Colony, and who displayed touching nostalgia for his former empire, merely a "sham" (*mnimyi*) Russian. True, that emigrant had forgotten most of his Russian—but then, so had the Russian officer who, through British captivity, ended up as a settler in the Cape Colony, and whose Russianness Goncharov does not question.[71]

The *Pallada* Russians knew they were regarded as "barbarians" by the people of East Asia, who had their own ancient hierarchies of civilizational superiority over all outsiders, but they treated this as quaint superstition. The Japanese language did not then possess a neutral term for "foreigners," so all were called "barbarians." The elite crew members of the *Pallada* were less indifferent, however, when encountering assumptions about Russian savagery among westerners they met on imperial frontiers. Dr. Verstfeld seems guilty of this prejudice. He expects, Goncharov supposes, to find among the *Pallada* officers exotic heroes of Russian folk tales or "people of savage exterior." Goncharov writes that Dr. Verstfeld is surprised to learn "that Goshkevich knew geology, and that we have many scientists, that we have a literature." Goncharov pities his ignorance, yet fails to conclude that his own typologies of supposedly "primitive" peoples may also unduly homogenize and devalue them. Ethnologic discrimination matters for representing one's own people but seems dispensable when dealing with "others." Goncharov protests the reduction of Russia's diversity to a pure type, but he is miffed to be made aware of his own gaffe of lumping the Americans and the English into one English nationality. "Well, who can make them out?" he complains. "I hear they pray the same, eat the same, and hate each other just the same, too!"[72]

Writing about Japan, Goncharov confidently assumes that the Japanese, for all their talk of European "barbarians," are deeply impressed with the Russians. Historian George Lensen's analysis of Japanese records shows this self-satisfaction not to be fully warranted. While appreciating the Russians' kindness, the Japanese were also shocked by the "barbarians'" uncouthness; they experienced physical revulsion and thought themselves superior and more civilized than their visitors. (The Americans, incidentally, were guilty of similar narcissism, just as unwarranted, in their travel writings about the Perry expedition.)[73] Russian bodies looked unpleasantly white to the Japanese, their noses too pointy. The Russians appeared effeminate, just as the Japanese appeared to the Russians. Traditional Japanese robes, described by Goncharov as "skirts," signaled to him the supposed Oriental predilection for homosexuality. The Japanese chuckled as they concluded the same about Russian men from their habit of shaking hands and kissing. Russian sailors lined up on the mast crossbars looked to them like "monkeys." Goshkevich labeled one Japanese translator as "the pockmarked one," probably not realizing that his own sobriquet among the Japanese was "the pockmarked barbarian." The translator whose face looked to Goncharov like a shovel referred in his diary to the portly Goncharov as a "pot-bellied barbarian." The Japanese mixture of repulsion and superiority seems a mirror image of the Russian one. In imperial encounters, western and eastern prejudices clashed, though the easterners at least stayed out of the lands of those they despised.[74]

Imperial Kaleidoscope

The kaleidoscope, a cylinder containing loose, multicolored objects, uses an arrangement of mirrors to create patterns out of the random heaps in which these objects fall. The optical reality is really a mirage: a false rendition of chaos as order, of formlessness as form. An arbitrary constellation of objects becomes available to the eye as symmetrical design.

The kaleidoscope is a fitting image for the processes of ordering that assist the transmutation of the raw experience of travel into a patterned narrative. It also captures the process of rendering an analytic account of such narratives. At each level, a confused mass of experiences or ideas becomes structured in a way that satisfies a craving for meaning and order shared by the travel writer and the analyst, not to mention their readers. The pattern of images in a kaleidoscope changes with the rotation of the cylinder. As

Goncharov organized his experience of travel into a book with specific theses, he chose the rotations that yielded the desired patterns. I have focused on one dimension of Goncharov's design—a fairly prominent one—and in the process have also rotated Goncharov's sprawling seven-hundred-page narrative to yield my own pattern. Mine is an imperial kaleidoscope.

Far from merely an unavoidable reality, these ordering processes are at the heart of the sense-making that defines the experience of both a (traveling) human and a humanist. But there are also asymmetries and jagged edges that contribute to the breakdown of ordered or intended meaning. These become visible when we zoom in on the interface between Goncharov's narrative optics and the experiential jumble it structures. Let's peer behind the tidy reflection produced by the kaleidoscope to glimpse the heap inside.

Studies of travel writing and colonial writing typically focus on representations of difference. Yet travelers also negotiate similarity on their journeys, and the interplay between similarity and difference in their texts can be quirky, unpredictable, even unsettling. As James Duncan argues, similarity can be as shocking to a traveler as difference, which makes "familiarizing gestures" as integral to travel narratives as the rhetoric of exoticism. Indeed, like most colonial texts, *The Frigate Pallada* features what Spurr calls "an inherent confusion of identity and difference." The same text may insist simultaneously on the colonizers' radical difference from and on their essential similarity with the colonized.[75]

Passages in *The Frigate Pallada* that stress sharp racial and ethnic difference sit alongside passages that stress similarities. While this chapter has so far highlighted the towering differences that dominate the travelogue's landscape, I now turn to the less pronounced features of similarity. Despite the travelogue's vast array of racial differences, Chinese bodies sometimes appear to Goncharov very similar to Russian ones, and black Africans under certain circumstances bear uncanny resemblances to white Russians. A Shanghai bazaar, with its noise, bustle, and motley outfits, is to Goncharov a near replica of a provincial Russian market where cooking and trading share the same space and luxuries and vulgar necessities are sold side by side. Functionally identical, the bazaar and the market differ only in content, a fact that actually puts the Russian stock in unflattering relief: Russian tar, bast fiber, and wooden dishes appear to be outshone by fancy Chinese tea, silk, and porcelain. Since Russia targeted China for trade rather than settlement, this positive description of Chinese wares and shared trading practices might have served as an enticing advertisement.

Spurr insists that both the similarities and the differences claimed by Europeans are always deployed for politically instrumental ends. While assertions of difference help establish European superiority, those of similarity augur eventual assimilation of the non-Europeans or their amenability to civilizing projects. Goncharov's portrayal of the Japanese largely follows this pattern. Some of Goncharov's assertions of similarity, however, lack a detectable political motivation. While stark racial, ethnic, and civilizational contrasts give *The Frigate Pallada* its structure, tiny flashes add nuance to this grid. Goncharov at times submits to his experience without worrying about it colliding with his conceptual framework. For example, the blacks in Cape Verde play what looks to Goncharov like a traditional Russian card game (*kozyri*). A jolly cartful of African pilgrims reminds Goncharov of Russian Gypsies, and the Malay waiter Richard reminds him of Russia's Tatar waiters. The Chinese are just like the English in their talent for detailed workmanship. The fault lines between the European and non-European, and even between black and white, sometimes appear fused in Goncharov's rushes of experience. A disinterested sense of human universality, rendered unsentimentally, illumines these rare glimpses.[76]

At times, Goncharov opts for a bemused nod at universal human follies. Indeed, traveling often tempers the belief in one's home culture's exceptionalism.[77] For Goncharov, it seems to challenge his assumption that certain flaws are uniquely Russian. When his inquiries about a broken window in his Cape Town hotel produce no quick replacement but only a month's worth of bland excuses, he concludes that the propensity for casual unconcern (*bespechnost'*) often thought of by Russians as their national trait, is in fact universally human. Further verification of this truth materializes for Goncharov in the Manila hotel. There, Goncharov has a comic first-ever experience with a shower: instead of the expected bathtub with a tap, he finds a cabinet with weird pipes. Though after much trial and error he manages to release "rain" from the pipes, he finds it impossible to stop the deluge. Meanwhile, the water has soaked his clothes, leaving him stranded in the shower room and deprived of a respectable manner in which to return to his private room. A Filipino hotel employee rescues the hapless Goncharov. His own inexperience turns out not to have been to blame: the newfangled invention has been broken for a year already. Connecting these two experiences with hotel amenities, Goncharov reiterates his conviction about such unconcern being universally human, rather than uniquely Russian. In Shanghai, having just avoided getting swindled by a Chinese storekeeper, who named an exorbitant price for an object worth much less, he concludes that "no corner of the world" is free from the temptation to rip off one's fellow man: "The enlightened, the half-enlightened, and the savages: all are subject to this weakness. Who took it from whom: we from the Orient or the Orient from us?"[78]

Anyone seeking logical or ideological consistency in *The Frigate Pallada* will do so in vain. For all the structuring to which Goncharov subjects his ample voyage material, his imperial kaleidoscope orders the chaos of the heap only imperfectly. This is not unusual for colonial writing or travel writing. Tim Youngs cautions readers not to seek consistency in travel narratives given their tension between objective and subjective description, reliance on fictional strategies, and the genre's hybrid nature. Edward Said's study of Orientalism highlighted this quality of imperial texts. Homi Bhabha has found them to be fundamentally and systemically ambivalent, always speaking in a "forked tongue." Spurr similarly concludes that the stresses of colonial situations cause texts to become fractured into multiple rhetorical forms. Taking a cue from psychoanalysis, Bhabha is interested in incoherence as a window onto the underlying stresses, anxieties, and neuroses of the colonizer, traumatized by the burdens of his own authority. Spurr, by contrast, focuses on the strategic uses of such incoherence. In his view, far from annulling the projection of power, internal inconsistencies play a crucial role in its operation. The shifting meanings and values are versatile tools to handle the diversity of colonial situations and tasks.[79]

Beyond Goncharov's handling of similarity and difference, inconsistency also marks his explanations of policies, processes, and motivations in imperial encounters. For example, Goncharov accepts the assurance of his French guide in Manila about the Spanish colonial authorities' benevolence toward indigenous populations, whose happiness seems absolute. However, on the very next page he reports the murder of twenty Spanish soldiers by clearly disgruntled locals, against whom a special military transport had to be dispatched from Spain. To take another example, while Goncharov presents those Africans who persist in rejecting European civilization as hardheaded ingrates, he is far from considering those who do accept it wise and prudent. Instead, he demeans them as weak. The true object of colonial desire is the resisting, not the submissive, native.[80]

Goncharov offers a similarly illogical explanation for the Europeans' continuing efforts to push indigenous Africans off their land. Frequent mentions throughout the African chapter of the Europeans' relentless displacement of native populations in no way hinder Goncharov from characterizing the European presence as an errand into the wilderness. The colonists, we are told, merely gather "endless empty spaces." The rhetoric of *terra nullius* (or "empty land") is seamlessly joined in *The Frigate Pallada* to evidence of plenty of people needing to be elbowed out. The inconsistency flexibly accommodates multiple needs: natives must be present as beneficiaries of European progress, but they also must be absent to minimize the brutality of conquest. The latter is described euphemistically. We read not of land capture, dispossession, extirpation, or conquest, but of tribes that were "pushed out," leaving behind "cleared" or "cleansed" places.[81]

Even considered on its own terms, the colonial logic of *The Frigate Pallada* sometimes breaks down. Noting the absence of settled Africans in the vicinity of Cape Town, Goncharov writes: "Together with wild animals, they depart toward the interior, as if luring (*zamanivaia*) the whites to pursue them ever further and to keep introducing Europe into Africa." In this bizarre image, the repellent effect of Europe-bearing whites is presented as an invitation. One wonders whom this gift of Europeanness is supposed to benefit, if the recalcitrant natives recoil from the munificence. The victims of pursuit are moreover presented as authors of their own doom, their very escape forcing white Europeans to keep pushing ahead. Youngs finds this to be a common device in British travel writing about Africa: "Africa and its people are to blame for provoking unwanted behavior in British explorers." English historian and politician Thomas Babington Macaulay, writing on British India, presents Bengalis as a people who invited conquest because they failed to project sufficient power in the region. The colonizers (and their like-minded observers) embed the colonized in their rhetorical projections of authority because, as Spurr explains, this authority needs to be "conferred by those who obey it" and thus be granted "its proper value." It seems, however, that, when pressed, Goncharov is willing to dispense with the people's conferral of authority and settle for its conferral by the land itself. In describing Nagasaki Bay, in which the Russians were treated as intruders, Goncharov claims that a terraced Japanese hill "lures one [*manit*] to climb it." The inhabitants' emphatically communicated prohibitions fail to curb Goncharov's flight of fancy. If the people's invitation cannot be construed, the beckoning of the land itself will suffice.[82]

Writing about travelogues, as about any text, invariably involves grouping similar images and distilling sequences of cognate ideas. Yet this poorly reflects the actual rhythm of this and many other travelogues. It is a kaleidoscopic mirage of analytical optics that disguises the heap within. Disparate ideas and clashing images abound in travelogues' narrative sequences; prejudice and approval zigzag with dizzying rapidity. The structure of travelogues fosters this: it is looser than the structure of plotted works of fiction such as novels. Sequences of impressions and musings simply accrue as traveler-narrators move through space. Structure and ordering certainly matter in travel writing, but they are less tight. A sequential summary of one representative seven-page passage will offer insight into the dramatic alterations of mood and tone in Goncharov's travelogue, often within the space of a few lines.

The passage in question precedes Goncharov's description of the first dinner at the Nagasaki governor's palace.[83] Goncharov initially stresses the spotless cleanliness of interiors and attires, which he contrasts in demeaning terms to Chinese filth. Even Japanese beggars, he claims, are preternaturally clean. The manners of the Japanese impress him, but their childish temporizing and deception frustrate him, causing him to say that "one pities them too much to beat them." In this one paragraph, we read genial complimenting of the Japanese and disparaging of the Chinese, followed by the deprecation of the Japanese as insubordinate children whom Russians may be in a position to punish. The paragraph concludes by ridiculing the Japanese policy of seclusion.

A detailed discussion of Japanese political dysfunction, which stymies such sensible changes as the abolition of the seclusion policy, follows on the next page. Goncharov then gloats about the Russian naval maneuvers that ignore Japanese prohibitions but incur no meaningful censure. The pathetic efforts of the Japanese to maintain appearances of sovereignty and authority, especially allusions to their laughable cannons, only make Russians "snicker." They disdainfully point to the Chinese, formerly so disinclined to open their ports to Europeans, who have been forced to open five. The tone is now spiteful.

But right away, Goncharov counterbalances this by compassionately putting himself in the shoes of the Japanese in order to dramatize their political dilemma. He sympathetically imagines the existential weight for their country, and for individual officials, of the decision to accommodate or reject western demands. In yet another pivot, this exercise in empathy ends with an image of the Japanese as a bunch of insubordinate schoolchildren who, upon the teacher's arrival, instantly confess their guilt, beg for mercy, and submit themselves to their elders' direction. The elders in question, Goncharov clarifies, may be the "sly" Americans, or a handful of spunky Russians, whose bayonet, "still blameless," he ominously notes, has glittered in the Japanese sun. Benign compassion imperceptibly morphs into condescension and malice, with ominous threats of violence.

This leads the way to a gruesome metaphor of Japan that has "suicidally" let vital sap out of its body, becoming arrested in enervated, pathetic childhood. This sap now needs to be replenished by either Americans or others, which will indubitably happen soon. A digression on hara-kiri customs follows, including a quotation from an unnamed "learned" source, calculated to horrify a European reader and to present any country that would invent such a custom as barbarous.

Having poured out this condescension mixed with aggressive posturing, and having denigrated the entire culture as a bloodless corpse teetering on the brink of extinction—unless magnanimous Greater Europeans come to the rescue—Goncharov softens his rhetoric yet again. He replaces the conquerors' drumbeat with the civilizers' lullaby. He presents western intrusion into Japan as a mission not of force but of assistance to the Japanese in achieving what they themselves secretly desire—which is why Goncharov predicts easy success. The Japanese are bored in their self-enclosure and curious of the larger world. Japanese commoners greedily grab Russian vodka, wine, biscuits, and candy lowered to them from the *Pallada.* Their eventual appreciation of the Europeans' trouble is all but assured: apathy is merely a mask over joyfulness, manifold talents, and lively curiosity. They resist because they are ignorant of the advantages of openness and of the good intentions that motivate its facilitators. They don't understand, Goncharov writes, that England and Russia could never have achieved their present greatness in the conditions of seclusion. As if cannons and bayonets have never cropped up in the narrative, the passage exudes benevolence.

Goncharov's thesis about a secret desire for rapprochement in no way complicates his assertion, a paragraph later, that the Japanese do not actually wish it, and are foolish to think that simply not wishing will suffice. They are unable to oppose intruders by force, he writes, and fear being unsuccessful if they do. Goncharov lists Greater Europeans' grievances against Japan: butchered Christians, imprisonment of captives, humiliation of envoys, and overall arrogance. This list makes revenge a palpable motivation in opening Japan, one that contradicts the notion of humanitarian assistance. The tone is vindictive. Putting the question of Japanese desires aside, Goncharov ultimately descends to naked power play, stating that no repulse is possible in view of Japan's lack of large seafaring ships. And with this, the account switches to a description of the visit to the Nagasaki governor.

As this summary shows, if one is intent on demonstrating Goncharov's tolerance and humanitarianism, as Soviet critics of the book were, then appropriate quotations are certainly available. To make Goncharov into an inveterate imperialist villain is equally possible. All it takes is to pick out from this textual salad the quotes conducive to one's taste. Yet either selection will render an incomplete image of the travelogue. Much of *The Frigate Pallada* is powered by alternating currents of sympathy and repulsion, benevolence and malice, sympathy and hostility, understanding and prejudice, altruism and aggression, ethnographic detachment and comedic ridicule. Even within just seven pages, we've seen it all.

Against the Grain of Colonial Authority

The Frigate Pallada strains to project an image of Russia as a confident and competent peer of European colonial empires. And yet, as is true of many colonial classics, it sometimes inadvertently subverts this goal, or destabilizes the ideological foundations of the imperial enterprise, or offers glimpses of the colonized people's agency that were meant to remain hidden. We thus learn something important about the operation of colonial texts when we attend to those rare moments in *The Frigate Pallada* when the narrator's colonial authority falters or strikes the modern-day reader in ways unintended by the author. Not infrequently, this happens when authority is projected onto non-European women, the most disenfranchised among imperial subjects, who serve as potent symbols of conquered lands. Interactions between European males and native women typically stand for interactions between European powers and their objects of conquest. The tale of Pocahontas is a good example.[84]

In Russian literature, this type of plot became powerfully established by Alexander Pushkin's 1821 narrative poem "The Prisoner of the Caucasus"—arguably the most important progenitor of the Russian literature of empire. The poem tells the story of a Circassian maiden who falls for a Russian captive and frees him, but then kills herself because her love is unrequited.[85] The Russian prisoner's lack of interest in the maiden primly departs from eroticized versions of such imperial romances. Yet Pushkin's interweaving of gender and imperialism, at its core, sends a traditional message about the ineluctable draw of superior Russian culture, embodied by the Russian male, which causes the Circassian maiden to renounce her own milieu. This colonial script is violated when colonized women prove impervious to the European male's desire or control. This is precisely what happens in a few evocative episodes of *The Frigate Pallada.*

The first of them involves an encounter in Hong Kong between two Russian men and a young Chinese woman. In this riveting scene, Goncharov and his fellow crewmember from the *Pallada,* Possiet, hire a Tanka boat after a night out on the town to transport them back to the *Pallada,* anchored offshore. The night is "sultry, glittering, and intoxicating." The boat is operated by an old Chinese woman and a beautiful fifteen-year-old, the latter becoming the object of Possiet's unwanted attention:

> "Two shillings!" the young girl announced. "For such a beauty, a hundred pounds sterling!" said my companion. "That's expensive" I noted. "Two shillings!" she repeated monotonously. "You're not from here, are you? You're too white. Where are you from? What's your name?" Possiet insistently questioned, moving nearer her. "I'm from Macao. My name is Etola," she answered in English, foreshortening some syllables in the Chinese manner. "Two shillings," she added after a moment's silence. "What a beauty!" my companion continued "Show me your hands. Tell me how old you are. Whom do you like better, us, English, or the Chinese?" "Two shillings," she kept answering. We approached the frigate. My companion held her hand; I ascended the ladder. "Tell me something, Etola," he kept asking, holding her hand. She kept her silence. "Tell me, what are you . . ." "Two shillings" she repeated. I laughed; he sighed. We paid the money and went to our cabins.[86]

In Goncharov's retelling, this is a humorous and titillating story about Possiet as a scorned would-be lover. The Chinese girl's thick-headedness and monotone repetition of the fare are also the target of ridicule: she is no Isolde to Possiet's Tristan. Yet the story begs to be read against the grain. For what is truly titillating is a temptation to violate its perspective by imagining the episode from the viewpoint of the Chinese girl rather than the white

Figure 5.3. Depiction of a Tanka boat, Macao. Goncharov's intended humorous portrayal of a crewmember rebuffed by the young girl handling the boat reveals the underlying power imbalance between the local Chinese and the Europeans.

European male. Like an overwritten sign, erased but not quite, her own story lurks in the text.[87]

She comes from Macao, then a poor and overpopulated Portuguese colony in China, which Goncharov mentions just two pages earlier as the source of the thirty thousand migrants who built Hong Kong. Britain's globalizing initiatives—establishing trading outposts in Asia, fostering labor mobility—frame the girl's presence in Hong Kong. Destitution likely brought her to this dangerous line of work, ferrying (white) men on a boat in the middle of the night. The older chaperone is her feeble protector in this high-risk job. It is tempting to read what Goncharov seems eager to portray as a materialistic focus on "two shillings" as an indigent's plea for mercy. Who else relies on her earnings? How many times has she been denied the fare due her to warrant this anxious staccato of remonstration?

The story presents the power dynamic by recording what it tries to deny. What Goncharov seems to find funny is that a debonair upper-class white European male is sexually rejected by his social inferior: a Chinese female pauper. Yet a closer look reveals, on the contrary, the precariousness of the young woman's position. In the confining space of the boat and of their business transaction, Possiet holds all the strings. He relentlessly seeks physical proximity to his victim, moving closer to her on the bench, touching her hand. In a perfect analog to imperial conquest—not the least, in this context, the Europeans' intrusion into Asian ports—Possiet's oppressive physical encroachments on Etola's space combine with steps toward epistemic mastery: an examination of her body, her skin color, her origin, her name. Her unwilling answers are punctuated by silences. Possiet desires knowledge and intimacy; she shrinks from both. He wants to gratify his ego and lust; she wants to earn a living and be left alone.

The language of this courtship is as "forked" as the British parliamentary debates that Said and Bhabha examined in their foundational works of postcolonial theory. On the one hand, Possiet's ardor may seem touching. By asking Etola personal questions, he would seem to care for her as an individual. He requests her compliance and respects her refusal. On the other hand, the reality of prostitution, a thriving industry that catered to Asia's European visitors, shadows this flirt from the start. Tanka boats in particular were famed for supplying Europeans with prostitutes, so this stereotype likely shapes Possiet's expectations. When Etola states the price of the fare, Possiet's counteroffer of a hundred pounds makes clear that he has in mind a fuller menu of services. Goncharov catches the innuendo, knowledgeably warning that this price is steep. Did he send Possiet a knavish wink? Both turn a deaf ear to the girl's desperation. As in most colonial writing, so in *The Frigate Pallada,* colonial settings become what Anne McClintock calls "porno-tropics for the European imagination."[88]

Granted, the annals of Russian serfdom offer rich evidence of more grievous sexual abuse of underage social inferiors than this ultimately harmless affair. Yet the colonial circumstances stamp their own meaning on this interaction. First, Goncharov's lighthearted and entirely permissive reaction may be difficult to find in Russian literary descriptions of parallel episodes at home, which at least since Karamzin's story "Poor Liza" tended to sympathize with the victims of sexual predators. Second, as he preens before Etola, demanding that she rate the Russian male's attractiveness vis-à-vis the Chinese and the English, Possiet reenacts the larger rivalry among the region's imperial powers—just as he reveals his own anxiety as to how exactly he stacks up. "Whom do you like better?" he harasses Etola: the Russians, the English, or the Chinese? For a Russian, outranking the English would have been, of course, the sweetest sexual compensation for actual political realities. While in most colonial narratives, European civilizers' narcissistic self-love needs no validation from the colonizer or else is easily conjured up, here the Russian officer seems less secure, and Etola ultimately withholds her validation.

A second episode also involves the importuning of colonized women who prove impervious to the European male's wishes. Yet the dynamic of the interaction is vastly different. On one of Goncharov's ethnographic sorties to the countryside surrounding Cape Town, he meets three African women whom he asks to identify their "tribe." The woman who replies shows none of the cooperation and helpfulness of the "Indian" from Pondicherry:

> "Fingo!" she said. "Mozambique," she then shouted. "Hottentot!" All three women began to loudly guffaw. It wasn't the first time I have heard this vulgar guffaw of black women. If you simply pass by—nothing happens. But if you ask a black beauty any question, such as her name or directions, she will lie, and her answer will be followed by her and her friends' laughter. "Bechuan! Kaffir!"—the wench [*baba*] kept on shouting at us. Quite a wench, indeed. Dressed exactly like our wenches: a kerchief on her head, something resembling a skirt around her waist, like in a *sarafan* [sleeveless Russian peasant tunic], and a shirt on top, sometimes with a scarf on her neck, sometimes without. Some women from the brown tribes are astoundingly similar to our suntanned village old women. The black ones, however, bear no similarity to anything [*ni na chto ne pokhozhi*]: all have thick lips, protruding jaws and chins, eyes black as tar, their whites yellowed, and a row of very white teeth. There is something terrible and evil about a smile on a black face.[89]

The "wench" flaunts her refusal to gratify white man's obsession for tabulating Africans. Her reaction makes one wonder how many times she must have heard these tedious questions before. What the Russian traveler apparently considered a perfectly natural inquiry appears to her as a white man's rote formula, a worn-out template deserving nothing more than ridicule. Rather than make herself more transparent, she brazenly lies, putting up a smokescreen. The shouting makes defiance palpable. A figure of noncompliance with European rule, she cleverly reverses the dynamic of power. Rather than provide the European with an opportunity to train his eye and master Africa, she makes herself unclassifiable and makes him into the butt of a joke. The white man's befuddlement becomes a merry spectacle for her African female companions.

Goncharov is discomfited by this obstreperous black woman who foils his classificatory zeal. From the perspective of this interaction, we see why the writer may have later so appreciated the convenience of having all ethnic representatives of southern Africa pinned down like specimens in a Cape Colony jail. There, laughing off a white man's questions was less of an option. Perhaps the woman's audacity momentarily raises her in the estimation of her chastened analyst, prompting him to declare the similarity of African women to Russian peasant women in their attire. He even briefly suspends the black/white dichotomy by commenting on the uncanny similarity of lighter-skinned old African women to their sunburnt Russian equivalents. Or perhaps, rather than ennobling, this comparison already moves in the direction of putting the African woman in her place. The well-practiced class superiority of Europeanized elite over Russian peasants, affirmed in a myriad of daily life rituals and public arrangements, and in this case layered onto a gender hierarchy, may function as a springboard for asserting a white man's racial superiority over a black woman. Does class prejudice, in other words, train one for racial prejudice? This does seem to be the direction of Goncharov's thoughts, since in the same breath, he asserts the radical racial inferiority of darker-skinned blacks in ways that resonate with his grotesque description of the San in the Cape Colony jail: thick lips, protruding jaws, the yellowed whites of their black-as-tar eyes. The conclusion to this portrait is a claim that a smile on a black face has something "terrible and evil" about it.

This mixture of similarity and difference illustrates Bhabha's ideas about the anxieties that underlie colonial ambivalence. Surprised by the challenge to his authority, Goncharov initially "ennobles" the black women by putting them on a par with whites. But the dynamic of colonial situations requires that the natives be put in their place. The real-life African is ungovernable. Goncharov makes her discursively governable by deploying scurrilous racial rhetoric. Bhabha explores resistance to the colonizer through camouflage or what he calls "sly civility": a mollifying promise of cooperation that feigns goodwill but in fact subverts the colonizer's wishes. The Indian natives from Bhabha's source, for example, make promises to the Christian missionary regarding their resolve to be baptized. Yet they slyly invoke the forthcoming harvest as an argument for postponement, to get the missionary off their backs. Goncharov's African interlocutor is bolder. Hers is not sly civility, but a spectacularly uncivil rebuff.[90]

Bronwen Douglas finds such "indigenous countersigns" of aboriginal agency throughout narratives about voyages of exploration. Explorers formed perceptions of indigenous people not in a vacuum, or from the safe distance of ship decks, but in actual cross-cultural encounters. Whether indigenous people chanced to greet European visitors with smiles or spears often determined subsequent long-standing characterizations of them as peaceful or savage. It is likely because the ethnic group of the Luoravetlans (Chukchi) posed a strong military challenge to Russian rule in Siberia that Goncharov feels justified labeling them "savage." He does not apply that epithet to the Sakha who accommodated to Russian rule. These rash judgments were products of wrestling with the puzzling or intimidating behavior of native people. Travel accounts channeled these judgments back to European publics, influencing ideas about essential racial traits of various populations.[91]

The black woman inscribes herself in *The Frigate Pallada* as precisely such an indigenous countersign. While allowing it to slip in, Goncharov must nonetheless suppress it. In order to recover a sense of his own superiority to an African "wench" who dared laugh at him, Goncharov must vilify her in his text. The smile through which she disrespected him becomes generalized into the "terrible and evil" smile of all black people. To merely record the conversation without such commentary would imperil the writer's image as a European white man in control of the situation. Racial debasement helps the narrator reassert his privileged status in the narrative. And it is through the narrative that he rights the slight he feels he has suffered in the actual interaction. As we have seen, Goncharov's imperialistic swagger in his description of Japan similarly compensates for the precariousness of the Russians' actual political control.

Goncharov pitches his encounter with the African "wenches" as a lesson on Africans' irrationality and rudeness. His story about the Chinese Tanka boat operator pokes fun at the girl's mundane materialism and a disappointing lack of famed Oriental allure. Yet what is arresting about both stories is how easily they lend themselves to being read against the grain. In spite of the shackles of Goncharov's colonial gaze and authority, the women's alternative, accidental stories—of noncompliance, evasion, and disrespect—bloom between his lines.

Diplomacy without the Gunboat

With the exception of some shoving and nonlethal shooting mentioned in the Korean section, *The Frigate Pallada* does not record any aggressive conduct on the part of the Russian crew. The aggressiveness—in the forms of racial and ethnic prejudice, imperial braggadocio, and unvarnished Eurocentrism—are all discursive in the travelogue. They reveal themselves less in the deeds of the Russian crew than in the narrator's manner of speaking. We trace these attitudes in the tone and images of Goncharov's descriptions, in his musings and impressions, in his thoughts about the order of the world in which he lives, including the meaning of its past and the desirable directions of its future. The harmful influence of such travel books as Goncharov's was that they habituated metropolitan readers to such attitudes, hierarchies, and manners of perceiving the world and its diverse populations. Our historical understanding of Russian culture, in particular, would benefit by greater attention to its affiliation with imperial projects and ideologies than has been devoted to this topic so far, especially by comparison with parallel efforts in other fields.

Yet despite that, and on a brighter note, I want to conclude this chapter by describing an episode from the history of the *Pallada* expedition that departs from the usual script of imperial conquest and domination. This will mean leaving aside the discursive vagaries of Goncharov's book and switching to a historical vantage point from which to reflect on interactions across the lines of ethnic, cultural, and political difference. The story that follows is based on historical sources, though Goncharov briefly described this episode in his sketch "Twenty Years Since," which he wrote much later, in 1879, and which has since been appended to *The Frigate Pallada*. He himself did not participate in these events, so he used eyewitness accounts of his fellow crewmembers from the *Pallada*. By the time these events transpired, he was already making his way through Siberia back to European Russia.

The story in fact begins quite tragically. During Putiatin's second mission to Japan, in December 1854, a tsunami caused by an earthquake flooded Shimoda, where the *Pallada*'s replacement, the *Diana,* was docked. A giant tidal wave wiped out most of Shimoda and the surrounding villages, filling harbors with debris and corpses. Out of a thousand homes, only sixteen were left standing. Whirling currents spun the *Diana* around like a top, causing

Figure 5.4. A tsunami in Shimoda, Japan, 1854. Goncharov by this point had left the expedition to return home, but later wrote about the event, downplaying the generous aid the Japanese provided to the Russian crew.

structural damage and putting her at risk of smashing against underwater rocks or coastal structures. A cannon broke free, killing one sailor and injuring two others. One Japanese official who from a distance watched the Russian sailors clinging to their frigate "like ants," bitterly reflected: "Why does Heaven not kill the thieves, but mistreat our own people?"[92]

The bad situation of the Russian crew could easily have become worse. However, both sides behaved at their best. Though themselves in peril, the Russians rescued Japanese survivors. They picked up an old woman from a drifting roof and two Japanese men from a junk (a third man, obeying prohibitions against boarding foreign vessels, refused aid and promptly perished). When the tidal wave subsided, the Russians offered medical help to shore communities, although the help was rejected. The Japanese, despite dealing with a horrific natural disaster themselves, extended generous aid to the Russians. They allotted a bay in Heda for the repairs of the badly damaged frigate. When it sank, they provided the Russian crew numbering five hundred men with shelter, winter clothing, and food, and later with artisans, materials, and tools for the construction of a new schooner.[93]

After the tsunami ebbed, the Japanese appreciated that the Russians went ashore to inquire about their condition and offered help. Goncharov's sketch of this episode in "Twenty Years Since," by contrast, is somewhat curt in its gratitude and appreciation for the Japanese sacrifices: "In general, though they themselves suffered from the earthquake, they rendered us all possible aid and services. The Japanese authorities sent us provisions and assisted all the needy." The very next sentence shifts to counterbalancing examples of Russian aid and generosity. In his retrospective account, Goncharov likely wished to avoid portraying the Russian empire as reliant on Japan's good graces.[94]

Putiatin himself, however, in a report penned on the spot and addressed to the head of the Navy, Grand Prince Konstantin, was more effusive. Having praised the zeal and competence of the Russian crew, he wrote:

> Neither can I leave unmentioned the readiness of the Japanese to give us all assistance and to supply us with all we needed. Officials who had been immediately sent by the government sympathized with our plight, hurriedly constructed houses to shelter us from the cold winter season, and tried by all means possible to alleviate our situation. Given the fact that in the village of Miyajima, near which we went ashore, not a single house remained that was not destroyed by the earthquake, one cannot praise enough their humanitarian care of us.

Perhaps most heartfelt were the blessings the *Diana*'s chaplain gave the Japanese in his memoir: "A good people; a truly good and humane one! May you good people prosper for many years, may you live and remember that your good turn saved up to five hundred persons, foreigners, who survive indebted for their life." As recorded in this memoir, not merely the government of Japan, but also private Japanese citizens spontaneously rendered generous aid to the Russians: a kimono taken off one's back and offered to a shivering Russian sailor, pots of hot tea and food brought from one's private stores, improvised shelters.[95]

Forces of nature orchestrated a curious reversal in the power dynamic of this imperial situation. Goncharov considered a similar reversal in asking "who should civilize whom," as he observed the Englishmen's rough treatment of the Chinese in Shanghai. In the tsunami episode, the cannon-toting Russian imperialists, the would-be openers of Japan (Putiatin's efforts were yet to bear fruit), found themselves at the mercy of their Japanese hosts for basic survival needs. Indeed, they had to relinquish their cannons once the *Diana* foundered. Alexander II's imperial decree later designated these cannons as a gift to the government of Japan in appreciation for the rescue. The Japanese, seemingly so dysfunctional in their mode of government—if Goncharov is to be believed—and in such dire need of civilizational upgrades, found themselves in a position to care for the well-being of the belligerent intruders and proved capable of mounting massive and complex assistance. At the time, the Russian government was unable to house and feed a crew this size in its own Pacific base in Kamchatka.[96] The Japanese managed, while themselves reeling from a catastrophe.

This episode also prompts reflection about the mutual perceptions of Russians and the Japanese, as crafted by Goncharov's narrative. With its diverse record of prejudice, Eurocentric superiority, and strident imperial rhetoric, *The Frigate Pallada* leaves one unprepared to predict this episode's outcome. With the exception of warm goodwill generated during ceremonial dinners—which, however, was rooted in the exigencies of diplomacy—the book's handling of human difference is not a cheery read. One is almost surprised that both sides acted humanely toward each other in a moment of peril. This natural disaster temporarily suspended the Russians' colonial posturing and lessened the distrust of the Japanese. The need to project imperial grandeur or civilizational superiority melted away on both sides. No longer figureheads of their states' political prestige, the Russians and the Japanese simply became people who helped their fellow man in need. But it took a tragedy for the posturing to simmer down.

Still, the flame remained alive. His imperial dreams unchastened, the dauntless Putiatin soon recommenced his negotiations and signed the Russo-Japanese Treaty of Shimoda, in February 1855. By then, however, the sixty Russian cannons were safely stowed away in Japanese barns. The one remaining Russian ship sank. Why did the Japanese choose to cooperate? They may have believed that other Russian expeditions would likely follow. The seclusion policy had by then been broken by the American and British treaties signed in the previous year. While the Japanese were prepared to grant the same concessions to the Russians, however, Putiatin upped the ante, demanding more.[97] Ridding the country of five hundred foreigners and acquiring expertise in western shipbuilding techniques may have also figured in the Tokugawa government's decision to assist the Russians in building the new schooner. The Tokugawa offered humanitarian aid to the Russians, however, before knowing that such training opportunities would become available, and there were other ways to send off the castaways. For example, Putiatin chartered a US schooner to transport a portion of the crew to the Kamchatka Peninsula. Because of the Crimean War, moreover, of which the Japanese were well aware, it was open season on Russian vessels and military personnel, with British and French navies cruising the Pacific waters. The American captain of a US clipper who had agreed, for an exorbitant price, to deliver another group of the shipwrecked Russians back to Europe reneged on the contract once his crew mutinied, fearing that a US vessel carrying Russian passengers could become the target of French and British attacks.[98] Diplomatically and politically, if there was ever an auspicious moment to rebuff or even annihilate the Russians, as some Japanese officials in fact recommended, that was it.[99]

But the opposite happened. More than their show of force, it was the Russians' weakness, and the shared experience of overcoming a disaster, that put the Japanese in a more cooperative mood. They agreed to the treaty when Russian aggression was no longer a looming danger. As one of the plenipotentiaries, the samurai Kawaji, noted in his diary, "The Russians were repeatedly humble in speech . . . their words tamed us greatly." In the words of Lensen, "Russian assistance to Japanese victims at the time of their own distress, and Japanese concern for Russian safety, as well as the cooperative building of the schooner *Heda,* helped create an atmosphere of greater trust and respect, if not friendship." Russians back home later viewed Putatin's opening of Japan in triumphalist tones, as a confirmation of Russia's global prestige and geopolitical might.[100] While these were certainly valid conclusions, the actual human interactions that contributed to this political process offer a window into a more complex dynamic, in which Russia's imperial heft, much diminished by the circumstances, had to contend with the indigenous agency of the Japanese. Rather than enacting their superiority, about which we read so much in *The Frigate Pallada,* the Russians showed solidarity with the suffering of the Japanese people. The Japanese, far from dysfunctional, indecisive, and generally handicapped by their lack of Europeanization, as *The Frigate Pallada* portrays them, proved morally and logistically capable of saving their would-be civilizers in their dire moment of need.

CHAPTER SIX

The Bestseller and Its Afterlife

Travelogues about distant corners of the world enjoy the privilege of staying in print longer than other books. Like a wheel, each leaves for long an indelible trace, or a rut, until the trail is blazed so well that all ruts merge into one broad road.

—Goncharov, "Better Late than Never" (1879)

It is to the novel *Oblomov* that Goncharov now owes his place in the Russian literary canon. Yet nineteenth-century audiences read his travelogue more eagerly than the novel. By all markers of publishing success, *The Frigate Pallada* became an undisputed imperial-era bestseller. Within nine months of his return to St. Petersburg in February 1855, Goncharov published separately the Japanese chapters as a separate book called *The Russians in Japan,* two months after they appeared in the journals. The first full account of the expedition appeared in 1858 as *The Frigate 'Pallada': Travel Sketches in Two Volumes* with the prestigious publishing house of Glazunov, which subsequently acquired copyrights to *The Frigate Pallada.* At a time when few Russian books saw two or three editions, *The Frigate Pallada* reached ten by the end of the nineteenth century. Even this fell short of meeting actual demand, since the long-term monopoly on the copyright kept the work out of reach for many. Reviews and articles routinely referred to *The Frigate Pallada* as a book that everyone had read. Prized for its exoticism, humor, and narrative flair, the book reached a socially and institutionally diverse audience that included not only those noblemen who traditionally consumed literature, but also government officials, students of military academies, women, and young readers—even schoolchildren.[1]

In its phenomenal popularity, *The Frigate Pallada* far surpassed the novel that secured Goncharov his place on Russian literature's Olympus. Compared to the travelogue's ten editions across the nineteenth century, *Oblomov* saw only six. In serial print culture, which for nineteenth-century Russia offers a more reliable measure of success than book editions, *The Frigate Pallada* also far outstripped *Oblomov,* gaining fame before it became a book.[2] Both works appeared, across four issues each, in the most popular journal of the time, *The Notes of the Fatherland.* Beyond that, fragments of the travelogue made sixteen additional appearances in five other journals, as compared with two excerpts of *Oblomov* published elsewhere. Many excerpts from *The Frigate Pallada* appeared in *The Naval Review*—the official organ of the Ministry of the Navy that organized the *Pallada* expedition and was known as a liberal periodical. The journal was founded by a proponent of reforms, Grand Prince Konstantin Nikolaevich, who headed the Ministry and to whom Goncharov dedicated the travelogue. Separate offprints of journal sketches were published to accommodate the public's voracious appetite, whetted for the book editions that followed.[3]

Such popularity was not a unique case. In the nineteenth century, travelogues were all the rage. One of the most popular, *Missionary Travels and Researches in South Africa,* by Scottish missionary and explorer David Livingston, sold seventy thousand copies within mere months of publication and eventually made its author a wealthy man and a national celebrity. Presumed dead on his later mission to Africa, Livingston was "found" near Lake Tanganyika by Welsh journalist Henry Morton Stanley. Stanley claimed to have greeted Livingston with an inquiring "Dr. Livingston, I presume?"—a phrase that became famous as a striking instance of adherence to British etiquette in a place where no other white men could be found for hundreds of miles. Stanley's account of this rescue voyage, *How I Found Livingston*, became an instant bestseller; his subsequent *In the Darkest Africa* went on to sell 150,000 copies in English. Already in its first year, Frances Trollope's controversial travelogue, *Domestic Manners of the Americans*, appeared in four editions, being one of about three hundred travel accounts about the United States published in Britain prior to the Civil War. The most popular Russian travelogue before Goncharov's, Nikolai Karamzin's *Letters of a Russian Traveler,* went through seven editions in its first thirty years, which for early nineteenth-century Russia was an amazing feat of popularity. From the late 1860s, Mark

Twain derived most of his income from travel writing. An account of his European travels, *A Tramp Abroad,* sold sixty-two thousand copies in its first year. Twain is best known today for his fiction, but was regarded by his contemporaries as primarily a travel writer. For Goncharov's contemporaries, similarly, his travel writing often upstaged his fiction.[4]

Goncharov's path to literary fame led through his novel because according to a reigning hierarchy of literary genres, only the recognized highbrow genres of fiction, poetry, or drama could elevate one to a literary pedestal. Laurels could not be earned for travel writing. When critics advocated that Goncharov should hold a place of honor in Russian literary history, they marginalized *The Frigate Pallada,* even though the work had been received with nearly unanimous praise of its artistic merits. The case for Goncharov's canonization simply could not rest on a travelogue; its status as light entertainment might even harm the author's cause.

The monthly *Action*'s opinion was that, while *The Frigate Pallada* would forever remain a favorite book of readers craving adventure and exoticism, Goncharov's reputation rested on three novels: *An Ordinary Story, Oblomov,* and *The Precipice.* The poet and critic Apollon Grigorev stood virtually alone in prizing *The Frigate Pallada*—the book most "greedily read by our entire public"—above Goncharov's fiction, which he found unimpressive.[5] Obituaries following Goncharov's death in 1891 presented the writer as "the author of *Oblomov,*" or at best of all three novels. Very few so much as mentioned the *Pallada* voyage or Goncharov's book about it. *The Frigate Pallada* was still greedily read—as recently as 1886, two editions of the book were printed, and three more appeared by the close of the century—but to honor the writer's contribution to Russian literature, the literary cognoscenti relied on his fiction.[6]

In the Soviet era, other reasons also endeared *Oblomov* to the political left in charge of repackaging imperial Russia's cultural patrimony. Under their care, *Oblomov* delivered marvelously a critique of the tsarist regime and its chief social deformation: a parasitic class of serf-owning gentry. *The Frigate Pallada* was a less likely platform for such critiques, though as we will see below, valiant efforts were made.

Between Information and Narration

In the nineteenth century, thirst for knowledge about faraway places drove readers' interests in travel literature. This was a big source of *The Frigate*

Pallada's success. Yet Goncharov's great achievement was to turn this fascinating content into a great read. From the start, reviewers remarked on his masterful storytelling, inimitable humor, and dazzling descriptions. These literary merits were acknowledged even by the book's detractors, and continue to garner praise today. Goncharov's travel writing was recently called "some of the best Russian prose ever written."[7] "Delight" was among the most commonly noted reactions to the book by nineteenth-century readers. One claimed that all Russian travel literature "was nothing when compared to Goncharov's letters, where with such mastery, vividness, and plasticity he depicted images of tropical nature, African and Indian ports, and the motley life of the East, in a word, all that for us then had the novelty of a bewitching world of fairy tales." That reader also noted the commercial results: "These letters were so vivid and fascinating that people gobbled them up like hot cakes (*ikh chitali vse naraskhvat*). When the whole travelogue appeared . . . it sold out in barely a month, and within a year a second edition was in demand."[8]

Yet the question of balance between information and narration stirred debate. Readers accustomed to older traditions of travel writing, which aimed above all to provide detailed information about distant lands, found *The Frigate Pallada* lacking. Although Goncharov supplied some historical, geographical, statistical, and ethnographic information, deftly interwoven among impressions, adventures, and dialogues, much more information was customarily crammed into travelogues well into the nineteenth century. Hawk's contemporaneous account of the Perry expedition serves as a good contrast, to say nothing of earlier explorer accounts of Captain Cook or Mungo Park. Russian readers accustomed to such fare demanded that a travel accounts' balance between instruction and delight be tilted toward the former. It mattered little that Goncharov shunned such models in his opening chapter. Explicitly rejecting dry scholasticism, he pitched his travelogue instead as an unassuming collection of impressions of what he saw with his own eyes.[9]

Yet even sympathetic reviewers found early editions of Goncharov's travel notes uninformative about the worlds he described. One reviewer brought up the example of the writer's visit to the cigar sweatshop in Manila and commented: "Yet how these eight to nine thousand people live, what they earn, what their life is like, whether it's hard or easy—unfortunately, the author had no opportunity to ask such questions." Many noted, in Goncharov's defense, that the author, being part of an official governmental expedition, was in charge of neither his itinerary nor the ports of call—nor the length of stay in various places. Beginning with the first full edition of 1858, this was explained in the introduction.[10]

S. Dydushkin, writing for *The Notes of the Fatherland,* argued that these constraints made the author's achievement all the more astounding. To his credit, Goncharov did not fill out his book with plagiarized excerpts from other travelogues, as was the habit among certain less scrupulous western authors. One will learn nothing from Goncharov's book about the political, social, or economic conditions of various countries, Dydushkin claims, but one will experience viscerally what it *feels like* to be there. *The Naval Review* acknowledged that scientific knowledge was not the book's purview, yet lauded Goncharov for the realism of his life-at-sea descriptions, his explanations of the technicalities of sailing, and his perfect grasp of naval terminology, which made Goncharov an exception to the usual dilettante writer. Coming from such a specialized journal, this praise would have cheered the writer's uncle, Tregubov, who taught little Ivan about sailing.[11]

The book's scanty knowledge value was thus acknowledged but largely excused. Interestingly, some voices on the radical left and radical right were less forgiving. Beyond the knowledge value of the book itself, they attacked the knowledgeability of its author. V. P. Popov, writing for the conservative journal *The Rumor,* deplored that an author who had such an unprecedentedly wide field of observation—unlike earlier Europe-bound Russian travelers such as Nikolai Karamzin or Denis Fonvizin—would prove so uncurious about the world. Popov painstakingly collated quotations from *The Frigate Pallada* where Goncharov confessed feeling too sleepy or lazy to partake of sightseeing opportunities. "With that attitude," Popov fulminated, "one supposes that the author beheld only that which chanced to turn up in front of his eyes. . . . Meanwhile, not one bump received on the roiling seas, not one mosquito bite, neither hunger nor cold, was ever forgotten!" It incensed Popov that the republished installments about Japan, which had earlier appeared in *The Naval Review* lacking maps and illustrations, would cost two silver rubles, while an annual subscription to the same journal cost five. (The first full edition of *The Frigate Pallada* sold at three and a half rubles.) Talent? Yes, Goncharov did have it, but according to *The Rumor,* he spent it on trifles. Beyond his bodily scrapes, the author wasted ink on international cuisine. If only he appended the recipes for the dishes he described eating, Popov scoffed, *The Frigate Pallada* could actually become "an interesting cookbook."[12]

The book does indeed have an earthy aspect, rich with the smells and tastes of Africa and Asia. And it is true that Goncharov does indulge in touristic gripes about bumpy rides on stormy seas, lizards, mosquitos, and shoddy hotels with broken showers that provided homes for scary creatures (which appear to have been geckos). Though armed with an admirable generalist's knowledge about the places he visited, Goncharov also displays his gaps. When missing precise terms, he resorts to circumlocutions. When stumped by the meaning of a social ritual, he confesses his confusion. His ignorance of the names of many fruits and plants he sees and tastes occasions some of the most amazing examples of estrangement in Russian literature prior to Leo Tolstoy. This literary technique is typically used to wean readers from rote perceptions by describing a familiar object in a starkly unfamiliar way, which often involves withholding the object's name. In his unabashed pose of a Russian "everyman," Goncharov is in fact closer to a modern tourist, more willing to acknowledge his ignorance than the heroic explorers of yore. According to Patrick Holland and Graham Huggan, such amateurishness is not necessarily a liability. It allows a narrator to claim authority as the "ordinary readers' representative in the field," free of specialists' biases. This made *The Frigate Pallada* "relatable" for most readers, even if some clearly had no taste for it.[13]

Alexander Herzen, the celebrated exiled socialist revolutionary, whose London-based journal *The Bell* was then still massively smuggled into Russia, was just as dismissive as his colleague on the right. Goncharov traveled the world, Herzen complained, without any intellectual preparation to comprehend the places he visited, which he portrayed from the loathsome perspective of a typical Russian landowner. (Goncharov actually grew up in a family of merchants.) Like Popov, Herzen saw the book as little more than an account of all the author ate between the Russian naval base in Kronstadt and Japan. The famous dissident's hostility may have been sharpened by the fact that, around the time the review was published, Goncharov left his job at the Department of Trade to assume, in early 1858, the position of a censor. Herzen alleged that the writer had participated in the voyage and subsequently written about it mainly to insinuate himself into the regime's good graces and prepare himself for this dishonorable profession. Herzen titled the review "An Extraordinary Story about the Censor Gon-Cha-Ro from Shi-Pan-Khu." This Asian coloring was clearly sarcastic. Shi-Pan-Khu was a transliteration into Cyrillic of the name for Japan in the Wu variety of Chinese, Cipan-guo; "extraordinary story" ironically called up *An Ordinary*

Story, the title of Goncharov's early novel. "Where else," Herzen provocatively asks, "can one perfect oneself in the art of censorship surgery—that is, of killing human speech—than in a country that since it dried out from the [Biblical] deluge has not uttered a single word?" This was, of course, an allusion to a Eurocentric assumption that Japan's seclusion policy meant the absence of cultural production.[14]

In the context of the book's reception, however, these two negative reviews were outliers, drowned by a chorus of accolades. Some defended Goncharov's travelogue against accusations of lack of scholarly rigor by noting that one should not judge a book by standards that are alien to it. Alexander Druzhinin, Goncharov's friend and the literary editor of *The Contemporary,* reviewing the 1855 volume *The Russians in Japan,* called the author "one of the most remarkable contemporary writers" and a worthy descendant of Nikolai Gogol and Alexander Pushkin, the founding fathers of Russian literature. This eminence by association was deepened by textual proximity to a landmark article on Gogol by the influential radical critic Nikolai Chernyshevsky, "Sketches of the Gogol Period of Russian Literature," which directly followed Druzhinin's review in the volume. In *The Notes of The Fatherland*, Dydushkin categorized Goncharov's travel notes as a work of art whose real value and novelty was in how, not in what, it related. To mark its importance, he positioned *The Russians in Japan* within the history of Russian travelogues, a strategy akin to how Chernyshevsky had approached Gogol's tales.[15]

Arguments about the work's classification continued with the appearance of the first full edition of 1858. Dmitry Pisarev, in a journal for ladies called *The Dawn,* agreed that the book's factual content was less important than its descriptive style. While contribution to knowledge was the typical measure of a travelogue's worth, the value of Goncharov's "purely artistic composition" was in its storytelling. Goncharov's close friend Ivan Lkhovsky, who later accomplished his own round-the-world voyage (which Goncharov seriously considered joining, but ultimately declined for health reasons), launched a major defense in *The Library for Reading.* Rather than distance the book from travel writing—as Pisarev and others before him had—Lkhovsky insisted that Russian readers needed to update their understanding of the genre's contemporary conventions. Travelogues nowadays, Lkhovsky wrote, give looser rein to fictionalizing strategies and unabashedly profile the author's self. Who would criticize Byron's *Childe Harold's Pilgrimage* for lack of maps, drawings, and learned research, Lkhovsky asked—or James Fenimore Cooper for failing to hire experts to assist him on his travels? No one demanded historical and political data of Dickens when he described the august spectacle of the source of the Nile. If Thackeray was allowed to describe the exotic Orient as if he were strolling around London squares, Goncharov should be free to describe Africa as if he were ambling around the Kovno province. Lkhovsky dismissed the pedantic gripes and advised readers to appreciate the book for what it was, rather than judge it against what it never aimed to become.[16]

Heeding this advice, the reviewer for *The Moscow Observer* agreed that serious discussions of countries and customs were not to be found in the pages of *The Frigate Pallada*, but that the author's personal impressions were at least captivating—"even delightful." *St. Petersburg News,* far from regretting the "dilletantism" of the author, heartily welcomed it. A public grown tired of stuffy foreign travelogues crammed with specialized, boring information would delight in Goncharov's street-level views, human-interest observations, personal asides, engaging storytelling, and humor. For most readers, people rather than places constituted the chief interest of the book, and especially the narrative's main hero: the author himself.[17]

The Russian Traveler and the World

Surprisingly, most readers found that the thinness of information in no way prevented Goncharov from capturing supremely reliable images of other nations and ethnicities. His Japanese were so lifelike—with their funny skirts and bows and chuckles—that they would unfailingly visit readers in their dreams, one reviewer predicted. Another credited Goncharov's uncanny powers of observation with summoning "a clear physiognomy of the Japanese," and a sense of their thoughts, feelings, and politics, too. These faithful characterizations—truth incarnate, to which the author "added nothing"—allowed readers to make "entirely probable conclusions" about the Japanese and other nations encountered by the *Pallada.* According to yet another reviewer, although ethnography, history, natural sciences, and geography gained nothing from Goncharov's book, he somehow succeeded in creating "faithful characterizations of certain nations and even sometimes to evaluate correctly the events themselves." In this regard, the author's "poetic intuition" produced results that were as reliable as "historical analysis." In other words, the book may not have been scholarly, but it was considered accurate.[18]

Among the sections of *The Frigate Pallada* most heavily promoted in reviews, Goncharov's images of Japan were on a par with his dazzling nature descriptions. Most commonly quoted was his description of the Nagasaki governor's dinner in honor of the Russian delegation, with its comically condescending comments about the Japanese officials and ceremonies, amazed reactions to Russia and the Russians by the Japanese, musings about the "ferule" of civilization (while the Russians stroke their cannons), and reveries about Japan's much needed civilizational upgrades.[19] Also popular were dramatic episodes of catching a fearsome shark and a hurricane that loosened the main mast, and descriptions of Manila in its picturesque decrepitude. Meanwhile, reviews almost never mentioned the Cape Colony and the successes of British imperial administration there. Though sections about Siberia were mentioned, critics never quoted them. The contrast between the machine-like British bourgeois and the goodly if lazy Russian landowner, however, ranked among the favorites. It was later included among passages particularly suitable for school anthologies in the journal of the Ministry of National Education.[20]

The Ministry of Foreign Affairs and the imperial political establishment clearly viewed Asia as vital to Russia's state interests. Why else go to all the trouble and expense of outfitting a naval expedition to Japan? Yet some readers failed to see any relevance to Russia of regions visited by the *Pallada.* At mid-century, Russia's stake in Asia still lacked public recognition and consensus. That the entire globe was a natural arena for their empire seemed more obvious to the British public than to Russians. Small wonder that as late as 1881, celebrating the recent Russian conquest of the fortress Geok Tepe, in today's Turkmenistan, Fyodor Dostoevsky wrote of Russia's imperial expansion and civilizing mission in Asia in the form of a polemic with these projects' opponents. Even then, public support for such missions was seen to be in need of shoring up.[21] Many Russians, at mid-century, did not yet see their empire globally. They needed to be patriotically admonished to take interest even in Siberia. This is something Goncharov hoped to change with his book. But the evidence of published reception shows less than astounding success.

The topic of Asia elicited limited commentary. Though he loved the book, Dydushkin, in *The Notes of the Fatherland,* declared Goncharov's reflection of his historical moment as peripheral to both European and Russian interests. For the reviewer, the true arena of modern history was Europe: "Asia is not the same as Europe when it comes to contemporary questions." Events such as the Taiping Rebellion could interest "us" only because the rebels tried to pass themselves off as Christians. Such Eurocentrism, incidentally, was also shared by Popov, who suggested that Goncharov's earnest Shanghai taunt—might the Chinese be in fact more fit to civilize the English than the other way round?—was the height of absurdity. To Dydushkin, Asia merited a Russian's attention only from a "cosmopolitan" point of view, as a continent that existed out there in the world and not because it was a sphere of vested Russian interests. Dydushkin saw "no connection" between the subjects and questions raised by Goncharov and those that engaged Russian society. Not meaning this critically, he simply thought that Goncharov's achievement lay elsewhere: in the art of painting nature.[22]

Some implied that the book's image of Europe's worldwide imperial expansion was unrelated to anything the Russian empire was doing: "We're not cramped at our own home. Our fatherland offers plenty to do for people who wish to serve it by the measure of their powers. A Russian warrior won't set out to build the Ashanti king's regiments [a reference to the Anglo-Ashanti wars on Africa's Gold Coast]. A Russian sailor won't go in and start establishing order on the waters of the Malay Archipelago."[23] That the Russian empire was contiguous often meant to Russians that it was no empire at all, but merely a sprawling "fatherland." What Russia's warriors were doing within its borders was supposedly a matter of domestic policy rather than imperialism.

Against such disavowals of political relevance, a few showed somewhat broader horizons. Writing for Russia's most popular newspaper, *The Northern Bee,* Lkhovsky appreciated that Goncharov's detailed descriptions of various Asian peoples corresponded to increased media attention to the region, "now that we constantly read about Singapore, Shanghai, Hong Kong, about Indians, Malays, the Chinese, and the Japanese." Putting the *Pallada* expedition's triumph in the context of Russia's half-century of efforts to access Japan, Lkhovsky exclaimed with pride: "the door to Japan has been thrown open by a Russian!" (The Americans were not mentioned in this or any other review.) Although the publisher's introduction to the 1858 edition presented *The Frigate Pallada* as primarily a work of literature, remarkably fit for specialist and child alike, it also claimed that the book widened Goncharov's circle of readers to include those who reached for it for reasons other than literature. What those reasons might be remained unspecified.[24] From the start, as they mentioned the little-known lands about which Goncharov supplied interesting information, many included Siberia. Nikolai Chernyshevsky provocatively claimed that Nagasaki was more familiar to the Russian public than Yakutsk. His radical colleague Dmitry Pisarev soon chimed in about Goncharov's fascinating description of Siberia, exhorting the Russian public to take greater interest in this vast territory still unknown to most Russians.[25]

The Frigate Pallada's flame flared up during the Anglo-Boer War of 1899–1902. Goncharov's account of the Cape of Good Hope, by then five decades old, richly reverberated in the Russian press, with some articles seeming little more than collages of quotations. Russian sympathies were firmly on the side of the Boers. The imperial government considered, and eventually rejected, the Boers' proposal to make their new South African state a Russian protectorate. Russian volunteers streamed to Transvaal to join the Boers' fight against the British. Reports that some British traders were making money from arms sales to the Boers even as their country was fighting a war with them inspired one reader to send to the popular Russian daily *The New Times* a letter reminding the public that this was a long-standing tradition among the British. His evidence was an excerpt from *The Frigate Pallada* that sarcastically noted arms sales by unscrupulous British merchants to the Xhosa during the British war against them, as well as Goncharov's critique of the British opium trade in China. *Moscow News* paid tribute to *The Frigate Pallada* for first acquainting the Russian public with the Boers and the Transvaal Republic. However, Goncharov's negative opinion of the Dutch civilizational achievements in southern Africa relative to the British ones was deemed biased and uncritical due to the author's reliance on British sources. While *The Frigate Pallada* would always remain a favorite of everyone, the article allowed, the Boer War showed Goncharov's starry-eyed optimism about British rule in Africa to be, sadly, misplaced. Incidentally, at the dusk of the tsarist era, some found Goncharov's optimism about Russia's civilizational uplift of Siberia and its "savages" to be just as naïve.[26]

Nonetheless, for the nineteenth-century Russian public, the book became notable for what it told the Russians about themselves rather than about the wider world. The issues of imperialism, colonialism, and race were broached indirectly, if at all. This, too, was not unusual. Though such topics are ubiquitous in scholarly studies of nineteenth-century travel literature today, its Victorian-era audiences mostly had nary a word to say about them. So natural seemed the imperial, Eurocentric worldview projected by most travel books that, like the air we breathe, it hardly deserved comment.

The traveler's persona Goncharov crafted in the book managed to please equally those who saw Russian identity as fully European and those who saw it as uniquely national. A reviewer from *The Library for Reading* deemed Goncharov's chapters on Japan—the ones in which Goncharov so comfortably inhabits the persona of Japan's would-be European civilizer, brimming with superiority—most valuable. These chapters in particular, according to the reviewer, "satisfy the contemporary demands made of a developed traveler, educated in the European manner, whom all certainly consider our talented writer to be."[27]

Others loved Goncharov's book for projecting a uniquely Russian manner of viewing the world. Russian readers flocked to the book, the argument went, because they could easily put themselves in the traveler's shoes. They were alienated by foreign travelers' sensibilities and outlooks on life, we read in *The Notes of the Fatherland*. They reacted warmly to *The Frigate Pallada* because Goncharov looked at the world through recognizably Russian eyes, in the manner they themselves would see it. Moreover, the review proclaimed, no genre was better suited to reflect the state of a given literature and society than travel writing, and Goncharov sensed the pulse of Russian society faultlessly.[28] The readers appreciated, as can be seen from such reviews, that *The Frigate Pallada* provided both the Russian lens through which to view the world and a mirror of Russia's contemporary condition. The lens was deemed comfortable and the mirror suitably flattering.

And yet it was the felicitous combination of Europeanness and Russianness that seemed to resonate most strongly in the reactions. That Goncharov appeared effortlessly European without ceasing to be Russian proved a particularly gratifying aspect. In his influential review for *The Contemporary*, which reverberated in others' reactions to *The Frigate Pallada* for the remainder of the century, Druzhinin proudly called Goncharov a "first-class European tourist," who only deepened his love of Russia under enchanting foreign skies. While being European, he was somehow better than Europeans by virtue of also being Russian. In Druzhinin's view, Goncharov's success rested on his spiritual affinity with Russian readers. Not for them were the histrionics of feverish, awe-struck tourists or the showy masculinity of dauntless explorers found in Western European travel accounts. Indeed, Goncharov's travelogue persona was a departure from heroic explorers who represented "ideal types of imperial masculinity," and who dominated western travel literature in this era of high imperialism.[29] Fear for his safety, health, and comfort prevented Goncharov from venturing out even on some sightseeing excursions, as *The Rumor* reviewer had peevishly noted, to say nothing of feats of exploration. According to Druzhinin, Goncharov struck a chord with the Russian audience because he apprehended the exotic new worlds dispassionately. Like all Russian travelers, he never pursued strong impressions, never craved novelty, and shunned affected and flashy descriptions. While most travel writers resemble footloose bachelors at a ball, Druzhinin writes, Goncharov comported himself like a stately married man. Most importantly, whether in the tropics or with the Nagasaki governor, he never lost his bearings as a Russian.[30]

Intoxicating Substance or Wholesome Reading for Youth?

When a new edition of *The Frigate Pallada* came out in 1879, most readers considered it long overdue. The popular press welcomed it as "a classic" and "one of the best works of our literature," occupying a place of honor on any Russian's bookshelf. No other travelogue, even to lands equally exotic, was said to have enjoyed the success of *The Frigate Pallada.* The book reportedly lost none of its freshness and read "as if written yesterday."[31]

Indeed, the public's adulation only grew. A reviewer for the most popular St. Petersburg daily, *The Voice*, captured the intoxicating experience of reading, and rereading, the book:

> I read *The Frigate Pallada* like a drunk drinks his wine: avidly, without measure. I may start from the middle, or from the last chapter. . . . On a whim, I randomly choose Singapore, or Eastern Siberia, or the episode with the captured shark, or the dinner with the Japanese, or the picture of the Augustinian monastery in Manila, or the figures of Russian sailors cast by fate to the deep south. In a word, I relate to *The Frigate Pallada* like a sybarite to a refined pleasure. The delights of the pictures match the delights of the storyline. The book of Mr. Goncharov excites imagination and—if I may be permitted to use a banal expression with regard to this masterpiece—flirts [*koketnichaet*] with the reader. . . . There's something tropical in this richness of images, in this inexhaustible suppleness of language, in this seemingly careless and accidental creation. . . . The book literally resembles a path through a tropical forest in a hilly countryside: you can't see what lies ahead and what you'll stumble upon, but all is rich and fragrant. At each turn you find enchanting surprises, unexpected turns, new images and colors.

The euphoric review concludes that "Mr. Goncharov was certainly born, if not for traveling, then for describing travels." Without a hint of pretentiousness or scholastic pedantry, it continues, his rich gallery of geographic and ethnographic images "will forever remain a beautiful monument of Russian literature." If only, it notes, Goncharov produced such travelogues about European Russia![32]

Among the ripples set in motion by *The Frigate Pallada*, literary polemics were but one. The book also had its impacts in government and education. Emperor Alexander II graciously received Goncharov's gift of the 1858 edition and offered the author a diamond-and-ruby ring worth 300 rubles. The 1855 volume about the Japanese leg of the journey, *The Russians in Japan*, was reprinted in 1857 in a journal for students of military academies, indicating its perceived relevance for training Russian officers.[33] The Emperor Alexander II's brother, Grand Duke Konstantin Nikolaevich, who had dispatched the *Pallada* to Japan, was spurred by the spectacular success of *The Frigate Pallada* to organize under ministry auspices a special "literary expedition" of 1855–1861 to areas near the Caspian, Black, and White Seas, the Urals, and the Far East. Such writers as A. F. Pisemsky, A. N. Ostrovsky, and G. P. Danilevsky joined this expedition. The Grand Duke asked them to create ethnographic descriptions of local populations on the model of *The Frigate Pallada*. Goncharov's assertion of Russia's colonizing mission in Siberia in particular became a cornerstone of the ministry's official ideology for representing the relations between the imperial center and its peripheral populations. Those writers, like Pisemsky, who questioned it—doubtful as he was about the capacity of some of Russia's ethnic minorities to become civilized—had their submissions to *The Naval Review* rejected.[34]

That *The Frigate Pallada* was excellent reading not only for adults but also for young people was always emphasized in its reception. As late as 1900, Anton Chekhov ranked *The Frigate Pallada* alongside the fairy tales of Hans Christian Andersen and the fiction of Nikolai Gogol as the best examples of literature that captivates adults and children alike. He had earlier recommended Goncharov's book to his brother as a travelogue that, miraculously, is not boring. Chekhov later reread *The Frigate Pallada* when preparing for his own trek through Siberia to Sakhalin Island, and he invokes it in his 1895 account of this journey, *Sakhalin Island*. At some point, Goncharov occupied the top perch in Chekhov's hierarchy of Russian writers, alongside Leo Tolstoy.[35]

Chekhov was not unique in this regard. For the remainder of the long Russian nineteenth century, a preference for even-tempered Goncharov, blissfully free of obsessions with the so-called "accursed questions"—knotty, hot-button social issues such as "the woman question," "the peasant question," or "the Jewish question"—elevated the writer for many readers over today's acknowledged giants of Russian literature. Compared to Dostoevsky's feverish, tormented fictions, to Tolstoy's restless individualism, and to Turgenev's melancholy, Goncharov seemed like a refreshing model of moderation, objectivity, and mental balance.[36]

For young readers, *The Frigate Pallada* was deemed to be informative about the world, and filled with sound judgments about it, from a Russian perspective to boot. The book's decorousness was also prized. One review reassured the public that one could with peace of mind leave Goncharov's volumes unattended in a roomful of young people and ladies.[37] *The Journal of the Ministry of National Education* recommended the book for school curricula, where it indeed found a place. Among its most suitable sections, the journal listed Goncharov's descriptions of London, remarks about the English character, arrival in Madeira, passages about Cape Town and environs, and the historical sketch about the Cape Colony, Japan, and the Ryukyu Islands. *The Pedagogic Leaflet* agreed that a more suitable reading for youth could hardly be found. It declared that such travelers as Goncharov were driven by the pursuit of truth, rather than material gain or power, which made their reports on natural history, ethnography, physical geography, and history particularly valuable for young readers. A popular illustrated weekly, *The Grainfield*, read mostly in bourgeois society, concurred that Goncharov's book was fun, wholesome family reading.[38] Because it proved such entertaining and educational reading for youth, *The Frigate Pallada* played a vital role in shaping and transmitting imperialist attitudes, and the cultural and racial stereotypes attached to non-European peoples. Russia's pedagogues who endorsed the book may have kept silent on these aspects, but it is fair to conclude that generations of Russians were taught to look at the world through their prism.

The *Pallada* in Soviet Rigging

In the wake of World War I, a wave of decolonizations in Africa and Asia delegitimized imperialism as a form of rule. The Soviet state officially proclaimed itself as anti-imperial—even as it engineered policies to maintain the territorial span of the tsarist empire.[39] It denounced imperialism, colonialism, and racism and excoriated the capitalist West for clinging to them.

So what might the Soviet trajectory be for a book that revels in the idea of capitalist profits from global trade, that promotes imperialism, colonialism, and their civilizing effects in Africa and Asia, that touts the phenomenal successes of the British bourgeoisie and its empire, that sounds unabashedly racist, and that shows Russia flexing its imperial muscle in Japan and managing Siberia in recognizably colonial ways? This was no easy question for a new regime. To sort it out took some time—a time that saw the spectacular rise of *Oblomov,* republished with stunning regularity. The story of *The Frigate Pallada* from the mid-twentieth century to today—this did not end with the Soviet era—is a story of sentences, pages, and chapters disappearing from certain popular editions. These deletions yield a record of what has made twentieth- and twenty-first century cultural authorities uncomfortable about Goncharov's portrayal of Russia and the global imperial world. Unsurprisingly, these issues revolve around imperialism, colonialism, and race.

Yet the new Soviet era also found its own attractions in travelogue, which was not at all suppressed. The new communist intelligentsia, raised on late imperial literary fare, would very likely have known and liked it. At a meeting in the Kremlin in 1934, Chairman of the Central Committee of the Soviet Union Mikhail Kalinin recommended it to aspiring peasant writers who finished party courses in creative writing. His speech was published on the front page of the main organ of the Union of Soviet Writers, *The Literary Gazette.* This endorsement from the highest perch of Soviet power paved the way to the travelogue's rehabilitation in Soviet culture. However, it left open the question of how the book might be reconstituted into nourishing ideological fare for Soviet society, the precise recipe for which Secretary Kalinin appears to have left to cultural commentators and literary critics. Apart from the famous Soviet epic, Mikhail Sholokhov's *And Quiet Flows the Don,* Goncharov's travelogue was the only modern title mentioned by Kalinin, who considered its language and form to be worthy models. Well into the late Soviet period, *The Frigate Pallada* appears to have been perused within party echelons. It is mentioned in Secretary General Leonid Brezhnev's 1978 memoir.[40]

The Frigate Pallada received curt mentions in Soviet celebrations of the hundred-and-twenty-fifth anniversary of Goncharov's birth in 1937.[41] As a preview of the friendlier reception to come, the official newspaper of the

Communist Party, *Pravda,* devoted a separate article to it in a celebratory full-page spread that built on Kalinin's endorsement. This prominent space was shared with only a biographical note, and articles on Lenin's ideas about "Oblomovism" and on Goncharov as a realist writer. In that context and layout, a separate feature on *The Frigate Pallada* was a notable distinction. Goncharov was presented as a writer who did not sympathize with his era's progressive politics, yet offered a valuable window onto the serf-owning system and the dawn of bourgeois social relations. The ideological contours of *The Frigate Pallada* were left murky save for approving mentions of the writer's critiques of a greedy English colonialist and patriarchal Japan. Though lacking the spellbinding draw of a novelistic plot, according to the article, the travelogue displayed its descriptive charms in abundance. It was "a solid and smartly made book" that entered "the golden fund of classical Russian literature." The *Pravda* spread shows that early Soviet intelligentsia considered *The Frigate Pallada* a core text of the Goncharov *oeuvre,* deserving of a Soviet stamp of approval.[42]

Nonetheless, the 1918, 1931, and 1948 multivolume editions of Goncharov's works did not include *The Frigate Pallada.* Except for the émigré Paris edition of 1935 and a radically abbreviated Soviet edition of 1940, Goncharov's travelogue had to wait for its reversal of fortune until after the Second World War. This reversal came in the form of the 1949 edition prepared by S. D. Muraveisky. The truncated 1940 edition was criticized for excessive suppression of the author's pro-capitalist leanings, given its expunging of passages about the British bourgeois trader, about comfort and luxury, and about Britain's colonial politics. Descriptions of lands other than Japan and Siberia barely figured in this edition.[43] The Muraveisky edition did better by using more surgical excisions, to preserve more of the original text while creating an acceptable version for the broad Soviet readership. This expurgated edition, which appears to have been aimed at young readers, included maps and illustrations and was published by a press specializing in geographic literature. It was republished twice, in 1951 and 1957. Until the 1980s, the Muraveisky edition became the Soviet era's standard textual variant for the general public.[44]

This was the period when frank and sharply critical assessments of tsarist imperialism, characteristic of the early decades of the Soviet period, were being replaced by a narrative of benevolent and progressive Russian rule over the state's far-flung multiethnic domains. The imperial and colonial aspects of Russian history were hidden, deemphasized, or silenced. "Friendship of peoples" rather than legacies of imperialism apparently united the Soviet Union. It is therefore small wonder that Muraveisky's "abbreviations" of *The Frigate Pallada* doubled as censorship cuts. Most fell into two broad categories: racial prejudice in Goncharov's portrayal of nonwhite populations, and Russia's imperial ambitions and politics. Taken together, these cuts identify the most objectionable aspects of *The Frigate Pallada* from the viewpoint of Soviet ideology.

While this is reason enough to take a closer look at these manipulative abbreviations, another reason to do so is their lasting legacy. The Soviet Muraveisky edition has outlived by a quarter century the Soviet Union itself. It continues as the book's popular format in Russia today, through a popular 2012 print edition and a 2015 audiobook brought to the market by the Eksmo publishing house, which specializes in mass-market paperbacks.[45] Muraveisky's emendations also enjoy a monopoly over the English-speaking world. Both English translations of the book, a 1965 partial one by N. W. Wilson (containing only five out of seventeen chapters) and a 1987 one by Klaus Goetze, are based on the Muraveisky edition. The Goetze translation is presented as "complete and unexpurgated," surprising misinformation given that Muraveisky made no secret in his preface of the book's abbreviated state. Moreover, given the fact that Goetze's rendering is merely approximate, rife with mistakes in the dictionary meaning of basic Russian words, readers who rely on this translation may have some difficulty recognizing the original, complete book.[46]

To start, Muraveisky did his best to temper the book's racialized representations of Africans. Although Goncharov's aversion to mulattoes, his insistence that black skin ought to glisten like a well-polished shoe, and his comparison of a Khoikhoi boy to a monkey passed through Muraveisky's sieve unaltered, in general his text greatly lessened the book's racism.[47] The African "wenches" who poked fun at Goncharov no longer have something "terrible and evil" in their smile in the Muraveisky text, and Africans are no longer so "ashamed of their skin" as to wear white gloves. Larceny is no longer listed as one of the typical San occupations; a comparison of them to troglodytes is omitted. Goncharov's disturbing inspection of the pitiful San in the Cape Colony jail, culminating in his expression of disbelief in the San's humanity, is expunged (Goncharov's racialized body scans of other Africans remain). Also gone is Goncharov's critique of Xhosa "savagery," in view of which he partly excused the British for treating them brutally. There is no trace left of the comparison of the British-Xhosa Wars to the

Russian empire's wars in the Caucasus. Only the subhead remains of the twenty-page sketch "The Cape Colony" ("Kapskaia koloniia"). Also missing is Goncharov's biased history of the British-Xhosa Wars and his wholehearted approval of British aggression, treachery, and ruthless extirpation of the Xhosa. Goncharov's appreciative designation of the British as the mythic heroes (*bogatyri*) who will wake up Africa, "the sleeping princess," makes no appearance in Muraveisky's text. Goncharov's exuberant praise for the Britons' civilizing potential is thus evidently diminished.[48]

Deracializing Goncharov's portrayal of Asians, or making them appear more dignified, seems to have been less of an imperative. Goncharov's comparisons of the Japanese to porcelain dolls, zombies, setters, and poodles, and of their "stupid" faces to shovels, were all retained. So was Goncharov's comment that the garlic aroma emanating from the Chinese causes flies to die in mid-flight. Further uplifted, however—Goncharov already censored himself on this subject—were Russia's own, "internal" Asians in Siberia. Muraveisky additionally removed Goncharov's perplexed question about Siberia's aborigines: "could these narrow-eyed, flat-nosed people really be Russian?" The readers would no longer know that Goncharov considered the Sakha to have been, until recently, half-human, half-animal, or that he viewed Luoravetlans as savages who required guidance in order to live like human beings.[49] They would also get no sense of the book's antisemitism: Goncharov's jocular denunciation of Dr. Wethered's Jewishness (only in spite of which he was a good chap), his comparison of Manila's cockfighting arena to Russian synagogues, or his indulgence for Goshkevich's obsession with "Yids."[50]

Consistent with this strategy, Muraveisky fretted more about the representation of those non-Russian Asians who were in the geopolitical orbit of the Soviet Union than those who were not. Japan was a declared enemy of the Soviet Union in the Second World War, and it joined the Western camp after the war. Korea, on the other hand, was a colonial victim of the Japanese empire. After the Second World War, Korea was split along the Thirty-Eighth Parallel between the Soviet- and American-occupied spheres of influence. Roughly concurrent with the Muraveisky edition, in June 1950, the Korean War erupted between the northern government, backed by the Soviet Union, and the southern government, backed by the United States. These were political reasons to treat Koreans as kindly as Siberians.

Muraveisky deleted Goncharov's comparison of inhospitable Koreans, accosted by the Russians, to dogs who would like to bite but do not dare. He also silenced the *Pallada*'s low-ranking Russian sailors' complaint that Korean traders were worse than Russia's own disreputable minorities: Poles and Circassians. He did, however, keep the mention that these sailors charitably threw rusks to the hungry Koreans. He considered it wise to remove the confrontation between the Koreans and the Russians, when the Russians fired blank cartridges at the throng of the Koreans who showered them with rocks. The edition's only trace of Russian aggressiveness was the hand-slapping of Koreans who tried to impede the Russians' movements. For the readers of this edition, little marred a fairly harmonious vision of Korean-Russian relations.[51]

The Russian mission to Japan arose in the Muraveisky edition in decidedly more peaceful and benevolent guise, cleansed of the imperial impetus that so clearly marked the original. Goncharov's Russians no longer stroke their sixty-pound cannons when contemplating the opening of Japan from the *Pallada*'s deck. Goncharov's bold proposal that the Russians take over Nagasaki through a surprise military attack disappears from the text. So does his conviction that force was necessary to accomplish Europe's political objectives. When a Westerner, however, recommends the cannons as the only way to open up Japan, no cuts are deemed necessary. Muraveisky kept Goncharov's sardonic definition of the "English way" of opening Japan: enter the Japanese ports, disembark without permission, and if the Japanese object, finagle a pretext for declaring war. Yet he deleted the writer's recommendation that the Russians should muster similar bravado, an option that appealed to Goncharov when he grew impatient with Putiatin's conciliatory strategy.[52]

Six pages of Goncharov's musings in advance of his visit to the Nagasaki governor ended up on Muraveisky's cutting-room floor. They revealed the mind of a boastful European civilizer, well habituated to thinking about the "Orient" in classically imperialistic terms. From his paternalistic pedestal, Goncharov condemned on these pages the absurdity of Japan's seclusion policy, comparing it to a "schoolhouse prank." The role of the European "teachers," according to Goncharov, was to discipline the childlike Japanese. He tantalized his readers with the persuasive power of the "Russian bayonet" and military power more broadly, for which the pathetic Japanese cannons would certainly be no match. Japan arose in this passage as a defenseless, enervated country, which only Europe's sap of life could bring back to life; the puny Japanese appeared to him too pathetic to be beaten. Goncharov's "industrial reverie" about European upgrades in Japan remained, but not the image of the Russian capital collaborating in this process with the western one. Goncharov's lecturing to his Japanese counterparts about the disadvantages of isolation—Russia did not become great by closing itself off from the outside world—was also expunged, likely due to its uncomfortable resonance with the Soviet Union's Cold War isolation from the West.[53] A similar fate befell Goncharov's programmatic statement about Russia's civilizing mission in Asia, a five-page section of the Korean chapter. This passage analyzed the East Asian "nations" through Orientalizing formulas, prophesying that they would "become human" only once they adopted European civilization and Christianity.[54]

Downplaying Russia's imperialism also proved necessary in the Siberian sections. Everything that could be aligned with the Soviet historical paradigm of Russian rule as a vehicle of progress, enlightenment, and economic development remained intact. Yet Goncharov's long passage probing Russian motives for civilizing Siberia, in which self-interest and profit were considered, only to be rejected, earned Muraveisky's disfavor. Information about resistance or hostility to Russian rule, and about the Russian government's efforts to subdue the region militarily, was left out. Soviet audiences were also shielded from Goncharov's fervor for Russian Orthodoxy's errand into the wilderness, such as his detailed account of bishop Innokentyi's Christianizing successes in Siberia, for which Goncharov crowned him a hero. They would not have known that Goncharov fervently wished Russians would reintroduce Christianity to Japan. Muraveisky kept the praise of the Russian government's refusal to reap profits from alcohol sale in Siberia, so contrary to the unscrupulousness of British opium-sellers. But he deleted the assimilatory goals invoked to rationalize this policy: Goncharov's idea that the imperial government's goal was to unite within the huge Russian "family" Siberia's indigenous ethnic groups, the "savage" youths of mankind. In the Siberian chapters alone, the cuts amount to about eight pages of text.[55]

In short, much work needed to be done to make *The Frigate Pallada* palatable to a broad Soviet audience. It had been a book that championed the tutelage of whites over benighted "colored" races, European and Russian imperialism and colonialism, and the worldwide expansion of Russia's commercial and political influence, by force if necessary. It had to become one that seemed innocent of such motives. So it is all the more surprising that, on the question of the book's politics, the dominant Soviet position settled on the notion that Goncharov's sentiments were anti-colonial and anti-imperialistic. One might wonder: How could such a trick be pulled off?

This new position was first presented by Muraveisky in the introduction to his doctored-up edition. Muraveisky cherrypicked quotations that could be construed as criticism of the west's imperial expansion, greedy capitalism, and exploitation of Africans and Asians, as well as the rapacious progress of British colonialism, unleashed by brutal wars of conquest. Goncharov's critical or merely snide comments about the British or the Americans (the positive ones were ignored) were interpreted by Muraveisky as criticisms of imperialism as such, not of its abuses. He portrays Russians as spectators, not participants in the global imperial pursuit of profits, markets, resources, and spheres of influence. What are the Russians doing in Japan? They merely wish to sign a trade treaty and establish relations with a neighboring state—a deceivingly innocuous formulation if ever there was one. Why do the Japanese not wish it? Because their feudalism blinds them. Russian cannons did not push Japan against the wall to impose unequal trade treaties. That is what Perry's Americans did. Goncharov had only sympathy for the people of Japan, Soviet readers were told.

Muraveisky also distorts the emotional register of Goncharov's remarks, twisting neutrality and even admiration into condemnation and sarcasm. He turns a blind eye to the book's racial and ethnic prejudices. He trusts in the Soviet reader's ability to distinguish Goncharov the political reactionary from Goncharov the great realist Russian writer. And yet, where Goncharov's account of world affairs circa 1850 yields an ideologically incorrect vision, Muraveisky adjusts it for the edification of Soviet readers, to protect them from adopting Goncharov's flawed perspectives. Thus we are informed that Goncharov fails to see things (like the flaws of the bourgeois social relations), exaggerates things (like the role of Christian missionaries), or ignores things (like class conflicts).[56]

The Colonial Question

Most Soviet analyses of *The Frigate Pallada* focused on purely literary questions such as the evolution of Goncharov's prose and novelistic technique, the generic features of travel writing, and the work's colorful survey of exotic places. Its connection to the politics of imperialism has received little attention, though this featured more prominently in the commentaries to the travelogue's intact editions, providing Soviet readers with guidance through this treacherous terrain. Here, too, the patterns established by Muraveisky proved influential. The commentaries followed Muraveisky in presenting the Russians circling the globe as strictly imperialism's observers, not its perpetrators. The purpose of Putiatin's mission was neatly pried out of its imperialist context. If gunboat diplomacy was decried, then only the Americans', never the Russians'. The *Pallada*'s cannons and Goncharov's enthusiasm for them as harbingers of civilization discreetly remained in the shadows. Nonetheless, in the 1950s and 1960s, a few Soviet critics directly took up the question of colonialism, which they saw, in the tradition of Marx and Lenin, as an outgrowth of capitalism.

A. G. Tseitlin, clashing with Muraveisky's earlier foray into the topic, reproached Goncharov for turning a blind eye to the evils of capitalism and colonialism in his zeal to idealize global trade. He accused Goncharov of callous disregard for the suffering of the Xhosa and the Madeirans, squeezed by the British profit-seekers the author naively held up as promoters of civilization. Yet Tseitlin also appreciated Goncharov's caustic remarks, so consonant with Engels and Marx, about the hypocritical and soulless British bourgeoisie. He applauded Goncharov for revising his admiration for the British traders in Shanghai and lambasting them for turning poison into cash. Being a sober-eyed realist, Goncharov could not help but observe the dark side of capitalism, Tseitlin wrote, even if he deemed it a necessary stage in human history. In an extension of this line of thought, K. Tiunkin, in his commentaries to many Soviet editions, appreciated that Soviet readers could still glimpse from the travelogue the historical truth of the transition from feudalism to bourgeois capitalism while disregarding the author's ignorant, mistaken judgment of those very processes.[57]

N. K. Piksanov and V. A. Mikhelson reached a conclusion opposite to Tseitlin's, painting *The Frigate Pallada* as a searing exposé of colonists' cruelty and greed and a spirited defense of subjugated natives. Yes, Goncharov showed that the world stage belonged to capitalism, but its historical performance made him bitter, they claimed. The British may have earned Goncharov's respect by building bridges in southern Africa, but Goncharov also showed their cruelty. (Piksanov neglects to disclose that Goncharov actually approved of spectacular displays of this cruelty, as in his comments on Cape Colony governor Harry Smith.) While Tseitlin claimed that Goncharov was mostly wrong, while sometimes being right, Piksanov concluded that the author was mostly right, while sometimes being wrong. For example, Goncharov mistakenly equated progress with bourgeois comfort, forgetting about its price for the Asian producers of cheap goods. Yet, overall, Piksanov painted Goncharov as a critic of colonialism. This became the default position of the Soviet literary establishment, which with slight permutations was reflected in all introductions and commentaries to the subsequent Soviet editions of *The Frigate Pallada* that bothered to broach the topic.[58]

It is important to realize that honest misunderstanding due to a reliance on a compromised text played no role in this phenomenon. Critics who cultivated the view of the book as an anti-colonial text worked with unexpurgated pre-revolutionary or Soviet editions. Moreover, beginning in the 1950s, the unexpurgated text of *The Frigate Pallada,* based on the last edition printed during Goncharov's lifetime in 1886, began to be republished in the many specialized or multivolume editions of Goncharov's works that intelligentsia readers, scholars, and libraries would purchase. The full version of *The Frigate Pallada* was widely available throughout the Soviet period.[59]

The most strident and detailed elaboration of the anti-colonial theory was a 1965 monograph by V. A. Mikhelson, *The Humanism of I. A. Goncharov and the Colonial Question.* Mikhelson sums up *The Frigate Pallada* as Goncharov's protest against the "colonial politics of global capitalism" and a "passionate challenge of Russian progressive thought against English, French, and American colonialism." Forced to confront some of Goncharov's sunny panegyrics to colonialism, Mikhelson explains them away as the author's mistakes, attributable to his ignorance of history or reliance on biased western sources. He claims that Goncharov "rips off the mask of civilization from the colonizer," fully in sympathy with the victims. The argument, most plausible in reference to the Shanghai chapter, rests on a careful selection of doctored passages and total ignorance of all contrary evidence. Deaf to the actual tone of Goncharov's descriptions, Mikhelson claims, for example, that Goncharov's idealized portrait of the Cape Colony's Mr. Bain drips with sarcasm. Goncharov's very act of comparing Britain's Xhosa wars with Russia's Caucasian wars proves to Mikhelson that the writer opposes colonial wars of expansion. The nadir of the book's racism—Goncharov's encounter with the San in the Cape Colony jail—furnishes Mikhelson with triumphant evidence of Goncharov's profound humanism: the Russian writer proclaims that the San prisoner is, after all, a human being. (That he does so while filled with repulsion, and in the context of profound doubts, does not enter Mikhelson's picture.)[60]

Mikhelson, as other Soviet critics, narrowed the theme of colonialism to the strictly non-Russian parts of Goncharov's itinerary. Once the traveling author sets foot in Siberia, this theme apparently vanished. If Goncharov's descriptions of Africa and Asia showed the operation of western imperialism, then those of Siberia apparently showed the humanitarian and peace-loving Russian alternative to imperialism, rather than a Russian version of the same. Mikhelson never even examined the Siberian chapters in his survey of Goncharov's treatment of the colonial question. According to him, Goncharov correctly and truthfully portrayed Siberia as a national homeland and as a domain of "the friendship of peoples" rather than a colonial site. Many Soviet critics steered clear of such outlandish propositions. Muraveisky, for example, summed up Goncharov's treatment of Siberia in the following way: "So far, [Goncharov] sees the sole source of progress in these regions in colonization, turning a blind eye to its negative sides, such as the merchants' and administrators' robbing of the local population. He notices only its positive sides, such as the introduction of agriculture, the beginnings of education, improved communications, etc., greatly exaggerating the role of the administration and missionaries as the bearers of Russian culture." Tseitlin likewise noted Goncharov's focus on Russia's progressive role in Siberia, yet chastised him for silence about tsarism's colonial practices there, especially the exploitation of the peoples of the Far East, as eastern Siberia is called in Russia.[61]

While the editions of the late 1950s and early 1970s largely followed Tsetlin's patterns, the idea of Goncharov's blind spots fell out of the introduction to the 1977 edition, which echoes Mikhelson's thesis of Goncharov's Siberia as a true-to-life antidote to the evils of western colonialism. Elena Krasnoshchekova later brought nuance to this contrast by discussing it in terms of Goncharov's unrealized social utopia.[62] Throughout the Soviet period, writers and critics from Siberia and the Far East used *The Frigate Pallada* to propound Russia's progressive influence on the region. Depending on whether they interpreted Goncharov's image of Siberia as positive or negative, they either supported or disagreed with the writer. For example, the Soviet poet of the Far East Petr Komarov, whose family resettled to the Amur region in 1918, claimed that Goncharov would have been astounded by Soviet progress in Siberia. In his 1948 poem "The Soviet Harbor," Komarov contrasts Siberia as the bleak domain of wild beasts about which one reads in Goncharov, with Siberia as a destination of "winged dreams," where the "miracle" of Soviet progress brought machines, workers' clubs, and schools. By contrast, the Siberian scholar, critic, and writer Gavriil Kungurov applauded Goncharov for breaking with the stereotypical image of Siberia as a cursed, forsaken place and for portraying it as a dynamic and prosperous region, in stark contrast to the stagnant Russian provinces. At the same time, Kungurov criticized Goncharov for failing to denounce the tsarist government's colonial policies and their negative impact on Siberia's indigenous populations.[63]

Soviet editors also felt the need to correct Goncharov's critical portrayal of the Taiping rebels in China. Muraveisky simply ignored Goncharov's criticisms and showcased instead those of Marx, who viewed the rebellion as a powerful welling up of the Chinese lower classes' opposition to a feudal regime and its European backers.[64] Later editions blamed Goncharov's failure to grasp the rebellion's historical meaning on his retrograde distaste for all revolutions. Only Mikhelson, dauntlessly arguing the implausible, asserted that Goncharov supported the Taiping rebels. Goncharov's overall portrayal of Russian behavior in China, in his view, illustrated such truths as "Russia and China always had common enemies" or that "the Russian people have always been the best friends of the Chinese people." Needless to say, these sentiments reflected wishful thinking about Sino-Soviet relations in the mid-1960s, soon to enter a rather tense phase that nearly erupted in a nuclear conflict, rather than any realities of Goncharov's travelogue or the *Pallada* mission.[65]

The late Soviet period saw a flurry of separate editions of *The Frigate Pallada*. Seven appeared between 1976 and 1986, many of them in the provincial presses of Saratov, Volgograd, Irkutsk, and Kaliningrad. *The Frigate Pallada* was translated, sometimes multiple times, but sometimes not fully, into Bulgarian, Czech, Chinese, English, Estonian, German, Hungarian, Japanese, Korean, Polish, and Romanian.[66]

The *Pallada* Sails On

The Frigate Pallada has kept pursuing its path through post-Soviet culture, sometimes imprinting new ruts, sometimes returning to old ones. New technologies have made the book available as an e-book and an audiobook. Recommended as wholesome, educational, and engaging reading for young people in the tsarist period, the book has come full circle to being marketed again to young audiences in Vladimir Putin's Russia. It is being reconsidered as Russia's signal contribution to not just national but "world literature"—a recent conception of literature that is concerned with the global circulation of literary works and overcoming western European dominance of the literary canon. Tsarist-era reviews routinely referred to *The Frigate Pallada* as a book that everyone had read. In 1955, Viktor Shklovsky spoke of it as a book that never left readers' desks. One 2015 edition chimes in: "Times change, technologies improve, speed increases, and *The Frigate,* as always, was read, is being read, and will be read."[67]

Beyond the excellent, copiously annotated, and unexpurgated scholarly "Nauka" edition of 1997 used in this book, *The Frigate Pallada* came out in the collected works of 2010 with a quite novel framing. In a substantial introduction to the entire set, noted Goncharov scholar Vladimir Melnik finds Goncharov's contemporary resonance so vivid as to call him "an author of the 21st century." He unhesitatingly proclaims *The Frigate Pallada* "the best description of circumnavigation in world literature," unmatched by any such work in European literature. For the first time, the unsigned commentary to the travelogue in this set presents the voyage and Goncharov's description of it with refreshing honesty. It stresses Russia's participation in imperial rivalries, thus moving away from the Soviet tradition of presenting Russia and the *Pallada* crew as mere observers.[68]

The commentary explains that as Great Britain, Holland, France, and the United States vied for colonies and spheres of influence in Asia in the mid-nineteenth century, "the Russian empire joined this race." At a time when all great powers found colonial and economic expansion into "weak and undeveloped" lands necessary, Russia lacked access to rich tropical possessions in Asia, but exhibited "ambition and desire to rival Britain in global influence." The *Pallada* expedition, we learn, demonstrated "Russia's effort to join colonial empires and, if not to directly annex, then possibly to include Japan, and maybe other territories, in its sphere of influence through diplomatic means." Goncharov's "merchant who becomes a colonizer" played an important role in the "eradication of artificial barriers between parts of the world, or in globalization, as we would say today." The commentary finds Goncharov's equation of civilization with European culture and with global trade to be cutting-edge, whereby those resisting such values are deemed to be "savages." This, we read, was not dissimilar to the sentiments animating Rudyard Kipling's famous poem "The White Man's Burden." For example, Goncharov blamed Africans for colonial wars launched against them, since they failed to perceive the civilizational benefits proffered by the British. In later parts of the travelogue, the commentary notes, especially in the Chinese sections, Goncharov sobers up to exploitative aspects of colonialism.

The commentary sums up comments about Siberia as Goncharov's valorization of a colonial asset: "Even if we don't have tropical possessions, Siberia, irrespective of its harsh climate, is possibly richer than English and French territories."[69]

Goncharov's travelogue continues to resonate with the concerns of post-Soviet Russian culture, which is seeking its own reconnections with imperial-era grandeur. The late Putin era has seen an expansive, one might say neo-imperial, foreign policy in places such as Georgia, Moldova, Ukraine, and even Syria which aims, as Russia's regional neighbors and western partners worry, to recapture the Soviet Union's territories and spheres of influence. Nostalgic references to the glorious traditions of the Romanov empire figure prominently in governmental and public discourse advocating such ventures. As the commentary to the 2010 edition of *The Frigate Pallada* shows, the refreshing honesty about the *Pallada* voyage as embedded in inter-imperial rivalries and about Goncharov as a colonial writer comes with a troubling sense of approval for such models of politics and authorship. At the very least, this commentary lacks any overtones of ideological distance or critique that customarily frame recent republications of western travel accounts purveying a similar diet of imperialistic swagger and racial prejudice.

The tsarist era's dominant view about the preponderance of narration over information in the travelogue, and the Soviet era's debates about the degree to which Goncharov's politics were wrong, have most recently been replaced by a tendency to authorize rather than question the information and ideas contained in *The Frigate Pallada*. This authorizing trend is on prominent display in the 2015 e-book version through what literary theorist Gerard Genete calls a paratext: supplementary material, provided in this case by the publisher, which frames the text for the reader and shapes its interpretation. In this e-book edition, such paratext consists of over 250 illustrations, many of them in color, and text boxes that comment on unfamiliar terminology, historical events referenced in the book, and various biographies. These materials, publishers note, make the book "a perfect gift for young readers and sophisticated bibliophiles alike."[70]

The cumulative effect of this massive encyclopedic paratext is to present *The Frigate Pallada* as a source of reliable information about the nineteenth-century world. By fleshing out Goncharov's references, the text boxes and illustrations authorize the supposed factuality of Goncharov's account, conveying an impression that young Russian people can confidently learn from the book. The text box information is for the most part correct. However, readers will instantly spot the problems in pitching *The Frigate Pallada* as, basically, a good textbook. These problems include the book's endorsement of Europe's and Russia's right to imperial supremacy over the non-western world, a sense of cultural superiority to it, and the vast record of ethnic and racial prejudice, still largely unaccounted for in Russian commentaries to *The Frigate Pallada*.

Thanks to both postcolonial theory and to studies of travel writing, we no longer consider such representations of non-western worlds in terms of mimetic fidelity and disinterested objectivity. What we have learned to do instead is to examine them as representations of a particular kind, based on morally dubious assumptions and questionable claims to truth, and enmeshed with the real-world operations of political power.[71] Yet postcolonial theory has encountered a great deal of resistance in Russian literary studies, especially in Russia itself—hence this analytical tradition has not led to any comprehensive rethinking of Russian cultural heritage or ways of presenting it to the public. This is why the 2015 e-book version of *The Frigate Pallada* so irresponsibly highlights the book's factuality while making no mention of its thick layers of prejudice. To a western audience this may well appear shocking. After all, even the publisher of Goetze's 1987 translation, which was sanitized of the most odious passages, felt compelled to include a disclaimer that renounced complicity with the book's demeaning stereotypes of non-western peoples.

The e-book edition of *The Frigate Pallada* makes no effort to question these stereotypes. One vivid example is a text box explaining that the "Hottentots" (Khoikhoi) and "Bushmen" (San) comprise a separate "racial type," a Capoid race (named so after the Cape of Good Hope). An opportunity to question Goncharov's racializing of Africans is lost. While the text box acknowledges the offensiveness of the term "Hottentot" (but not "Bushmen"), it blithely endorses this usage by claiming that it remains an accepted term in the Russian language. Another example of supplementary material that authenticates questionable notions is supplied by English engravings of Boers sparring with Zulu warriors, done in a manner entirely sympathetic to the Boers. While sympathy for the white man in any conflict with the African people correctly reflects Goncharov's bias, these engravings, absent any commentary, make the bias appear justified. (Never mind that the preponderance of the Zulu-themed engravings is out of place in a book that barely mentions the Zulu, who lived north east of the Cape Colony.)[72]

Moreover, the e-book edition violates Goncharov's actual text by eliminating the last three chapters of *The Frigate Pallada* describing Goncharov's journey though Siberia, along with the "Twenty Years Since" sketch, traditionally included with *The Frigate Pallada* since the nineteenth century. Following the chapter "From Manila to the Shores of Siberia," the e-book simply breaks off, informing readers that in the summer of 1854 Goncharov disembarked on the Siberian coast and began his overland journey to St. Petersburg.[73] The readers for whom the e-book is the only contact with Goncharov's travelogue will have no idea that he actually described this journey. One can only speculate about the reasons for this surreptitious excising of Siberia from the travelogue. Perhaps Goncharov's description of Russia's largest Asian colony as desolate and underdeveloped struck the editors as a jarring contrast to Goncharov's enthused images of British imperial successes in Africa or Asia. Or perhaps the very portrayal of Siberia in recognizably colonial terms proved objectionable. Either way, a disavowal of Goncharov's Siberian chapters, or at least a disinclination to feature them for broad readership, appears to be a trend in the early twenty-first century. The popular print and audiobook editions by Eksmo likewise omit these chapters.[74]

Amazingly, not only does Goncharov's book about the *Pallada* expedition continue its course in twenty-first century Russian culture, a new frigate "*Pallada,*" built and named in honor of the flagship that delivered Putiatin's team to Japan, keeps sailing the seven seas. Its journeys—though so far literarily unremarkable—are no less symbolic.

What happened to the original vessel? Its fifty-two cannons removed, transferred to the *Diana,* and then gifted to the Japanese, the original *Pallada,* aged and badly battered by storms and typhoons, was scuttled in January 1856 in the well-hidden bay of Emperor's Harbor, located in the Tatar Strait, between the Sea of Okhotsk and the Sea of Japan, across from Sakhalin Island. It remains there to this day. The decision to sink it was prompted by a concern that the frigate might become a British or French war trophy. In the Soviet period, the submerged wreck, more famous for literary than for military reasons, continued to exert a magnetic pull. One description in the chief communist organ *Pravda* of the eighty-year wreck of the *Pallada* claimed that its wooden fragments, thanks to the literary fame imparted to the ship, were treated like "relics" when washed ashore. Some Soviet poets paid respect to the legendary vessel that found its resting place at the bottom of the sea.[75] In 1962, a team of researchers from a Moscow naval institute, "enchanted since childhood by Goncharov's romantic narration," undertook an underwater expedition in order to behold the *Pallada* with their own eyes and photograph its remnants.[76]

The original *Pallada* was built in St. Petersburg on the British model, which was copied from an American model. The new frigate *Pallada* was built in 1989, to the design of a Polish architect trained in Poland and Russia, as a replica of an early twentieth-century three-mast sailing ship.[77] Its construction was outsourced to the Polish shipyard in Gdańsk, the birthplace of the 1980s Solidarity movement that opposed the Moscow-supported Communist regimes across Eastern Europe. The new *Pallada* is owned and operated by the Far Eastern State Technical Fisheries University, based in Vladivostok (the city's name means "Ruler of the East"). Vladivostok is today Russia's largest Pacific port and home to its Pacific Fleet. It was founded in 1860, after the annexation of the Amur from China, by order of Count Nikolai Muravev, the governor-general of Siberia whom Goncharov so idolized for his energetic efforts to expand the empire. The new *Pallada* is used as a training vessel for young cadets and competes in international sailing events. Beyond sailing skills, young generations of Russian seamen are meant to acquire "patriotic education" in the course of their training on the new *Pallada.*[78]

The symbolism of the expeditions undertaken by the namesake of Putiatin's *Pallada* furthers this goal. In 2004, the ship completed a religious cruise of Asia called "Be Blessed, Far East," which commemorated the hundredth anniversary of "the heroic defense of Port Arthur" in the Russo-Japanese War. Its ports of call were in Japan (Nagasaki), South Korea, and China. The crew included both cadets and Orthodox clergymen who performed services at the fallen Russian sailors' burial places. The new *Pallada* carried a hundred-year old Port Arthur icon of the Triumph of the Most Holy Mother of God, which had failed to be delivered to Port Arthur before the famous 1904 battle, but finally reached its original destination.[79]

Among several circumnavigations accomplished by the new *Pallada,* the one in 2007–2008 celebrated the 190th anniversary of the circumnavigation of the globe by the Baltic Russian Faddei Bellinshausen and by Mikhail Lazarev, discoverers of the Antarctic continent in 1820. The voyage also honored the fiftieth anniversary of the Russian Vostok research station in Antarctica. In 2011, the new *Pallada* completed the voyage of the original *Pallada,* truncated in 1854 by the Crimean War and the frigate's poor condition, by reaching the shores of North America, and visiting Alaska, Seattle, and San Francisco. The voyage commemorated the 270th anniversary of the Russian discovery of America and the fiftieth anniversary of Yuri Gagarin's pioneering space flight. By order of President Vladimir Putin, in 2014 the ship's commander was awarded the prestigious Order of Alexander Nevsky. In his thanks for the award, the commander affirmed that "Russia was, is, and will always be a great naval and fishing power."[80] In 2014–2015 the new *Pallada* celebrated the seventieth anniversary of the Great Patriotic War, as World War II is known in Russia. In October 2015, it became the first Russian ship to acquire an iconostasis, a wall of icons that demarcates the holiest space in Russian Orthodox churches.[81] The pious Yevfimy Putiatin would be pleased.

Though none of these commemorative itineraries replicates the voyage of Putiatin's frigate, they collectively honor the legacy of the ship Goncharov's book made famous. The symbolic meanings attached to the new *Pallada*'s transoceanic cruises glorify the Russian tradition of exploration and colonization, the projection of Russian naval and state power, Russia's role in the global world order, and Russian nationalism, in which Orthodox Christianity again plays an important role.[82] In the epigraph to this chapter, Goncharov likens travelogues to wheels whose indelible traces merge into "one broad road." In this wonderful image, he blurs the distinction between textual and real-world journeys, between an imprint of words on a page and an imprint of wheels on the ground. Seen this way, travel books inspire imaginative journeys—and actual ones, such as those of the new *Pallada*. Yet they also frame the contours of the known world and one's own place in it. They nudge some readers out of armchairs, influencing their dispositions as travelers. They also configure the worldliness of those who stay put. Most fundamentally, they impart meaning to the journeys that gave rise to them. Russia's historic mission to Japan inspired Goncharov's travelogue. For the broad Russian public, his travelogue has indelibly shaped the meaning of that mission and of that moment in Russian and global history.

Appendix

Goncharov's Sources

Listed here are relevant sources that Goncharov knew before the voyage, or that he consulted either in preparation for the voyage or when composing *The Frigate Pallada*. Main sources used in compiling this list: T. I. Ornatskaia, "Istoriia sozdaniia Fregata Pallada," in I. A. Goncharov, *Fregat "Pallada." Ocherki puteshestviia v dvukh tomakh* (Leningrad: Nauka, 1986), 763–787; V. I. Mel'nik, *I vdrug—na more!: Literaturnye klasski na Dal'nem Vostoke* (Vladivostok: Dal'izdat, 2012), 76–77; and *PSS* 3, 839–845 and notes.

Arbousset, T., and F. Daumas. *Narrative of an Exploratory Tour to the North-East of the Colony of the Cape of Good Hope.* Trans. John Croumbie Brown. Cape Town: Robertson, 1846.

Barrow, John. *An Account of Travels into the Interior of Southern Africa in the Years 1797 and 1798.* London: T. Cadell, jun., and W. Davies, 1801–1804.

Beechey, Frederick William. *Narrative of a Voyage to the Pacific and Beering's Strait: To Co-operate with the Polar Expeditions, performed . . . in the years 1825, 26, 27, 28.* London : H. Colburn and R. Bentley, 1831.

Belcher, Edward. *Relations des voyages du "Sulphur" et du "Samarang" (Bornéo, les portes de Chine, les Manilles, Célèbes, la Corée, le Japon, les Philippines)* (Paris). French translation of Belcher, Edward. *Narrative of a Voyage Round the World : Performed in Her Majesty's Ship Sulphur, during the years 1836–1842,* 2 vols. London: H. Colburn, 1843.

Bichurin, Nikita Iakovlevich. [Father Iakinf], *Kitai, ego zhiteli, nravy, obychai, prosveshchenie.* St. Petersburg: Tip. Imperatorskoi akademii nauk, 1840.

Bille, Steen. *Korvetten Galatheas Rejse omkring Jorden.* 1853.

Botkin, Vasilii P. *Pis'ma ob Ispanii.* St. Petersburg, 1847.

Böhtlingk, Otto von. *Über die Sprache der Jakuten.* St. Petersburg, 1851. [Goncharov incorrectly cites the title as *Über die jakütische Sprache.*]

Broughton, William Robert. *A Voyage of Discovery to the North Pacific Ocean . . . in the years 1795, 1796, 1797, 1798.* London: T. Cadell and W. Davies, 1804.

Chase, John Centlivres. *The Cape of Good Hope and the Eastern Province of Algoa Bay.* London: P. Richardson, 1843.

The Cape of Good Hope Almanac and Annual Register for 1853. Compiled by B. J. Van de Sandt de Villiers. Cape Town: Van de Sandt de Villiers and Tier, 1852.

Cook, James. *A New Voyage Round the World, in the Years 1768, 1769, 1770, and 1771,* 2 vols. 1774.

———. *A Voyage towards the South Pole, and round the world . . . in the years 1772, 1773, 1774, and 1775.,* 2 vols. 4th ed. London: W. Strahan and T. Cadell, 1784.

[Duncan, Archibald]. *Opisanie primechatel'nykh korablekrushenii, v raznoe vremia sluchivshihksia. Sochinenie gospodina Dunkena.* Trans. V. M. Golovnin. St. Petersburg, 1822. Russian translation of Archibald Duncan, *The Mariner's Chronicle, Containing Narratives of the Most Remarkable Disasters at Sea, such as Shipwrecks, Storms, Fires, and Famines.* 6 vols. London, 1804–1808.

Gedenshtrom, Matvei M. *Otryvki o Sibiri.* St. Petersburg, 1830.

Golovnin, Vasily. *Zapiski flota kapitana Golovnina o prikliucheniiakh ego v plenu u iapontsev v 1811, 1812, i 1813 godakh.* 1816. [*Notes of the Fleet Captain Golovnin about his Adventures in Japanese Captivity in the Years 1811, 1812, and 1813*].

Gualtieri, Guido. *Relazioni della ventua degli Ambasciatori Giapponesi a Roma, sino alla partita di Lisbona.* Rome, 1586. German translation 1587, French translations 1585 and 1586.

Hagenaer, Hendrik. *Opisaniie o Iapone, soderzhavshee v sebe tri chasti, to est': izvestie o Iapone i o vine goneniia na khristiian v Iapone i posledovanie stranstvovaniia Genrika Gagenara, kotoroe ispravnoiu landkartoiu i izriadnymi figurami ukrasheno.* Trans. Ivan Gorlitskii. St. Petersburg, 1734.

Hall, Basil. *Account of a Voyage of Discovery to the West Coast of Corea and the Great Loo-Choo Island in the Japan Sea.* London: John Murray, 1818.

Hayashi, Shihei. *San kokf tsou ran to sets, ou, Aperqu général des trois royaumes. Traduit de l'original japonais-chinois par Mr. J. Klaproth.* Paris, 1832.

Horsburgh, James. *The India Directory, or Directions for Sailing to and from the East Indies, China, New Holland, Cape of Good Hope, Brazil, and the Interjacent Ports.* London, 2nd ed. 1817, 3rd ed. 1826.

Humboldt, Alexander von. *Puteshestvie barona Aleksandra Gumbol'dta, Erenberga i Roze v 1829 godu po Sibiri i k Kaspiiskomu moriu.* St. Petersburg, 1837. Possibly also Humboldt, Alexander von. *Asie centrale. Recherches sur les chaînes des montagnes et la climotologie comparée.* 3 vols. Paris: Gide, 1843.

Kaempfer, Engelbert. *A History of Japan, Giving an Account of the Ancient and Present State and Government of that Empire. . . .* Trans. J. G. Scheuchzer. London, 1727.

"Das Kap der guten Hoffnung." *Die Gegenwart: Eine encyclopädische Darstellung der neuesten Zeitgeschichte für alle Stände.* Vol. 4, 507–554. Leipzig: F. A. Brockhaus, 1850.

Karamzin, Nikolai M. *Pis'ma russkogo puteshestvennika.* St. Petersburg, 1797–1801.

Krasheninnikov, Stepan P. *Opisanie zemli Kamchatki.* St. Petersburg, 1755.

Litke, Fedor L. *Puteshestvie vokrug sveta na voennom shliupe 'Seniavin' v 1828–1829 gg.* St. Petersburg, 1834–1836.

Mallat, J. *Les Philipines; histoire, géographie, moeurs, agriculture, industrie et commerce des colonies espagnoles dans l'Océanie.* Paris: A. Bertrand, 1846.

The Nautical Magazine

Nopitsch, Wilhelm Herman. *Kaufmännische Berichte: gesammelt auf einer Reise um die Welt mit der Kriegs-Corvette Galathea in den Jahren 1845, 46 und 47.* Hamburg: Perthes, Besser, & Mauke, 1849.

Park, Mungo. *Travels in the Interior Districts of Africa.* 3rd ed. London: W. Bulmer, 1799.

Shchukin, Nikolai S. *Poezdka v Iakutsk.* St. Petersburg, 1833.

Siebold, Philipp Franz von. *Nippon. Archiv zur Beschreibung von Japan und dessen Neben- und Schutzländern: Jezo mit den Südlichen Kurilen, Krafto, Koorai und den Liukiu-Inseln.* 7 vols. Leiden, 1832–1852.

Smith, Andrew. *Report of the Expedition for Exploring Central Africa from the Cape of Good Hope.* Cape Town: The Government Gazette Office, 1836.

Smith, Thornley. *South Africa Delineated: or, Sketches Historical and Descriptive, of Its Tribes and Missions, and of the British Colonies of the Cape and Port-Natal.* London: J. Mason, 1850.

Sutherland, John. *Memoir Respecting the Kaffers, Hottentots and Bosjemans of South Africa.* 2 vols. Cape Town: Pike and Philip, 1845–1846.

Thunberg, Carl Peter. *Resa uti Europa, Africa, Asia: Förrättad åren 1770–1779.* Upsala, 1788–1793. Known to Goncharov in German (1792–1793), French (1794), or English (1795) translations.

Vancouver, George. *A Voyage of Discovery to the North Pacific Ocean, and Round the World . . . in the Years 1790–1795.* 3 vols. London: G. G. and J. Robinson, 1798.

Vaillant, François le. *Puteshestvie G. Val'iana vo vnutrennost' Afriki, cherez Mys Dobroi Nadezhdy v 1780, 81, 82, 83, 84 i 85 godakh.* Moscow: Tip. I. Zelennikova, 1793. Russian translation of Vaillant, François le, *Voyage de M. Le Vaillant dans l'Intérieur de l'Afrique, par le Cap de Bonne Espérance, dans les années 1780, 81, 82, 83, 84 et 85.* Paris: Leroy, 1790.

Veniaminov, Ivan Evseevich (Bishop Innokentii). *Zapiski ob ostrovakh Unalashkinskogo otdela.* St. Petersburg, 1840.

———. *O sostoianii pravoslavnoi tserkvii v Rossiiskoi Amerike.* 1840.

Vrangel', Ferdinand P. *Puteshestvie po severnym beregam Sibiri i po Ledovitomu moriu sovershennoe v 1820–1824 gg.* St. Petersburg, 1841.

Werne, Ferdinand. *African Wanderings, or an Expedition from Sennaar to Taka, Basa and Beni-Amer, with a Particular Glance at the Races of Bellad Sudan.* Trans. from the German by J. R. Johnston. London: Longman, Brown, Green, and Longmans, 1852.

Wilkes, Charles. *Narrative of the United States Exploring Expedition: During the Years 1838, 1839, 1840, 1841, 1842.* 5 vols. Philadelphia: Lea and Blanchard, 1845.

Notes

Introduction

1. *PSS* 2, 10, and *PSS* 3, 399.
2. The full Russian title is *Fregat "Pallada." Ocherki puteshestviia v dvukh tomakh* (*The Frigate Pallada. Travel Sketches in Two Volumes*). On Goncharov's apprehensions, see B. M. Engel'gardt, "Putevye pis'ma I. A. Goncharova iz krugosvetnogo plavaniia," *Literaturnoe nasledstvo,* vol. 22–24 (Moscow: Zhurnal'no-Gazetnoe ob"edinenie, 1935), 356. The English translations are Ivan Goncharov, *The Voyage of the Frigate 'Pallada,'* ed. and tr. N. W. Wilson (London: The Folio Society, 1965); and Ivan Goncharov, *The Frigate Pallada,* tr. Klaus Goetze (New York: St. Martin's Press, 1987). Despite assurances to the contrary, Goetze's translation is not complete; it also has serious errors.
3. John J. Stephan, "The Crimean War in the Far East," *Modern Asian Studies* 3.3 (1969): 257–277.
4. Susanna Soojung Lim, *China and Japan in the Russian Imagination, 1685–1922* (London: Routledge, 2013), 9, and her "Whose Orient Is It? *Frigate Pallada* and Ivan Goncharov's Voyage," *Slavic and East European Journal* 53.1 (2009): 23; David Schimmelpenninck van der Oye, *Russian Orientalism: Asia in the Russian Mind from Peter the Great to the Emigration* (New Haven: Yale University Press, 2010), 229. Viktor Shklovsky argued that the sharp conflict caused by the Crimean War "determines the flow of narration like underwater mountains and sandbars change the direction of the sea currents"; Viktor Shklovskii, "I. A. Goncharov, avtor 'Fregata Pallada,'" in *Izbrannoe v dvukh tomakh,* vol. 1 (Moscow: Khudozh. lit., 1983), 379.
5. In this, Goncharov complements another subject of a recent micro-historical study, Baron von Ungern-Sternberg, featured in Willard Sunderland, *The Baron's Cloak: A History of the Russian Empire in War and Revolution* (Ithaca: Cornell University Press, 2014). While Ungern was a busy historical actor, he left little record of his thoughts. Goncharov, by contrast, did little of historical significance, yet left a rich record of his ideas.

6. On Russians' tendency to view themselves as European in Asia, see Sunderland, *The Baron's Cloak,* 55–56. Goncharov reserved his fleeting doubts about the Europeanness of Russians for his private correspondence from the voyage; see Engel'gardt, "Putevye pis'ma," 386. See also Madina Tlostanova, "The Janus-faced Empire Distorting Orientalist Discourses: Gender, Race, and Religion in the Russian/(post)Soviet Constructions of the 'Orient,'" Worlds and Knowledge Otherwise, web dossier, Center for Global Studies and the Humanities, Duke University, Spring 2008, p. 2, https://globalstudies.trinity.duke.edu/wp-content/themes/cgsh/materials/WKO/v2d2_Tlostanova.pdf. On exaggerated claims to Europeanness as an expression of a feeling of inferiority, see also Elena Andreeva, *Russia and Iran in the Great Game: Travelogues and Orientalism* (New York: Routledge, 2007), 10–11.
7. The important predecessor to *The Frigate Pallada,* Nikolai Karamzin's popular travelogue about Western Europe, *Letters of a Russian Traveler* (1789–1790), similarly appealed to the Russian public by stressing Russo-European compatibility; see Andrew Kahn, "Nikolai Karamzin's Discourses of the Enlightenment," in Nikolai Karamzin, *Letters of a Russian Traveller* (Oxford: Voltaire Foundation, 2003), 503. Goncharov achieves this by viewing the worlds of Africa and Asia through the lens of a culturally confident European.
8. Efforts to integrate the Russian empire in the history of European imperialism include Mark Von Hagen and Karen Barkey, eds., *After Empire: Multiethnic Societies and Nation Building* (Boulder: Westview, 1997); Dominic Lieven, *Empire: The Russian Empire and Its Rivals* (New Haven: Yale University Press, 2000); [n.a.], *Rossiiskaia imperiia v sravnitel'noi perspektive* (Moscow: Novoe izd-vo, 2004); Alexei Miller and Alfred J. Rieber, eds., *Imperial Rule* (Budapest: Central European University Press, 2004); Jane Burbank and Frederick Cooper, *Empires in World History: Power and the Politics of Difference* (Princeton: Princeton University Press, 2010); and Martin Aust, Ricarda Vulpius, and Alexey Miller, eds., *Imperium inter pares. Rol' transferov v istorii Rossiiskoi imperii (1700–1917)* (Moscow: Novoe lit. obozrenie, 2010). The Russian empire also figures in an influential work on global nineteenth-century history: Jürgen Osterhammel *The Transformation of the World: A Global History of the Nineteenth Century* (Princeton: Princeton University Press, 2014).
9. George Lensen, *Russia's Japan Expedition of 1852 to 1855* (Gainesville: University of Florida Press, 1955), vii. Historians of East Asia have long been aware of the limitations of the Perry-centric approach, yet it lives on in Western perceptions.
10. Larry Wolff, "The Global Perspective of Enlightened Travelers: Philosophic Geography from Siberia to the Pacific Ocean," *European Review of History—Revue Européenne d'Histoire* 13.3 (2006): 437–453; Joyce E. Chaplin, *Round about the Earth: Circumnavigation from Magellan to Orbit* (New York: Simon and Schuster, 2012).
11. In the order of reference, Anthony Pagden, *Lords of All the Worlds: Ideologies of Empire in Spain, Britain and France c. 1500–c. 1850* (New Haven: Yale University Press, 1995), 4; Ann Laura Stoler, "Considerations on Imperial Comparisons," in *Empire Speaks Out: Languages of Rationalization and Self-Description in the Russian Empire,* ed. Ilya Gerasimov, Jan Kusber, and Alexander Semyonov (Boston: Brill, 2009),

38–39; Vladimir Bobrovnikov, "Russkii Kavkaz i frantsuzskii Alzhir: sluchainoe skhodstvo ili obmen opytom kolonial'nogo stroitel'tva?" in *Imperium inter pares. Rol' transferov v istorii Rossiiskoi imperii (1700–1917),* ed. Martin Aust, Ricarda Vulpius, and Alexey Miller (Moscow: Novoe lit. obozrenie, 2010), 203; Willard Sunderland, "Empire without Imperialism? Ambiguities of Colonization in Tsarist Russia," *Ab Imperio* 2 (2003): 112. See also Stoler, "Considerations," 43–47.

12. Andreeva, *Russia and Iran,* 42–43.
13. On extension of sea power as a demonstration of Russia's European character, see Richard Wortman, *Visual Texts, Ceremonial Texts, Texts of Exploration* (Boston: Academic Press, 2014), 263.
14. David M. Wrobel, *Global West, American Frontier: Travel, Empire, and Exceptionalism from Manifest Destiny to the Great Depression* (Albuquerque: University of New Mexico Press, 2013), 5.
15. Mark Bassin, *Imperial Visions: Nationalist Imagination and Geographic Expansion in the Russian Far East, 1840–1865* (Cambridge: Cambridge University Press, 1999), 6. For travel-writing scholar Tim Youngs, the social salience of travel writing rests on the following: "It records our temporal and spatial progress. It throws light on how we define ourselves and on how we identify others. Its construction of our sense of 'me' and 'you,' 'us' and 'them,' operates on individual and national levels and in the realms of psychology, society, and economics"; Tim Youngs, *The Cambridge Introduction to Travel Writing* (Cambridge: Cambridge University Press, 2012), 1. The hybridity of the genre makes its definition somewhat contestable. Youngs's fine and serviceable version is: "predominantly factual, first-person prose accounts of travels that have been undertaken by the author-narrator" (3).
16. Existing studies include: T. A. Roboli, "Literatura 'puteshestvii,'" *Russkaia proza* (Leningrad, 1926); Reuel K. Wilson, *The Literary Travelogue: A Comparative Study with Special Relevance to Russian Literature from Fonvizin to Pushkin* (The Hague: Martinus Nijhoff, 1973); Viktor Guminskii, *Otkrytie mira, ili, Puteshestviia i stranniki* (Moscow: Sovremennik, 1987); Andreas Schönle, *Authenticity and Fiction in the Russian Literary Journey, 1790–1840* (Cambridge, MA: Harvard University Press, 2000); Derek Offord, *Journeys to a Graveyard: Perceptions of Europe in Classical Russian Travel Writing* (Dordrecht: Springer, 2005); Sara Dickinson, *Breaking Ground: Travel and National Culture in Russia from Peter I to the Era of Pushkin* (Amsterdam: Rodopi, 2006); Andreeva, *Russia and Iran;* Amartya Mukhopadhyay, *India in Russian Orientalism: Travel Narratives and Beyond* (New Delhi: Manohar, 2013); Anne E. Gorsuch and Diane P. Koenker, eds., *Turizm: The Russian and East European Tourist under Capitalism and Socialism* (Ithaca: Cornell University Press, 2006); Daniel Brower and Susan Layton, "Liberation through Captivity: Nikolai Shipov's Adventures in the Imperial Borderlands," in *Orientalism and Empire in Russia,* ed. Michael David-Fox, Peter Holquist, and Alexander Martin (Bloomington: Slavica, 2006), 270–290; and Katya Hokanson, "Russian Women Travelers in Central Asia and India," *Russian Review* 70 (2011): 1–19.
17. Mary Louise Pratt, *Imperial Eyes: Travel Writing and Transculturation*, 2nd ed. (1992; London: Routledge, 2008), 3.

18. George Lensen, *The Russian Push toward Japan: Russo-Japanese Relations, 1697–1875* (Princeton: Princeton University Press, 1959), 344; Lensen, *Russia's Japan Expedition,* xi, 146; Lensen "The Historicity of *Fregat Pallada,*" *Modern Language Notes* 68.7 (1953): 462–466.
19. Ilya Vinkovetsky, *Russian America: An Overseas Colony of a Continental Empire, 1804–1867* (Oxford: Oxford University Press, 2011), 38, 48–49; see also his "Circumnavigation, Empire, Modernity, Race: The Impact of Round-the-World Voyages on Russia's Imperial Consciousness," *Ab Imperio* 1–2 (2001): 191–210. On the *Pallada* library, see *PSS* 3, 446n1. It was unloaded in the port of Ayan, on the Pacific shore of Siberia, but afterward its trail goes cold.
20. James Duncan and Derek Gregory, "Introduction," in *Writes of Passage: Reading Travel Writing,* ed. James Duncan and Derek Gregory (New York: Routledge, 1999), 7; Simon Gikandi, *Maps of Englishness: Writing Identity in the Culture of Colonialism* (New York: Columbia University Press, 1996), 97.
21. George Lensen, "Introduction," in *War and Revolution: Excerpts from Letters and Diaries of the Countess Olga Poutiatine,* tr. and ed. George Lensen (Tallahassee: Diplomatic Press, 1971), 5–11; N. K. Piksanov, "'Fregat Pallada' Goncharova," *Uchenye zapiski Moskovskogo gos. universiteta. Kafedra russkoi literatury,* kn. 2, vyp. 118 (Moscow: MGU, 1946), 36.
22. George A, Lensen, *Report from Hokkaido: The Remains of Russian Culture in Northern Japan* (Hakodate: The Municipal Library of Hakodate, 1954), 65–66; V. I. Mel'nik, *I vdrug—na more! Literaturnye klassiki na Dal'nem Vostoke* (Vladivostok: Dal'izdat, 2012), 57–58; *PSS* 3, 434. The Japanese refugee, Tachibana Kosai (Russian name Vladimir Yosifovich Yamatov), became the first professor of Japanese at the University of St. Petersburg and joined the Russian Ministry of Foreign Affairs (Lensen, *Report,* 65–66).
23. Before the expedition, Possiet authored a book on naval armaments that also won the Demidov Prize (Mel'nik, *I vdrug,* 78; *PSS* 3, 421). On Goncharov, see Milton Ehre, *Oblomov and His Creator: The Life and Art of Ivan Goncharov* (Princeton: Princeton University Press, 1973), 44–45.
24. The Russians' image of their empire as a "gift" to the imperial minorities is treated in Bruce Grant, *The Captive and the Gift: Cultural Histories of Sovereignty in Russia and the Caucasus* (Ithaca: Cornell University Press, 2009).
25. David Spurr collates a useful survey of these tropes in *The Rhetoric of Empire: Colonial Discourse in Journalism, Travel Writing, and Imperial Administration* (Durham: Duke University Press, 1993). As defined by a key scholar of Europe's culture of imperialism, Edward Said, "Orientalism" was a system of knowledge and cultural description, mostly of dubious scholarly rigor, that projected stereotyped and prejudiced understandings of the peoples of the East, or "the Orient." According to Said, Orientalism was a form of conceptual conquest that bolstered Europe's goals of political control. See Edward W. Said, *Orientalism* (1978; New York: Vintage, 1994). For a window onto the debates surrounding the applicability of Said's Orientalism framework for the study of Russian empire, see Nathaniel Knight, "Grigor'ev in Orenburg, 1851–1862: Russian Orientalism in the Service of Empire?" *Slavic Review*

59.1 (2000): 74–100; and polemical responses to Knight's skepticism in a forum convened by the journal *Kritika: Explorations in Russian and Eurasian History* 1.4 (2000), especially Adeeb Khalid's article "Russian History and the Debate over Orientalism," 691–699.

26. Carl Thompson, *Travel Writing* (New York: Routledge, 2011), 28, 30; Youngs, *Cambridge Introduction,* 166.
27. [I. A. Goncharov], "Vsepoddanneishii otchet general-ad'iutanta grafa E. V. Putiatina o plavanii otriada voennykh sudov v Iaponiiu i Kitai, 1852–1855," *PSS* 3, 162–224; the expedition's other documents are reprinted in *PSS* 3, 87–161. During the voyage, Goncharov kept an "official journal" (what he referred to as "*kazennyi zhurnal*") and a private diary. Neither of these sources, nor the drafts of *The Frigate Pallada,* nor correspondence with publishers are extant (*PSS* 3, 446). Justified reservations about treating *The Frigate Pallada* as a fully reliable historical document are raised in the following sources: Engel'gardt, "Putevye pis'ma"; Lensen, "The Historicity"; William W. McOmie, "The Russians in Nagasaki, 1853–54: Another Look at Some Russian, English, and Japanese Sources," *Acta Slavonica Japonica* 13 (1995): 42–60.
28. Barbara Heldt, "'Japanese' in Russian Literature: Transforming Identities," in *A Hidden Fire: Russian and Japanese Cultural Encounters, 1868–1926,* ed. J. Thomas Rimer (Stanford: Stanford University Press, 1995), 171.
29. Linda Colley, *The Ordeal of Elizabeth Marsh: A Woman in World History* (New York: Pantheon Books, 2007). For recent examples in Russian historiography, see Sunderland, *The Baron's Cloak;* and Stephen N. Norris and Willard Sunderland, *Russia's People of Empire: Life Stories from Eurasia, 1500 to the Present* (Bloomington: Indiana University Press, 2012).
30. For the list of editions, see Goncharov, *PSS* 3, 394–395, and *PSS* 6, 6. For a few editions missing from the *PSS* lists, see A. D. Alekseev, *Bibliografiia I. A. Goncharova* (Leningrad: Nauka, 1968), 16–19. *The Frigate Pallada* also had a vastly wider journalistic imprint than *Oblomov.* In the twentieth century, *Oblomov*'s success outstripped that of *The Frigate Pallada.* The Russian titles of Goncharov's three novels, in the order of mention, are *Obyknovennaia istoriia* (1847), *Oblomov* (1859), and *Obryv* (1869). Goncharov's friend Anatoly Koni complained in 1911 that the long term monopoly on the copyright to *The Frigate Pallada* kept the work out of reach for many; see Ekaterina Pravilova, *A Public Empire: Property and the Quest for the Common Good in Imperial Russia* (Princeton: Princeton University Press, 2014), 255.
31. The commentators included Nikolay Dobrolyubov, Dmitry Pisarev, Nikolay Chernyshevsky, and Alexander Herzen. On inclusion in school curricula, see N. K. Piksanov, "Goncharov i kolonializm," *Materialy iubileinoi Goncharovskoi konferentsii* (Ul'ianovsk, 1963), 23. On the overall popularity of *The Frigate Pallada,* see *PSS* 3, 534n1; N. K. Piksanov, ed., *I. A. Goncharov v vospominaniiakh sovremennikov* (Leningrad: Khudozh. lit., 1969), 202, 226; A. G. Tseitlin, *I. A. Goncharov* (Moscow: Izd-vo Ak. nauk SSSR, 1950), 146; and Piksanov, "'Fregat Pallada,'" 40.
32. A. P. Chekhov, *Ostrov Sakhalin,* in *Sochineniia,* vol. 14–15 (Moscow: Nauka, 1978), 34, 890; van der Oye, *Russian Orientalism,* 76; Vladimir Nabokov mentions *The Frigate*

Pallada in his 1930 novel *The Defense* (New York: Vintage, 1990), 33; A. B. Davidson and V. A. Makrushin, *Oblik dalekoi strany* (Moscow: Vostochnaia literatura, 1975), 303–304; M. I. Kalinin, "Pisatel' dolzhen byt' masterom svoego dela," *Literaturnaia gazeta* 62 [May 18] (1934): 1; Leonid Brezhnev, *Tselina* (Moscow: Izd-vo politicheskoi lit., 1978), 61; Shklovskii, "I. A. Goncharov," 381; *I. A. Goncharov v vospominaniiakh,* 190; on the 1878 remark about "the rose," see A. D. Alekseev, *Letopis' zhizni i tvorchestva I. A. Goncharova* (Moscow: Izd-vo AK nauk SSSR, 1960), 232.

33. Emperor Alexander II's brother, Grand Duke Konstantin Nikolaevich, who headed the Naval Ministry, dispatched writers to the distant reaches of the Russian empire and ordered them to produce ethnographic descriptions modeled on *The Frigate Pallada* (*PSS* 3, 527–528n4). As a literary model for the second half of the nineteenth century, the only rival for *The Frigate Pallada* was the travelogue about the Caucasus by Russia's national poet, Alexander Pushkin, *A Journey to Erzurum* (*Puteshestvie v Arzrum,* 1836).

34. Lensen, *Russia's Japan Expedition;* Lensen, *The Russian Push;* William McOmie, *The Opening of Japan, 1853–1855* (Folkestone: Global Oriental, 2006). I have benefited greatly from these excellent works on the Russian mission to Japan but hope to complement them by vindicating the travelogue's literary dimension as worthy of study itself.

35. There has been little critical work on race in Russian literature. Empire studies have never become the academic juggernaut comparable to parallel developments in English, French, or Spanish literary studies. On race and Russian literature, see Catherine Theimer Nepomnyashchy, Nicole Svobodny, and Ludmilla A. Trigos, eds., *Under the Sky of My Africa: Alexander Pushkin and Blackness* (Evanston: Northwestern University Press, 2006); and Henrietta Mondry, *Exemplary Bodies: Constructing the Jew in Russian Culture, since the 1880s* (Boston: Academic Studies Press, 2009). Book-length studies of imperialism in Russian literature include Susan Layton, *Russian Literature and Empire: Conquest of the Caucasus from Pushkin to Tolstoy* (Cambridge: Cambridge University Press, 1994); Ewa Thompson, *Imperial Knowledge: Russian Literature and Colonialism* (Westport, CT: Greenwood Press, 2000); Myroslav Shkandrij, *Russia and Ukraine: Literature and the Discourse of Empire from Napoleonic to Postcolonial Times* (Montreal: McGill-Queen's University Press, 2001); Izabela Kalinowska, *Between East and West: Polish and Russian Nineteenth-Century Travel to the Orient* (Rochester: University of Rochester Press, 2004); Harsha Ram, *The Imperial Sublime: A Russian Poetics of Empire* (Madison: University of Wisconsin Press, 2003); Katya Hokanson, *Writing at Russia's Borders* (Toronto: University of Toronto Press, 2008); Olga Maiorova, *From the Shadow of Empire: Defining the Russian Nation through Cultural Mythology, 1855–1870* (Madison: University of Wisconsin Press, 2010); Sanna Turoma, *Brodsky Abroad: Tourism, Empire, Nostalgia* (Madison: University of Wisconsin Press, 2010); and Edith Clowes, *Russia on the Edge: Imagined Geographies and Post-Soviet Identity* (Ithaca: Cornell University Press, 2011).

36. Among those who have held the travelogue's literary merit in very high regard are Barbara Heldt, "'Japanese' in Russian Literature," 171; and V. Mel'nik, "Pisatel' XXI veka," in I. A. Goncharov, *Sobranie sochinenii,* vol. 1 (Moscow: Knizhnyi klub

"Knigovek," 2010), 7, 42. Appreciating the "impeccable style" of this "calm and collected narrative," Vsevolod Setchkarev spoke of *The Frigate Pallada* in the following terms: "Its wealth of nuances, its judicious reserve, its humor, and its conscious avoidance of anything the least bit tinged with sensationalism required deliberate, intelligent reading. The precise, carefully constructed language deserves to be savored sentence by sentence"; Vsevolod Setchkarev, *Ivan Goncharov: His Life and His Works* (Würtzburg: Jal Verlag, 1974), 110.

37. This has been more observable in the Western critical tradition, which has reacted to rote Soviet readings of *Oblomov* as a satire on the sins of the landowning class. See, for example, Ehre, *Oblomov,* 154–232; and Setchkarev, *Ivan Goncharov,* 127–161. For a critique of the idealizations of Oblomovism, see also Tseitlin, *I. A. Goncharov,* 197–201. On Oblomovka as a cross between idyll and anti-utopia, see E. Krasnoshchekova, *Ivan Aleksandrovich Goncharov: Mir tvorchestva* (St. Petersburg: "Pushkinskii fond," 1997), 258.
38. *PSS* 2, 19. On evidence that Goncharov himself saw Stolz as a repository of positive values, see his "Luchshe pozdno chem nikogda" (1879), in I. A. Goncharov, *Sobranie sochinenii v vos'mi tomakh,* vol. 8 (Moscow: Khudozh lit, 1980), 115.
39. Anne Lounsbery, "The World on the Back of a Fish: Mobility, Immobility, and Economics in *Oblomov,*" *Russian Review* 70.1 (2011): 44, 48. Marijeta Bozovich also connects *Oblomov* with *The Frigate Pallada* in her "Bol'shoe puteshestvie 'Oblomova': Roman Goncharova v svete 'prosvetitel'noi poezdki,'" *Novoe literaturnoe obozrenie* 6 (2010): 130–145.

1. From London to Cape Town, or How to Run a Successful Empire

1. *PSS* 2, 7.
2. Jürgen Osterhammel, *The Transformation of the World: A Global History of the Nineteenth Century* (Princeton: Princeton University Press, 2014), 122, 452–453, 454, 455, 458. See also H. V. Bowen, "British Conceptions of Global Empire, 1756–83," *Journal of Imperial and Commonwealth History* 26.3 (1998): 1–27. On Britain's global turn in the late eighteenth century, see Linda Colley, *The Ordeal of Elizabeth Marsh: A Woman in World History* (New York: Pantheon Books, 2007), esp. xxiv–xxvii.
3. Susanna Soojung Lim, "Whose Orient Is It? *Frigate Pallada* and Ivan Goncharov's Voyage," *Slavic and East European Journal* 53.1 (2009): 25.
4. Such travelogues are examined in Elena Andreeva, *Russia and Iran in the Great Game: Travelogues and Orientalism* (New York: Routledge, 2007).
5. Carl Thompson, *Travel Writing* (New York: Routledge, 2011), 62–129.
6. See Evgeny Sergeev, *The Great Game, 1856–1907: Russo-British Relations in Central and East Asia* (Baltimore: John Hopkins University Press, 2013), 345, 347 (the quoted general was Leonid Sobolev). Though he did not invent it, the India-born English writer Rudyard Kipling popularized the term The Great Game, which speakers of Russian today also use (*Bol'shaia igra*). For the term's actual origin in the 1840s British government correspondence, see Seymour Becker, "The 'Great Game': The

History of an Evocative Phrase," *Asian Affairs* 43.1 (2012): 61–80. The term used in imperial Russia, "the tournament of shadows" (*turniry tenei*), was coined in 1837 by the Russian chancellor, Count Karl Nesselrode (Sergeev, *The Great Game,* 7).

7. V. I. Mel'nik, *I. A. Goncharov v kontekste russkoi i mirovoi literatury* (Moscow: Gos. Akademiia slavianskoi kul'tury, 2012), 129–130, 133; see also N. K. Piksanov, "*Fregat Pallada* Goncharova," *Uchenye zapiski Moskovskogo gos. universiteta. Kafedra russkoi literatury,* kn. 2, vyp. 118 (Moscow: MGU, 1946), 27–28.

8. *I. A. Goncharov v vospominaniiakh sovremennikov,* ed. O. A Demikhovskaia and E. K. Demikhovskaia (Ul'ianovsk: "Region-Invest," 2012), 176; on Putiatin's Anglophilism, see Voin A. Rimskii-Korsakov, *Baltika-Amur. Povestvovanie v pis'makh o plavaniiakh, prikliucheniiakh i razmyshleniiakh komandira shkuny 'Vostok'* (Khabarovsk: Khabarovskoe knizhnoe izd-vo, 1980), 47; and George Lensen, "Introduction," in *War and Revolution: Excerpts from Letters and Diaries of the Countess Olga Poutiatine,* tr. and ed. George Lensen (Tallahassee: The Diplomatic Press, 1971), 5; on Goncharov's memories of his uncle, see Milton Ehre, *Oblomov and His Creator* (Princeton: Princeton University Press, 1973), 10, 16.

9. B. M. Engel'gardt, "Putevye pis'ma I. A. Goncharova iz krugosvetnogo plavaniia," *Literaturnoe nasledstvo,* vol. 22–24 (Moscow: Zhurnal'no-Gazetnoe ob"edineniie, 1935), 346–368.

10. Mary Louise Pratt, *Imperial Eyes: Travel Writing and Transculturation,* 2nd ed. (London: Routledge, 2008), 60–61.

11. On travel narratives' engagement with the social and political tensions back in the travelers' home country, see Tim Youngs, *Travellers in Africa: British Travelogues, 1850–1900* (Manchester: Manchester University Press, 1994).

12. *PSS* 2, 40.

13. N. M. Karamzin, *Pis'ma russkogo puteshestvennika* (1797–1801; Leningrad: Nauka, 1984), 330.

14. *PSS* 2, 44; and [I. A. Goncharov], "Vsepoddanneishii otchet general-ad'iutanta grafa E. V. Putiatina o plavanii otriada voennykh sudov v Iaponiiu i Kitai, 1852–1855," *PSS* 3, 162.

15. On tourism and anti-tourism, see James Buzard, *The Beaten Track: European Tourism, Literature, and the Ways to Culture, 1800–1918* (Oxford: Clarendon Press, 1993), 80–154.

16. Dominic Lieven gives the Russian army its due in his *Russia against Napoleon: The True Story of the Campaigns of 'War and Peace'* (New York: Viking, 2010).

17. *PSS* 2, 46–47.

18. *PSS* 2, 41, 58.

19. *PSS* 2, 48. The readers of Goncharov's earlier novel, *An Ordinary Story,* would have actually recognized in Goncharov's London his St. Petersburg. Shown through the eyes of a provincial youth, the Russian capital arose in that novel as similarly impersonal, oppressive, and cold, a description patterned on Nikolai Gogol's famous story "Nevsky Prospect"; see Ivan Goncharov, *Obyknovennaia istoriia, PSS* 1, 203, 204.

20. *PSS* 2, 43. By consulting guidebooks for 1851 and 1852, Goncharov's early English translator, N. W. Wilson, identified some of these institutions and corroborated Gon-

charov's account of London's impressive array of attractions, which included a demonstration of the Cantelonian system of hatching eggs by steam heat. See N. W. Wilson's note to I. A. Goncharov, *The Voyage of the Frigate 'Pallada,'* ed. and tr. N. W. Wilson (London: The Folio Society, 1965), 38, 39.

21. *PSS* 2, 43–44.
22. Buzard, *The Beaten Track,* 80.
23. *PSS* 2, 46.
24. *PSS* 2, 49, 50. Both admiring and critical comments largely build upon Karamzin's judgments about the English, from his *Letters of a Russian Traveler.* The occasional tone of ridicule, however, is Goncharov's own. On Goncharov and Karamzin, see Elena A. Krasnoshchekova "'Fregat Pallada': 'Puteshestvie' kak zhanr (N. M. Karamzin i I. A. Goncharov)," *Russkaia literatura* 4 (1992): 12–31.
25. *PSS* 2, 51, and *PSS* 3, 229, notes to 50–52.
26. Goncharov's contrast reverses Karamzin's praise of the quiet domestic life of the English, in which he saw the deep imprint of the Enlightenment, and his critique of Russian high society's addiction to salon life's superficial glitter (Karamzin, *Pis'ma,* 364–367).
27. *PSS* 2, 61; see also 45 and 53. The Russian phrase for "paper sheets" is *bumazhnye odeiala.*
28. *PSS* 2, 64–66 (passage about the Russian landowner), and 67.
29. Ingrid Kleespies, *A Nation Astray: Nomadism and National Identity in Russian Literature* (DeKalb: Northern Illinois University Press, 2012), 121–126. In a reading that does not venture beyond Goncharov's London chapter, Kleespies exaggerates the negativity of Goncharov's portrayal of the English. So does Derek Offord in *Journeys to the Graveyard, Perceptions of Europe in Classical Russian Travel Writing* (Dordrecht: Springer, 2005), 201. Though fairly balanced overall, Milton Ehre seems more taken with Oblomov than was Goncharov; see Ehre's *Oblomov and His Creator* (Princeton: Princeton University Press, 1973), 154–232.
30. Steve Clark, "Introduction," in *Travel Writing and Empire: Postcolonial Theory in Transit,* ed. Steve Clark (New York: Zed Books, 1999), 14–15.
31. *PSS* 2, 15–16. Goncharov misquotes the famous English patriotic song and naval hymn "Rule Britannia" (*PSS* 3, 544–545 n. to p. 16). It should also be noted that Goncharov never visited India. His critique of English exploitation echoes Karamzin, who described the English as charitable at home but greedy in the colonies (Karamzin, *Pis'ma,* 372).
32. Liah Greenfeld, *Nationalism: Five Roads to Modernity* (Cambridge, MA: Harvard University Press, 1992), 222–235.
33. *PSS* 2, 12, 88.
34. *PSS* 2, 93.
35. I. A. Goncharov, letter of September 20 / October 20 to Avraam S. Norov, I. A. Goncharov, *Fregat 'Pallada': Ocherki puteshestviia v dvukh tomakh* (Leningrad: Nauka, 1986), 681; Greenfeld, *Nationalism,* 222.
36. One reviewer wrote: "Irrespective of his evident lack of sympathy for the British, the image of this civilizing nation, possibly against the author's will, comes from under

his pen as grandiose and attractive. This could not be otherwise: as a friend of civilization, in support of which he wrote many a warm page, and as a poet, the author could not avoid being struck by this image, known throughout the world, even if it is perhaps not very pleasant to look at." See M. F. de Pule, rev. of *Fregat Pallada* (1858), by I. A. Goncharov, *Atenei* 6 (1858), 12.

37. On emptiness and silence as tropes of colonial writing about southern Africa, see J. M. Coetzee, *White Writing: On the Culture of Letters in South Africa* (New Haven: Yale University Press, 1988), 163–177. Coetzee sees in this convention a certain "historical will" to misrepresent the South African land as uninhabited (177). Goncharov uses such tropes in his descriptions of Japan.

38. *PSS* 2, 107, 111. While analyzing *The Frigate Pallada* through the lens of "sleep" and "awakening," which accurately captures Goncharov's cultural schema in its broadest contours, Elena Krasnoshchekova nonetheless ignores this schema's entanglement in the ideology of imperialism; see E. A. Krasnoshchekova, *Ivan Aleksandrovich Goncharov: Mir tvorchestva* (St. Petersburg: Pushkinskii Fond, 1997).

39. E. Siu [E. Sue], "Atar-Giul'. Otryvok iz romana. Perevod s frantsuzskogo," by I. A. Goncharov, *PSS* 1, 534–546; *PSS* 4, 169.

40. For Golovnin's account of the Cape of Good Hope, see his "Puteshestvie shliupa 'Diana' iz Kronshtadta v Kamchatku, sovershennoe pod nachal'stvom flota lejtenanta Golovnina v 1807, 1808 i 1809 gg.," in Vasilii Golovnin, *Sochineniia* (Moscow, Leningrad: Izd-vo Glavsevmorputi, 1949), 17–123. On the naval and cultural history of Russian visits to the Cape of Good Hope, see A. B. Davidson and V. A. Makrushin, *Oblik dalekoi strany* (Moscow: Vostochnaia literatura, 1975); the Dutch Boer's account of Golovnin's escape appears on pp. 266–267. Aleksei Vysheslavtsev followed Goncharov's itinerary and wrote about it in his *Ocherki perom i karandashem iz krugosvetnogo plavaniia v 1857, 1858, 1859 i 1860 godakh* (St. Petersburg: Tip. Morskogo ministerstva, 1862); see Davisdon and Makrushin, *Oblik,* 331–337.

41. Davisdon and Makrushin, *Oblik,* 359–361.

42. Adam Smith, *An Inquiry into the Nature and Causes of the Wealth of Nations,* vol. 2 (1776; Oxford: Clarendon Press, 1976), 626.

43. My overview of the history of South Africa is based on Leonard Thompson, *A History of South Africa* (New Haven: Yale University Press, 1990), 1–69; Richard Elphick and Hermann Giliomee, eds., *The Shaping of South African Society, 1652–1840* (Middletown: Wesleyan University Press, 1989); T. R. H. Davenport and Christopher Saunders, *South Africa: A Modern History,* 5th ed. (New York: St. Martin's Press, 2000); Carolyn Hamilton, Bernard K. Mbenga, and Robert Ross, eds. *The Cambridge History of South Africa,* vol. 1 (Cambridge: Cambridge University Press, 2010); Siegfried Huigen, *Knowledge and Colonialism: Eighteenth-Century Travellers in South Africa* (Leiden: Brill, 2009), 9; and Christopher Saunders and Iain R. Smith, "Southern Africa, 1795–1910," in *The Oxford History of the British Empire,* vol. 3, ed. Andrew Porter (Oxford: Oxford University Press, 1999), 597–623.

44. Mungo Park, *Travels in Interior Districts of Africa* (1799; Durham: Duke University Press, 2000); David Livingstone, *Missionary Travels and Researches in South Africa*

(1857; New York: Harper and Brothers, 1858); Chinua Achebe, "An Image of Africa: Racism in Conrad's *Heart of Darkness*," in *Hopes and Impediments: Selected Essays, 1965–1987* (New York: Anchor Books, 1988), 12.

45. Willard Sunderland, "The 'Colonization Question': Visions of Colonization in Late Imperial Russia," *Jahrbücher für Geschichte Osteuropas* 48 (2000): 210–232; Willard Sunderland, *Taming the Wild Field: Colonization and Empire on the Russian Steppe* (Ithaca: Cornell University Press, 2004), the citation from Klyuchevsky appears on p. 4. The notion of frontier colonization as formative for Russian national history preceded by nearly half a century Victor Turner's famous frontier thesis regarding US history; see Mark Bassin, "Turner, Solov'ev, and the 'Frontier Hypothesis': The Nationalist Signification of Open Spaces, *Journal of Modern History* 65 (1993): 473–511.

46. Fyodor Dostoevsky reprinted a report on the Society's work in his journal: "Vopros o kolonizatsii," *Vremia* 9 (1861). On European colonial migrations in a global context, see "O Evropeiskikh pereseleniiakh v deviatnadtsatom veke," *Biblioteka dlia chteniia* 135 (1856): 1–32; and I. Berezin, "Metropoliia i kolonii," *Otechestvennye zapiski* 117 (1858): 81–98, 349–370, and 118 (1858): 74–115. Examples of fictional treatments of colonization are novels of D. V. Grigorovich and G. P. Danilevskii that appeared in the 1850s–1860s; see Sunderland, *Taming the Wild Field,* 97, 168.

47. *PSS* 2, 130, 140, 175, 177.

48. *PSS* 2, 155.

49. Throughout, Goncharov uses the term "colored" (*tsvetnye*) to mean any nonwhites, whether indigenous people of southern Africa or people of mixed racial ancestry. In today's South Africa, the term "coloured" more narrowly denotes people from mixed unions of southern African people (mostly Khoisan women) with Europeans or southern Asians.

50. *PSS* 2, 138, 148, 217. Incidentally, tigers are not native to Africa, but some Afrikaners called leopards tigers (see Wilson's note to Goncharov, *The Voyage of the Frigate 'Pallada,'* 75). It is also possible that Goncharov tossed in an occasional tiger to his narrative as part of stock exotica, as does the narrator of *Robinson Crusoe*: Daniel Defoe, *Robinson Crusoe* (1799; New York: Norton, 1975), 98.

51. [Goncharov], "Vsepoddanneishii otchet," *PSS* 3, 168. Goncharov mentions that photographs were taken on this and other occasions (*PSS* 2, 204, 225). Unfortunately, they have not been preserved. Evert Johannes Van Dyck was listed as a driver for the Worcester omnibus in the Cape Almanach of 1853 (see Davidson and Makrushin, *Oblik,* 318).

52. *PSS* 2, 185–186 (Stellenbosch), 193, 196–197 (Paarl), 214 (Worcester); see also 197, 210, 217.

53. Geoffrey Nash, "Politics, Aesthetics, and Quest in British Travel Writing on the Middle East," cited in *Travel Writing in the Nineteenth Century: Filling the Blank Spaces,* ed. Tim Youngs (London: Anthem Press, 2006), 55–70; Reuel K. Wilson, *The Literary Travelogue* (The Hague: Martinus Nijhoff, 1973), xii.

54. *PSS* 2, 150, 191. See also "Measuring Worth Is a Complicated Question," MeasuringWorth, n.d., http://www.measuringworth.com.

55. [Goncharov], "Vsepoddanneishii otchet," *PSS* 3, 162.

56. *Les quatre mendiants* is a French dessert consisting of nuts and dried fruits; as is fitting for this image, the phrase means "four beggars"; *PSS* 2, 179, 190.
57. Rimskii-Korsakov, *Baltika-Amur,* 69; V. P. Botkin's commentary about the English on Gibraltar in *Pis'ma ob Ispanii* (1847), which was known to Goncharov (*PSS* 3, 487). The paragraph's passages come from *PSS* 2, 155, 158.
58. James Belich, *Replenishing the Earth: The Settler Revolution and the Rise of the Anglo-World, 1783–1939* (Oxford: Oxford University Press, 2013), 374–377.
59. According to J. B. Peires, the Great Trek reflected dissatisfaction of the Dutch not with the British rule, but with the colonial government. The abolition of slavery hit the Boers economically because they conducted most transactions by barter, so were unable to pay cash wages. See J. B. Peires, "The British and the Cape, 1814–1834" in *The Shaping,* ed. Elphick and Giliomee, 500. On the Great Trek, see also Thompson, *A History,* 87–100; and *Illustrated History of South Africa: The Real Story,* 3rd ed. (New York: Reader's Digest, 1994), 114–125.
60. This can be seen in the account of A. E. Vrangel', "S mysa Dobroi Nadezhdy," *Morskoi sbornik* 1 (1859): 1–14 ("Smes'"). Vrangel does not invoke Goncharov but seems clearly in dialogue with him.
61. I. A. Goncharov, letter of September 20 / October 20 to Norov and Goncharov, *Fregat 'Pallada',* 681.
62. *PSS* 2, 160.
63. On the affinity between the Afrikaners and the Oblomovites, see Henrietta Mondry, "A Formalist Reading of the Chapter on the Cape Province from Goncharov's Book *Frigate Pallada,*" in *The Waking Sphinx: South African Essays on Russian Culture,* ed. Henrietta Mondry (Johannesburg: University of the Witwatersrand Library, 1989), 130–143.
64. *PSS* 2, 160.
65. Ronald L. Meek, *Social Science and the Ignoble Savage* (Cambridge: Cambridge University Press, 1976), 2. For a view of Goncharov's approach to nomadism as more positive—indeed, linked to Russian national identity—see Kleespies, *A Nation Astray.* Kleespies's argument relies on a more metaphoric understanding of nomadism, almost as equivalent to travel itself, whether actual or imaginary.
66. *PSS* 2, 154.
67. Barrow is cited in Huigen, *Knowledge and Colonialism,* 159; Coetzee, *White Writing,* 30–31.
68. Pratt, *Imperial Eyes,* 61; Coetzee, *White Writing,* 32, cited in Pratt, 61.
69. *PSS* 2, 166–167. On travelogues' inconsistency, see Tim Youngs, *The Cambridge Introduction to Travel Writing* (Cambridge: Cambridge University Press, 2012), 173; and David Spurr, *The Rhetoric of Empire: Colonial Discourse in Journalism, Travel Writing, and Imperial Administration* (Durham: Duke University Press, 1993), 168–169.
70. *PSS* 2, 247, 250.
71. Goncharov reflects on the activities of the historical Andrew Geddes Bain (1796–1864) quite accurately, see *PSS* 3, 585–586; and Davidson and Makrushin, *Oblik,* 310–311.

72. *PSS* 3, 585–586.

73. The longstanding rivalry between the British and the Dutch in southern Africa culminated in the Boer Wars of the 1880s–1900s. A discovery of rich diamond and gold deposits in the independent Boer Transvaal Republic and the Orange Free State led the British to intensify their annexation efforts. The particularly vicious Second Boer War (1899–1902), which horrified European public opinion, ended in British victory; see Davenport and Saunders, *South Africa,* 213–232, esp. 228; and *Illustrated History,* 238–261. Russia, where the pro-Boer sentiment ran high, sent volunteers; see Apollon Davidson and Irina Filatova, *The Russians and the Anglo-Boer War, 1899–1902* (Cape Town: Human and Rousseau, 1998).

74. *PSS* 2, 200, 217.

75. Thompson, *A History,* 73–80; *Illustrated History,* 102–109, 133–137; *The Shaping,* ed. Elphick and Giliomee, 432–471, 480–490; Martin Legassick, *The Struggle for the Eastern Cape, 1800–1854: Subjugation and the Roots of South African Democracy* (Johannesburg: KMM, 2010).

76. I. A. Goncharov, letter of March 19, 1953, to E. P. and N. A Maikov, in B. M. Engel'gardt, "Putevye pis'ma," 376. The sketch appears in *PSS* 2, 154–174.

77. For an explanation of the terminology used for Africa's ethnic groups in this books, see "Note on Primary Sources, Transliteration, Ethnonyms, and Place Names."

78. "Das Kap der guten Hoffnung," *Die Gegenwart: Eine encyclopädische Darstellung der neuesten Zeitgeschichte für alle Stände,* vol. 4 (Leipzig: F. A. Brockhaus, 1850), 507–554; see *PSS* 2, 158, and *PSS* 3, 578, n. to p. 158.

79. See I. A. Goncharov, *Fregat 'Pallada': Ocherki puteshestviia,* ed. and intro. by S. D. Muraveiskii (Moscow: Gos. izd-vo geograficheskoi literatury, 1949), republished in 1951 and 1957.

80. *PSS* 2, 156, emphasis in source.

81. *PSS* 2, 155–156, 165, 166. The encyclopedia mentions increasing profits and progress of commerce, industry, and agriculture. It stresses the colony's "boundless" potential, "Das Kap," 520, 554.

82. *PSS* 2, 160, 167. In the 1980s, the question of the British Empire's profitability was debated among historians, some of whom argued that Britain lost money on its empire. Proposing an appropriately nuanced conception of profit, Osterhammel rejects such arguments in *The Transformation,* 455–458.

83. *PSS* 2, 154.

84. *PSS* 2, 155, 158.

85. *PSS* 2, 156, 157, 158, 217. The Boers' Great Trek also led them, according to Goncharov, into "empty" space up north (*PSS* 2, 162). The German encyclopedia employs the same rhetoric (see, for example, "Das Kap," 531, 534).

86. Though it, too, takes the settlers' side, the German encyclopedia mentions as the root cause the violence of the Dutch against the native tribes and their steady push beyond colonial boundaries ("Das Kap," 532).

87. "Das Kap," 536; see also 533. On the Xhosa's conflicts with colonial society, see J. B. Peires, *The House of Phalo: The History of the Xhosa People in the Days of Their Inde-*

pendence (Berkeley: University of California Press, 1982); Peires, "The British and the Cape"; and Legassick, *The Struggle.*

88. *PSS* 2, 157, 168; see also 172.
89. Justin Livingstone, "*Missionary Travels,* Missionary Travails: David Livingstone and the Victorian Publishing Industry," in *David Livingstone: Man, Myth, and Legend,* ed. Sarah Worden (Edinburgh: National Museums Scotland, 2012), 33–51.
90. *PSS* 2, 155, 157, 163.
91. Andreas Kappeler, *The Russian Empire: A Multiethnic History,* tr. Alfred Clayton (New York: Longman, 2001), 183; see his treatment of the Caucasian war on 179–185; Charles King, *The Ghost of Freedom: A History of the Caucasus* (Oxford: Oxford University Press, 2008), 45. See also V. O. Bobrovnikov et al., eds., *Severnyi Kavkaz v sostave Rossiiskoi imperii* (Moscow: Novoe lit. obozrenie, 2007).
92. King, *The Ghost of Freedom,* 91–92; on the war more generally, see 20–98. On Russian views of Shamil, see Austin Jersild, *Orientalism and Empire* (Montreal: McGill-Queen's University Press, 2002), 110–125.
93. Some of Goncharov's terminology would have also resonated with Russia's Caucasian lexicon. For example, "peaceable Hottentots" (*mirnye gottentoty;* 168) calls to mind "peaceable highlanders" (*mirnye gortsy*), which denoted the Caucasians who were amenable to Russian rule. While comparisons to French Algeria were more common, Caucasus-Africa parallels were also in the air. Another Russian traveler who soon followed in Goncharov's African footsteps called Chief Sandile "a Kaffir Shamil" (*kafrskii Shamil,* see A. Vysheslavtsev, *Ocherki parom,* 85, cited in *PSS* 3, 582, n. to p. 173).
94. *PSS* 2, 239; see also 156.
95. Legassick, *The Struggle,* 78, 97; Martin Legassick and Robert Ross, "From Slave Economy to Settler Capitalism," in *The Cambridge History of South Africa* (Cambridge: Cambridge University Press, 2010), 311. On contemporary accounts of Smith, see Richard Price, *Making Empire: Colonial Encounters and the Creation of Imperia Rule in Nineteenth-Century Africa* (Cambridge: Cambridge University Press, 2008), 193; and Peires, *The House of Phalo,* 113–115, 165–169.
96. *PSS* 2, 171. For a prototype of Goncharov's Harry Smith, see "Das Kap," 548–552. In truth, many colonists petitioned for Smith's dismissal; see Legassick and Ross, "From Slave Economy," 311.
97. *PSS* 2, 171–171. On Maqoma, see Price, *Making Empire,* 108–109; and *Illustrated History,* 133–136. On Maqoma's retort, see Legassick, *The Struggle,* 79. Smith was also partial to having Xhosa chiefs kiss his feet (Peires, *The House of Phalo,* 165).
98. King, *The Ghost of Freedom,* 87; and Austin Jersild and Neli Melkadze, "The Dilemmas of Enlightenment in the Eastern Borderlands: The Theater and Library in Tbilisi," *Kritika: Explorations in Russian and Eurasian History* 3.1 (2002): 27–49.
99. Sir Charles Talbot (1801–1876) is mentioned in *The Frigate Pallada* on p. 127; see also *PSS* 3, 570 n. to p. 127. Sir George Cathcart (1791–1854) is mentioned in *The Frigate Pallada* on p. 173; see also *PSS* 3, 582 n. to p. 173.
100. J. B. Peires, *The Dead Will Arise: Nongqawuse and the Great Xhosa Cattle-Killing Movement of 1856–7* (Johannesburg: Ravan Press, 1989), 72. The Russian episode

in fact belongs to a tragic chapter in Xhosa history called the Cattle-Killing Movement. A particularly lethal cattle disease, brought by a Dutch ship, spread in the colony and decimated Xhosa cattle. When the epidemic reached catastrophic levels, the Xhosa began indiscriminate slaughter of all cattle, acting on a young girl's prophecy that this will cleanse the land of contagion and bring back the spirits of their ancestors. With the main source of their sustenance thus obliterated, only a quarter of the Xhosa survived the ensuing starvation (Peires, *The Dead,* 317, 319).

101. Michael Barnett, *Empire of Humanity: A History of Humanitarianism* (Ithaca: Cornell University Press, 2011), 15; Adam Hochschild, *Bury the Chains,* cited in Barnett, *Empire of Humanity,* 57.

102. Philip D. Curtin designates 1830–1852 as Britain's age of humanitarianism; see his *The Image of Africa: British Ideas and Action, 1780–1850* (Madison: University of Wisconsin Press, 1964). Peter Stamatov, *The Origins of Global Humanitarianism: Religion, Empires, and Advocacy* (Cambridge: Cambridge University Press, 2013), 177.

103. Alan Lester and Fae Dussart, *Colonization and the Origins of Humanitarian Governance: Protecting Aborigines across the Nineteenth-Century British Empire* (Cambridge: Cambridge University Press, 2014), 21.

104. Jane Burbank and Frederick Cooper, *Empires in World History: Power and the Politics of Difference* (Princeton: Princeton University Press, 2010), 290–293.

105. *PSS* 2, 167.

106. Matt Matsuda, *Pacific Worlds: A History of Seas, Peoples, and Cultures* (Cambridge: Cambridge University Press, 2012), 165; "Das Kap," 554. See also Thompson, *A History,* 64.

107. *PSS* 2, 165.

108. *PSS* 2, 173, 174, and *PSS* 3, 583 n. to pp. 173–174. In truth, although Cape laws no longer needed ratification, they could be vetoed by London, which would continue to appoint governors. Full independence for South Africa came only in 1934. On the establishment of the Cape's representative government, see Legassick and Ross, "From Slave Economy," 311–313.

109. Dmitrii A. Badalian, "Poniatie *konstitutsiia* v Rossii XVIII–XIX vekov," in *'Poniatiia o Rossii: K istoricheskoi semantike imperskogo perioda,* vol. 1, ed. A. Miller, D. Sdvizhkov, and I. Shirle (Moscow: Novoe lit. obozrenie, 2012), 151–174. Until the late nineteenth century, the word "constitution" was often replaced in Russian public discourse by euphemisms, such as "legal order" or "European political institutions" (Badalian, 151, 162).

110. *PSS* 3, 829. For the report's description of the political changes at the Cape, see [I. A. Goncharov], "Vsepoddanneishii," 168–169. Another member of the expedition, K. N. Possiet, referred to "the constitution" in his notes on the Cape published in the Naval Ministry's journal, a widely read but elite publication (K. N. Pos'et, "O plavanii fregata 'Pallada" iz Anglii na Mys Dobroi Nadezhdy i v Zondskii proliv, v 1853 godu," *Morskoi sbornik* 9 [1853]: 233–245, 244).

111. Thompson, *A History,* 64; Legassick and Ross, "From Slave Economy," 316–317.
112. *PSS* 2, 197.
113. Burbank and Cooper, *Empires,* 314.

2. Pineapples in Petersburg, Cabbage Soup on the Equator

1. *PSS* 2, 303, 541; see also 41, 86, 99, 510, 515, 668.
2. The definition is Manfred B. Steger's, from his *Globalization: A Very Short Introduction* (Oxford: Oxford University Press, 2013), 9. Similarly, Jürgen Osterhammel defines globalization as "accelerated and spatially extended mobilization of resources across the boundaries of states and civilizations"; see his *The Transformation of the World: A Global History of the Nineteenth Century* (Princeton: Princeton University Press, 2014), 911.
3. Jonathan Israel, *Dutch Primacy in World Trade, 1585–1740* (Oxford: Oxford University Press, 1989), 3; Janet Abu-Lughod, *Before European Hegemony: The World System A.D. 1250–1350* (New York: Oxford University Press, 1989).
4. Jürgen Osterhammel and Niels P. Petersson, *Globalization: A Short History* (Princeton: Princeton University Press, 2003), 49–56, 57, 150; and Osterhammel, *The Transformation,* xx. See also Barry K. Gills and William R. Thompson, *Globalization and Global History* (London: Routledge, 2006).
5. John Darwin, *After Tamerlane: The Rise and Fall of Global Empires, 1400–2000* (New York: Bloomsbury Press, 2000), 224, 223, 245.
6. Darwin, *After Tamerlane,* 237–238.
7. Osterhammel and Petersson, *Globalization,* 28, 80.
8. The statistics come from Osterhammel and Petersson, *Globalization,* 76–80 (Tom Standage's "internet" comparison is cited on 77). The total number of voluntary migrants for 1815–1914 is eighty-two million, which is triple the rate of post-1945 levels (Osterhammel, *The Transformation,* 154). The Russians statistics are corrected to account for Osterhammel's more detailed figures from *The Transformation,* 148. In the years 1871–1916 alone, over eight million people left areas of European Russia for imperial peripheries in the east and the south; see Willard Sunderland, "The 'Colonization Question': Visions of Colonization in Late Imperial Russia," *Jarbücher für Geschichte Osteuropas* 48 (2000): 213.
9. Gary B. Magee and Andrew S. Thompson, *Empire and Globalisation: Networks of People, Goods, and Capital in the British World, c. 1850–1914* (Cambridge: Cambridge University Press, 2010), xi, 16–17, 240; Asa Briggs, *The Age of Improvement, 1763–1867* (New York: David McKay Company, 1959), 389.
10. C. A. Bayly, *The Birth of the Modern World, 1780–1914: Global Connections and Comparisons* (Malden, MA: Blackwell, 2004).
11. Susanna Soojung Lim stresses the global dimension of Goncharov's portrayal of Asia in her *China and Japan in the Russian Imagination, 1685–1922* (London: Routledge, 2013); and her article "Whose Orient Is It? *Frigate Pallada* and Ivan Goncharov's Voyage," *Slavic and East European Journal* 53.1 (2009): 19–39.

12. Cited in Matt K. Matsuda, *Pacific Worlds: A History of Seas, Peoples, and Cultures* (Cambridge: Cambridge University Press, 2012), 192.
13. Philip D. Curtin, *Cross-Cultural Trade in World History* (Cambridge: Cambridge University Press, 1984), 251.
14. Briggs, *The Age of Improvement,* 392–393.
15. John K. Fairbank, "The Creation of the Treaty System," in *The Cambridge History of China,* vol. 10, ed. Denis Twitchett and John K. Fairbank (Cambridge: Cambridge University Press, 1978), 213–263.
16. Darwin, *After Tamerlane,* 271–272.
17. Leonard Gomes, *The Economics and Ideology of Free Trade: A Historical Review* (Northampton, MA: Edward Elgar, 2003), 4–5; Ronald Findlay and Kevin H. O'Rourke, *Power and Plenty: Trade, War, and the World Economy in the Second Millennium* (Princeton: Princeton University Press, 2009), 367–368.
18. Osterhammel, *The Transformation,* 455.
19. Findlay and O'Rourke, *Power and Plenty,* 365–378; Gomes, *The Economics and Ideology of Free Trade,* 34, 249.
20. Vincent Barnett, *History of Russian Economic Thought* (London: Routledge, 2005), 20. Smith's ideas gained wide popularity in Russia, see T. V. Artem'eva, "Adam Smit v Rossii," *Filosofskii vek. Almanakh,* vyp. 19 (2002): 39–66.
21. L. V. Kuprianova, *Tamozhenno-promyshlennyi protektsionizm i rossiiskie predprinimateli (40–80-e gody XIX veka)* (Moscow: Rossiiskaia Ak. nauk, Institut Rossiiskoi istorii, 1994), 8–78; E. V. Ereshko, "Protektsionizm i fritrederstvo v tamozhennoi politike Rossiiskoi imperii," *Istoricheskaia i sotsial'no-obrazovatel'naia mysl'* 1 (2009): 73–77; Walter McKenzie Pintner, *Russian Economic Policy under Nicholas I* (Ithaca: Cornell University Press, 1967), 237–249.
22. For discussions of Russian debates about protectionism and free trade, see I. G. Blium in, *Ocherki ekonomicheskoi mysli v Rossii v pervoi polovine XIX veka* (Moscow and Leningrad: Izd-vo Ak. nauk Soiuza SSR, 1940), 50–61, 129–136, 137–172; and J. F. Normano, *The Spirit of Russian Economics* (New York: The John Day Company, 1945), 12–35. Arguments advocating caution are well reflected in one source mostly contemporaneous to Goncharov: A. Semenov, *Izuchenie istoricheskikh svedenii o Rossiiskoi vneshnei torgovli i promyshlennosti s poloviny XVII-go stoletiia po 1858 god,* 3 vols. (St. Petersburg: I. I. Glazunov, 1859), 3:410–413.
23. Osterhammel, *The Transformation,* 455.
24. Vernon John Puryear, *International Economics and Diplomacy in the Near East* (Stanford: Stanford University Press, 1935), 6, 222. For the diplomatic and geopolitical genesis of the Crimean War, linked to rivalry over Asia, see also David Gillard, *The Struggle for Asia, 1828–1914: A Study in British and Russian Imperialism* (Mondon: Methuen, 1977); and Jane Burbank and Frederick Cooper, *Empires in World History: Power and the Politics of Difference* (Princeton: Princeton University Press, 2010), 340–341.
25. Osterhammel, *The Transformation,* 455.
26. Charles Brandon Boynton, *The Russian Empire, Its Resources, Government and Policy* (Cincinnati: Moore, Wilstach, Keys & Co., 1856), esp. 192–208.

27. Alfred J. Rieber, *Merchants and Entrepreneurs in Imperial Russia* (Chapel Hill: University of North Carolina Press, 1982), 71–73.
28. These are 1859 estimates by a Russian statistician, cited in Pintner, *Russian Economic Policy*, 3.
29. Rieber, *Merchants and Entrepreneurs*, 149–151; Jacob W. Kipp, "M. Kh. Reutern on the Russian State and Economy: A Liberal Bureaucrat during the Crimean Era, 1854–1860," *Journal of Modern History* 47.3 (1975): 437–459.
30. Burbank and Cooper, *Empires in World History*, 158.
31. Anthony Pagden, *Lords of All the Worlds: Ideologies of Empire in Spain, Britain and France c. 1500–c. 1850* (New Haven: Yale University Press, 1995), 115.
32. John Gallagher and Ronald Robinson, "The Imperialism of Free Trade," *Economic History Review*, Second Series, 6 (1953): 3, 13; Bernard Semmel, *The Rise of Free Trade Imperialism: Classic Political Economy, the Empire of Free Trade and Imperialism 1750–1850* (Cambridge: Cambridge University Press, 1970), 1–13; and Burbank and Cooper, *Empires in World History*, 248.
33. *PSS* 2, 482.
34. Anthony Preston and John Major, *Send a Gunboat! A Study of the Gunboat and Its Role in British Policy, 1854–1904* (London: Longmans, 1967); and James Cable, *The Political Influence of Naval Force in History* (London: Macmillan Press, 1998). The Crimean War can be seen as a case of Western Europeans' gunboat diplomacy with regard to Russia; with few exceptions, the war did not involve major naval battles, but relied instead on bombardment from French and British ships of Crimea's harbors and coastal fortresses.
35. Darwin, *After Tamerlane*, 12–15, 199–206, 263–294; Findlay and O'Rourke, *Power and Plenty*, 353–357; Osterhammel, *The Transformation*, 251, 650; Kenneth Pomeranz, *The Great Divergence: Europe, China, and the Making of Modern World Economy* (Princeton: Princeton University Press, 2000), 15–17. The precise causes of the "great divergence" are disputed, but historians have moved away from seeing it as an inexorable process stemming from Europe's inherent superiority. All historians cited in this note stress that state action and the military backing of trade greatly contributed to Europe's global economic ascendancy.
36. On Canton, see Matsuda, *Pacific Worlds*, 178. On Shanghai, see Fairbank, "The Creation of the Treaty System," 227–228.
37. *PSS* 2, 275–276.
38. David Igler, *The Great Ocean: Pacific Worlds from Captain Cook to the Gold Rush* (Oxford: Oxford University Press, 2013), 34; Mary Louise Pratt, *Imperial Eyes: Travel Writing and Transculturation*, 2nd ed. (London: Routledge, 2008), 72.
39. *PSS* 2, 467.
40. A. J. von Krusenshtern, *Voyage around the World in the years 1803, 1804, 1805, and 1806, by the Order of His Imperial Majesty Alexander the First*, 2 vols. (1813; New York: De Capo Press, 1968), 2:290, 292.
41. *PSS* 2, 367, 388. On Pogodin, see Nicholas V. Riasanovsky, "Asia through Russian Eyes," in *Russia and Asia: Essays on the Influence of Russia on the Asian Peoples*, ed. Wayne S. Vucinich (Stanford, CA: Hoover Institution Press, 1972), 14.

42. In the sketch "Twenty Years Since" (1874), serving as the closing chapter of *The Frigate Pallada,* Goncharov falsely claims that the British transported the Russians as shipwrecks, not as prisoners of war (*PSS* 2, 737). He might have been bound by official face-saving reports, or he might have knowingly lied. Given his personal contacts with the fellow officers, which continued beyond the expedition, it is unlikely he was ignorant of their real fate. See *PSS* 3, 794–795; George Lensen, *The Russian Push toward Japan: Russo-Japanese Relations, 1697–1875* (Princeton: Princeton University Press, 1959), 340–342; and George Lensen, *Russia's Japan Expedition of 1852 to 1855* (Gainesville: University of Florida Press, 1955), 102–110, 139–140.
43. With locations in London, New York, Calcutta, Manila, and Cape Town, the Boston firm Russell & Co. operated globally and was involved in opium trade in China (*PSS* 3, 665 n. to p. 414). It created "the largest merchant steam fleet in East Asia" (John C. Perry, *Facing West: Americans and the Opening of the Pacific* [London: Praeger, 1994], 78; see also Igler, *The Great Ocean,* 33–34). Throughout *The Frigate Pallada,* Goncharov mistakenly refers to Cunningham as Russia's consul, rather than a vice consul; see Shaohua Diao, "I. A. Goncharov i Kitai," in *Ivan A.Gončarov: Leben, Werk und Wirkung,* ed. Peter Thiergen (Cologne: Böhlau Verlag, 1994), 339. On Cunningham's multiple assignments, see Lensen, *Russia's Japan Expedition,* 180n13; and William McOmie, *The Opening of Japan, 1853–1855* (Folkestone: Global Oriental, 2006), 178.
44. Arkhimandrit Avvakum (Chetsnoi), *Dnevnik krugosvetnogo plavaniia na frigate "Pallada" (1853 god). Pis'ma iz Kitaia (1857–1858 gg.)* (Tver: Tverskoi gos. universitet, 1998), 77. For the mention of the Shanghai coal, see McOmie, *The Opening,* 180–182.
45. Lensen, *Russia's Japan Expedition,* 103–109; and Lensen, *The Russian Push,* 339.
46. *PSS* 2, 151, 231, 235, 266, 409, 544.
47. On cultural hybridity among trade diasporas prior to the eighteenth century, see Curtin, *Cross-Cultural Trade.*
48. *PSS* 2, 143, 556, 694. Félix had toured Russia.
49. *PSS* 2, 231.
50. *PSS* 2, 230, 289, 291, 436, 438.
51. Lim, *China and Japan,* 7.
52. On the importance of naval networks for connecting international government and business elites, see Ilya Vinkovetsky, *Russian America: An Overseas Colony of a Continental Empire, 1804–1867* (Oxford: Oxford University Press, 2011), 48–49.
53. Francis L. Hawks, *Narrative of the Expedition of an American Squadron to the China Seas and Japan, Performed in the Years 1852, 1853, and 1854 under the Command of Commodore M. C. Perry, United States Navy* (New York: D. Appleton and Co., 1856), 124, 125–126, 134, 151–152, 176. Hawks based his narrative on Perry's papers, official documents of the expedition, and accounts of other officers.
54. Carl Thompson, *Travel Writing* (London: Routledge, 2011), 144–145.
55. *PSS* 2, 431, 435–436.
56. For Perry's account of Bettelheim, see Hawks, *Narrative of the Expedition,* 176, 258–259, 572. On Bettelheim's extravagant excesses on the Ryukyu, which involved lodging his family illegally in the local temple, see George Kerr, *Okinawa: The History of an Island People* (Rutland, VT: Charles E. Tuttle Co., 1958), 279–296.

57. "Additional Instructions from the Russian Ministry of Foreign Affairs to Vice-Admiral Putiatin" (February 27, 1853), published in Edgar Franz, *Philipp Franz von Siebold and Russian Policy and Action on Opening Japan to the West in the Middle of the Nineteenth Century* (Munich: Iudicium, 2005), 223.
58. *PSS* 2, 509–510.
59. *PSS* 2, 254, 256, 259, 267, 273.
60. *PSS* 2, 256; Matsuda, *Pacific Worlds,* 103–113. The quote is on 112.
61. Voin A. Rimskii-Korsakov, *Baltika-Amur. Povestvovanie v pis'makh o plavaniiakh, prikliucheniiakh i razmyshleniiakh komandira shkuny 'Vostok'* (Khabarovsk: Khabarovskoe knizhnoe izd-vo, 1980), 92. On Goncharov's Singapore, see *PSS* 2, 263, 270–271.
62. *PSS* 2, 272.
63. Karl Marx, *The Communist Manifesto* (1848; New York: Norton, 2013), 64–65.
64. *PSS* 2, 272.
65. *PSS* 2, 273. The naturalist Charles Darwin was similarly shocked that the Tahitians consumed their pineapples wastefully, like turnips; Charles Darwin, *The Voyage of the Beagle,* 4th ed. (1839; New York: Bantam, 1972), 352.
66. Milton Ehre, *Oblomov and His Creator: The Life and Art of Ivan Goncharov* (Princeton: Princeton University Press, 1973), 152.
67. Ehre, *Oblomov and His Creator,* 144; Ingrid Kleespies, *A Nation Astray: Nomadism and National Identity in Russian Literature* (DeKalb: Northern Illinois University Press, 2012), 114.
68. *PSS* 2, 85. The Russian phrase is "*puteshetvuiu, sledovatel'no, naslazhdaius'*."
69. *PSS* 2, 273.
70. Findlay and O'Rourke, *Power and Plenty,* 353–355; Darwin, *After Tamerlane,* 12–13, 15, 199–206, 263. Burbank and Cooper, in *Empires in World History,* show Asian empires to have been successful also at managing multi-ethnicity and state building.
71. On this disjunction, see also Lim, *China and Japan,* 84.
72. *PSS* 2, 273, 285, 288, 386; Pratt, *Imperial Eyes,* 82. On Jardine, Matheson & Co., see "Return to China," *Economist*, July 4, 2015, 57.
73. *PSS* 2, 280–281. The affluence of Asian merchants was indeed a historical reality. In the 1850s, the fortune of the Cantonese merchant Howqua (Wu Bingjian) was several times greater than that of his contemporary and Britain's richest man, Nathan Rothschild; see Matsuda, *Pacific Worlds*, 182. On Perry, see Hawks, *Narrative of the Expedition*, 151–152.
74. Karl Marx, *Dispatches for the New York* Tribune*: Selected Journalism of Karl Marx*, ed. James Ledbetter (London: Penguin, 2007), 29.
75. My account of the Opium Wars is primarily based on Immanuel Hsü, *The Rise of Modern China* (New York: Oxford University Press, 1970), 168–195; and on John K. Fairbank, "The Creation of the Treaty System," 213–263. See also Zheng Yangwen, *The Social Life of Opium in China* (Cambridge: Cambridge University Press, 2005); Julia Lovell, *The Opium War: Drugs, Dreams and the Making of China* (London: Picador, 2011), 2; Carl A. Trocki, *Opium, Empire, and the Global Political Economy: A*

Study of the Asian Opium Trade, 1750–1950 (London: Routledge, 1999), 169; and Carl A. Trocki, *Opium and Empire: Chinese Society in Colonial Singapore, 1800–1910* (Ithaca: Cornell University Press, 1990), 50.

76. Jonathan D. Spence, *God's Chinese Son: The Taiping Heavenly Kingdom of Hong Xiuquan* (New York: Norton, 1996), 201; Karl Marx, "Revolution in China and in Europe" (published June 14, 1853), *Dispatches,* 3; Hsü, *The Rise of Modern China,* 219; Lovell, *The Opium War,* 9.
77. *PSS* 2, 431, 432.
78. Diao, "I. A. Goncharov i Kitai," 338; Lensen, *Russia's Japan Expedition,* 5.
79. George Feifer, *Breaking Open Japan: Commodore Perry, Lord Abe, and American Imperialism in 1853* (New York: Smithsonian Books / Collins, 2006), 321; "Secret Instructions" to Vice Admiral Putiatin from the Russian Ministry of the Navy, dated August 14, 1852, in the "Appendix" to Franz, *Philipp Franz von Siebold,* 211–212. For some, hitchhiking imperialism was "a badge of weakness and passivity" rather than avoidance of the stigma; see Stephen R. Platt, *Autumn in the Heavenly Kingdom: China, the West, and the Epic Story of the Taiping Civil War* (New York: Knopf, 2012), 37. See also Lensen, *Russia's Japan Expedition,* 129.
80. Joseph Fletcher, "Sino-Russian Relations, 1800–62," in *The Cambridge History of China,* vol. 10, ed. Denis Twitchett and John K. Fairbank (Cambridge: Cambridge University Press, 1978), 342–349; Hsü, *The Rise of Modern China,* 268; Sarah C. M. Paine, *Imperial Rivals: China, Russia, and Their Disputed Frontier* (Armonk, NY: M. E. Sharpe, 1996), 64–67.
81. *PSS* 2, 396, and *PSS* 3, 660 n. to p. 396, and 675 n. to p. 441. See also McOmie, *The Opening,* 179–180.
82. Fletcher, "Sino-Russian Relations," 335; Karl Marx, "Russian Trade with China," *Dispatches for the New York* Tribune (published April 7, 1857), 17–19; M. I. Sladkovskii, *Istoriia torgovo-ekonomicheskikh otnoshenii narodov Rossii s Kitaem (do 1917 g.)* (Moscow: Nauka, 1975), 210. In ten years' time, the Kiakhta trade would be decimated by the competition of tea shipped more cheaply from Canton, predominantly by the British. For this information I thank Robert Geraci, author of the forthcoming *Imperial Bazaar: Ethno-National Dimensions of Commerce in Russian Eurasia.*
83. Goncharov's account was included in a recent Chinese collection of historical documents about the Taiping Rebellion in Shanghai (Diao, "I. A. Goncharov i Kitai," 340).
84. Hsü, *The Rise of Modern China,* 270; Platt, *Autumn,* xxiii; Osterhammel, *The Transformation,* 120–121.
85. Among the lucky ones, the ratio of ethnic Manchus to the Han Chinese was 350 to 1; see Lovell, *The Opium War,* 44–45.
86. Though the Taiping Rebellion is not one of his case studies, Michael Adas discusses such movements in *Prophets of Rebellion: Millenarian Protest Movements against the European Colonial Order* (Chapel Hill: University of North Carolina Press). The Taiping belief system also had doctrinal similarities with American Mormonism,

which Perry happened to note; see Hawks, *Narrative of the Expedition,* 170; and Osterhammel, *The Transformation,* 548.

87. Philip A. Kuhn, "The Taiping Rebellion," in *The Cambridge History of China,* vol. 10, ed. Denis Twitchett and John K. Fairbank (Cambridge: Cambridge University Press, 1978), 269.
88. Spence, *God's Chinese Son,* 193.
89. W. G. Beasley, "The Foreign Threat and the Opening of the Ports," *Cambridge History of Japan,* vol. 5, ed. Marius B. Jansen (Cambridge: Cambridge University Press, 2008), 267–268; Igler, *The Great Ocean,* 34; Hawks, *Narrative of the Expedition,* 171.
90. All three missions are described in Spence, *God's Chinese Son,* 192–209.
91. Stephen Platt, *Autumn,* xxvi.
92. *PSS* 2, 410, 424.
93. *PSS* 2, 429.
94. Ehre, *Oblomov and His Creator,* 5.
95. Letter of E. V. Putiatin to L. G. Seniavin of 10 [22] December, 1853, *PSS* 3, 119–121. On Muravev, see *Graf Nikolai Nikolaevich Murav'ev-Amurskii,* vol. 2, ed. Ivan Barsukov (Moscow, 1891), 104–105. On Putiatin's visit to the imperial camp, see Avvakum, *Dnevnik,* 75.
96. Goncharov replicates this description of the Shanghai insurrection, with its narrative flare and humor expunged, in the official account of the expedition he later penned in Putiatin's name. This report was published in the Naval Ministry's journal, *Morskoi sbornik,* in 1856; see *PSS* 3, 185–186.
97. *PSS* 2, 434–435.
98. *PSS* 2, 424–425; *PSS* 3, 186–187.
99. *PSS* 2, 434, 697.
100. Platt, *Autumn,* xxvi; *PSS* 2, 429–430.
101. *PSS* 2, 605.
102. *PSS* 2, 261–262, 287–278, 414 (see also 217, 221, and 446); and Osterhammel, *The Transformation,* 288 (see 283–295 for his discussion of "colonial cities").
103. *PSS* 2, 137, 157, 283, 414, 441, 548.
104. *PSS* 2, 423.
105. The most elaborate anti-colonial characterization of *The Frigate Pallada* is V. A. Mikhel'son, *Gumanizm I. A. Goncharova i kolonial'nyi vopros* (Krasnodar: Krasnodarskii gos. pedagog. institut, 1965). Even some Chinese scholars consider Goncharov's portrayal of China as anti-colonial; see, for example, Diao, "I. A. Goncharov i Kitai." See also Peter Hulme, *Colonial Encounters: Europe and the Native Caribbean, 1492–1797* (London: Methuen, 1986), 253–254.
106. *PSS* 2, 430.
107. *PSS* 2, 422, 430. On the Cantonese, see *PSS* 3, 668 n. to p. 430. Goncharov's fellow crew-member witnessed Canton boys making throat-cutting gestures at the sight of foreigners (Rimskii-Korsakov, *Baltika-Amur,* 99).
108. See "Instructions from the Russian Ministry of Foreign Affairs to Vice-Admiral Putiatin" (August 23, 1852), in Franz, *Philipp Franz von Siebold,* 213.

109. *PSS* 2, 397, 412, 526.
110. Mark Bassin, *Imperial Visions: Nationalist Imagination and Geographic Expansion in the Russian Far East, 1840–1865* (Cambridge: Cambridge University Press, 1999).
111. *PSS* 2, 552–555, 562–563, 568, 572.
112. That the southern Ussuri was the cradle of the Manchu dynasty shows the radical extent of China's concessions; Paine, *Imperial Rivals*, 29, 61, 66, 70.
113. Karl Marx, "The British and Chinese Treaty," *Dispatches for the New York* Tribune, 40–41.
114. Paine, *Imperial Rivals*, 79; for Paine's description of what she calls the Russians' "masterful bluff" (64), see 57–70. See also Fletcher, "Sino-Russian Relations," 342–348. For the Russian view of this episode, see N. A. Samoilov, "Rossiia i Kitai," in *Rossia i vostok*, ed. S. M. Ivanov and B. N. Mel'nichenko (St. Petersburg: Izd-vo S.-Peterburgskogo universiteta, 2000), 267–271. On Chinese views, see the volumes edited by the Institute of Modern History of the Chinese Academy of Sciences, *Sha E qin Hua shi* [*The History of Tsarist Russia's Aggression against China*], 2nd ed., 4 vols. (Beijing, 2007). Victor Zatsepine also briefly characterizes them in *Beyond the Amur: Frontier Encounters between China and Russia, 1850–1950* (Vancouver: UBC Press, 2017), xi–xiii.

3. Prying Open Japan, Prospecting Korea

1. *PSS* 2, 313–314. In Russian, a "locked casket" is *zapertoi larets*.
2. For examples of this antiseptic view that span the Soviet and post-Soviet periods, see B. M. Engel'gardt, "'Puteshestvie vokrug sveta I. Oblomova': Glavy iz neizdannoi monografii B. M. Engel'gardta," *Literaturnoe nasledstvo*, vol. 102 (*I. A. Goncharov. Novye materialy i issledovaniia*) (Moscow: IMLI RAN "Nasledie," 2000), 24–82; A. R. Sadokova, "Iaponiia i iapontsy vo 'Fregate Pallada'"; I. A Goncharova, *Vostok v russkoi literature XVIII–nachala XX veka* (Moscow: IMLI RAN, 2004), 216–233.
3. Marius B. Jansen, *The Making of Modern Japan* (Cambridge, MA: Harvard University Press, 2000), 64; William McOmie, *The Opening of Japan, 1853–1855* (Folkestone: Global Oriental, 2006), xi. See also Andrew Gordon, *A Modern History of Japan: From Tokugawa Times to the Present* (Oxford: Oxford University Press, 2003), 17–19.
4. George Feifer, *Breaking Open Japan: Commodore Perry, Lord Abe, and American Imperialism in 1853* (New York: Smithsonian Books / Collins, 2006), 38–43; George Lensen, *The Russian Push toward Japan: Russo-Japanese Relations, 1697–1875* (Princeton: Princeton University Press, 1959), 9–14; George Lensen, *Russia's Japan Expedition of 1852 to 1855* (Gainesville: University of Florida Press, 1955), xv.
5. Matt Matsuda, *Pacific Worlds: A History of Seas, Peoples, and Cultures* (Cambridge: Cambridge University Press, 2012), 101; William Heine, *With Perry to Japan*, tr. and ed. Frederic Trautmann (Honolulu: University of Hawaii Press, 1990), 75. Heine was a German illustrator hired for Perry's expedition.
6. Lensen, *The Russian Push*, 14.

7. *PSS* 2, 326; John J. Stephan, *The Russian Far East: A History* (Stanford: Stanford University Press, 1994), 38. Rezanov acted on his own initiative and not the government's order. Golovnin's famous account of his captivity, which Goncharov studied carefully, mentions Rezanov's attacks. The Soviet edition of Golovnin's account, incidentally, portrays the attacks as wholly justified, on account of the islands being simply "Russian land"; see V. M. Golovnin, *Zapiski flota kapitana Golovnina o prikliucheniiakh ego v plenu u iapontsev v 1811, 1812, i 1813 godakh* (1816; Khabarovsk: Khabarovskoe knizhnoe izd-vo, 1972), 500n19.
8. Akira Iriye, "Japan's Drive to Great-Power Status," in *The Emergence of Meiji Japan*, ed. Marius B. Jansen (Cambridge: Cambridge University Press, 1995), 283–285, 293; Michael Auslin, *Negotiating with Imperialism: The Unequal Treaties and the Culture of Japanese Diplomacy* (Cambridge, MA: Harvard University Press, 2004), 146–200.
9. On the United States' and Russia's push to the Pacific, see David Igler, *The Great Ocean: Pacific Worlds from Captain Cook to the Gold Rush* (Oxford: Oxford University Press, 2013); Ilya Vinkovetsky, *Russian America: An Overseas Colony of a Continental Empire, 1804–1867* (Oxford: Oxford University Press, 2011); and Mark Bassin, *Imperial Visions: Nationalist Imagination and Geographical Expansion in the Russian Far East, 1840–1865* (New York: Cambridge University Press, 1999).
10. Lensen, *Russia's Japan Expedition,* vii, xxiii, and *The Russian Push;* John Curtis Perry, *Facing West: Americans and the Opening of the Pacific* (London: Praeger, 1994).
11. Lensen, *Russia's Japan Expedition,* 2, 3, 4, 6, 69. The repairs in Portsmouth and in the Cape of Good Hope alone exceeded five weeks' time, which amounted to Putiatin's lag behind Perry. Putiatin knew already on Cape Verde, in February 1853, that Perry had reached the shores of China (Lensen, *Russia's Japan Expedition,* 3).
12. Viktor Shklovskii, "I. A. Goncharov, avtor 'Fregata Pallada,'" in his *Izbrannoe v dvukh tomakh,* vol. 1 (Moscow: Khudozh. lit., 1983), 379. Putiatin was so versed in Orthodox ritual that he used to correct the ship chaplain; A. M. Linden, "Zapiski A. M. Lindena," *Russkaia starina* 4 (1905): 135.
13. "Secret Instructions" to Vice-Admiral Putiatin from the Russian Ministry of the Navy, dated August 14, 1852; and "Additional Instructions" from the Russian Ministry of Foreign Affairs to Vice-Admiral Putiatin, dated February 27, 1853, both included in the "Appendix" to Edgar Franz, *Philipp Franz von Siebold and Russian Policy and Action on Opening Japan to the West in the Middle of the Nineteenth Century* (Munich: Iudicium, 2005), 203–224.
14. I thank William McOmie for offering me helpful guidance on the subject of Russia's non-race with America.
15. Feifer, *Breaking Open Japan,* 5; Lensen, *The Russian Push,* 318; McOmie, *The Opening,* 92; Perry, *Facing West,* 84.
16. Francis L. Hawks, *Narrative of the Expedition of an American Squadron to the China Seas and Japan, Performed in the Years 1852, 1853, and 1854 under the Command of Commodore M. C. Perry, United States Navy* (New York: D. Appleton and Co., 1856), 415. Hawks apparently does not bother to discriminate between Japanese and Chinese officials (only the latter were called "mandarins").

17. Lensen, *Russia's Japan Expedition,* 83, 132.
18. Arkhimandrit Avvakum (Chestnoi), *Dnevnik krugosvetnogo plavaniia na frigate "Pallada" (1853 god). Pis'ma iz Kitaia (1857–1858 gg.)* (Tver: Tverskoi gos. universitet, 1998), 82–83. Rimsky-Korsakov corroborated Putiatin's stinginess, *PSS* 3, 418n3.
19. Lensen, *The Russian Push,* 317–318. The Japanese later offered the Russians preferential treatment by promising to grant them trade before any other nation. In what seems like a case of uncoordinated diplomacy due to problems with communications, this promise was not kept; see Lensen, *Russia's Japan Expedition,* 64, 117; and McOmie, *The Opening,* 461.
20. On the gift exchange with the Americans, see Hawks, *Narrative of the Expedition,* 413.
21. Lensen, *The Russian Push,* 300–301, 329, 338–339, 344–354; Lensen, *Russia's Japan Expedition,* 128–129.
22. McOmie, *The Opening,* xvi, 456–465; Lensen, *The Russian Push,* 337; Lensen, *Russia's Japan Expedition,* 134, 153, 154. McOmie persuasively argues that the real breakthrough was the favorable reply of the Roju to Nesselrode's letter, and that Perry's treaty, unlike Putiatin's, was too limited to have any real impact, especially on trade.
23. Lensen, *Russia's Japan Expedition,* 129.
24. Lensen, *Russia's Japan Expedition,* 81, 150; *PSS* 3, 417.
25. Kunitake's remark comes from a compilation of his writings in *Japan Rising: The Iwakura Embassy to the USA and Europe 1871–1873,* ed. Chushichi Tsuzuki and R. Jules Young (Cambridge: Cambridge University Press, 2009), 350; for other examples, see Lensen, *The Russian Push,* 161; McOmie, *The Opening,* xiii, 475. The Japanese anime film is titled *Bakumatsu-no Spasibo* (dir. Satoshi Dezaki, 1997). It aired in Russia under the title *A Difficult Friendship* (*Trudnaia druzhba*), see *Kommersant,* February 19, 1998, http://www.kommersant.ru/doc/192892.
26. *PSS* 2, 606.
27. Hawks, *Narrative of the Expedition,* 79 (Putiatin's letter was dated November 12, 1853). P. F. von Siebold publicized this view in a pamphlet *Urkundliche Darstellung der Bestrebungen von Niederland und Russland zur Eröffnung Japans für die Schiffahrt und den Seehandel aller Nationen* (1854). Its Russian translation appeared in *Morskoi sbornik* 15.2 (1855): 1–41. McOmie finds merit in von Siebold's argument (*The Opening,* 458–460). On von Siebold's contributions to the planning of the Russian Expedition of 1852–1854, see Franz, *Philipp Franz von Siebold;* and Herbert Plutschow, *Phillip Franz von Siebold and the Opening of Japan: A Reevaluation* (Folkestone: Global Oriental, 2007), 80–107. Franz discovered that both the "Additional Instructions" for Putiatin from the Russian Ministry of Foreign Affairs and the Russian Treaty of Shimoda were based on von Siebold's drafts. Von Siebold visited Russia on Nesselrode's invitation in early 1853. Though widely, and falsely, perceived as a Russian spy, von Siebold seemed to freely dispense political advice about how to open Japan to just about any western entity that would listen. His offer of services to the Americans was rejected.
28. Hawks, *Narrative of the Expedition,* 78–79, 452. For critiques of Hawks's allegations see Franz, *Philipp Franz von Siebold,* 92; and McOmie, *The Opening,* 440.

29. Lensen, *Russia's Japan Expedition,* 119. Putiatin bought the Chinese language copies of European treaties in the Shanghai printing office of *The North China Herald;* see Avvakum, *Dnevnik,* 73. For the text of both treaties, see Lensen, *Russia's Japan Expedition,* 122–125, 158–160.
30. What Goncharov interprets as cowardice was actually a justifiable concern that Japan's own shore guards may take the cannon salutes to be hostile and start firing back (*PSS* 453–454, 467, 486; see also Lensen, *Russia's Japan Expedition,* 41–42).
31. Although originally headed for Edo, Putiatin was told in the instructions he received on the Bonin Islands to sail instead to Nagasaki. This sudden change was based on von Siebold's advice to the Russian government; Franz, *Philipp Franz von Siebold,* 217. For Japanese reactions to the Russians, see Feifer, *Breaking Open Japan,* 218–223; Lensen, *Russia's Japan Expedition,* 130–132; Shintaro Nakamura, *Iapontsy i russkie: iz istorii kontaktov* (Moscow: Progress, 1983), 169; McOmie, *The Opening,* 215–220.
32. Golovnin, *Zapiski flota kapitana.*
33. The Russian title was *Russkie v Iaponii v kontse 1853 i v nachale 1854 godov (Iz putevykh zametok)* (St. Petersburg, 1855).
34. Edward W. Said, *Culture and Imperialism* (New York: Vintage, 1994), 62.
35. Mary Louise Pratt, *Imperial Eyes: Travel Writing and Transculturation,* 2nd ed. (London: Routledge, 2008), 9, 66.
36. *PSS* 2, 314.
37. *PSS* 2, 316, 370.
38. *PSS* 2, 325. Though ungenerous, this was not inaccurate; see the description of Tokugawa Japan as "a police state par excellence" in Lensen, *The Russian Push,* 12.
39. *PSS* 2, 326, 348; McOmie, *The Opening,* 96–98, 142–143. Unbeknownst to Goncharov, it was Japanese custom not to invoke the name of the Emperor publicly.
40. *PSS* 2, 318. Matthew Perry, when asked the same question, replied with supreme diplomacy that dispatching a letter on many ships "was a greater compliment to their emperor—probably!" (Lensen, *Russia's Japan Expedition,* 9).
41. *PSS* 2, 314. Goncharov's word for "caressing" is *laskaia.*
42. Edward W. Said, *Orientalism* (New York: Vintage, 1979), 92, emphasis in source.
43. See Lowell Tillett, *The Great Friendship: Soviet Historians on the Non-Russian Nationalities* (Chapel Hill: University of North Carolina Press, 1969). The Russian title of Pushkin's poem is "Klevetnikam Rossii."
44. *PSS* 2, 450.
45. McOmie, *The Opening,* 164; see also Voin A. Rimskii-Korsakov, *Baltika-Amur. Povestvovanie v pis'makh o plavaniiakh, prikliucheniiakh i razmyshleniiakh komandira shkuny 'Vostok'* (Khabarovsk: Khabarovskoe knizhnoe izd-vo, 1980), 137. For Rimsky-Korsakov's other critical remarks about Putiatin see 47, 129–130; for an episode in which the Japanese negotiators outsmarted Putiatin, see 236–237.
46. A. J. von Krusenshtern, *Voyage around the World in the years 1803, 1804, 1805, and 1806, by the Order of His Imperial Majesty Alexander the First,* vol. 1 (1813; New York: De Capo Press, 1968), ch. 12.
47. McOmie, *The Opening,* 164; *PSS* 2, 341, 348. Lensen supplies the governor's name in *The Russian Push,* 312; Goncharov refers to him as "the governor of Nagasaki."

48. *PSS* 2, 330, 331, 339–340, 345, 371. The pun contrasts *krainii Vostok* and *krainiaia skuka*. Today the standard Russian term for the Far East is *dal'nii Vostok*.
49. Steve Clark, "Introduction," in *Travel Writing and Empire: Postcolonial Theory in Transit*, ed. Steve Clark (New York: Zed Books, 1999), 11.
50. In addition to Hawks, *Narrative of the Expedition* (e.g., 391) such sentiments also suffuse William Heine's account (*With Perry to Japan*).
51. *PSS* 2, 329, 334, 346, 368.
52. *PSS* 2, 474.
53. *PSS* 2, 467–468, 599; Lensen, *Russia's Japan Expedition*, 42–43, 52–54, 146–147.
54. *PSS* 2, 482, 484–485. On the Russian empire's coopting of elites, see Jane Burbank and Frederick Cooper, *Empires in World History* (Princeton: Princeton University Press, 2010), 251, 276; Andreas Kappeler, *The Russian Empire: A Multiethnic History*, tr. Alfred Clayton (New York: Longman, 2001).
55. *PSS* 2, 334. When the Russians traipse around the harbor in little sloops, Goncharov claims that they do so in defense of "the rights of Europeans," teaching the Japanese that "water belongs to all" (*PSS* 2, 384). One wonders if this rule would apply equally to Japanese sloops in view of St. Petersburg embankments.
56. *PSS* 2, 334.
57. *PSS* 2, 372. The full scene spans 350–356.
58. *PSS* 2, 353.
59. *PSS* 2, 353; and *PSS* 3, 642 n. to p. 353.
60. *PSS* 2, 353–354.
61. *PSS* 2, 351. Goncharov added "we" to this passage only in the edition of 1879, see *PSS* 3, 266.
62. *PSS* 2, 355, 356, 449–450.
63. *PSS* 2, 330, 349–350; and Heine, *With Perry*, 67–68.
64. *PSS* 2, 472.
65. In a fitting coincidence, the term "realpolitik" was coined in the year of Perry's and Putiatin's visits to Japan, 1853, though the phenomenon certainly predates the term; see Jürgen Osterhammel, *The Transformation of the World: A Global History of the Nineteenth Century* (Princeton: Princeton University Press, 2014), 398. See also *PSS* 2, 471.
66. Susanna Soojung Lim, "Whose Orient Is It? *Frigate Pallada* and Ivan Goncharov's Voyage," *Slavic and East European Journal* 53.1 (2009): 29. Rimsky-Korsakov also favored Perry's more militant tactics and disparaged what he saw as Putiatin's ineptness and meekness; see McOmie, *The Opening*, 167–168; and *PSS* 2, 374, 390–392.
67. *PSS* 2, 470–471.
68. *PSS* 2, 320. These were typically fake "discoveries," which involved "making one's way to the region and asking the local inhabitants if they knew any big lakes, etc. in the area, then hiring them to take you there, whereupon with their guidance and support, you proceeded to discover what they already knew" (Pratt, *Imperial Eyes*, 198).
69. Pratt, *Imperial Eyes*, 200–201, 205, 209, 213.
70. *PSS* 2, 321.

71. David Spurr draws attention to the exposure of such "fundamental economics of perception" in George Orwell's essay "Marrakech" (1939). "One sees what it profits one to see, what one has a share or stake in, a claim upon," Spurr writes, commenting on the following passage from Orwell: "In a tropical landscape one's eye takes in everything except the human beings. It takes in the dried-up soil, the prickly pear, the palm tree and the distant mountain, but it always misses the peasant hoeing his patch. He is the same colour as the earth, and a great deal less interesting to look at" (cited in David Spurr, *The Rhetoric of Empire: Colonial Discourse in Journalism, Travel Writing, and Imperial Administration* [Durham: Duke University Press, 1993], 191–192).
72. *PSS* 2, 197, 369. Pratt calls the estranging of people from land, culture, and history "textual apartheid," see her *Imperial Eyes,* 52, 60.
73. *PSS* 2, 321–322.
74. *PSS* 2, 386. On what Pratt calls the trope of *disponibilité,* see her *Imperial Eyes,* 201.
75. Hawks, *Narrative of the Expedition,* 309–311.
76. *PSS* 2, 322, 372.
77. *PSS* 2, 319, 320, 387–386; Pratt, *Imperial Eyes,* 58.
78. *PSS* 2, 314; Krusenshtern, *Voyage around the World,* 1: ch. 4. Goncharov's information about Japan's natural resources comes from his predecessor in Japan: Golovnin, *Zapiski flota kapitana,* see *PSS* 3, 608, 625–626.
79. McOmie, *The Opening,* 147, 163, 182; Rimskii-Korsakov, *Baltika-Amur,* 120, 122, 124, 141, 147. The *Vostok,* which transported Goncharov to the Siberian port of Ayan, ran on Sakhalin coal (*PSS* 2, 631).
80. Charles Stuart Cochrane, *Journal of a Residence and Travels in Colombia during the Years 1823 and 24* (1825), cited in Pratt, *Imperial Eyes,* 146.
81. Pratt, *Imperial Eyes,* 59.
82. *PSS* 2, 347.
83. Sarah Tarlow, *The Archaeology of Improvement in Britain, 1750–1850* (Cambridge: Cambridge University Press, 2007), 20; and Raymond Williams, *The Country and the City* (1973; New York: Oxford University Press, 2011), 61–62.
84. Joseph Andrews, cited in Pratt, *Imperial Eyes,* 147; and Perry McDonough Collins, *Siberian Journey Down the Amur to the Pacific, 1856–1857,* 2nd ed., ed. Charles Vevier (Madison: University of Wisconsin Press, 2011), 187.
85. *PSS* 2, 454.
86. Krusenshtern, *Voyage around the World,* 2:65–66; Collins, *Siberian Journey,* 252, 298.
87. Krusenshtern, *Voyage around the World,* 2:286; Charles Darwin, *The Voyage of the Beagle,* 4th ed. (1839; New York: Bantam, 1972), 420.
88. *PSS* 2, 531–532, 541, 563, 568.
89. Lensen, *The Russian Push,* 423–424; see also George A. Lensen, *Report from Hokkaido: The Remains of Russian Culture in Northern Japan* (Hakodate: The Municipal Library of Hakodate, 1954), 152–155. The embrace of the use-it-or-lose it approach to Manchuria by the Russians and the Japanese was also a leading cause of the 1904 war between them.

90. *PSS* 2, 493, 501.

91. Basil Hall, *Account of a Voyage of Discovery to the West Coast of Corea and the Great Loo-Choo Island* (Philadelphia: Abraham Small, 1818), 188, 192, 193, 200. Kerr confirms that from the founding of the principality in the fourteenth century up to the opening by the Europeans in the middle of the nineteenth, the Ryukyu people governed themselves without the use of arms; see George Kerr, *Okinawa: The History of an Island People* (Rutland, VT: Charles E. Tuttle Co., 1958), 3.

92. Pratt, *Imperial Eyes,* 44; *PSS* 2, 496, 507.

93. *PSS* 2, 506–509. Kerr, *Okinawa,* 249–275; on erratic Bettelheim's deceitful and egregiously disrespectful treatment of the Ryukyuans, see 279–296. It should be noted that travelogue accounts exaggerated the prosperity of the Ryukyu Islands. A steady stream of natural disasters in the first half of the nineteenth century, compounded by the burdens of victualing increasing numbers of ships (accepting payments from whom was prohibited by law), led to sharp economic decline (Kerr, *Okinawa,* 241–245).

94. *PSS* 2, 505, 509, 512; see also Heine, *With Perry,* 38, 56, 58.

95. *PSS* 2, 496.

96. *PSS* 2, 501.

97. *PSS* 2, 496.

98. I refer here to the ambivalence internal to individual texts. For anti-imperial critiques formulated in the age of the Enlightenment, see Sankar Muthu, *Enlightenment against Empire* (Princeton: Princeton University Press, 2003). Muthu argues that anti-imperialist political thinking virtually disappeared by the mid-nineteenth century (5). It resurfaced, however, toward the century's end. On Chekhov, see Edyta Bojanowska, "Chekhov's *The Duel,* or How to Colonize Responsibly," in *Chekhov for the 21st Century*, ed. Carol Apollonio and Angela Brintlinger (Bloomington, IN: Slavica, 2012), 31–48.

99. *PSS* 2, 497. On Perry's claim on the Ryukyu Islands, which ignored his government's explicit instructions, see Kerr, *Okinawa,* 297–341. Kerr offsets the whitewashed official story of Perry's expedition by unofficial critiques voiced by the Commodore's own chagrined officers.

100. *PSS* 2, 499; Hawks, *Narrative of the Expedition,* 230, 332, 352–356; Willard Sunderland, "Imperial Space: Territorial Thought and Practice in the Eighteenth Century," in *Russian Empire: Space, People, and Power, 1700–1930*, ed. Jane Burbank, Mark von Hagen, and Anatolyi Remnev (Bloomington: Indiana University Press, 2008), 52. (The Russian plaques bore the inscription *Zemlia Rossiiskogo Vladeniia.*) Today, post-colonial parodies of such arbitrary acts of possession are used for political protest. Australia's Koori activists planned to claim the British Isles by planting the Aboriginal flag in England in 1988, around the bicentenary of Captain Cook's landing in Botany Bay; see Matsuda, *Pacific Worlds,* 165.

101. *PSS* 2, 503–504, 514; Said, *Culture and Imperialism,* 64.

102. *PSS* 2, 448, 520.

103. *PSS* 2, 338.

104. Lensen, *Russia's Japan Expedition,* ix.

105. *PSS* 2, 350, 364, 388.
106. *PSS* 2, 342. Insisting on escorts served an important public-relations function in *sakoku*-era Japan. For foreigners to be publicly seen as coming onto Japanese land unassisted by Japanese officials would undermine the image of the government as capable of enforcing Japanese laws.
107. *PSS* 2, 341, 344; Osterhammel, *The Transformation,* 68, 72.
108. *PSS* 2, 357, 359; Lensen, *Russia's Japan Expedition,* 59.
109. On the Japanese perception of Goncharov as one of the main negotiators, see [Kadzukhiko Savada (Saitama)], "I. A. Goncharov glazami iapontsev," in *Ivan A. Gončarov: Leben, Werk und Wirkung*, ed. Peter Thiergen (Cologne: Böhlau Verlag, 1994), 127; Yoshikazu Nakamura, "I. A. Goncharov u iapontsev," in *Literatura i iskusstvo v sisteme kul'tury*, ed. B. B. Pitorovskii (Moscow: "Nauka," 1988), 411–420; and Aleksandr Genis, "Goncharov o iapontsakh i iapopntsy o Goncharove," *Novoe literaturnoe obozrenie* 12 (1995): 451–453. Goncharov reportedly planned to save the material about negotiations for a separate book. No such records have been preserved; see Lensen, *Russia's Japanese Expedition,* viii. Lensen summarizes Nesselrode's letter and the Japanese reply in *The Russian Push,* 326–328.
110. *PSS* 2, 360, 461, 462.
111. *PSS* 2, 464, 479; Hawks, *Narrative of the Expedition,* 443. On Russian tea and sugar, see Lensen, *Russia's Japan Expedition,* 46, 53.
112. *PSS* 2, 475; Lensen, *Russia's Japan Expedition,* 49–50.
113. *PSS* 2, 464–465. On Japanese reactions, see Nakamura, "I. A. Goncharov u iapontsev," 418; see also Lim, *China and Japan,* 87.
114. *PSS* 2, 361, 363–364. Many of Goncharov's sympathetic comments about Japan come from Golovnin's account (Golovnin, *Zapiski flota kapitana,* 299, 305, 331).
115. *PSS* 2, 362, 457.
116. W. G. Beasley, "The Foreign Threat and the Opening of the Ports," *Cambridge History of Japan,* vol. 5, ed. Marius B. Jansen (Cambridge: Cambridge University Press, 2008), 273–277; Lensen, *Russia's Japan Expedition,* xxiv-xxv; McOmie, *The Opening,* 137–139, 193–201. See also *PSS* 2, 487.
117. *PSS* 2, 361, 455, 478, 483. Goncharov also contrasted China's resistance to westernization to Russia's successful course of it, but later deleted this passage; see *PSS* 3, 306 (note to p. 603, l.26).
118. *PSS* 2, 329. The Americans viewed the curiosity of the Japanese as a sign of intelligence; Hawks, *Narrative of the Expedition,* 306–307.
119. Goncharov, "Twenty Years Since" (Cherez dvadtsat' let), *PSS* 2, 712–740. See also Lensen, *Russia's Japan Expedition,* 104, 105, 141; and McOmie, *The Opening,* 464. Of the Japanese artisans who helped construct the schooner, Captain Mizuno Hironori later wrote that "these workmen were the first to learn the art of occidental shipbuilding"; cited in Lensen, *The Russian Push,* 339.
120. After the war, the 1899 *Pallada* was recovered, renamed the *Tsugaru*, and recommissioned by the Imperial Japanese Navy; see Hansgeorg Jentschura, Dieter Jung, and Peter Michael, *Warships of the Imperial Japanese Navy, 1869–1945*, tr. A. Preston and J. D. Brown (Annapolis, MD: Naval Institute Press, 1977), 102.

121. Lensen, *Russia's Japan Expedition,* xi, 146; Lensen *The Russian Push,* 344; Lensen "The Historicity of *Fregat Pallada,*" *Modern Language Notes* 68.7 (1953): 462–466; *PSS* 2, 381.
122. Key-Hiuk Kim, *The Last Phase of the East Asian World Order: Korea, Japan, and Chinese Empire, 1860–1882* (Berkeley: University of California Press, 1980), 330; Iriye, "Japan's Drive," 293, 294; Feifer, *Breaking Open Japan,* 304, 305; Lensen, *Russia's Japan Expedition,* xxvi.
123. *PSS* 3, 196; Lensen, *Russia's Japan Expedition,* 71; Lim, "Whose Orient Is It?" 34n22.
124. *PSS* 2, 594–595; Susanna Soojung Lim, *China and Japan in the Russian Imagination, 1685–1922: To the Ends of the Orient* (London: Routledge, 2013), 78.
125. *PSS* 2, 597, 598, 599, 615, 517; Martina Deuchler, *Confucian Gentlemen and Barbarian Envoys: The Opening of Korea, 1875–1885* (Seattle: University of Washington Press, 1977), 92.
126. *PSS* 2, 598–599; A. S. Pushkin, *Sobranie sochinenii v piati tomakh,* vol. 4 (St. Petersburg: Bibliopolis, 1994), 221; Hawks, *Narrative of the Expedition,* 194, 250.
127. *PSS* 2, 374, 600, 618–619; see also Lensen, *Russia's Japan Expedition,* 71.
128. *PSS* 2, 613, 618–619. On the renaming by Britons and Americans, see Hawks, *Narrative of the Expedition,* 230; Pat Barr, *The Coming of the Barbarians* (London: Macmillan, 1967), 25; and Perry, *Facing West,* 92. On the Russians' renaming of Korean sites, see Lensen, *Russia's Japan Expedition,* 71; and B. Engel'gardt, "Putevye pis'ma I. A. Goncharova iz krugosvetnogo plavaniia," *Literaturnoe nasledstvo,* vol. 22–24 (Moscow: Zhurnal'no-Gazetnoe ob"edinenie, 1935), 325. On Goncharov Island, see *PSS* 3, 409n3; "Mayang-do," http://kp.geoview.info/mayangdo,1874458; and Mayang Island Missil Base description, Nuclear Threat Institute (NTI), Washington, DC, March 1, 2003, http://www.nti.org/learn/facilities/213/.
129. On Oblomov's gown, see *PSS* 5, 7 (*vostochnyi khalat*).
130. *PSS* 2, 601, 602, 604; Dipesh Chakrabarty, *Provincializing Europe: Postcolonial Thought and Historical Difference* (Princeton: Princeton University Press, 2000), 8.
131. *PSS* 2, 601–602. The Chinese term for "fatherland" then in use was "Guojia," which denoted a "family-state" as early as the third century BC. By the nineteenth it acquired the meaning of a "nation" or "fatherland." I thank Richard VanNess Simmons for helping me check up on Goncharov's Russian sinologist.
132. *PSS* 2, 604.
133. Gordon, *A Modern History,* 10; Kerr, *Okinawa,* 3. Today, three-fifths of the American military personnel in Japan are stationed on the once idyllic Okinawa, a staggering proportion in view of the fact that the island represents merely 0.6 per cent of Japan's territory. As of late, plans to expand these bases and airstrips stirred Okinawans to stage protests; see "Base Issues," *Economist,* April 25, 2015, 37–39; Martin Fackler, "Premier's Push for U.S. Base in Okinawa Stirs Protests," *New York Times,* July 5, 2015, A4, 9.
134. *PSS* 2, 387, 466, 603, 609.
135. *PSS* 2, 351–352, 355, 361, 365.
136. *PSS* 2, 355.
137. *PSS* 2, 355.

138. *PSS* 2, 614, 616–617, 621.
139. *PSS* 2, 600, 611.
140. *PSS* 2, 617.
141. Jansen, *The Making of Modern Japan,* 355–361. The full account is available in *The Iwakura Embassy, 1871–73: A True Account of the Ambassador Extraordinary and Plenipotentiary's Journey of Observation through the United States of America and Europe,* 4 vols. (Chiba: The Japan Documents, 2002).
142. *Japan Rising,* 328; the full excerpt from Kume Kunitake's report on Russia appears on 326–350. For full text, see *The Iwakura Embassy, 1871–73,* 4:9–104. Russian scholars suspect an influence of Britain's anti-Russian propaganda on the views of the Japanese, see N. Iu. Krainiuk, N. A. Samoilov, et al., "Rossiia i Iaponiia," in *Rossia i vostok*, ed. S. M. Ivanov and B. N. Mel'nichenko (St. Petersburg: Izd-vo S.-Peterburgskogo universiteta, 2000), 413. Marquis de Custine's travel account of Russia was titled *La Russie en 1839* (1843). On the *Meiji gekkan* ranking, see Togawa Tsuguo, "The Japanese View of Russia before and after the Meiji Restoration," in *A Hidden Fire: Russian and Japanese Cultural Encounters, 1868–1926*, ed. J. Thomas Rimer (Stanford: Stanford University Press, 1995), 215.
143. *Japan Rising,* 350.

4. Eastward Ho!

1. *PSS* 2, 633. For the saying cited in the epigraph, see *PSS* 2, 696.
2. Seymour Becker, "Contributions to a Nationalist Ideology: Histories of Russia in the First Half of the Nineteenth Century," *Russian History/Histoire Russe* 13.4 (1986): 331–353. The Russians did not use the phrase "manifest destiny" in referring to their own continental expansion, though they viewed it in such terms. In the rest of this chapter, I therefore adopt this phrase for the Russian context.
3. See, for example, Lord Macaulay's famous 1833 speech to the House of Commons, cited in Anthony Pagden, *Peoples and Empires: Europeans and the Rest of the World, from Antiquity to the Present* (London: Phoenix Press, 2001), 159.
4. B. M. Engel'gardt, "Putevye pis'ma I. A. Goncharova iz krugosvetnogo plavaniia," *Literaturnoe nasledstvo*, vol. 22–24 (Moscow: Zhurnal'no-Gazetnoe ob"edineniie, 1935), 380, 402, 403.
5. *PSS* 3, 411–412.
6. *PSS* 2, 9.
7. On the Yakutsk-Ayan route see James R. Gibson, *Feeding the Russian Fur Trade: Provisioning of the Okhotsk Seaboard and the Kamchatka Peninsula, 1639–1856* (Madison: University of Wisconsin Press, 1969), 85.
8. *PSS* 2, 676.
9. *PSS* 2, 703–704.
10. My description of Siberia prior to the Russian conquest is based on Alan Wood, *Russia's Frozen Frontier: A History of Siberia and the Russian Far East, 1581–1991*

(London: Bloomsbury, 2011), 1–24; Igor V. Naumov, *The History of Siberia* (London: Routledge, 2006), 3–49. The saying about Mendeleev's Table is cited in Sergey Glebov, "Siberian Ruptures: Dilemmas of Ethnography in an Imperial Situation," in Roland Svetkovski and Alexis Hofmeister, eds., *An Empire of Others: Creating Ethnographic Knowledge in Imperial Russia and the USSR* (Budapest: Central European University Press, 2014), 282. On Siberia's linguistic diversity, see James Forsyth, *A History of the Peoples of Siberia, Russia's North Asian Colony, 1581–1990* (Cambridge: Cambridge University Press, 1992), 10.

11. Andreas Kappeler, *The Russian Empire: A Multiethnic History* (New York: Longman, 2001), 21–59.
12. Naumov, *The History of Siberia,* 58; Wood, *Russia's Frozen Frontier,* 26; W. Bruce Lincoln, *The Conquest of a Continent: Siberia and the Russians* (New York: Random House, 1994), 33–92; and Willard Sunderland, "Ermak Timofeevich," in *Russia's People of Empire: Life Stories from Eurasia: From 1500 to the Present,* ed. Stephen Norris and Willard Sunderland (Bloomington: Indiana University Press, 2012), 17–24.
13. Mark Bassin, *Imperial Visions: Nationalist Imagination and Geographic Expansion in the Russian Far East, 1840–1865* (Cambridge: Cambridge University Press, 1999), 19; Wood, *Russia's Frozen Frontier,* 3; for a brief overview of the conquest of Siberia and the Far East, see Kappeler, *The Russian Empire,* 33–38, 200–204.
14. Wood, *Russia's Frozen Frontier,* 18.
15. Alan Wood, "Introduction: Siberia's Role in Russian History," in *The History of Siberia: From Russian Conquest to Revolution,* ed. Alan Wood (London: Routledge, 1991), 3.
16. Mark Bassin, "Geographies of Imperial Identity," in *The Cambridge History of Russia,* vol. 2, ed. Dominic Lieven (Cambridge: Cambridge University Press, 2006), 60; Wood, *Russia's Frozen Frontier,* 70. The turn-of-the-century Russian historian Pavel Miliukov also regarded Siberia as Russia's "first colony"; see Anatolii Remnev, "Vdvinut' Rossiiu v Sibir'. Imperiia i russkaia kolonizatsiia vtoroi poloviny XIX-nachala XX vv.," *Ab Imperio* 3 (2003): 135–136.
17. Yuri Slezkine, *Arctic Mirrors: Russia and the Small Peoples of the North* (Ithaca: Cornell University Press, 1994), 21–22; Lincoln, *The Conquest,* 86, 96, 183–189; Etkind, *Internal Colonization,* 83; Ilya Vinkovetsky, *Russian America: An Overseas Colony of a Continental Empire, 1804–1867* (Oxford: Oxford University Press, 2011), 54; Naumov, *The History,* 107.
18. N. N. Rodigina, *Drugaia Rossiia: Obraz Sibiri v russkoi zhurnal'noi presse vtoroi poloviny XIX-nachala XX veka* (Novosibirsk: NGPU, 2006), 325; Naumov, *The History,* 99. On colonization in the nineteenth-century, see Willard Sunderland, *Taming the Wild Field: Colonization and Empire on the Russian Steppe* (Ithaca: Cornell University Press, 2004); and his article "The 'Colonization Question': Visions of Colonization in Late Imperial Russia," *Jahrbücher für Geschichte Osteuropas* 48 (2000): 210–232. Sunderland treats in greater detail the first half of the nineteenth century in "Making the Empire: Colonists and Colonization in Russia, 1800–1850," Ph.D. diss., Indiana University, 1997.

19. L. M. Dameshek and A. V. Remnev, at al., *Sibir' v sostave rossiiskoi imperii* (Moscow: Novoe lit. obozrenie, 2007), 345; Forsyth, *A History,* 115, 156; Etkind, *Internal Colonization,* 77. On genocidal campaigns, see James Forsyth, "The Siberian Native People before and after the Russian Conquest," in *The History of Siberia,* ed. Alan Wood, 80.
20. Nikolai Iadrintsev, *Sibirskie inorodtsy, ikh byt i sovremennoe polozhenie* (1891; Tiumen': Iu. Mandriki, 2000), 6, 151–172; see also Iadrintsev's *Sibir' kak koloniia* (1882; St. Petersburg: I. M. Sibiriakov, 1892); Forsyth, *A History,* 156–158, 161; and Anatolii Remnev, "'Russkoe delo' na Aziatskikh okrainakh: 'Russkost'' pod ugrozoi ili 'somnitel'nye kul'turtregery,'" *Ab Imperio* 2 (2008): 169. See also James Forsyth, "The Siberian Native People"; and Wood, *A Frozen Frontier,* 95–117. On Speransky's reforms, see Lincoln, *The Conquest,* 155–162; and Naumov, *The History,* 91–98.
21. Janet M. Hartley, *Siberia: A History of the People* (New Haven: Yale University Press, 2014), 39–40; Slezkine, *Arctic Mirrors,* 28–29; John J. Stephan, *The Russian Far East: A History* (Stanford: Stanford University Press, 1994), 25. On the challenges of administering Siberia, see Hartley, *Siberia,* 100–114. On the discrepancy between policy and practice, see Slezkine, *Arctic Mirrors,* 20–22; and Kappeler, *The Russian Empire,* 36. I owe the term "under-governed" to Ilya Vinkovetsky.
22. Rodigina, *Drugaia Rossiia,* 323; Naumov, *The History,* 94; Lincoln, *The Conquest,* 158; Goncharov's "Across Eastern Siberia" ("Po Vostochnoi Sibiri," 1891), *PSS* 3, 59; Sergey Glebov, "Siberian Middle Ground: Languages of Rule and Accommodation on the Siberian Frontier," in *Empire Speaks Out: Languages of Rationalization and Self-Description in the Russian Empire,* ed. Ilya Gerasimov, Jan Kusber, et al. (Boston: Brill, 2009), 141.
23. Willard Sunderland, "Empire without Imperialism? Ambiguities of Colonization in Tsarist Russia," *Ab Imperio* 2 (2003): 102–103. On Siberia's separate legal status, see Anatolii Remnev, "Regional'nye parametry imperskoi 'geograficheskoi vlasti' (Sibir' i Dal'nii Vostok)," *Ab Imperio* 3–4 (2000): 354.
24. Stephen Watrous, "The Regionalist Conception of Siberia, 1860 to 1920," in *Between Heaven and Hell: The Myth of Siberia in Russian Culture,* ed. Galya Diment and Yuri Slezkine (New York: St. Martin's Press, 1993), 113–132; Dmitry von Mohrenschildt, *Toward a United States of Russia: Plans and Projects of Federal Reconstruction of Russia in the Nineteenth Century* (Rutherford: Fairleigh Dickinson University Press, 1981), 85–130; Glebov, "Siberian Ruptures," 292–293. Some exiled radicals did toy with the idea of Siberia's separation from Russia, transformation into the United States of Siberia, and establishment of a federal union with the United States of America; see A. V. Remnev, *Samoderzhavie i Sibir': administrativnaia politika vtoroi poloviny XIX-nachala XX vekov* (Omsk: Omskii gos. universitet, 1997), 21. On the limited appeal of Siberian regionalism, see Remnev, "Regional'nye parametry," 354; and Remnev, "Vdvinut' Rossiiu," 157.
25. Hartley, *Siberia,* 246; Alec Luhn, "Russia Bans Siberian Independence March," *Guardian,* August 5, 2014.
26. Comparing himself and other travelers who disembarked in Ayan to Robinson Crusoe, Goncharov writes: "So what if Siberia is not an island, that there are towns

and civilization there? It takes two, three, or five thousand versts to get to them!" (*PSS* 2, 634). Vinkovetsky calls the vast distances and geographical barriers of Russia's continental empire "ocean substitutes" (Vinkovetsky, *Russian America,* 12). On mail delivery times, see Remnev, *Samoderzhavie i Sibir',* 44; Philip Curtin, *Cross-Cultural Trade in World History* (Cambridge: Cambridge University Press, 1984), 252; and *PSS* 2, 682. See also Wood, *Russia's Frozen Frontier,* 70. Indeed, contiguity can blur coloniality even for scholars sympathetic to colonial approaches to Russian history. Inexplicably, given his sources and his historical outline of a classic colonial situation, Etkind presents Siberia as a land where Russia colonized *its own land,* as it were, as distinct from "external" colonization of such non-Russian territories as the Caucasus (Etkind, *Internal Colonization,* 72–90).

27. Vladimir Bobrovnikov, "Russkii Kavkaz i frantsuzskii Alzhir: sluchainoe skhodstvo ili obmen opytom kolonial'nogo stroitel'tva?" in *Imperium inter pares. Rol' transferov v istorii Rossiiskoi imperii (1700–1917),* ed. Martin Aust, Ricarda Vulpius, and Alexey Miller (Moscow: Novoe lit. obozrenie, 2010), 198, 201.
28. Remnev, *Samoderzhavie i Sibir',* 18–52.
29. *PSS* 2, 657, 707, 737; Slezkine, *Arctic Mirrors,* 53; Rodigina, *Drugaia Rossiia,* 324.
30. Remnev, "Regional'nye parametry," 350; Anatolii Remnev, "Rossiia i Sibir' v meniaiushchemsia prostranstve imperii, XIX—nachalo XX veka" in *Rossiiskaia imperiia v sravnitel'noi perspektive* (Moscow: Novoe izd-vo, 2004), 310.
31. David Collins, "Russia's Conquest of Siberia: Evolving Russian and Soviet Historical Interpretations," *European Studies Review* 12 (1982): 17–44. See also Lowell Tillett, *The Great Friendship: Soviet Historians on the Non-Russian Nationalities* (Chapel Hill: University of North Carolina Press, 1969). For Forsyth's account of the conquest's Soviet mythology, see his *A History,* 109–111.
32. Sunderland, "Empire without Imperialism?" 111–113. For an account of Russian colonization that considers its imperialistic aspects, see Sunderland, *Taming the Wild Field.*
33. On the plurality of imperialisms, see Nicholas Thomas, *Colonialism's Culture: Anthropology, Travel, and Government* (Princeton: Princeton University Press, 1994). On the plurality of colonizations, see James Belich, *Replenishing the Earth: The Settler Revolution and the Rise of the Anglo-World, 1783–1939* (Oxford: Oxford University Press, 2013), 177–218. See also Ann Laura Stoler, "Considerations on Imperial Comparisons," in *Empire Speaks Out: Languages of Rationalization and Self-Description in the Russian Empire,* ed. Ilya Gerasimov, Jan Kusber, et al. (Boston: Brill, 2009), 37–38; and Forsyth, *A History,* 109.
34. The single exception is "a colony of houses" in one spot on the Lena River (*PSS* 2, 706).
35. See, for example, *PSS* 2, 605, 651, 673, 680.
36. Sunderland, "The 'Colonization Question,'" 212–213; Sunderland, "Empire without Imperialism?" 103–106.
37. Engel'gardt, "Putevye pis'ma" 402; *PSS* 3, 122. In his 1867 autobiography, Goncharov replaced the term he used in the travelogue, "North American possessions," with "North American colonies"; "Avtobiografiia," in I. A. Goncharov, *Sobranie sochinenii v vos'mi tomakh,* vol. 7 (Moscow: Khudozh lit, 1980), 222. However, as Sunderland notes, the term was more widely used for overseas possessions.

38. *PSS* 2, 702.
39. Yuri Slezkine, "Introduction," in *Between Heaven and Hell,* ed. Diment and Slezkine, 2.
40. Mark Bassin, "Inventing Siberia: Visions of the Russian East in the Early Nineteenth Century," *American Historical Review* 96.3 (1991): 763–794 (quotations come from 782 and 784). For changing myths about Yermak, see Sunderland, "Ermak Timofeevich." For changing conceptions of the Russian empire as a whole, see Bassin, "Geographies of Imperial Identity." On the Russian-American parallel, see Bassin's "Turner, Solov'ev, and the 'Frontier Hypothesis': The Nationalist Signification of Open Spaces," *Journal of Modern History* 65.3 (1993): 473–511.
41. Slezkine, *Arctic Mirrors,* 81 (see 73–92 for Russia's nationalist polemics surrounding Siberia); Galya Diment, "Exiled from Siberia: The Construction of Siberian Experience by Early-Nineteenth-Century Irkutsk Writers," in *Between Heaven and Hell,* ed. Diment and Slezkine, 52, 60; Rodigina, *Drugaia Rossiia,* 139–145, 261–266; A. S. Khomiakov, *Stikhotvoreniia i dramy* (Leningrad: Sovetskii pisatel', 1969), 277 (the line in Russian is "*Sibiri bole net: otnyne zdes' Rossiia*"); Anatolyi Remnev, "Siberia and the Russian Far East in the Imperial Geography of Power," in *Russian Empire: Space, People, Power, 1700–1930,* ed. Jane Burbank, Mark von Hagen, and Anatolyi Remnev (Bloomington: Indiana University Press, 2007), 441; and Glebov, "Siberian Ruptures," 283.
42. I. N. Berezin, "Metropoliia i koloniia," *Otechestvennye zapiski* 117 (1858): 81–98, 349–370 and 118 (1858): 74–115; Remnev, "Siberia and the Russian Far East," 440; Remnev, "Regional'nye parametry," 347–348; Mark Bassin, *Imperial Visions: Nationalist Imagination and Geographical Expansion in the Russian Far East, 1840–1865* (Cambridge: Cambridge University Press, 1999), 12–13; Bassin, "Geographies of Imperial Identity," 52; and Olga Maiorova, *From the Shadow of Empire: Defining the Russian Nation through Cultural Mythology, 1855–1870* (Madison: University of Wisconsin Press, 2010), 6.
43. *PSS* 2, 633, 634, 645, 657.
44. *PSS* 2, 644, 660, 686. I thank Serguei Oushakine for drawing my attention to the perceptions surrounding nomadism; see a forum convened by Oushakine on "Unsettling Nomadism," *Ab Imperio* 2 (2012). See also *PSS* 2, 672, for Goncharov's assertion that the Sakha were not really nomads, which means that construing their presence as not mitigating the land's "emptiness" involved more than their nomadism.
45. *PSS* 2, 661.
46. Slezkine, *Arctic Mirrors,* 59; Vinkovetsky, *Russian America,* 96. Scholars distinguish two types of assimilationist process in the Russian empire. In Vinkovetsky's explanation (96), Russification (*russifikatsiia*) was "an aggressive and coordinated government policy aimed at cultural transformation." Russianization (*obrusenie*), by contrast, was a voluntary "interactive cultural process" by which Russianness took root in indigenous communities without the authorities' steering. In the tsarist period, Russification was pursued mostly in the western provinces. See also Alexei Miller, *The Romanov Empire and Nationalism* (Budapest: Central European University Press, 2008), 45–65.
47. *PSS* 2, 672, 673.

48. *PSS* 2, 668. One cameo of this diversity comes in Goncharov's description of the Lena River settlers: "Population here is mixed (*smes' v narode*). . . . Among them are Poles, Jews, and also descendants of Yakuts. Everyone likes the Jews: they are good at trade and move the country forward" (*PSS* 2, 703). Many self-identified Russians in Siberia were in fact Russified Ukrainians and Belarusians (Remnev, "Vdvinut' Rossiiu," 150–152).
49. *PSS* 2, 706, 709–710.
50. Of classical provenance, the "smoke of the fatherland" trope appears in the poetry of Derzhavin and Griboedov; see *PSS* 3, 594; and Ingrid Kleespies, *A Nation Astray: Nomadism and National Identity in Russian Literature* (DeKalb: Northern Illinois University Press, 2012), 131. Serfdom did not exist among the European settler society, with the exception of the Demidov ironworks (Lincoln, *The Conquest,* 159). However, aboriginal people were sometimes enserfed by settlers or their own elites empowered by the colonial regime. Since free men could be taxed, slavery was banned by the order of Empress Anna Ioannovna in 1733. Limited, household-level slavery was also traditionally practiced by Siberian aborigines (Forsyth, *A History,* 29, 62, 163). Commenting elsewhere that people in Siberia socialize across estates and professional lines, Goncharov implicitly critiques the social exclusions of Russia's European society (*PSS* 2, 679).
51. *PSS* 2, 674.
52. An earlier traveler to these parts, Ferdinand P. Vrangel', provides a more exhaustive and fairly respectful ethnographic account of the peoples of eastern Siberia in his *Puteshestvie po severnym beregam Sibiri i po Ledovitomu moriu sovershennoe v 1820–1824 gg.* (1841; Izd-vo Gavsevmorputi, 1948). Goncharov knew this popular travelogue and claimed that all educated Siberians owned a copy (696).
53. *PSS* 2, 626. Goncharov praises the Evenki for domesticating reindeer and portrays the Evenki as kind, industrious, and honest. Another far-eastern people, the Koryaks, emerge in *The Frigate Pallada* as quintessential noble savages. Exceedingly kind, they evenly share food within the community even in famines, which they suffer often in their habitat (*PSS* 2, 642, 651, 692–693).
54. Glebov, "Siberian Middle Ground," 128. On the cultural anthropology of the Sakha people prior to the Russian conquest, see A. P. Okladnikov, *Yakutia before Its Incorporation into the Russian State* (Montreal: McGill-Queen's University Press, 1970), 227–448.
55. Forsyth, *A History,* 55–69. Forsyth's history of Siberia incorporates substantially the history of its indigenous people. See also Anna Reid, *The Shaman's Coat: A Native History of Siberia* (London: Weidenfeld and Nicolson, 2002). Most histories of Siberia are narratives of the Russian conquest and administration of Siberia. For a critique of this tendency, see Glebov, "Siberian Middle Ground," 122–123.
56. *PSS* 2, 641, 645–647, 657–659, 660, 663, 672, 690. For the emendation about the Sakha women in the 1879 edition, see *PSS* 3, 315 (to p. 659, l.8).
57. *PSS* 2, 633, 681, 705 (*prirodnye khoziaeva*). Forsyth claims that few Sakha actually converted. Since baptism came with a *yasak* waiver, sham conversions were common; Forsyth, *A History,* 165.

58. *PSS* 2, 693–694.
59. *PSS* 2, 661, 672, 705. On Bushkov, see 659.
60. *PSS* 2, 673 (compare with 164). On the Sakha raids, see Forsyth, *A History,* 59–60. On the "diapers of oblivion," see Petr A. Slovtsov, cited in Slezkine, *Arctic Mirrors,* 76.
61. Stephan, *The Russian Far East,* 23. In a letter of September 1854 to A. A. Kraevsky, Goncharov mentions that the Cossacks "oppressed" the Sakha (Engel'gardt, "Putevye pis'ma," 423).
62. *PSS* 2, 691–692. On the incomplete conquest of the Chukchi, see Forsyth, *A History,* 150; and Reid, *The Shaman's Coat,* 184. On their American connections, see Vrangel', *Puteshestvie,* ch. 7. A contemporary, post-colonial Luoravetlan-Russian writer, Yury Rytkheu, highlights this in his fictionalized family chronicle *The Chukchi Bible* (Brooklyn, NY: Archipelago Books, 2011). On the extirpation order, see Kappeler, *The Russian Empire,* 154; and Forsyth, *A History,* 145–151. Forsyth compares the Chukchi Wars to the resistance of North American Indians. The Russian government waged campaigns of extirpation also against the Bashkirs. The failure of these campaigns, and non-Russians' resistance more generally, led the Russian empire to adopt a policy of flexibility and restraint (Kappeler, *The Russian Empire,* 154).
63. Mary Louise Pratt, *Imperial Eyes: Travel Writing and Transculturation,* 2nd ed. (London: Routledge, 2008), 8–9.
64. Remnev, "Regional'nye parametry," 355–356; Ilya Vinkovetsky, "Circumnavigation, Empire, Modernity, Race: The Impact of Round-the-World Voyages on Russia's Imperial Consciousness," *Ab Imperio* 1–2 (2001): 191–210; and Remnev, *Samoderzhavie,* 37.
65. Remnev, "Vdvinut' Rossiiu," 136–137.
66. Sunderland, "Making the Empire," 52, 57–58.
67. Remnev, "Regional'nye parametry," 351.
68. *PSS* 2, 691, 697–698, 703, 708. Even when mentioning the ongoing Gold Rush in Siberia, Goncharov adopts the lens of the peasants, who complain that the influx of gold-seekers has caused an increase in food prices (704–705).
69. *PSS* 2, 655. "Free and easy parts" is my translation of *mesta privol'nye.*
70. *PSS* 2, 684.
71. Ilya Vinkovetsky, *Russian America: An Overseas Colony of a Continental Empire, 1804–1867* (Oxford: Oxford University Press, 2011), 156; see also 154–180.
72. *PSS* 3, 62, 769–771 (Goncharov's term for "becoming humanized" is *gumaniziruetsia*).
73. On Innokenty's reaction to the Crimean War, see Engel'gardt, "Putevye pis'ma," 420. The nationalists worried that translating the Bible would weaken Russificatory processes; see Robert Geraci, *Window on the East: National and Imperial Identities in Late Tsarist Russia* (Ithaca: Cornell University Press, 2001). See also Robert Geraci and Mikhail Khodorkovsky, eds., *Of Religion and Empire: Missions, Conversions, and Tolerance in Imperial Russia* (Ithaca: Cornell University Press, 2001).
74. *PSS* 2, 654, 660.
75. For a contrary view, see Kleespies, *A Nation Astray,* 126–141, and her "Russia's Wild East? Domesticating Siberia in Ivan Goncharov's *The Frigate Pallada,*" *Slavic and*

East European Journal 56.1 (2012): 21–37. For Kleespies, Goncharov's domestication and Russification of Siberia conflicts with the notion of the work's imperial boosterism. On the contrary, I see these strategies and ideas as interconnected. Both Bassin (*Imperial Visions,* 186–190), and E. Krasnoshchekova, (*I. A. Goncharov: Mir tvorchestva* [St. Petersburg: Pushkinskii fond, 1997], 209–210), stress the boosterist enhancements in Goncharov's vision of Siberia, as noted by Kleespies.

76. One missionary's claim that "there is no place in Siberia where the Russians haven't set foot" inspires the writer's ebullient praise: "Amazing words!" (*PSS* 2, 687). On demography data, see Willard Sunderland, "Russians into Iakuts? 'Going Native' and Problems of Russian National Identity in the Siberian North, 1870–1914," *Slavic Review* 55.4 (1996): 822. Even in 1926, the Sakha accounted for ninety percent of the Yakutsk region's population (Reid, *The Shaman's Coat,* 123). On Goncharov's refusal to disembark, see *PSS* 3, 312 (n. to p. 642, l.36) and Engel'gardt, "Putevye pis'ma," 408.
77. Engel'gardt, "Putevye pis'ma," 408; Stephan, *The Russian Far East,* 45.
78. A. M. Linden, "Zapiski A. M. Lindena," *Russkaia starina* 4 (1905): 116. In the post-Crimean period, the government began to question the colonizing prowess of Russian peasants, which Goncharov assessed so highly. Doubt was cast on their agricultural and Russianizing capabilities (see Remnev, "'Russkoe delo'").
79. *PSS* 2, 667–674.
80. Engel'gardt, "Putevye pis'ma," 416, 423. For similar impression of Yakutsk, see Vrangel', *Puteshestvie,* ch. 1–2; and Adolph Erman, *Travels in Siberia Including Excursions Northward, Down the Obi to the Polar Circle, and Southwards, to the Chinese Border,* vol. 2 (London: Longman, 1848), 364–400.
81. A. V. Remnev, *Rossiia Dal'nego Vostoka. Imperskaia geografiia vlasti XIX-nachala XX vekov* (Omsk: Izd-vo Omskogo gos. universiteta, 2004), 124; Bassin, "Geographies of Imperial Identity," 60.
82. Peter C. Perdue, *China Marches West: The Qing Conquest of Central Eurasia* (Cambridge, MA: Harvard University Press, 2005), 164.
83. Vaniukov is cited in Remnev, *Rossiia Dal'nego Vostoka,* 122. Muravev is cited in V. V. Alekseev et al., *Aziatskaia Rossiia,* 291.
84. Bassin, *Imperial Visions,* 3; Forsyth, *A History,* 215–216.
85. *PSS* 2, 629.
86. Engel'gardt, "Putevye pis'ma," 326, 328; Linden, "Zapiski," 115, 121. See also Goncharov's official expedition report in *PSS* 3, 197–199. *The Frigate Pallada* makes no mention of any sailors dying in the Amur fiasco or of relative mortality statistics overall.
87. Engel'gardt, "Putevye pis'ma," 420; Goncharov, "Iz vospominanii i rasskazov o morskom plavanii," *PSS* 3, 52; and his "Po vostochnoi Sibiri," *PSS* 3, 59–60.
88. Andrew Higgins, "Russia Looks to Populate Its Far East. Wimps Need Not Apply," *New York Times,* July 14, 2016, A6; Andrew Higgins, "Vladivostok Lures Chinese Tourists (Many Think It's Theirs)," *New York Times,* July 24, 2016, A9.
89. A. N. Maikov, "Otryvok iz pis'ma k A. F. Pisemskomu," *Sankt Peterburgskie vedomosti* 176 [August 11] (1854): 863–864. I thank Alexey Vdovin for sharing this text with me. These patriotic and imperial sentiments also found an outlet in Apollon

Maikov's poetry inspired by the Crimean War; see A. N. Maikov, *Polnoe sobranie sochinenii,* vol. 1 (St. Petersburg: A. F. Marks, 1914), 297–312.

90. Maikov, "Otryvok," 864, also reprinted in *PSS* 3, 520 (see also *PSS* 3, 471); Fyodor Dostoevsky, "Geok Teppe. What Does Asia Mean to Us?" in *A Writer's Diary,* vol. 2 (1881; Evanston: Northwestern University Press, 1993–1994), 1368–1378; Sunderland, "Empire without Imperialism?" 102; and Engel'gardt, "Putevye pis'ma," 419–420.
91. Solidarity with Maikov's argument infuses especially Part II, Chapter 8, of *The Frigate Pallada* ("From Yakutsk"); see *PSS* 2, 680, 685 (discussed below).
92. *PSS* 2, 680–682.
93. *PSS* 2, 695; Matvei M. Gedenshtrom, *Otryvki o Sibiri* (St. Petersburg, 1830). For Bassin's discussion of this polemic and what he terms as Goncharov's "hysterical" outburst, see his *Imperial Visions,* 186–190.
94. *PSS* 2, 685, emphasis in source.
95. Slezkine, *Arctic Mirrors,* 99; Stephan, *The Russian Far East,* 23–24; Forsyth, *A History,* 161 (see also 158, 160, 185, 218–219, 226).
96. *PSS* 2, 678, 681; Engel'gardt, "Putevye pis'ma," 408–409; Goncharov, "Po vostochnoi Sibiri," *PSS* 3, 64–72.
97. Goncharov, "Po Vostochnoi Sibiri" (1891), *PSS* 3, 55–79.
98. Goncharov, "Dva sluchaia s morskoi zhizni," *PSS* 3, 22. The article was published in Maikov's journal for youth, *Podsnezhnik* 2 (1858). Here, Goncharov does use the term "colonization" (*kolonizatsiia*).
99. *PSS* 2, 677. On Goncharov's polemic with Chaadaev, see Krasnoshchekova, *I. A. Goncharov,* 174–181.
100. *PSS* 2, 678.
101. Remnev, "Siberia and the Russian Far East," 445–446; Berezin, "Metropoliia i koloniia," 87, 91.
102. Remnev, *Samoderzhavie i Sibir',* 20–28, 33. On western political thought, see Jennifer Pitts, *A Turn to Empire: The Rise of Imperial Liberalism in Britain and France* (Princeton: Princeton University Press, 2005).
103. *PSS* 2, 155; "Das Kap der guten Hoffnung," *Die Gegenwart: Eine encyclopädische Darstellung der neuesten Zeitgeschichte für alle Stände,* vol. 4 (Leipzig: F. A. Brockhaus, 1850), 554.
104. Stoler, "Considerations," 40. Though he passed in silence Siberia's perennial administrative abuses in *The Frigate Pallada,* Goncharov alludes to them more openly in "In Eastern Siberia," published in a more relaxed censorship climate. There, Goncharov writes that Siberia suffered a plight worse than serfdom: a "governmental yoke" (*chinovnich'e igo*), likely continuing to this day ("Po Vostochnoi Sibiri," *PSS* 3, 59).
105. Alice L. Conklin, *A Mission to Civilize: The Republican Idea of Empire in France and West Africa, 1895–1930* (Stanford: Stanford University Press, 1997), 2.
106. Michael Barnett, *Empire of Humanity: A History of Humanitarianism* (Ithaca: Cornell University Press, 2011), 61, 222. Citation from Burke is on 61.
107. Rimsky-Korsakov's travel notes initially appeared in *The Naval Review* (*Morskoi sbornik*). With abbreviations, they are reprinted in Voin A. Rimskii-Korsakov,

Baltika-Amur. Povestvovanie v pis'makh o plavaniakh, prikliucheniiakh i razmyshleniiakh komandira shkuny 'Vostok' (Khabarovsk: Khabarovskoe knizhnoe izd-vo, 1980), 320.

5. Russians Confront Human Diversity

1. *PSS* 2, 257. In Russian, Goncharov's initial question was "*Otkuda ty rodom?*"
2. *PSS* 2, 42.
3. Ivan Goncharov, *The Frigate Pallada,* tr. Klaus Goetze (New York: St. Martin's Press, 1987); see "Note to the Reader" preceding the Table of Contents.
4. This oversight cannot be blamed on the Soviet practice of printing "abbreviated" editions of *The Frigate Pallada* which censored passages that might sully the Russian writer's benevolent image. Scholars have always had access to full, unexpurgated academic editions of *The Frigate Pallada.* A more likely reason is that race and imperialism are simply not part of a typical conceptual toolkit for a scholar of Russian literature, nor are they research priorities in the field.
5. B. M. Engelgardt considered Goncharov's descriptions of various ethnicities to be remarkably free of prejudice, as accomplished artistically as they were psychologically true. In his view, *The Frigate Pallada* was "suffused with deep sympathy, understanding of life, and respect for human dignity. It is 'humane' [*gumanna*] in the highest sense of the word, and its subtle humor is filled with supreme humanity [*chelovechnost'*]"; see B. M. Engel'gardt "'Puteshestvie vokrug sveta I. Oblomova': Glavy iz neizdannoi monografii B. M. Engel'gardta," *Literaturnoe nasledstvo*, vol. 102 (I. A. Goncharov. Novye materialy i issledovaniia) (Moscow: IMLI RAN "Nasledie," 2000), 67. Soviet scholar V. A. Mikhelson posited far-fetched arguments about Goncharov's "humanistic" anti-colonialism in his *Gumanizm I. A. Goncharova i kolonial'nyi vopros* (Krasnodar: Krasnodarskii gos. pedagog. institut, 1965). In post-Soviet times, Elena A. Krasnoshchekova characterized Goncharov's stereotypes as fairly benign and at any rate eventually overcome by the author's psychological depth and a belief in human universality; see her "'Mir Iaponii' v knige I. A. Goncharova 'Fregat Pallada,'" *Acta Slavica Iaponica* 11 (1993): 106–125; and her *Ivan Aleksandrovich Goncharov: Mir tvorchestva* (St. Petersburg: Pushkinskii Fond, 1997), 194–197. Goncharov's portrayal of the Japanese has been praised as a model of tolerance by A. R. Sadokova in "Iaponiia i iapontsy vo 'Fregate Pallada' I. A Goncharova," in *Vostok v russkoi literature XVIII- nachala XX veka* (Moscow: IMLI RAN, 2004), 216–233. Any broaching of racial prejudice in *The Frigate Pallada,* except as a sin of western colonialists, has been scrupulously avoided in Soviet and Russian criticism. Western scholarship has taken a less antiseptic view of the matter, though it tends simply not to focus on the book's prejudices, perhaps because, as typical of the age, they are not seen as meriting attention; see, for example, Milton Ehre, *Oblomov and His Creator: The Life and Art of Ivan Goncharov* (Princeton: Princeton University Press, 1973). The historian George Lensen, among others, has briefly criticized Goncharov's demeaning stereotypes of

the Japanese in his *Russia's Japan Expedition of 1852 to 1855* (Gainesville: University of Florida Press, 1955). Susanna Soojung Lim has also noted them in *China and Japan in the Russian Imagination, 1685–1922: To the Ends of the Orient* (London: Routledge, 2013). To my knowledge, the first mention of Goncharov's prejudices as being racial, as opposed to merely ethnic or cultural, was made by Peter Drews in his "Die Darstellung nichteuropäischer Völker in I. A. Gončarovs *Fregat 'Pallada,'*" in *Ivan A. Gončarov: Leben, Werk und Wirkung,* ed. Peter Thiergen (Cologne: Böhlau Verlag, 1994), 287–303.

6. For a fascinating story of an African-American emigrant from the United States who encountered no racial barriers in late imperial Russia in his spectacular rise as an entrepreneur, see Vladimir Alexandrov, *The Black Russian* (New York: Atlantic Monthly Press, 2013).

7. The term "travelee" was introduced by Mary Louise Pratt to mean the communities impacted and described by travelers; see her *Imperial Eyes: Travel Writing and Transculturation,* 2nd ed. (London: Routledge, 2008), 8.

8. Nancy Stepan, *The Idea of Race in Science: Great Britain 1800–1960* (Hamden, CT: Archon Books, 1982), 4; Philip D. Curtin, *The Image of Africa: British Ideas and Action, 1780–1850* (Madison: University of Wisconsin Press, 1964), 244–245.

9. Colette Guillaumin, "The Idea of Race and Its Elevation to Autonomous Scientific and Legal Status," in *Sociological Theories: Race and Colonialism* (Paris: Unesco, 1980), 42; Karl Hall, "'Rasovye priznaki koreniatsia glubzhe v prirode chelovecheskogo organizma': neulovimoe poniatie rasy v Rossiiskoi imperii," in *'Poniatiia o Rossii:' K istoricheskoi semantike imperskogo perioda,* vol. 2, ed. A. Miller, D. Sdvizhkov, and I. Shirle (Moscow: Novoe lit. obozrenie, 2012), 194–258 (esp. 224–239); David Bindman, *Ape to Apollo: Aesthetics and the Idea of Race in the 18th Century* (London: Reaktion Books, 2002), 151. On the imperial context of Russian brain research see Marina Mogilner, *Homo Imperii: A History of Physical Anthropology in Russia* (Lincoln: University of Nebraska Press, 2013), 251–266.

10. The most horrendous case was that of Saartjie Baartman, known as "the Hottentot Venus." Brought to Europe from the Cape Colony, she was widely displayed in ethnic shows. Upon Saartjie's death, a plaster mold was made of her body; her sexual organs, anus, and brain were removed and preserved in jars in a natural history museum in France. Her remains were transferred to South Africa and reburied there only in 2002, after lengthy negotiations. See Gilles Boëtsch and Pascal Blanchard, "From Cabinets of Curiosity to the 'Hottentot Venus': A Long History of Human Zoos," in *The Invention of Race,* ed., Nicolas Bancel, Thomas David, and Dominic Thomas (New York: Routledge, 2014), 185–194. On Robert Knox, author of the influential book *The Races of Man* (London: H. Renshaw, 1850), see Patrick Harries, "Warfare, Commerce, and Science: Racial Biology in South Africa," in *The Invention of Race,* ed. Bancel et al., 170–182. On the visual culture of race, see "Introduction" to *The Invention of Race,* ed. Bancel et al., 2.

11. Robert C. J. Young, *Colonial Desire: Hybridity in Theory, Culture, and Race* (London: Routledge, 1995), 91, 94. On racial scientists reading travel literature, see Bronwen Douglas, "Seaborne Ethnography and the Natural History of Man," *Journal of Pa-*

cific History 38.1 (2003): 13. On Galton, see David M. Wrobel, *Global West, American Frontier: Travel, Empire, and Exceptionalism from Manifest Destiny to the Great Depression* (Albuquerque: University of New Mexico Press, 2013), 51. Galton is also considered a founder of racial anti-Semitism later used in the extermination policies of the Third Reich.

12. By contrast to the reified category of race, Nikolay Zakharov proposes "racialization" as an interactive process involving "making," "becoming," and "doing." As such, racialization connects discourse of race with social relations and political practices. See Zakharov, *Race and Racism*, 3, 65–70.

13. Hall, "'Rasovye priznaki'"; and Vera Tolz, "Diskursy o rase: imperskaia Rossiia i Zapad v sravnenii," in *'Poniatiia o Rossii:' K istoricheskoi semantike imperskogo perioda*, vol. 2, ed. A. Miller, D. Sdvizhkov, and I. Shirle (Moscow: Novoe lit. obozrenie, 2012), 145–193 (see esp. 161–162). For an abbreviated English-language version of Tolz's article, see "Discourses of Race in Imperial Russia (1830–1914)" in *The Invention of Race*, ed. Bancel et al., 130–144. On Russian physical anthropology, see Mogilner, *Homo Imperii*. If the editor's wholehearted endorsement of "racial science" and the lack of scholarly apparatus can be ignored, an anthology of tsarist-era writings on race is available in V. B. Avdeev, *Russkaia rasovaia teoriia do 1917 goda: Sbornik original'nykh rabot russkikh klassikov*, 2 vols. (Moscow: "FERI-V," 2001). On Chaadaev, see Nikolay Zakharov, *Race and Racism in Russia* (Houndsmills: Palgrave Macmillan, 2015), 30.

14. Ann Laura Stoler, "Racial Histories and Their Regimes of Truth," *Political Power and Social Theory* 11 (1997): 198.

15. *PSS* 2, 155. Patrick Brantlinger, *Rule of Darkness: British Literature and Imperialism, 1830–1914* (Ithaca: Cornell University Press, 1988), 173–197, esp. 183.

16. Douglas, "Seaborne Ethnography," 4; and Vera Tolz, "Diskursy o rase," 185–186.

17. *PSS* 2, 12; Hall, "'Rasovye priznaki,'" 196–210. The rhetoric of "tribes" conferred Biblical legitimacy on the idea of race. Historian Mikhail Pogodin urged the white conquest of Africa and Asia by making "the tribe of Japeth" (the white race) responsible for subduing "Shem and Ham"; see Nicholas Riasanovsky, *Nicholas I and Official Nationality in Russia, 1825–1855* (Berkeley: University of California Press, 1959), 158–161. Goncharov's source that used "race" and "tribe" interchangeably was "Das Kap der guten Hoffnung," *Die Gegenwart: Eine encyclopädische Darstellung der neuesten Zeitgeschichte für alle Stände*, vol. 4 (Leipzig: F. A. Brockhaus, 1850), 511–514. James Cowles Prichard used "race" interchangeably with "tribe"; many eighteenth-century polemics about race did not use the word "race" at all. See Michael Banton, *Racial Theories*, 2nd ed. (Cambridge: Cambridge University Press, 1998), 39; and his *The Idea of Race* (London: Tavistock Publications, 1977), 28.

18. Surprisingly, racial theorizing sometimes coincided with political radicalism. Eighteenth-century theorists of race were often abolitionists who wrote treatises against color discrimination and who did not equate Africans with simians. However, their "endlessly reproduced charts" helped solidify demeaning perceptions of Africans and the very notion of human hierarchy (Bindman, *Ape to Apollo*, 201–203). Robert Knox inveighed against colonial depredations of the white race, which crippled "coloured" societies around the globe (Banton, *The Idea of Race*, 48).

19. *PSS* 2, 160, 174, 506, 668; B. M. Engel'gardt, "Putevye pis'ma I. A. Goncharova iz krugosvetnogo plavaniia," *Literaturnoe nasledstvo* 22–24 (1935): 409–410. For comedic effect, Goncharov also strings together the names of Siberia's ethnic groups along with those of animals in his letter from Siberia: "no one lives here yet, only the Tungus, the Ulch, the Orochon, bears, elk, sable, and otters roam around (*kochuiut*)" (Engel'gardt, "Putevye pis'ma," 408).
20. Richard Elphick and Hermann Giliomee, eds., *The Shaping of South African Society, 1652–1840* (Middletown: Wesleyan University Press, 1989), 4–7 (the Khoikhoi and the San are currently treated as a common ethnic group, the Khoisan); Robert M. Lewis, "Wild American Savages and the Civilized English: Catlin's Indian Gallery and the Shows of London," *European Journal of American Studies* 3.1 (2008): 3–4; and Terry Jay Ellingson, *The Myth of the Noble Savage* (Berkeley: University of California Press, 2001), 244. For the case of the San corpse, see Stepan, *The Idea of Race,* 3; and Harries, "Warfare," 175. On Dickens, see Laura Peters, *Dickens on Race* (Manchester: Manchester University Press, 2013), 1. Dickens was responding to London's popular "Zulu Kaffir" show from 1853. It coincided with shows displaying the San and Australian aborigines. Indigenous groups were also a big part of the Crystal Palace Exhibit and the Great Exposition of 1851 (Ellingson, *The Myth,* 244–245).

    For an explanation about the names used in this book to describe African and Siberian ethnic groups, see "Note on Primary Sources, Transliteration, Ethnonyms, and Place Names," this volume.
21. *PSS* 2, 141. Goncharov's likely source was Thornley Smith, *South Africa Delineated* (London: J. Mason, 1850).
22. *PSS* 2, 206.
23. *PSS* 2, 206, emphasis in source. In Russian, the epithet describing the San is *"nedosozdannoe, zhalkoe sushchestvo."*
24. *PSS* 2, 458–459.
25. David Spurr, *The Rhetoric of Empire: Colonial Discourse in Journalism, Travel Writing, and Imperial Administration* (Durham: Duke University Press, 1993), 76–78.
26. Conrad's Marlow confesses: "No, they were not inhuman. Well, you know, that was the worst of it—this suspicion of their not being inhuman. . . . They howled and leaped, and spun, and made horrid faces; but what thrilled you was just the thought of their humanity—like yours—the thought of your remote kinship with this wild and passionate uproar. Ugly." Joseph Conrad, *Heart of Darkness and The Secret Sharer* (New York: Bantam, 1987), 59.
27. The passage about the San (*PSS* 2, 205–207) is excised, for example, from the influential Soviet edition of Muraveiskii: I. A. Goncharov, *Fregat 'Pallada': Ocherki puteshestviia,* ed. S. D. Muraveiskii (Moscow: Gos. izd-vo geograficheskoi literatury, 1951), missing from p. 218. It is also missing in Goetze's English translation: Goncharov, *The Frigate Pallada* (1987), 167.
28. Charles Darwin, *The Voyage of the Beagle,* 4th ed. (1839; New York: Bantam, 1972), 176–178, 183, 196.
29. Michel Foucault, *Discipline and Punish,* cited in Spurr, *The Rhetoric of Empire,* 16.

30. Pratt, *Imperial Eyes,* 63.
31. Building on Pratt's creative conflation of "imperial I/eye," scholars of travel writing Patrick Holland and Graham Huggan label the voyeuristic tendencies of traveling narrators as "the roving 'I.'" Drawn to surfaces, such roving I's "seek out difference," projecting onto bodies "fears and fantasies of the ethnicized cultural 'other.'" See Patrick Holland and Graham Huggan, *Tourists with Typewriters: Critical Reflections on Contemporary Travel Writing* (Ann Arbor: University of Michigan Press, 1998), 15, 19.
32. *PSS* 2, 109, 205; Harries, "Warfare," 176. Skin taken off cadavers of black slaves was tanned for such things as instrument cases also in United States colleges; see Craig S. Wilder, *Ebony & Ivy: Race, Slavery, and the Troubled History of America's Universities* (New York: Bloomsbury Press, 2013), 199.
33. *PSS* 2, 110–111, 205, 534–535; Young, *Colonial Desire,* 96; Darwin, *The Voyage,* 258; Francis L. Hawks, *Narrative of the Expedition of an American Squadron to the China Seas and Japan, Performed in the Years 1852, 1853, and 1854 under the Command of Commodore M. C Perry, United States Navy* (New York: D. Appleton and Co., 1856), 125.
34. Engel'gardt, "Putevye pis'ma," 385, 414. For the mountain passage, Goncharov hired two Sakha: he was pulled by the one in front of him, to whose belt he held on, and was pushed from behind by the other one. Goncharov skips these details when mentioning the nosebleed in *The Frigate Pallada* (642, 644).
35. *PSS* 2, 237–239; Hawks, *Narrative,* 125.
36. *PSS* 2, 49, 601.
37. Stepan, *The Idea of Race,* xvii; Stoler, "Racial Histories," 198; Jane Burbank and Frederick Cooper, *Empires in World History: Power and the Politics of Difference* (Princeton: Princeton University Press, 2010), 289.
38. Mark Bassin, "Geographies of Imperial Identity," in *Cambridge History of Russia,* vol. 2, ed. Dominic Lieven (Cambridge: Cambridge University Press, 2008), 45–63; David Schimmelpenninck van der Oye, *Russian Orientalism: Asia in the Russian Mind from Peter the Great to the Emigration* (New Haven: Yale University Press, 2010), 239.
39. *PSS* 2, 247. The Cantonese, perceived as "brown," were the exception. See Walter Demel, "Wie die Chinesen gelb wurden: Ein Beitrag zür Frühgeschichte der Rassentheorien," *Historische Zeitschrift* 255.3 (1992): 625–666. "Yellow race" is missing, for example, from Johann Blumenbach's influential division of human kind into five races: Caucasian, Mongolian, Ethiopian, American, and Malay.
40. *PSS* 2, 250, 256, 258 (*raznoobraznye gruppy raznotsvetnykh tel*), 261–262, 265.
41. *PSS* 2, 267.
42. *PSS* 2, 135; Wilder, *Ebony & Ivy,* 188.
43. Brantlinger, *Rule of Darkness,* 184.
44. Susanna Soojung Lim, "Whose Orient Is It? *Frigate Pallada* and Ivan Goncharov's Voyage," *Slavic and East European Journal* 53.1 (2009): 31.
45. Goncharov echoes typical nineteenth-century European travelers, who tended to valorize what they perceived as Japan's surprisingly clean, rational, and orderly modernity

against China's dirtiness and incomprehensibility; see Susan Schoenbauer Thurin, "Introduction," *Nineteenth-Century Travels, Explorations and Empires: Writings from the Era of Imperial Consolidation, 1835–1910,* vol. 4 (London: Pickering and Chatto, 2004), x.

46. *PSS* 2, 327, 341, 350, 363 (*krainii Vostok* vs. *krainii Zapad*); on teeth-blackening, see 376, 465, 468.
47. *PSS* 2, 323–330; Young, *Colonial Desire,* 60.
48. Quotations appear in *PSS* 2, 335, 357, 456, 459. On the interpreters' prostrations, see 360, 457, 458, 461, 475, 483. See also 318–319, 330, 350.
49. *PSS* 2, 335–336, 460–461.
50. Lensen, *Russia's Japan Expedition,* 145; Lim, *China and Japan,* 86–88; William W. McOmie, "The Russians in Nagasaki, 1853–54: Another Look at Some Russian, English, and Japanese Sources," *Acta Slavonica Japonica* 13 (1995): 42–60.
51. Aleksandr Genis, "Goncharov o iapontsakh i iapontsy o Goncharove," *Novoe literaturnoe obozrenie* 12 (1995): 451–453; see also [Kadzukhiko Savada (Saitama)], "I. A. Goncharov glazami iapontsev," in *Ivan A. Gončarov: Leben, Werk und Wirkung,* ed. Peter Thiergen (Cologne: Böhlau Verlag, 1994), 125–133.
52. *PSS* 2, 150, 427, 565. On the racialization of Jews in Russia, see Mogilner, *Homo Imperii,* 217–250. Goncharov misspells the name of Dr. Thomas Allman Wethered, who moved from East India to serve as the main army surgeon in Cape Town, as "Whetherhead" (*PSS* 3, 574 n. to p. 142).
53. *PSS* 2, 150.
54. PSS 2, 338; Hawks, *Narrative of the Expedition,* 438. For the photographs of the Russians' blackface performance, see the online English-language Russian news magazine *Sputnik,* "The Frigate Pallada Sailing the Pacific," Sputnik International, October 9, 2011, http://sptnkne.ws/b4S8. On racism as an urgent problem in contemporary, post-Soviet Russian society, see Zakharov, *Race and Racism.* On the persistence of racialization in the Soviet period, despite overt disavowals of it, see Eric D. Weitz, "Racial Politics without the Concept of Race: Reevaluating Soviet Ethnic and National Purges," *Slavic Review* 61.1 (2002): 1–29, and a debate on this question included in the same issue of the journal.
55. *PSS* 2, 109, 128; Darwin, *The Voyage,* 61, 95–96.
56. Willard Sunderland, "Russians into Iakuts? 'Going Native' and Problems of Russian National Identity in the Siberian North, 1870–1914," *Slavic Review* 55.4 (1996): 806–825; Ilya Vinkovetsky, "Circumnavigation, Empire, Modernity, Race: The Impact of Round-the-World Voyages on Russia's Imperial Consciousness," *Ab Imperio* 1–2 (2001): 191–210; on built-in flexibility of imperial repertoires of power, see Burbank and Cooper, *Empires in World History.*
57. Sunderland, "Russians into Iakuts?" 814–816; Vinkovetsky, "Circumnavigation," 201–209; and Susan Smith-Peter, "Creating a Creole Estate in Early Nineteenth-Century Russian America," *Cahiers du Monde Russe* 51.2–3 (2010): 441–459.
58. *PSS* 2, 772; Adolph Erman, *Travels in Siberia Including Excursions Northward, Down the Obi to the Polar Circle, and Southwards, to the Chinese Border,* vol. 2 (London: Longman, 1848), 175.
59. *PSS* 2, 674; Engel'gardt, "Putevye pis'ma," 423.

60. Anatolyi Remnev, "Siberia and the Russian Far East in the Imperial Geography of Power," in *Russian Empire: Space, People, Power, 170–1930,* ed. Jane Burbank, Mark von Hagen, and Anatolyi Remnev (Bloomington: Indiana University Press, 2007), 448. One government official estimated that it takes roughly ten years to remake a Russian colonist into a Kamchadal; see A. V. Remnev, "Sdelat' Sibir' i Dal'nii Vostok russkimi. K voprosu o politicheskoi motivatsii kolonizatsionnykh protsesov XIX-nachala XX veka," in *Kul'tura russkikh v arkheologicheskikh issledovaniiakh,* ed. L. V. Tataurova (Omsk: Izd-vo Omskogo pedagog. universiteta, 2002), 24.

61. *PSS* 2, 659, 662, 664, 700.

62. On the Sakha as "primitive," see Willard Sunderland, "Making the Empire: Colonists and Colonization in Russia, 1800–1850," Ph.D. diss., Indiana University, 1997, 90. On Sakha as lingua franca, see James Forsyth, *A History of the Peoples of Siberia, Russia's North Asian Colony, 1581–1990* (Cambridge: Cambridge University Press, 1992), 165; Erman, *Travels in Siberia,* 2:374; and Anna Reid, *The Shaman's Coat: A Native History of Siberia* (London: Weidenfeld and Nicolson, 2002), 124. On the imperial government's skepticism about Russian settlers' Russifying potential, see Anatolii Remnev, " 'Russkoe delo' na Aziatskikh okrainakh: 'Russkost' ' pod ugrozoi ili 'somnitel'nye kul'turtregery,' " *Ab Imperio* 2 (2008): 169. For Goncharov's letter to Kraevsky, see Engel'gardt, "Putevye pis'ma," 423–424. See also *PSS* 2, 659 and Goncharov's letter to S. A. Tolstaia, November 11, 1870, in *I. A. Goncharov. Literaturno-kriticheskie stat'i i pis'ma,* ed. I. A. Rybasov (Leningrad: Khudozh. lit., 1938), 264.

63. *PSS* 2, 255, 551, 612. Polish nobility, or *szlachta,* from the former areas of the Polish-Lithuanian Commonwealth that Russia annexed in the eighteenth century, were commonly referred to as "*litva,*" which also means "Lithuanians"; see Sergey Glebov, "Siberian Middle Ground: Languages of Rule and Accommodation on the Siberian Frontier," in *Empire Speaks Out: Languages of Rationalization and Self-Description in the Russian Empire,* ed. Ilya Gerasimov, Jan Kusber, and Alexander Semyonov (Boston: Brill, 2009), 129.

64. *PSS* 2, 58.

65. *PSS* 2, 274; A. B. Davidson and V. A. Makrushin, *Oblik dalekoi strany* (Moscow: Vostochnaia literatura, 1975), 301.

66. *PSS* 2, 128, 373.

67. *PSS* 2, 76–78, 291–292, 315, 465.

68. *PSS* 2, 20, 84. Alexander Etkind, *Internal Colonization: Russia's Imperial Experience* (Malden, MA: Polity, 2011). A serious limitation of this study, however, is Etkind's failure to define and delimit his concept of the "internal." Indeed, he systemically uses the historical evidence of "external" colonization to support his thesis about Russia's "internal" colonization, which has the unfortunate effect of obscuring the reality of Russia's imperial expansion into non-ethnically Russian spaces.

69. *PSS* 2, 49, 205, 597, 617. On skin-touching scenes, see Kate Ferguson Marsters, "Introduction," in Mungo Park, *Travels in the Interior Districts of Africa,* ed. K. F. Marsters (1799; Durham: Duke University Press, 2000), 24. On the Japanese onlookers, see George Lensen, *The Russian Push Toward Japan* (Princeton: Princeton University Press, 1959), 352, 380–381.

70. *PSS* 2, 187.
71. *PSS* 2, 128, 218.
72. *PSS* 2, 187, 438, 614.
73. George Lensen, "The Historicity of *Fregat Pallada*," *Modern Language Notes* 68.7 (1953): 462–466. For American accounts of the Perry expedition, see Hawkes, *Narrative of the Expedition*; and Wilhelm Heine, *With Perry to Japan: A Memoir*, tr. F. Trautmann (Honolulu: University of Hawaii Press, 1990).
74. Lensen, *Russia's Japan Expedition*, 146–147 (see also 46, 48–49, 52–53, 56, 81); Savada, "I. A. Goncharov glazami iapontsev," 128. Translated into Russian, Goncharov's Japanese sobriquet was *briukhastyi varvar*. Japanese officials' diaries also refer to Goncharov as a "tactician" and a "joker," see Yoshikazu Nakamura, "I. A. Goncharov u iapontsev," in *Literatura i iskusstvo v sisteme kul'tury*, ed. B. B. Pitorovskii (Moscow: "Nauka," 1988), 419. Russians' encounters with Siberian aborigines featured similar parallels. While some aborigines smelled revolting to the Russians, the smell of Russians has been known to make some aborigines faint; see Yuri Slezkine, *Arctic Mirrors: Russia and the Small Peoples of the North* (Ithaca: Cornell University Press, 1994), 57.
75. Thompson, *Travel Writing*, 9; James Duncan, "Dis-Orientation: On the Shock of the Familiar in a Far-away Place," in *Writes of Passage: Reading Travel Writing*, ed. James Duncan and Derek Gregory (New York: Routledge, 1999), 151–163; Spurr, *The Rhetoric of Empire*, 7.
76. *PSS* 2, 47, 112, 143, 180, 291.
77. For a study that puts this in focus, see Wrobel, *Global West*.
78. *PSS* 2, 228, 419, 550–551.
79. Tim Youngs, *The Cambridge Introduction to Travel Writing* (Cambridge: Cambridge University Press, 2012), 173; Edward Said, *Orientalism* (1978; New York: Vintage, 1994); Homi K. Bhabha, *The Location of Culture* (London: Routledge, 1994), 122; Spurr, *The Rhetoric of Empire*, 7, 168–169.
80. *PSS* 2, 157, 562–563.
81. *PSS* 2, 156, 159, 168.
82. *PSS* 2, 197, 321; Tim Youngs, *Travellers in Africa: British Travelogues, 1850–1900* (Manchester: Manchester University Press, 1994), 160; Spurr, *The Rhetoric of Empire*, 11; on Macaulay, see Brantlinger, *Rule of Darkness*, 80.
83. *PSS* 2, 350–356 (all quotations in the remainder of this section come from this passage).
84. Ania Loomba, *Colonialism/Postcolonialism* (London: Routledge, 2005), 128–145.
85. For interpretations of the poem ("Kavkazskii plennik" in Russian) in the imperial context, see Bruce Grant, *The Captive and the Gift: Cultural Histories of Sovereignty in Russia and the Caucasus* (Ithaca: Cornell University Press, 2009), 10–18; Katya Hokanson, *Writing at Russia's Border* (Toronto: Toronto University Press, 2008), 23–72; Harsha Ram, *The Imperial Sublime: A Russian Poetics of Empire* (Madison: University of Wisconsin Press, 2003), 186–196; Susan Layton, *Russian Literature and Empire: Conquest of the Caucasus from Pushkin to Tolstoy* (Cambridge: Cambridge University Press, 1994), 15–35, 89–109; and Stephanie Sandler, *Distant Plea-*

sures: Alexander Pushkin and the Writing of Exile (Stanford: Stanford University Press, 1989), 145–164.

86. *PSS* 2, 290.
87. My notion of partial erasure extends Homi Bhabha's concept of ambivalent mimicry in colonial situations, when the natives appear the same, but not quite, to their colonizers; see his essay "Of Mimicry and Man" in *Location,* 121–131.
88. Cited in Loomba, *Colonialism/Postcolonialism,* 131.
89. *PSS* 2, 130.
90. Bhabha elaborates the notion of "sly civility" in essays such as "Sly Civility" and "Signs Taken for Wonders"; see Bhabha, *The Location,* 132–174. For the story about the Christian missionary, see 146–148.
91. *PSS* 2, 691; Douglas, "Seaborne Ethnography."
92. George Lensen, *Russia's Japan Expedition of 1852 to 1855* (Gainesville: University of Florida Press, 1955), 89. For Goncharov's "Twenty Years Since," see *PSS* 2, 732–738; for Putiatin's account see E. V. Putiatin, "Raport General-Adiutanta Putiatina Ego Imperatorskomu Vysochestvu Upravliaiushchemu Morskim Ministerstvom," *Morskoi sbornik* 7 (1855): 231–243.
93. Lensen, *Russia's Japan Expedition,* 85–97.
94. *PSS* 2, 735.
95. Putiatin, "Raport," 242; Lensen, *Russia's Japan Expedition,* 94; Lensen, *The Russian Push,* 336.
96. I. A. Goncharov, letter to E. P. and N. A. Maikov, May 25, 1853, in Engel'gardt, "Putevye pis'ma," 380.
97. Lensen, *The Russian Push,* 332–334.
98. Lensen, *Russia's Japan Expedition,* 106–108.
99. Lensen, *The Russian Push,* 335.
100. Lensen, *Russia's Japan Expedition,* 121. For the quotation from Kawaji, see Lensen, *The Russian Push,* 335. On Russian triumphalism, see, for example, [I. I. L'khovskii], rev. of *Fregat 'Pallada'* (1858), by I. A. Goncharov, *Severnaia pchela* 102 (1858): 2.

6. The Bestseller and Its Afterlife

1. The full title of the 1855 book about Japan was *The Russians in Japan at the End of 1853 and the Beginning of 1854 (from Travel Notes)* (*Russkie v Iaponii v kontse 1853 i nachale 1854 godov (Iz putevykh zametok)*). The full Russian title of the first complete edition of 1858 is *Fregat 'Pallada': Ocherki puteshestviia v dvukh tomakh.* In Goncharov's lifetime, other editions of the travelogue, either as separate books or as parts of Goncharov's collected works, appeared in 1862, 1879, 1884, and twice in 1886. After Goncharov's death, three more editions followed by the close of the century (in 1895, 1896, and 1899) and two more prior to the Bolshevik Revolution (in 1912 and 1916). See *PSS* 3, 394–395; and A. D. Alekseev, *Bibliografiia I. A. Goncharova* (Leningrad: "Nauka," 1968), 16–26. On the markers of publishing success, see Abram I. Reitblat, *Ot Bovy k Bal'montu i drugie raboty po istoricheskoi sotsiologii russkoi literatury*

(Moscow: Novoe lit. obozrenie, 2009), 73–82. On the copyright monopoly, see Ekaterina Pravilova, *A Public Empire: Property and the Quest for the Common Good in Imperial Russia* (Princeton: Princeton University Press, 2014), 255.

2. *The Frigate Pallada* was never fully serialized in any one venue, but most chapters appeared in the years 1855–1856 in a wide range of popular journals for the general public. For enthusiastic reception of these fragments, see Nikolai A. Nekrasov, "Zametki o zhurnalakh za oktiabr' 1855 goda," *Polnoe sobraniie sochinenii i pisem,* vol. 9 (Moscow: Gos. izd-vo khudozh. lit., 1959), 337 (published originally in *Sovremennik* 11 [1855]: 71–87); and *Biblioteka dlia chteniia* 134 (1855): 2–3 (otd. 6). On *Oblomov*'s editions, see *PSS* 6, 6.
3. On the travelogue's journalistic footprint, see *PSS* 3, 394–395, 450; *PSS* 6, 6; and Alekseev, *Bibliografiia,* 11. *The Naval Review* was read by the Navy, government officials, and, increasingly, the general public. Nikolai Chernyshevsky, a major critic, called it "one of the most remarkable phenomena in our literature." The journal was not subject to political censorship but remained under the direct supervision of Grand Prince Konstantin Nikolaevich; see A. B. Davidson and V. A. Makrushin, *Oblik dalekoi strany* (Moscow: Vostochnaia literatura, 1975), 327–328. Goncharov later briefly tutored Prince Konstantin's son in literature; Vsevolod Setchkarev, *Ivan Goncharov. His Life and Works* (Würzburg: Jal-Verlag, 1974), 256.
4. On Livingston and Stanley, see Patrick Brintlinger, *Rule of Darkness: British Literature and Imperialism, 1830–1914* (Ithaca: Cornell University Press, 1990), 180; on Trollope, see Robert M. Lewis, "Wild American Savages and the Civilized English: Catlin's Indian Gallery and the Shows of London," *European Journal of American Studies* 3.1 (2008): 4; on Karamzin, see Andreas Schönle, *Authenticity and Fiction in the Russian Literary Journey, 1790–1840* (Cambridge, MA: Harvard University Press, 2000), 6; on Twain, see David M. Wrobel, *Global West, American Frontier: Travel, Empire, and Exceptionalism from Manifest Destiny to the Great Depression* (Albuquerque: University of New Mexico Press, 2013), 29, 72–73.
5. V. P. Ostrogorskii, "Ocherki literaturnoi deiatel'nosti I. A. Goncharova," *Delo* 3 (1887): 153; Apollon Grigor'ev, "I. S. Turgenev i ego deiatel'nost'. Po povodu romana *Dvorianskoe gnezdo,*" *Literaturnaia kritika* (Moscow: Izd-vo khudozh. lit., 1967), 332–333 (first published in *Sovremennik* 1 [1859]).
6. For examples of obituaries, see [M. M. Stasiulevich], "I. A. Goncharov," *Vestnik Evropy* 10 (1891): 859–865; [unsigned], "I. A. Goncharov," *Novoe vremia* 5585 [September 16] (1891): 1; Iu. Nikolaev, "Literaturnye zametki. I. A. Goncharov," *Moskovskie vedomosti* 261 [September 21] (1891): 3–4; A Nezelenov, "Ivan Aleksandrovich Goncharov," *Russkoe obozrenie* 5 (1891): 548–560; A Volynskii, "Literaturnye zametki. I. A. Goncharov," *Severnyi vestnik* 10 (1891): 152–163. Among the obituaries that mentioned *The Frigate Pallada* were A. Vvedenskii, "I. A. Goncharov," *Niva* 39 (1891): 850; I. A. Ivanov, "Ivan Aleksandrovich Goncharov," *Russkie vedomosti* 256 [September 17] (1891): 2; [unsigned], *Russkaia mysl'* 10 (1891): 171–172; [unsigned], *Pravitel'stvennyi vestnik* 203 [September 17] (1891): 2; [unsigned], "Ivan Aleksandrovich Goncharov," *Istoricheskii vestnik* 46.11 (1891): 549–552. In the period 1886–

1900, both the novels and the travelogue appeared in the collected works editions of 1886, 1879, and 1899. In addition, *The Frigate Pallada* in this period had two separate publications, while *Oblomov* had none. See Alekseev, *Bibliografiia,* 16–19.

7. See Barbara Heldt, "'Japanese' in Russian Literature: Transforming Identities," in *A Hidden Fire: Russian and Japanese Cultural Encounters, 1868–1926,* ed. J. Thomas Rimer (Stanford: Stanford University Press, 1995), 171.
8. G. N. Potanin, "Vospominaniia o Goncharove," *Istoricheskii vestnik* 2 (1903): 118, cited in T. I. Ornatskaia, "Istoriia sozdaniia *Fregata 'Pallada,'*" in I. A. Goncharov, *Fregat Pallada* (1986), 781.
9. *PSS* 2, 13. In a letter to the Maikov family, Goncharov ridiculed pedantic travelogues of exploration. With self-irony, he compared his own lengthy letter about England to an introduction to august-sounding "A Voyage Around the World, in 12 Volumes, with Plans, Sketches, the Map of Coastal Japan, and the Drawings of Port Jackson, Costumes, and Portraits of the Inhabitants of Oceania, by I. Oblomov"; see B. Engel'gardt, "Putevye pis'ma I. A. Goncharova iz krugosvetnogo plavaniia," *Literaturnoe nasledstvo*, vol. 22–24 (Moscow: Zhurnal'no-Gazetnoe ob"edinenie, 1935), 356.
10. The comments on Manila appeared in V. F. Kenevich, rev. of *Russkie v Iaponii* (1855), by I. A. Goncharov, *Biblioteka dlia chteniia* 35 (1856): 32. Interviews that defended Goncharov against the charge of insufficient factuality included S. Dydushkin, rev. of *Russkie v Iaponii* (1855), by I. A. Goncharov, *Otechestvennye zapiski* 104 (1856): 40; N. A. Dobroliubov, rev. of *Fregat 'Pallada'* (1858), by I. A. Goncharov, *Polnoe sobranie sochinenii v deviati tomakh,* vol. 3 (Moscow: Gos. Izd-vo khudozh. lit., 1962), 160; rev. of *Fregat 'Pallada'* (1858), by I. A. Goncharov, *Zhurnal Ministerstva narodnogo prosveshcheniia* 4 (1868): 242–243. See also "Predislovie ot izdatelia," in Ivan Goncharov, *Fregat Pallada. Ocherki puteshestviia* (St. Petersburg: A. I. Glazunov, 1858), ii.
11. Dydushkin, rev. of *Russkie v Iaponii,* 41, 47; [unsigned], rev. of *Fregat 'Pallada'* (1858), by I. A. Goncharov, *Morskoi sbornik* 6 (1858): 24; N. Rykachev, rev. of *Fregat 'Pallada'* (1858), by I. A. Goncharov, *Morskoi sbornik* 5 (1862): 7–17, and 6 (1862): 23–40.
12. V. P. Popov, "Krugosvetnyia puteshestviia g. Goncharova," *Molva* 12 (1857): 136–137. On pricing, see rev. of *Fregat 'Pallada'* (1858), by I. A. Goncharov, *Moskovskoe obozrenie* 2 (1859): 6.
13. Patrick Holland and Graham Huggan, *Tourists with Typewriters: Critical Reflections on Contemporary Travel Writing* (Ann Arbor: University of Michigan Press, 1998), 33; the quotation paraphrasing their argument comes from Carl Thompson, *Travel Writing* (London: Routledge, 2011), 92.
14. A. I. Herzen, "Neobyknovennaia istoriia o tsensore Gon-Cha-Ro iz Shi-Pan-Khu," *Sobranie sochinenii v tridtsati tomakh,* vol. 13 (Moscow: Izd. Ak nauk SSSR, 1958), 104 (original publication in *Kolokol* 6 [December 1] [1857]: 49). Goncharov's censor reports can be found in André Mazon, *Un Maitre du Roman Russe: Ivan Gontcharov, 1812–1891* (Paris: Librairie Ancienne Honoré Champion, 1915), 344–421.
15. [A. V. Druzhinin, unsigned], rev. of *Russkie v Iaponii* (1855), by I. A. Goncharov, *Sovremennik* 55 (1856): 1–26; Dydushkin, rev. of *Russkie v Iaponii,* 49.
16. D. I. Pisarev, rev. of *Fregat 'Pallada'* (1858), by I. A. Goncharov, *Polnoe sobranie sochinenii i pisem v dvenadtsati tomakh,* vol. 1 (Moscow: "Nauka," 2000), 70–73 (first

published, unsigned, in *Rassvet* 1.2 [1859]: 68–79); [I. I. L'khovskii, signed I. L.], rev. of *Fregat 'Pallada'* (1858), by I. A. Goncharov, *Biblioteka dlia chteniia* 150 (1858): 1–11.

17. Rev. of *Fregat 'Pallada'* (1858), by I. A. Goncharov, *Moskovskoe obozrenie,* 6; rev. of *Fregat 'Pallada'* (1858), by I. A. Goncharov, *Sanktpeterburgskie vedomosti* 105 [May 17] (1858): 621–622.
18. In the order of mention, Kanevich, rev. of *Russkie v Iaponii,* 44; Dydushkin, rev. of *Russkie v Iaponii,* 43; M. F. de Pule, rev. of *Fregat Pallada* (1858), by I. A. Goncharov, *Atenei* 6 (1858): 12. Pisarev too praised the author for capturing "national types" in scenes from everyday life (Pisarev, rev. of *Fregat 'Pallada,'* 72).
19. In addition to Dydushkin's review, such passages can be found in rev. of *Morskoi sbornik* (1855), *Otechestvennye zapiski* 102 (1855): 66–72; rev. of *Russkie v Iaponii* (1855), by I. A. Goncharov, *Sanktpeterburgskie vedomosti* 271 [December 10] (1855): 1457–1458. Full seven out of eight pages of Chernyshevsky's review are taken up by a quote from the scene of the Nagasaki governor's dinner; N. G. Chernyshevskii, rev. of *Morskoi sbornik* (1855), *Polnoe sobraniie sochinenii v piatnadtsati tomakh,* vol. 2 (Moscow: Gos. Izd-vo khudozh. lit., 1949), 592–599 (originally published in *Sovremennik* 10 [1855]: 29–54).
20. See [I. I. L'khovskii], rev. of *Fregat 'Pallada'* (1858), by I. A. Goncharov, *Severnaia pchela* 102 [May 13] (1858): 1–2; de Pule, rev. of *Fregat Pallada,* 11–14; rev. of *Fregat 'Pallada,' Zhurnal Ministerstva.*
21. Fyodor Dostoevsky, *A Writer's Diary,* vol. 2 (Evanston: Northwestern University Press, 1994), 1368–1378.
22. Dydushkin, rev. of *Russkie v Iaponii,* 49; Popov, "Krugosvetnyia," 136.
23. [Druzhinin], rev. of *Russkie v Iaponii,* 8–9.
24. [I. I. L'khovskii], rev. of *Fregat 'Pallada'* (1858), by I. A. Goncharov, *Severnaia pchela* 102 (1858): 2; and "Predislovie of izdatelia" (1858), vi.
25. Chernyshevskii, Rev. of *Morskoi sbornik,* 592; Pisarev, rev. of *Fregat 'Pallada,'* 73.
26. A. B. Davidson and V. A. Makrushin, *Oblik dalekoi strany* (Moscow: Vostochnaia literatura, 1975), 303–304; A. Lykoshin, "I. A. Goncharov ob Anglichanakh (pis'mo v redaktsiiu)," *Novoe vremia* 8556 [December 21] (1899): 4; N. Ovsiannikov, "I. A. Goncharov i Bury," *Moskovskie vedomosti* 317 [November 17] (1899): 3; on Siberia, see D. Ovsianiko-Kulikovskii, "I. A. Goncharov," *Vestnik Evropy* 6 (1912): 208–209. On Russian reactions to the Anglo-Boer War, see Apollon Davidson and Irina Filatova, *The Russians and the Anglo-Boer War, 1899–1902* (Cape Town: Human and Rousseau, 1998); and Allison Blakely, *Russia and the Negro: Blacks in Russian History and Thought* (Washington: Howard University Press, 1986), 37.
27. Kenevich, rev. of *Russkie v Iaponii* (1855), 44.
28. Dydushkin, rev. of *Russkie v Iaponii,* 35–40.
29. Thompson, *Travel Writing,* 53.
30. [Druzhinin], rev. of *Russkie v Iaponii,* esp. 7–9, 19–20, 25. On Russian travel writing and the construction of national identity, see Derek Offord, *Journeys to the Graveyard, Perceptions of Europe in Classical Russian Travel Writing* (Dordrecht: Springer, 2005).

31. Rev. of *Fregat Pallada* (1879), by I. Goncharov, *Golos* 106 (1879): 2; Rev. of *Fregat Pallada* (1879), by I. Goncharov, *Niva* 31 (1879): 618. *The Notes of the Fatherland* was unique in considering the reissue superfluous, dismayed by the mentality of a store-owner (*lavochnik*) that apparently imprinted itself on the travelogue; see rev. of *Fregat Pallada* (1879), by I. Goncharov, *Otechestvennye zapiski* 245 (1879): 254–261. See also Goncharov's "Preface" to this edition in *PSS* 3, 81–83.
32. G. A. Larosh, "Po povodu '*Fregata Pallady*' v novom izdanii," *Golos* 137 (1897): 1–2.
33. The journal was *Zhurnal dlia chteniia vospitannikam voenno-uchebnykh zavedenii* [*Journal for Reading by Students of Military Academies*]; A. D. Alekseev, *Bibliografiia I. A. Goncharova* (Leningrad: "Nauka," 1968), 11. On the ring, see Mazon, *Un Maitre,* 341.
34. *PSS* 3, 527–528n4. See also Aleksei Vdovin, "Literatory v roli orientalistov na sluzhbe u imperii: sluchai A. F. Pisemskogo," *"Ideologicheskaia geografiia" Rossiiskoi imperii: Prostranstvo, granitsy, obitateli* [a collective electronic monograph] (Tartu: 2012), 120–123, www.ruthenia.ru/territoria_et_populi/texts/1.4.Vdovin.pdf; and Vdovin's "Russkie pisateli i etos tsivilizatorskoi missii: 'literaturnaia ekspeditsiia' Morskogo ministerstva (1855–1861)," *Ab Imperio* 1 (2014): 109n66.
35. Anton P. Chekhov, letter to G. I. Rossolimo (January 21, 1900) in *Pis'ma,* vol. 9 (Moscow: Nauka, 1980), 19; and letter to M. P. Chekhov (April 1879) in *Pis'ma,* vol. 1 (Moscow: Nauka, 1974), 29. For the reference to *The Frigate Pallada,* see A. P. Chekhov, *Ostrov Sakhalin,* in *Sochineniia,* vol. 14–15 (Moscow: Nauka, 1978), 34. The book appears in Chekhov's list of sources consulted in preparation for the voyage (item 36), see Chekhov, *Sochineniia,* 14–15:890. On Chekhov's literary ranking, see A. P. Chekhov, "Literaturnyi tabel o rangakh" (1886), *Sochineniia,* vol. 5 (Moscow: Nauka, 1976), 143. Chekhov later cooled toward *Oblomov,* which made him question this judgment; see Chekhov, letter to A. S. Suvorin (May 1889) in *Pis'ma,* vol. 3 (Moscow: Nauka, 1976), 201–202. His high regard for *The Frigate Pallada,* however, remained unchanged.
36. V. Azbukin, *I. A. Goncharov v russkoi kritike (1847–1912)* (Orel: Tip. M. L. Mirkina, 1916), 249–254; see also A. V. Krukovskii, "Goncharov i ego tvorchestvo," *Zhurnal Ministerstva narodnogo prosveshcheniia* 9 (1912): 93–111; and D. S. Merezhkovskii, *Vechnye sputniki. Portrety iz vsemirnoi literatury* (1897; St. Petersburg: Nauka, 2007), 195–213. Krukovskii ranked *Oblomov* above Tolstoy's *War and Peace,* Gogol's *Dead Souls,* and Dostoevsky's novels. By virtue of his sober outlook on life, Merezhkovskii proclaimed Goncharov an heir to Pushkin, superior to Dostoevsky, Turgenev, and Tolstoy.
37. [I. I. L'khovskii], rev. in *Severnaia pchela,* 1; the book was recommended for young readers also in such reviews as [A. V. Druzhinin], rev. in *Sovremennik,* 21; and de Pule, rev. in *Atenei,* 15.
38. Rev. of *Fregat 'Pallada,' Zhurnal Ministerstva,* 242–243; rev. of *Fregat Pallada* (1879), by I. A. Goncharov, *Pedagogicheskii listok* 3–4 (1879): 264–265; rev. of *Fregat Pallada, Niva,* 618. N. K. Piksanov reports that the travelogue was taught in high schools and universities in his "Goncharov i kolonializm," *Materialy iubileinoi Goncharovskoi*

konferentsii (Ul'ianovsk, 1963), 23. Prominent Russian pedagogue Vasilii I. Vodovozov modeled the teaching of *The Frigate Pallada* in the context of travel literature in his *Slovesnost' v obraztsakh i razborakh,* 6th ed. (St. Petersburg: L. F. Panteleev, 1905), 163–177.

39. Terry Martin, *The Affirmative Action Empire: Nations and Nationalism in the Soviet Union, 1923–39* (Ithaca: Cornell University Press, 2001).

40. M. I. Kalinin, "Pisatel' dolzhen byt' masterom svoego dela," *Literaturnaia gazeta* 62 [May 18] (1934): 1; Leonid I. Brezhnev, *Tselina* (Moscow: Izd-vo politicheskoi lit., 1978), 61. Most likely, Brezhnev did not write his memoirs but shepherded a team of ghostwriters. This additionally shows the degree to which *The Frigate Pallada* became a cultural touchstone.

41. E. Koval'chik, "I. A. Goncharov," *Komsomol'skaia pravda* 137 [June 17] (1937): 3; I. Kubikov, "I. A. Goncharov," *Krasnaia zvezda* 138 [June 17] (1937): 4.

42. D. Zaslavskii, "Fregat 'Pallada,'" *Pravda,* 165 [June 17] (1937): 4.

43. The textual form of *The Frigate Pallada* was fairly stable in the nineteenth century. Goncharov made the most substantial revisions to the edition of 1879. With very few exceptions, from the author's death in 1891 to the mid-twentieth century, the edition of 1886—the last one to be printed during Goncharov's lifetime—became canonical. On the post-revolutionary editions that omit the travelogue, the Paris and the 1940 Soviet editions, see Alekseev, *Bibliografiia,* 27 (item 187), 31 (items 235 and 244), 35 (item 282), and 36 (item 297). A reviewer of the 1940 edition was so disappointed with the cuts that he resorted to quoting from the pre-revolutionary edition of 1899; see V. N. Zlobin, rev. of *Fregat 'Pallada,'* by I. A. Goncharov (1940), *Literaturnoe obozrenie* 14 (1940): 39–42. The 120-page chapter on the Cape of Good Hope was reduced to three pages; only four pages remain of Goncharov's forty on Singapore and Hong Kong; see I. A. Goncharov, *Fregat 'Pallada': Ocherki puteshestviia* (Moscow: Voenmorizdat, 1940). Zlobin establishes his right to write about Goncharov's travelogue by invoking Kalinin's endorsement (41).

44. I. A. Goncharov, *Fregat 'Pallada': Ocherki puteshestviia,* ed. and intro. by S. D. Muraveiskii (Moscow: Gos. izd-vo geograficheskoi literatury, 1949). As regards the emendations, Muraveiskii merely notes that this is a "somewhat abbreviated edition" (60). The two republications are: I. A. Goncharov, *Fregat 'Pallada': Ocherki puteshestviia,* ed. and intro. by S. D. Muraveiskii (Moscow: Gos. izd-vo geograficheskoi literatury, 1951); I. A. Goncharov, *Fregat 'Pallada': Ocherki puteshestviia,* ed. and intro. by S. D. Muraveiskii (Moscow: Gos. izd-vo geograficheskoi literatury, 1957). Sanitizing books on sensitive topics was frequently done in the Soviet period. On the Muraveisky-style edits to *Uncle Tom's Cabin,* see John MacKay, *True Songs of Freedom: Uncle Tom's Cabin in Russian Culture and Society* (Madison: University of Wisconsin Press, 2013), 88–89.

45. Ivan A. Goncharov, *Fregat "Pallada": Putevoi dnevnik krugosvetnogo puteshestviia* [print] (Moscow: Eksmo, 2012), and [audiobook] (Moscow: Eksmo, 2015). The Eksmo press does not mention the source text; based on my own comparison, I concluded that it is the Muraveisky edition. Longer cuts in the audiobook that are consis-

tent with the Muraveisky edition, discussed below, include: the sketch about the history of the Cape Colony, pp. 154–174 (CD 1, track 40); the encounter with the San ("Bushman") in the Cape Colony jail, pp. 205–207 (CD 1, track 50); Goncharov's musings about Japan that precede his first visit to the Nagasaki governor, pp. 350–356 (CD 1, track 82, min. 8:50), and the passage about Russia's civilizing mission in Asia, pp. 600–605 (CD 2, tr. 69, min. 2:50). The audiobook additionally skips the chapters on Madeira, Java, Hong Kong, Ryukyu, and Siberia.

46. Ivan Goncharov, *The Voyage of the Frigate 'Pallada,'* ed. and tr. N. W. Wilson (London: The Folio Society, 1965); Ivan Goncharov, *The Frigate Pallada,* tr. Klaus Goetze (New York: St. Martin's Press, 1987). Wilson names the Muraveisky edition as his source text (14) while Goetze does not (I have concluded that he uses the Muraveisky edition by comparing the versions). Wilson selected for his translation the chapters on England, the Cape of Good Hope, Japan, Shanghai, and Manila. The St. Martin's Press's assurance to readers about the "complete and unexpurgated" status of their translation appears in "Note to Readers," two pages before the Table of Contents (unnumbered). Among the howlers in Goetze's translation one finds the rendition of the Russian *baba* (wench, old woman, usually of a lower class) as "grandmother," of *med'* (copper) as "honey," and of *sukhar'* (rusk or dry biscuit) as, alternately, "sweatmeats" or "sugar" (118, 214, 529, 537).

47. In what follows, references to Muraveisky's changes will come from I. A. Goncharov, *Fregat 'Pallada': Ocherki puteshestviia*, ed. and intro. by S. D. Muraveiskii (Moscow Gos. izd-vo geograficheskoi literatury, 1951), hereafter *FPM*. These will be followed by the page number in the corresponding text of the current academic edition used in this book (*PSS* 2). For examples of racialized passages that Muraveisky retained, see *FPM* 159, cf. 109, and *FPM* 192, cf. 174–175.

48. In the order of examples: *FPM* 67, cf. 12; *FPM* 173, cf. 130; *FPM* 182, cf. 141; *FPM* 218, cf. 205–207; *FPM* 244, cf. 239; *FPM* 192, cf. 154–174; *FPM* 154, cf. 111.

49. *FPM* 347, cf. 350; *FPM* 623, cf. 672; *FPM* 630, cf. 681; *FPM* 634–635, cf. 691–692.

50. *FPM* 190, cf. 150–151; *FPM* 408, cf. 427; *FPM* 410, cf. 410; *FPM* 532, cf. 565.

51. *FPM* 561, cf. 599; *FPM,* 568, cf. 612; *FPM* 573, cf. 618–619.

52. *FPM* 318, cf. 314; *FPM* 343, cf. 347; *FPM* 429–430, cf. 450; *FPM* 566, cf. 609; *FPM* 448, cf. 472.

53. *FPM* 347, cf. 350–356. On the cut in an industrial reverie, see *FPM* 433, cf. 545.

54. *FPM* 562–563, cf. 600–605.

55. *FPM* 634–635, cf. 691–694; *FPM* 634, cf. 686–691; *FPM* 603, cf. 652; *FPM* 429, cf. 449. The religious dimension was also trimmed elsewhere. Muraveisky deleted the report that the *Pallada* crew said prayers for the Grand Prince Konstantin on his birthday, and the title of the imperial hymn sung on this festive occasion, "God Save the Tsar" ("*Bozhe Tsaria khrani*"); *FPM* 343, cf. 346; *FPM* 634, cf. 685.

56. S. D. Muraveiskii, "I. A. Goncharov i ego plavanie na frigate 'Pallada,'" in *FPM,* 3–60.

57. A. G. Tseitlin, *I. A Goncharov* (Moscow: Izd-vo Ak. nauk SSSR, 1950), 125–133. Tseitlin reiterated this position in his commentary ("Primechaniia") to *The Frigate Pallada* in I. A. Goncharov, *Sobranie sochinenii v vos'mi tomakh,* vol. 3 (Moscow:

Gos. izd-vo khudozh. lit., 1952), 445–462. See K. Tiun'kin's commentaries to the following editions: I. A. Goncharov, *Fregat "Pallada." Ocherki puteshestviia v dvukh tomakh,* 2 vols. (Moscow: Goslitizdat, 1957); I. A. Goncharov, *Sobranie sochinenii v shesti tomakh,* vol. 2–3 (Moscow: Gos. izd-vo khudozh. Lit, 1959); I. A. Goncharov, *Sobranie sochinenii v shesti tomakh,* vol. 2–3 (Moscow: Biblioteka "Ogonek," Izd-vo "Pravda," 1972). Tiun'kin paints Goncharov overall as a critic of imperialism, yet he allows that the writer's judgment was occasionally clouded by his overriding concern with enlightenment, civilization, and progress, which he mistakenly linked to trade, colonization, or bourgeois capitalism.

58. N. K. Piksanov, "Goncharov i kolonializm," *Materialy iubileinoi Goncharovskoi konferentsii* (Ul'ianovsk, 1963), 23–53. Piksanov's frank and strikingly nonjudgmental assessment of Goncharov's enthusiasm for capitalism and comfort can be found in his earlier article, "'Fregat Pallada' Goncharova," *Uchenye zapiski Moskovskogo gos. universiteta. Kafedra russkoi literatury,* kn. 2, vyp. 118 (Moscow: MGU, 1946), 27–42. E. A. Krasnoshchekova questioned, in the early post-Soviet period, Soviet accounts of Goncharov's attacks on western colonialism in an article comparing Goncharov and Karamzin; see E. A. Krasnoshchekova, "'Fregat Pallada': 'Puteshestvie' kak zhanr (N. M. Karamzin i I. A. Goncharov)," *Russkaia literatura* 4 (1992): 28–29.

59. The unexpurgated version of *The Frigate Pallada* appeared in the following Soviet editions: Goncharov *Sobranie sochinenii v vos'mi tomakh,* vol. 2–3 (1952); Goncharov, *Fregat "Pallada"* (1957); Goncharov, *Sobranie sochinenii v shesti tomakh* (1959); Goncharov, *Sobranie sochinenii v shesti tomakh* (1972); I. A. Goncharov, *Sobranie sochinenii v vos'mi tomakh,* vol. 2–3 (Moscow: Khudozh. lit., 1977–1978). In the late Soviet period, *The Frigate Pallada* appeared in two unexpurgated single-title editions, the second of which was aimed for academic readers: I. A. Goncharov, *Fregat 'Pallada': ocherki puteshestviia v dvukh tomakh* (Moscow: Sovetskaia Rossiia, 1976), afterword by E. Krasnoshchekova; and I. A. Goncharov, *Fregat 'Pallada': ocherki puteshestviia v dvukh tomakh,* ed. T. I. Ornatskaia (Leningrad: Nauka, 1986), Literaturnye pamiatniki series.

60. V. A. Mikhel'son, *Gumanizm I. A. Goncharova i kolonial'nyi vopros* (Krasnodar: Krasnodarskii gos. pedagog. institute, 1965), 10, 89, 91, 113, 118, 120, 274.

61. Mikhel'son, *Gumanizm,* 274; *FPM* 57–58; Tseitlin, "Primechaniia," I. A. Goncharov, *Sobranie sochinenii,* vol. 3 (1952), 457–458.

62. [Unsigned and untitled commentary], I. A. Goncharov, *Sobranie sochinenii v vos'mi tomakh,* vol. 3 (Moscow: Khudozh. lit., 1977), 509. E. Krasnoshchekova, "'Fregat 'Pallada' v tvorchestve I. A. Goncharova," in I. A. Goncharov, *Fregat Pallada: ocherki puteshestviia v dvukh tomakh* (Moscow: Sovetskaia Rossiia, 1976), 592.

63. Petr S. Komarov, "Sovetskaia gavan'," *Lirika* (Moscow: Izd-vo Sovetskaia Rossiia, 1968), 238–239; G. F. Kungurov, "Ocherki krugosvetnogo puteshestviia na fregate "Pallada" (I. A. Goncharov o Sibiri i sibirakakh)," *Ocherki russkoi i zarubezhnoi literatury* (Irkutsk: Irkutskii gos. pedagog. institut, 1966), 3–26.

64. *FPM,* 35.

65. Mikhel'son, *Gumanizm,* 125, 139, 153–155.

66. B. L. Kandel', "Bibliografiia I. A. Goncharova. Ukazatel' proizvedenii Goncharova i literatury o nem (na russkom i innostrannykh iazykakh, 1965–1987), *Literaturnoe*

nasledstvo, vol. 102 (Moscow: IMLI RAN, "Naslediie," 2000), 677–678, 696–700; Alekseev, *Bibliografiia,* 44–67 (these two sources cover the publication history up to 1986). Only small excerpts of *The Frigate Pallada* appeared in the non-Russian languages of the Soviet Union (in Tatar and Tadzhik). A full translation appeared only in one European language of the Soviet Union: Estonian.

67. [Unsigned], "Annotatsiia," in Ivan Goncharov, *Fregat 'Pallada'* [e-book] (Moscow: Eksmo, 2015), 2.
68. V. Mel'nik, "Pisatel' XXI veka," in I. A. Goncharov, *Sobranie sochinenii,* vol. 1 (Moscow: Knizhnyi klub "Knigovek," 2010), 7, 42. The 2015 Eksmo e-book edition likewise presents the book in the context of world literature.
69. [Unsigned], commentary to Goncharov, *Sobranie sochinenii,* vol. 2 (2010), 362–270.
70. "Annotatsiia," in Goncharov, *Fregat"Pallada"* [e-book] 2, http://www.litres.ru/goncharov-ivan-aleksandrovich/fregat-pallada/.
71. Tim Youngs, *The Cambridge Introduction to Travel Writing* (Cambridge: Cambridge University Press, 2012), 9–10, 163–164; Thompson, *Travel Writing,* 130–167.
72. Goncharov, *Fregat "Pallada"* [e-book], 120, 138, 145.
73. Goncharov, *Fregat "Pallada"* [e-book], 478.
74. Goncharov, *Fregat "Pallada"* [print] (Eksmo, 2012), and [audiobook] (Eksmo, 2015). Unlike the e-book, the Eksmo audiobook edition preserves the sketch "Twenty Years Since."
75. Zaslavskii, "Fregat 'Pallada,'" 4; Riurik Ivnev, "Fregat 'Pallada,'" *Izbrannoe* (1944; Moscow: Khudozhestvennaia lit., 1985), 135 (Ivnev, born in Tiflis, was a Silver Age poet who became a secretary to Anatoly Lunacharsky, the first Soviet Minister of Education). See also Georgii Koreshov, "Podarok Vodolaza" (1950), http://vm.msun.ru/Litsalon/Korehov/Kor_gl2.htm. The tradition of a poetic eulogy goes back to Goncharov's own time, when his friend Vladimir Benediktov published a poem about the travelogue's exotic charms in *The Notes of the Fatherland*; see Benediktov, "I. A. Goncharovu," *Otechestvennye zapiski* 120 (1858): 639–640.
76. V. Azhazha, "Svidanie s 'Palladoi,'" *Izvestiia* 230 [September 27] (1962): 4.
77. Pallada (tallship), Wikipedia entry, https://en.wikipedia.org/wiki/Pallada_(tall ship).
78. Uchebnoe parusnoe sudno 'Pallada,' "Obshchie svedeniia," http://dalrybvtuz.ru/pallada/history/obschie-svedeniya/.
79. Sputnik International, May 21, 2004, "Frigate Pallada Ends Religious Cruise," http://sptnkne.ws/b4S5; Under the Theodosian Walls Blog, November 24, 2008, "Port Arthur Icon and the Triumph of the Most Holy Theotokos," https://horologion.wordpress.com/2008/11/24/port-arthur-icon-of-the-triumph-of-the-most-holy-theotokos/.
80. Uchebnoe parusnoe sudno 'Pallada,' "Istoriia pokhodov," http://dalrybvtuz.ru/pallada/history/istoriya-pohodov/; Uchebnoe parusnoe sudno 'Pallada,' "Dmitrii Medvedev vruchil kapitanu 'Pallady' Orden Aleksandra Nevskogo," http://dalrybvtuz.ru/pallada/news/2014-10-10-dmitriy-medvedev-vruchil.htm.
81. Uchebnoe parusnoe sudno 'Pallada,' "Istoriia pokhodov," http://dalrybvtuz.ru/pallada/history/istoriya-pohodov/.

82. In its nostalgic reenactment of national-imperial glory, the replica of the *Pallada* resembles the five-million-dollar replica of Cook's ship *Endeavor* that in 1770 raised the British flag in Botany Bay. The *Endeavor* replica was commissioned to honor the European settlement in Australia; Matt Matsuda, *Pacific Worlds: A History of Seas, Peoples, and Cultures* (Cambridge: Cambridge University Press, 2012), 161–162.

Acknowledgments

The exhilaration of working on this book has made me count my blessings in becoming a scholar, more than in any previous project. The text began as a chapter in a long-term, larger study of empire and the Russian classics, but soon grew into a project all its own. However vast I saw the project's intellectual horizons to be, and however interdisciplinary its engagements, writing a study of a single book that few people have read seemed a risky move. I am therefore very grateful for the encouragement I received from the people whose counsel I sought early on: Jane Burbank, Michael Gordin, and William Mills Todd III. Of course, books need editors willing to publish them. For the second time now, I have been very fortunate to find one in Kathleen McDermott of Harvard University Press, who not only expertly guided the work to the printed page but also has been a most valuable and perceptive interlocutor.

Writing this book has been a great intellectual adventure. The research gave me new perspectives on Russian culture and history, and beyond that, opened up to me the cultures and histories of many other parts of the world. I was lucky to have many guides helping me along the way. In the project's earliest stages, at the Institute for Advanced Study's School of Historical Studies in Princeton, I benefited greatly from the advice of Nicola Di-Cosmo, Jonathan Israel, and Michael van Walt van Praag, and of my fellow members Judith Byfield, Yaacob Dweck, Matthew Mosca, Kim Lane Scheppele, and Nikolay Tsyrempilov. Finding firm footing in areas outside my expertise would have been impossible without the generous colleagues who read sections of the book's advanced draft: Thomas Conlan, Sheldon

Garon, Jeanne-Marie Jackson, David Chioni Moore, and Richard N. Price. I am very grateful for their guidance.

Equally substantial is the debt of gratitude I owe to my colleagues in the Slavic field who read all or parts of this manuscript, and whose scholarship and collegiality have been a constant source of inspiration. They include Julie Buckler, Nancy Condee, Caryl Emerson, Robert Geraci, Michael Gordin, Bruce Grant, Katya Hokanson, Peter Holquist, Marina Mogilner, Serguei Oushakine, Cathy Popkin, Gabriella Safran, Valeria Sobol, William Mills Todd III, Emily Van Buskirk, Ilya Vinkovetsky, and Larry Wolff. This book is much enriched by their knowledge and wisdom. I thank Yanni Kotsonis, William McOmie, Abram Reitblat, and Alexey Vdovin for help with specialized questions. I am also immensely grateful to both my anonymous press reviewer and to Willard Sunderland, whose copious and erudite notes struck a perfect balance between rigorous critique and productive advice, and whose research has had great impact on mine.

A major impetus for this work came from the American Council of Learned Societies. Its Frederick Burkhardt Residential Fellowship for Recently Tenured Scholars allowed me to spend a blissful and productive year at the School of Historical Studies, from 2013 to 2014. I was able to remain at the Institute for Advanced Study the following year, thanks to Piet Hut's kind invitation to join the Program in Interdisciplinary Studies. I also received substantial support from Rutgers University, and especially my wonderful colleagues in the Department of Germanic, Russian, and East European Languages and Literatures.

Audiences at many institutions where I presented my work in progress provided invaluable feedback as well as opportunities to think through this project's various dimensions in greater depth. My great thanks go to: at Princeton University, the East Asian Studies Program lecture series, the *Kruzhok* hosted by the Program in Russian, East European, and Eurasian Studies, and the 2015 conference on "The Global 1860s" organized by Linda Colley and Matthew Karp; at Harvard University, the Davis Center Seminar and the lecture series funded by the Gochman Dean's Fund; the Slavic departments at the University of Southern California and the University of Toronto; the 2015 workshop on "Russia's Races" at New York University; the 2016 University of Pennsylvania conference on "Translating Race in Eurasia"; the 2014 conference on "Russia in East Asia" at Columbia University's Harriman Institute; and my co-panelists and audiences at the conferences of the Association for Slavic, East European, and Eurasian

Studies and the American Association of the Teachers of Slavic and East European Languages.

My research benefited from the resources of the Princeton and Harvard library collections and the services of dauntless librarians Karen Dennis at the Institute for Advanced Study and Jim Niessen at Rutgers University. Maria Tuya offered generous help with scanning images and Sascha Hosters assisted me in research. I thank Michael Siegel from Rutgers University for his excellent work on the maps, and Andrew Rubenfeld for his expert indexing. The book's style gained much from my copyeditor at Harvard University Press, Julia Kirby, whose powers of preserving nuance while increasing ease of reading are truly magical.

I am very grateful to the support of my family, including my mother, Małgorzata, and my father-in-law, Salvatore DiMauro. Many thanks go to my siblings, Maja, Maciej, and Tosia, who gave my sons summer fun while their mother was planted in front of her laptop. To my beloved sons, Yash and Elio, whom I've watched grow and mature in the past few years along with this manuscript, I am happy to say: Mom is back!

Finally, my profound thanks go to my husband, Giorgio DiMauro, a fellow PhD in Slavic studies, at once my most demanding critic and my greatest fan. He has encouraged me when energy faltered and ordered me to stop tinkering when it was clearly the sensible thing to do. His enthusiasm has sustained and cheered me as we talked through ideas and drafts. The joys of both my intellectual and real-life journeys would be vastly diminished without him. I dedicate this book to him.

Index